OTTOMAN SEAPOWER
AND LEVANTINE DIPLOMACY
IN THE AGE OF DISCOVERY

D1545849

SUNY SERIES IN
THE SOCIAL AND ECONOMIC HISTORY
OF THE MIDDLE EAST

DONALD QUATAERT, EDITOR

Issa Khalaf, *Politics in Palestine: Arab Factionalism and Social Disintegration, 1939–1948*

Rifa'at 'Ali Abou-El-Haj, *Formation of the Modern State: The Ottoman Empire, Sixteenth to Eighteenth Centuries*

M. Fuad Köprülü, *The Origins of the Ottoman Empire*, translated and edited by Gary Leiser

Guilian Denoeux, *Urban Unrest in the Middle East: A Comparative Study of Informal Networks in Egypt, Iran and Lebanon*

Zachary Lockman, ed., *Workers and Working Classes in the Middle East: Struggles, Histories, Historiographies*

Palmira Brummett, *Ottoman Seapower and Levantine Diplomacy in the Age of Discovery*

OTTOMAN SEAPOWER
AND LEVANTINE DIPLOMACY
IN THE AGE OF DISCOVERY

PALMIRA BRUMMETT

STATE UNIVERSITY OF NEW YORK PRESS

Published by
State University of New York Press, Albany

For information, address State University of New York
Press, State University Plaza, Albany, N.Y., 12246

Production by Diane Ganeles
Marketing by Lynne Lekakis

Library of Congress Cataloging-in-Publication Data

Brummett, Palmira Johnson, 1950–
    Ottoman seapower and Levantine diplomacy in the age of discovery /
by Palmira Brummett.
        p.   cm. — (SUNY series in the social and economic history of
the Middle East)
    Includes bibliographical references and index.
    ISBN 0-7914-1701-8 (alk. paper). — ISBN 0-7914-1702-6 (pbk. :
alk. paper)
    1. Turkey—Commerce—Middle East—History—16th century.
    2. Middle East—Commerce—Turkey—History—16th century.
    3. Mercant marine—Turkey—History—16th century. 4. Navigation—
Turkey—History—16th century. 5. Turkey—History—Bayezid II,
1481–1521. I. Title. II. Series.
HF3756.5.Z7M6283   1994
382′.09561056—dc20   92-44704
                                                          CIP

10 9 8 7 6 5 4 3 2 1

For Ma and Pa:
Elaine Bassi and John Kemmett Johnson
Lovers of Learning

Contents

Contents

Illustrations

Maps

Plates

A Note on Transliteration

There is no single standard or satisfactory romanization of Ottoman Turkish. In this work, the Library of Congress romanization has been utilized for Arabic and Persian names, and the customary, if inadequate, transliteration based on modern Turkish has been used for Turkish names (Sadeddin, not Sʿad al-Dīn). Whereas modern Turkish employs both dotted and undotted capital "I"s, only the undotted capital "I" will be used here. Because the Ottoman Empire is the primary focus here, a Turkish preference has been given to names which might otherwise be romanized, hence Ismail Safavi rather than Ismāʿīl Safāwī. Names such as ʿAlā ad-Dawla or Shaibānī Khān, which might be either romanized or placed in Turkish transliteration, have been rendered according to language of the sources regarding them used here and according to geographic area of operation. Beg has been preferred for the title spelled alternately bey, bāy, bek, and so forth, although Bāy has been preserved where the word occurs as part of a name in Arabic. Place names are rendered with modern spellings, giving preference to modern Turkish place names in Anatolia and to Italian spellings in the Aegean (where there are often Greek alternatives). Words such as sultan, shah, pasha, sheikh and Sunni, which have acquired a common status in English usage, are not translitered, and Shiʿi is preferred over other options found in English transliteration. Because the manuscripts cited do not always employ a recto/verso pagination system, the designations "a" and "b" have been employed for manuscript page notation.

Acknowledgments

Many people have assisted me in bringing this work to publication. The ideas included here were inspired by the work and scholarship of Halil Inalcık, Frederic Lane, Eliyahu Ashtor, and Andrew Hess. I would like to thank the advisors who guided me through this study in its initial stages: Halil Inalcık, John Woods, and Richard Chambers. Invaluable editorial advice was provided by Donald Quataert, Felicia Hecker, Jahan Kuhn, and James Fitzgerald. The Bunting Institute provided time for reflection and writing. To the many friends and colleagues, who provided intellectual insights, expert criticism, and moral support, I am most grateful. Among them are: Mohamad Tavakoli, Carol Lansing, Paolo Cherchi, John Guilmartin, Bruce Masters, Selim Deringil, Dan Goffman, Linda Darling, Rifaʿat Abou-El-Haj, Roderic Davison, Doug Howard, Uli Schamiloglu, Elaine Johnson, Caroline Berg, and Ann Wagner. I was fortunate to have use of the bountiful resources of the University of Chicago Library, the Newberry Library in Chicago, and the Süleymaniye Kütüphanesi in Istanbul, as well as the invaluable assistance of Bruce Craig, John Tedeschi, and Muammer Ülker at those institutions. The University of Tennessee Department of History provided support; and the University of Tennessee Cartography Lab produced the maps included in this study. Andras Riedlmayer provided suggestions for miniatures along with anecdotes on the private lives of the Ottoman elites. I am grateful to the British Library, the Isabella Stewart Gardner Museum, and the Österreichisches Nationalbibliothek for permission to reproduce miniatures from their collections. Earlier versions of parts of this work appeared in *The International History*

Review, v. 11, n. 4 (1989); *New Perspectives on Turkey*, nos. 5–6 (1991); and *Studies on Ottoman Diplomatic History*, v. 5 (1990). Finally, I would like warmly to acknowledge the spiritual, material, and intellectual support of my husband and family. Any technical errors, of which I hope there are few, or gaps in reasoning, of which there are perchance more, may be credited directly to the author.

Plate 1: Ottoman Sultans (1421–1512)
Murad II, Mehmed II, Bayezid II
Source: Courtesy of Österreichische Nationalbibliothek, Album 48, A.F. 50.

Plate 2: Ottoman Sultans (1512–1566)
Selim I, Süleiman I
Source: (Same as Plate 1)

CHAPTER 1

Introduction:
The Physical and Historiographic Space

What if the Ottomans had discovered America? Or, more to the point, what if the Ottomans had colonized America? Naval supremacy, gunpowder, talent, resources, that intangible ethos of empire—all the factors assembled which comprise the historiographic success formula were the Ottomans' preserve at the turn of the sixteenth century. Yet, this is not a study of the New World or even of the Age of Discovery in its usual sense because in 1503, as the first Portuguese traders traced their tentative path back to Lisbon, their holds full of Indian pepper, the dominant power in the Euro-Asian world turned its hegemonic ambitions and formidable navy not west after the Atlantic fantasy but east.[1] The Ottoman Empire in less than twenty years expanded its territorial control south and eastward, there to engage the Portuguese in the Persian Gulf and Indian Ocean. This work takes as its focus the processes by which that expansion occurred. Its topic is not so much the physical clash of empires, but its prelude—the political, economic, and rhetorical mechanisms by which Ottoman competitors, one by one, were removed from contention for control of the Levant.

The sixteenth century has been called the "Age of Discovery," a period when the voyaging empires of western Europe endeavored to capture the revenues of the oriental trade and, in the process, came upon and conquered the Americas. The term Age of Discovery is, of course, no longer much in vogue. Historians and history department class offerings have now turned their attentions to the recipients as well as the bearers of this particularly European form of "discovery." Yet, the weight of Age of Discovery vintage historiography has continued to focus disproportionate attention on certain discoveries, or conquerors and imperialists, and on certain rhetorics of conquest in certain geographic spheres, at the expense of others.

European historiography on the sixteenth century has been overwhelmingly structured in terms of the Age of Discovery, and the increasing power of Western Europe that it announced; Columbus' voyages are its central drama, and the spectre of the coming Industrial Revolution sets its tone. In that framework, the Ottoman Empire has been not a protagonist but something to be circumvented as the globe was to be circumnavigated: an obstacle, though not an insurmountable one, to the shift of the balance of power inexorably westward. Although the Age of Discovery paradigm is currently being deconstructed, the story of early sixteenth-century Ottoman hegemony in the Levant remains firmly under the shadow of what the empire would become, the late nineteenth century "Sick Man of Europe," a colonized and imperialized dependent of latter day European dominance. This study is intended to tell a story less structured by later outcomes. It assumes a different world map, centering not on Lisbon, Antwerp, Amsterdam, Paris, or London, but on Istanbul, Cairo, and Tabriz. The objectives of Ottoman expansion in the sixteenth century were the same as those of the European voyages of discovery: wealth, power, glory, religious legitimation. The territories promised to King Emmanuel of Portugal by the pope were the same as those coveted by the Ottomans; the only dilemma was whether one sailed west or east to reach them. Here, too, there was an obstacle, but the obstacle was Safavid Iran, not the Muslim alter ego of the European accounts, but a fellow pretender to the Ottoman claims to empire.

The sixteenth century was indeed a pivotal period in which shipping and gunpowder technologies along with accumulations of wealth brought the achievement of world hegemony closer to realization for a select few monarchs. The turn of the sixteenth century signaled a recasting of the boundaries of "world" sovereignty in terms of seapower; for four centuries thereafter naval hegemons would contend to expand their spheres of influence within that recast world. Accompanying the rearticulation of boundaries in the sixteenth century world order came a rearticulation of the language of diplomacy and the rhetoric of empire. Command of the sea drew the claims of rulers well beyond the limits circumscribed by the march of their armies in a single campaign season. Seapower meant that the feats of Alexander or of the Caesars no longer marked the outer limits of imaginable conquest.

Moving out in four great sweeping arcs from Lisbon, London, Amsterdam, and Antwerp, the monarchs of the Atlantic seafaring empires set out in four directions to journey to southeastern Asia: one route arced northeast (heading overland through Muscovy and Iran); a second moved northwest (across the Atlantic and toward the Arctic, seeking a northwest passage); a third arc went southeast (around the horn of Africa and into the Indian Ocean); while a fourth arc went southwest (around the tip of South America and across the Pacific). Ultimately, only the routes tracing the two southern arcs were successful, bringing the Portuguese, the English, and the Dutch naval control in the Indian Ocean and South Pacific. No sea route materialized through the northwest passage. Distance, inhospitable climate, and the English failure to negotiate favorable trading conditions with Iranian monarchs, made the long overland route through Muscovy unprofitable. Conversely, the southern seaborne arcs brought to the western European voyaging empires the wealth and far flung bases that they used to support their claims to world hegemony.

Within the bounds of the two arcs that swept eastward lay Euro-Asia, a territory stretching from the Balkans to South Asia, governed by Muslim rulers who controlled the traditional land-based routes and the Mediterranean outlets of the eastern trade.[2] For the west European merchant states, this territory was something to be circumvented, a land mass dominated by Turkic dynasties and slave states, commercial middlemen between the source areas of the eastern trade and the European consumers. But historically it was not a closed block, cut off and distinct from the commercial, political, and cultural spheres of interconnected empires in Europe, Africa, and East Asia. This study concerns itself with this region between the eastern arcs—the playing out there of the tensions between contending claims to universal sovereignty, the articulation of state policy, and the mechanisms of conquest and of trade by which a new sixteenth-century world order was forged.

The intent of this study is to alter the boundaries of historiography on the Euro-Asian sphere and on the incorporation of the Ottoman Empire into constructions of the sixteenth-century world order. The following premises are essential to that analysis: the Ottoman state was a merchant state endowed with economic intentionality; the development of Ottoman seapower was a crucial

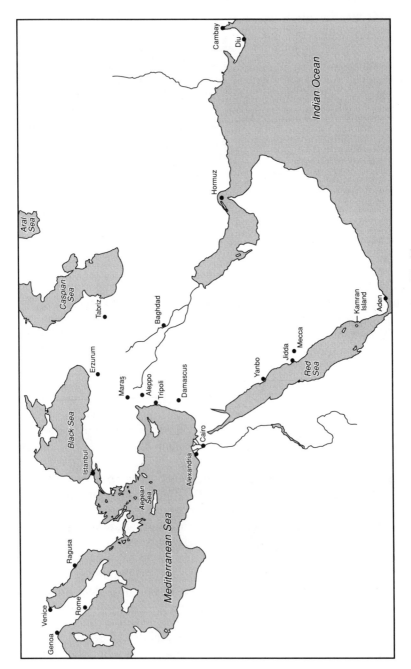

Figure 1. The Euro-Asian World.

factor in the reconfiguration of the early sixteenth-century balance of power; the Ottomans were inheritors of Euro-Asian commercial patterns and cannot be assessed as a separate and isolationist block set apart by Islamic philosophy or slave state military ethos; and, finally, analysis of the political and economic processes of the Age of Discovery cannot assume the later outcomes of western European world hegemony as inevitable. By merchant state, here, is meant a state which invests part of its accumulated wealth in trading ventures for profit and whose elite military classes do likewise; it consciously attempts to compete with other states for the control of commercial revenues; it designs its foreign policy with the clear intention of acquiring control of sources of commercial revenue rather than simply acquiring land for purposes of colonization and agricultural exploitation.

Much has been written about the ambitions of the Atlantic seafaring states. The universalist claims of the Portuguese and Spanish were guaranteed by a papal bull of 1493 granting title in rather flamboyant fashion to: ". . . all islands or mainlands whatever, found or to be found . . . in sailing towards the west and south."[3] The scope of European ambition, then, appeared limited, at any rate to the west, only by the bounds of papal imagination. In fact, it was limited, as were the ambitions of its Asian counterparts, by the range of its navies, number of its cannon, and extent of its economic resources.

Claims of universal sovereignty were not an invention of the late medieval world. Christianity and Islam had posed claims to universal sovereignty and world community for their god-kings. Before the advent of Islam and the conversion of Europe to Christianity, Alexander the Great and the Caesars had become favored models for leaders with somewhat less spiritual claims. The Ottoman sultans and the Hapsburg emperors in the sixteenth century would aspire to resurrect the Roman Empire. Sultan Mehmed the Conqueror (d. 1481) had claimed that imperial glory in 1453 when he took the old eastern Roman capital, Constantinople. Rome had long since lost its position as western hegemon. But Constantinople/Istanbul, under the Ottoman dynasty, was the capital of an empire which came to control a greater territory, from Belgrade to the Yemen and from the Crimea to North Africa, than it had under the Byzantines.[4] Then, Sultan Süleiman the Magnificent (ruled 1520–1566), whose reign is generally considered the golden age of Ottoman power and prestige, would challenge the Hapsburg emperor's claim to the title of Caesar.[5] This competition for title signified the struggle of

European and Asian potentates for the rhetorical terrain of public image. The nature of the Ottoman expansion in the sixteenth century, however, suggests that it was not only the conquests of Julius or Augustus that Süleiman and his father and grandfather wished to duplicate but also the unfulfilled ambitions of Alexander.[6] Once Constantinople and Cairo fell, the lands of India and China, too, came within the purview of Ottoman ambitions.[7]

Once Constantinople had been conquered and rebuilt, and Ottoman control consolidated in the southern Balkan peninsula, Mehmed II's successors turned their attention to conquest on their eastern frontiers. It was not rich agricultural lands and commercial entrepôts alone that attracted the Ottoman gaze eastwards.[8] The sultan required imperial and religious legitimation to match his imperial capital. Hegemony in the Muslim world demanded not papal endorsement but control over Mecca, Medina, and Jerusalem and the title, "Protector of the Holy Cities." It was this title to which the sovereigns of Muslim states aspired and for which they contended: the Ottoman sultans Bayezid II (1481–1512) and Selim I (1512–1520), the Safavid Shah Ismail (1501–1524) in Iran, and the Uzbeg Shaibānī Khān (1500–1510) in Transoxania. In the early years of the sixteenth century, the Mamluk sultans, who were in the final years of their long reign over Egypt and Syria, and suffering both internal revolt and the incursions of the infidel Portuguese into the Red Sea, were still the nominal overlords of the Islamic world. They were the protectors of the Holy Cities and harbored a claimant to the long defunct Abbasid caliphate. The caliphs, still formally honored as successors to the prophet Muhammad, had lost temporal power by the thirteenth century and the spiritual allegiance of segments of the Muslim community long before that. Abbasid puppets during the Mamluk regime, however, still provided a seal of religious legitimacy on the reigns of monarchs who otherwise lacked the legitimation either of piety or of descent. Many Muslim dynasties, including the Ottoman and Safavid, constructed false genealogies linking them to the Prophet Muhammad, but they also coveted the Mamluk claims which derived from control of the Holy Cities and of the puppet caliph. The Mamluks bore the insults of these other contenders who each proposed his own entitlement and fitness to protect the routes of the pilgrimage (*hajj*), and assume the legacy of the Prophet's rule. For the Ottomans, a felicitous combination of commercial and political ambitions could be fulfilled through deposing the Mamluks, and gaining title not only to the Holy Cities but also to the customs posts for the eastern trade. The Mamluks, however, were only the intermediaries for this trade. Once they were conquered, the Ottomans could attempt directly the conquest of the Indian Ocean. The pilgrim routes to Mecca, after all, traversed not only Syria and North Africa but the sea routes from India as well. Ottoman ships launched from the Red Sea and Persian Gulf would be charged with defending the *hajjis* enroute from South Asia.[9] Thus, both the lure of trading profits and the clear direction of conquest indicated by the dictates of legitimacy in the Muslim world drew the Ottomans eastwards through the Euro-Asian commercial corridors. There Ottoman universalist claims would intersect with those of the Portuguese—one mighty seaborne empire against another.

Empire building, in this era, was dependent upon the ability to mobilize irresistable armies and navies. Seaborne states expanded at the expense of those without ships. Naval power in turn was dependent upon access to the resources for shipbuilding, cannon founding, crew mobilization, and provisioning. Once these resources were secured, other factors became decisive for the expansionist enterprise. These were: the successful prevention of enemy coalitions through shrewd alliances and the securing of domestic tranquility through a combination of force, administrative expertise, and legitimation of sovereignty. Where the latter was lacking it was eagerly sought after in the forms of military success, and religious sanction. Lacking then were only the opportunity and occasion to attack neighboring states. Attacks on Muslim competitors were legitimized by means of a *fetva* (statement of concurrence with *şeriat* Islamic law) and by accusations of "heresy" against the designated enemy. Forays against Christian competitors were justified as *jihad* or war against the infidel. For Christian states intent on going to war, the same purposes were served respectively by papal bulls and by declarations of "holy war."

Much of the eastern Mediterranean region had been lost to the direct control of European states in the drawn out and spasmodic conflicts of the Crusades.[10] In 1453, the Ottoman Sultan Mehmed the Conqueror's long anticipated capture of Constantinople ended European visions of a reconstructed eastern Roman Empire. The shock waves this conquest sent through European Christendom found expression in the papacy's renewal of crusading rhetoric. But no coalition of European states would emerge to challenge the Ottoman Turks. Political and economic imperatives dictated otherwise, and the rhetoric of holy war would not suffice to articulate the image of empire in the sixteenth-century world order.

The Ottoman state became the irresistible force of the early sixteenth-century Levantine world. It accomplished its objectives (control of trade and territory plus the humiliation of its foes) through a combination of carefully formulated alliances, formidable firepower, and precisely applied naval action. These factors eventually secured the defeats of its Muslim competitors, Ismail Safavi in Iran in 1514 and the Mamluks in Egypt and Syria in 1516–1517, while gaining for the Ottomans access to control of the eastern trade and the routes of the *hajj*. With conquest came wealth and legitimacy. Control of commerce, however, was a prerequisite as well as an effect of Ottoman conquest. By securing and manipulating the mechanisms of trade in the eastern Mediterranean the Ottomans paved the way for their actual incursions, beginning in 1505, east to the Red Sea and Indian Ocean. The power to control commerce was as much a factor in the expansion of the Ottoman state as the power to forge cannon.

The participants in the struggle for hegemony in the Euro-Asian sphere were not equal in power, resources, range of action, or governmental organization. Expanded possibilities, actual and rhetorical, were granted to states which commanded seapower. The primary competitors here were the Ottomans in Anatolia and the Balkans, the Mamluks in Egypt and Syria, the Safavids in Iran and Iraq, the Portuguese, and the Venetians. Of these, Venice is of particular significance in this study because it was Venice that the Ottoman state replaced as the dominant naval power in the eastern Mediterranean. All of these contenders but the Safavids in the early sixteenth century were merchant states with economies, in greater or lesser part, organized to develop and exploit customs revenues. The Mamluks and Safavids were not naval powers. Iran had never developed as a seapower in the Persian Gulf, and the Mamluks had failed to maintain the reputation for naval dominance in the Mediterranean established by their predecessors, the Fatimids, during the Middle Ages. Venice was a seafaring republic whose success derived from well ordered merchant fleets and the energetic exploitation of its Mediterranean middleman position in the East-West trade. But Venice lacked the economic and military resources to dominate the eastern Mediterranean basin. The Portuguese and Ottoman empires, in contrast, were merchant states with resources to match their expansionist ambitions. Their development of navies and artillery, combined with wealth in the form of commercial, manpower, agricultural, mineral, and timber resources, permitted them to compete, as dominant powers, for control of the Euro-Asian sea frontiers.

The context for this study is the period of Ottoman expansion, during the reigns of sultans Bayezid II (1481–1512) and Selim I (1512–1520), beginning with the Ottoman-Venetian wars of 1499–1503 and culminating in the Ottoman conquest of Syria and Egypt in 1516–1517, which ended two and a half centuries of Mamluk rule. While the Ottomans were concluding a period of protracted warfare with Venice and its allies, a new challenger for the role of Euro-Asian hegemon was gaining power in Iran. Shah Ismail Safavi, sheikh of the Safavid order of dervishes and charismatic military leader, conquered Tabriz in 1501 and, within ten years, had seized Baghdad, united Iran, and begun the process of converting predominantly Sunni Iran to Shiʿism. The ascendancy of Ismail coincided temporally with the Portuguese navigations to East Africa and India, which constituted a military and economic challenge to Mamluk control of the Red Sea and the Mediterranean outlets of the oriental trade. The Mamluks, based in Cairo and claiming sovereignty over Arabia as well as Egypt and Syria, held a monopoly on the spice trade and controlled the caravan routes north through the Hijaz and west from the Persian Gulf into Aleppo, Damascus, and Beirut.[11] Mamluk commercial interests, however, were only part of the complex network of economic exchange which transferred goods from the Indian Ocean to northern and western Europe. The Portuguese assault on the Asian trade also threatened the revenues of Venice and the Ottoman state, primary intermediaries after the Mamluks in the conduct of the East-West trade.

At the beginning of the sixteenth century, Ottoman expansion was blocked on their southeastern frontiers by longtime rivals, the Mamluks, and by new challengers, the Safavids and the Portuguese. The Ottoman western frontiers at the same time can be divided roughly into a sea zone, where Ottoman preeminence in the eastern Mediterranean had been demonstrated decisively during the Ottoman-Venetian wars (1499–1503), and a land zone where Ottoman armies were actively extending the sultan's control over Balkan territory until a stalemate was reached in the later sixteenth century. No concerted resistance to Ottoman expansion coalesced in either the sea or land frontier zones during the period under discussion. Conditions on the Austro-Hungarian front were chaotic, and Hapsburg power was not consolidated in Hungary until after the Ottoman conquest of Egypt. On the eastern salient,

Sultan Selim, in the course of his short but illustrious reign, defeated Ismail, in 1514 at Çaldıran in eastern Anatolia, and conquered the Mamluk territories in 1516–1517, thereby bringing Egypt, Syria, and the Holy Cities of Mecca and Medina into Ottoman hands. Under Selim's successor, Süleiman the Magnificent (d. 1566), the Ottomans pursued the quest for control of the Persian Gulf and Indian Ocean but ultimately failed. It was not until the second half of the sixteenth century, however, that this outcome, like that of the eventual stalling of Ottoman western expansion, would become apparent. Thus, this work considers the period 1503–1517 as one in which Ottoman commercial and military spheres were expanding to satisfy Ottoman ambitions for "world" hegemony. Hindsight regarding the eventual limitations of that expansion should not distort the assessment of its processes. Thus, for example, the superiority of Atlantic type merchantmen over galleys had yet to be determined, and the decision, made eventually by Sultan Süleiman to make Vienna the preeminent objective of Ottoman campaigns, had yet to be made. The primary thrust of Ottoman ambitions in the early sixteenth century was eastward, proceeding through economic zones which predated Ottoman rule, and engaging the mechanisms of Ottoman diplomacy and conquest to establish control over the revenues of the eastern trade.

European historiography, anachronistically, has focused on the Hapsburg and even Russian challenges to Ottoman hegemony. An analysis of Ottoman empire building in the Age of Discovery is better served by an assessment of the struggles between the Ottomans and Venice on the one hand and the Ottomans, Mamluks, and Safavids on the other. By the time the East became an important terrain of struggle for Russia, its competitors would be the British and not the Ottomans. The Hapsburgs (claiming the title of Holy Roman Emperor), characterized as the European bulwark against the "Terrible Turks," played only a secondary role in the Ottoman expansion eastwards.[12] Timing, within the sixteenth-century framework here, is crucial to an understanding of the balance of power in the Euro-Asian sphere. The Hapsburg power, which eventually accrued to the emperor, Charles V (1519–1558), cannot be projected back into the early decades of the century when his grandfather Maximilian I (1493–1519) contended with King Wladislas II of Hungary (1471–1516) and others for control of the Balkans. Their struggle is characteristic of the forces within Europe which militated against the presentation of a united Christian-state front against the Ottomans. For the Ottoman rulers before Sultan Süleiman I, the Hapsburgs were one of several forces on their second front which enjoined caution and the signing of a peace treaty before operations eastward could be conducted. The Ottoman first front at the turn of the sixteenth century was the eastern salient. No single ruler in Europe could contend with the military power of the Ottoman sultan in the early sixteenth century. The European states, mindful of the Ottoman landing at Otranto on the Italian coast in 1480, feared a "Muslim invasion" from the east, much more than Bayezid II or Selim I feared any joint Christian operation from the west.

European states in the early sixteenth century endeavored to form alliances that would maintain the balance of power and contain Ottoman expansion. Yet these attempts were often purely rhetorical, lacking in men and arms. They were thwarted by the active pursuit of individual political aspirations on the part of the monarchs of Europe. Coalitions of Christian monarchs eyed each other's territories. In 1508, for example, the League of Cambrai was formed to annex Venetian territory. The Hapsburg Maximilian I allied with Pope Julius II, Ferdinand of Aragon, Louis of France, and the city-states of Mantua and Ferrara, hoping to advance his own territorial ambitions on the Italian mainland at the expense of Venice. Wladislas II of Hungary supported Venice. Three short years later Maximilian was again allied with the pope in the Holy League, against their erstwhile ally, Louis of France. These rivalries for European territory, wealth, and prestige sapped the resources of all the contending monarchs. None provided substantial financial support for an alliance against the Ottomans. Communal loyalties could not stand in the way of more immediate territorial and commercial ambitions.

While the struggle for European dominance was hotly contested with rhetoric and arms by the pope, the emperor, France, Spain, and the Italian city-states, a similar realignment of power was transforming the political terrain on the eastern borders of the Ottoman state. At the beginning of the century, just as the Portuguese began to use their ship-mounted cannon to dominate the coasts of Africa and India, the Safavid Shah Ismail initiated the series of land campaigns which would reunite Iran. Shah Ismail, who, like the Ottomans, was interested in controlling the revenues of the eastern trade, was the lynchpin of early sixteenth-century Levantine diplomacy. He negotiated with the Portuguese, Venetians, the French, the Holy Roman emperor, the pope, and the Mamluks, in pursuit of his own claims to universal sovereignty.

His military victories and the success of Safavid religious proselytizing deterred the Ottoman expansion eastward and helped define the parameters of the succession struggle for the Ottoman
throne. European monarchs hastened to explore the possibilities
for political and commercial relations with his militarily successful
Muslim state. States like Venice looked to Ismail to contain Ottoman power where the efforts of European competitors had failed to
do so. The consolidation of Ismail's power in Iran, a region which
had been politically fragmented for two centuries, combined with
the expanding of the Ottoman and Portuguese empires into the
Euro-Asian space, required new political and rhetorical configurations—expressed in the formation of alliances and the conduct of
diplomacy. Such configurations had never been based strictly on
polarizations of Christian-Muslim, or orient-occident. They had,
however, always been determined by economic interest and by the
organization of the commercial space.

Boundaries

The boundaries dealt with in this work are both physical and
historiographic: the extent and nature of sovereign claims, and the
nature, process, and intentions of conquest. Territory and borders
are relative terms when applied to the sixteenth century. Like images of universal sovereignty, they are not readily reducible to specific spaces and exact lines. A state's territory was that area from
which taxes could be collected and troops levied until another state
seized those prerogatives. But territory was also imagined—the
areas to which a sovereign laid claim or to which imperial edicts
were sent without any firm guarantees that their authority would
be respected. Territory could be a rhetorical construct designed to
ward off or intimidate competing claimants. It did not necessarily
reflect a ruler's ability to command obedience. The organization of
day-to-day government and commerce functioned essentially on a
local level, administered by provincial governors, chieftains, head-
men, and judges (*kadis*). These governors could withdraw their allegiance from one sovereign and give it to another or proclaim
their own autonomy. If they did, depending upon their distance
from the center, it might be some time before the offended ruler
could or did respond. Conquest was also relative. Conquest was defined not in terms of chunks of territory but in terms of routes
defended and fortresses garrisoned. It meant the occupying of

towns, the setting up of customs posts, and the sending of central government agents. Frontiers then were large and porous, the borders of one empire melding into those of another with many independent or semi-independent governors in between. Contention for authority within these frontier zones is an important indicator of the nature and ambitions of sixteenth-century empires. The significance of such frontiers has been illustrated by Andrew Hess in his pioneering work on the Ibero-African frontier, a work which has not received due recognition because of the undue privileging of certain frontiers, like the American and Indian Ocean frontiers, at the expense of others within the Age of Discovery framework.[13] Sixteenth-century monarchs were not preoccupied with drawing boundaries so much as they were with controlling agricultural and mineral resources, taxing trade, and demanding the submission of subordinates and opponents (whether or not that submission was accompanied by financial gain). These acts of submission provided both a basis for territorial claims, and security, however temporary, against the threat of attack. They also lent honor to the name of the sovereign, legitimizing in concrete fashion his exercise of authority. Sixteenth-century boundaries, then, might better be measured in troops, taxes, and acts of submission than in lines on a map.

The amorphous nature of late medieval boundaries notwithstanding, some terms are needed to discuss the range of armies and of traders and the sixteenth-century monarchs' consciousness of their limits. Travel accounts of this period focus on descriptions of cities and trade routes, generally neglecting their hinterlands. These narratives suggest the ways in which empire was imagined. This study, too, focuses on trade routes to conceptualize zones by which the Ottoman economies of conquest and of trade can be analyzed. The zones of commerce through which the Ottomans operated stretched from the Mediterranean to the Indian Ocean, drawing on the resources and personnel of a series of interconnected regions. For purposes of this study, which links Ottoman expansion eastward and Ottoman naval development to the attempt to control international trade, three commercial zones can be delineated.[14] The first is the island-coast zone, which comprised the trade from the Ottoman coast westward through the Aegean and into the Adriatic. The hallmark commodity of this zone was grain. The second zone is the Anatolia-Syria zone, which comprised the east-west overland caravan, and eastern Mediterranean sea trades from Iran, into eastern Anatolia and Syria and on to west Anatolia.[15]

This zone stretched from Istanbul to Aleppo to Tabriz to the head of the Persian Gulf. The hallmark commodities of this zone were silk, spices, and lumber. The third zone is the eastern Mediterranean-Indian Ocean zone. It stretched from Istanbul to Alexandria to Jidda to the coasts of India and Malacca.[16] Its primary avenues were the sea-lanes and its hallmark commodities were spices and copper. The boundaries of these zones are overlapping. They correspond not to political borders but, rather, to markets, to the limitations of transport, and to the energies and relationships of traders.

While the energies of states like the Ottoman and Portuguese were directed at garrisoning commercial entrepôts and transit points in order to collect customs taxes, the energies of individual traders were directed at circumventing the boundaries imposed by political overlords, and overcoming the limits posed by technology, by weather, and by predators whose only investment was in arms. State rationale was not necessarily merchant rationale. The organization of commercial activity was usually outside the immediate control of the state. Commerce survived between state controls. This is not to say that the Ottoman state and the members of the ruling military class behaved without commercial motivation or that they never acted as merchants. The boundaries delineating state servants from commercial entrepreneurs were not fixed. Often individual state agents themselves, in order to make a profit, were integrated into the commercial networks. At issue are the ways that members of the *askeri* (military-administrative) class disposed of the capital they accumulated and the meaning of that disposition for assessing the nature of the Ottoman economy. The Ottoman state, traditionally, has been portrayed as a land-based military state whose motivation for expansion can be explained solely in terms of the acquisition of arable land to broaden the tax base which in turn was used to support the ruling elites. Its concerns, then, are assumed to have been limited to political rather than commercial boundaries.[17] Rather, the Ottoman state was a sea based power whose conquests were directed not only at the acquisition of arable land but also at dominating or controlling the trade entrepôts and commercial networks across the zones described above. As a commercial power, the Ottoman state produced a ruling class whose members, (including the sultan, his sons, and the pashas) accumulated wealth that could be and was invested in commercial endeavor.[18]

Participation of the Ottoman state in trade was tied to the nature of transport facilities and to the initiative of various individuals within the state system. Agricultural hinterlands controlled by *askeri* provided not only the raw materials but also part of the capital for investments in trade across and between economic zones. To the extent that governments (such as the Ottoman, Mamluk, and Venetian) and their ruling military classes controlled shipping, food commodities (especially grain), and the revenues from landed estates, the adoption of trading functions by these governments and their functionaries was a logical extension of the accumulation of wealth.[19] By monopolizing trade (in certain commodities) and the distribution of agricultural revenues and surpluses, these governments became, in effect, big traders. Further, naval power gave some of these states the ability to limit or manipulate the long distance commercial ventures of competing states or individuals in a manner inconceivable when land-based military power alone was employed. Navies were visible when in port, but their movements were not readily charted as were those of cumbersome and slow moving armies. Fleets could appear offshore or at the side of a merchant vessel without warning. Their force was one of intimidation as well as firepower.

Ottoman expansion eastward and the development of foreign policy in the Levant proceeded by stages of negotiation and conquest, which correspond in their area of focus to the intersecting zones of trade described above. Each stage of Ottoman expansion (coastal-Aegean, Egypt and Syria, the Red Sea to the Indian Ocean) was mediated by naval supremacy. Analysis of each stage, in this work, will correspond to an assessment of the commercial policy and characteristic commodity of each trading zone. This essential linking of economic intent to offensive action and to the conduct of diplomacy exposes the nature of the Ottoman state in the context of the struggle for world power that characterized the early sixteenth century.

Historiography

Historiography generally has excluded the Oriental empires from the competition for world economic power. The Chinese sailed to Africa in the early fifteenth century. Then one day the ships apparently just stopped coming.[20] The Mongols "swept" across the steppes for the love of conquest, pastures, and space. The Ottoman armies marched to Yemen, Tabriz, Vienna. Yet this marching seems somehow merely instinctual, a reaction of blood, training, or temperament. One might suppose that this apparent Oriental failure to be an economic contender was a state of mind rather than an act of will, a matter of naiveté or arrogance rather than of power and its limits. Eurocentric historiography has not disarmed the Ottomans, instead it has mentally incapacitated them, thereby dispensing with the need to evaluate economies of conquest and disposing of the issue of competition with European states for markets rather than territory.[21]

This study, instead, proposes that the Ottoman state or components thereof had a plan that extended beyond the mobilization of troops, the organization of bureaus, and the assignment of military fiefs (*timars*); and that this plan imagined world hegemony, intended to exploit the customs revenues of the Indian Ocean ports, and envisioned a condition of dominance founded on naval supremacy among merchant competitors. These chapters explore some of those possibilities, linking Levantine commercial activity to Ottoman ambitions for world power and to the ramifying effects of those ambitions on its merchant competitors. The implications for further debate and research are: (*a*) a reassessment of the impact of Ottoman naval development on the world economy; (*b*) a revision of analyses of Ottoman economic policy in the context of mercantile ambitions; and (*c*) an examination of the details of participation by the Ottoman state, its merchants, and the Ottoman *askeri* class in the trade of the Levant and beyond.[22]

What exactly do we know about the economy of the sixteenth-century Ottoman Empire? The documentation in the Ottoman archives increases dramatically for the latter half of the sixteenth century and this is reflected in the scholarship of historians like Mehmed Genç, Bruce McGowan, Daniel Goffman, and Suraiya Faroqhi.[23] The pioneering work of Halil Inalcık on the fifteenth-century organization of commerce has not been followed up by the development of a systematic analytical and theoretical framework for the assessment of Ottoman commerce, and the integration of regional and international trading activity into the broader context of Ottoman agriculture, labor, and taxation systems. Here the work done on other areas such as India can provide some guidelines for the development of a comprehensive economic history premised on the notion that there existed a world economic system in the fifteenth century and that states and state agents were motivated to active participation in, and assertion of control over, commercial networks.[24]

Some research has been done on the early sixteenth century

since the great European historian, Wilhelm Heyd, characterized it as the period of "two great catastrophes": the Portuguese navigations and the Ottoman conquest of Cairo. In particular the works of Vittorino Godinho, Frederic C. Lane, Niels Steensgaard, and Eliyahu Ashtor have demonstrated that the Indian Ocean spice trade to the Levant was not destroyed by the Portuguese.[25] These works however, have not dealt with the transition period from Mamluk to Ottoman dominance. Rather they have documented the volume of spice trade in the fifteenth century and then in the reign of Süleiman I and after to show that the trade revived. This focus on *revival* perpetuates the assumption that the Portuguese cut off the eastern Mediterranean trade in the early decades of the sixteenth century. One result of this framing of the Levant trade is the minimization of the importance of the Ottoman conquests.[26] They become significant when attention is shifted away from western Europe and the New World discoveries, and back to the Euro-Asian sphere. There, the most important aspect of the Portuguese navigations was their contribution, through the consequent realignment of power, to the establishment of Ottoman political and commercial hegemony.

As long as the eastern Mediterranean trade in the early sixteenth century is viewed uni-dimensionally, as a direct outcome of Portuguese naval activity, the Ottoman naval expansion has no commercial significance. Fernand Braudel, for example, wrote that only when the great discoveries had robbed the Levant of much of its appeal did the Ottomans extend their influence into that area, noting that the occupation of Egypt did not occur until twenty years after Vasco da Gama's voyage.[27] He proposed that Ottoman hegemony developed only when Europe lost interest, thereby simultaneously discounting both Ottoman naval supremacy and the generally keen interest in the eastern Mediterranean trade evidenced among European states long after the advent of the Portuguese in the Indian Ocean. Analyses of the Ottoman state are still dominated by the assumption that naval and commercial affairs were tangential to the central state concerns of military-agricultural organization.[28] The Ottoman navy, however, played a considerable role in shaping Ottoman foreign affairs. It was a major determining factor in Venetian, Rhodian, and Mamluk foreign policy considerations. Ottoman naval power forced Venice and Rhodes into dependency relationships with the Ottomans in order to ensure the provisioning of their territories with grain and other commodities. Rhodes, for example, geared its military and economic activities to Ottoman naval maneuvers. Food stockpiling, licensing of ships, mobilization of noncombatant citizens, and even corsair activities were regulated according to the perceived threat of the Ottoman fleet.[29] The Mamluks placed themselves in another form of dependency relationship, also based on naval potential, with the Ottomans. In the Mamluk case, the need was for ships, shipbuilders, artillery, materials, and seamen to man a fleet against the Portuguese. Both power politics and the organization of trade on the east-west axis from the Mediterranean to the Indian Ocean were thus a function of the nature of Ottoman naval power in the early sixteenth century.

Imagining the Ottoman state as a commercial entity requires a reconceptualization of both the state itself and its typical modes of action. The notion of the Ottoman "state" has tended to be coterminous either with sultanic authority or with the operations of the central government. The latter is the usage employed here. "State," however, must be broken down into its separate relations and functions and must be understood as only one nexus of power. Failure to do so results, among other things, in the equation of the ideal of sultanic edict (*kanun*) with the actual processes of day-to-day legal and commercial operations. The state is then represented as acting only in a unitary fashion. This model obscures the complex interactions of notables, dynasty, and the merchant classes. It also contributes to the image of the Ottomans as somehow unique, not engaged in the commercial behaviors that characterized both their predecessors and their neighbors.

The avenues for exploring the relationships between Ottoman policy and the mechanisms of trade are limited by the nature and availability of Ottoman sources for the early sixteenth century. The *mühimme* (important affairs) registers do not cover the early decades of this century and *gümrük* (customs) registers, where available, do not break down trade revenues by commodity in most cases. Some pioneering work has been done using court records, but those, too, are restricted to certain cities for certain years. The questions, however, can be framed even though some must remain unanswered, and that framing alters the evaluation of the Ottoman state and its contextualization within the frameworks of European and world history. How was the state concerned with markets and could it increase profits? What were supply, demand, prices, raw materials, capital, products, technology, organization, mercantile institutions, profit? What was the level of consumption, of agricultural surpluses, and the extent of commandeering? What was the relationship between agriculture and commercial capital? Who exploited surpluses and how? What was the extent of pasha, notable family, and state agents' involvement as merchants?[30] Notable here will refer to members of the *askeri* class or to members of the Ottoman dynasty, who had access to power through the accumulation of wealth and political influence. The *askeri* class controlled the bulk of the wealth in Ottoman society although not all *askeri* were wealthy. Non-*askeri* members of the merchant class, money changers, and tax farmers might amass large fortunes as well. Contemporary scholarship on European notables, in Italy, for example, and on patron-client relations, provides theoretical models by which these relationships can be approached. If the Ottoman state discouraged initiative by confiscating estates, how consistent was that policy and how often and by what means was it circumvented? Were the goods of the "political classes" recycled into commerce instead of pious endowments (*evkaf*) or, through confiscation, into the state treasury? Can one distinguish between state commerce, partnership commerce, and individual commerce?[31] Neither the intersection of merchant, state, and notable interests nor the participation by various classes in large-scale investment in trade have been carefully investigated for the Ottoman Empire in the pre-seventeenth century period. How flexible were commercial systems (changes of route, bidding for products, campaign requisitions, production), and to what extent did the Ottoman state actually control trade within its borders? The traditional model of sixteenth-century absolutism tends to presume that Ottoman state control of trade was pervasive, but that was clearly not the case. What exactly were the mechanisms of trade and the distinctions between absolute and relative decline in trade? What were the rhythms of dramatic change? That is, which factors significantly altered the conduct of trade and which did not, for example: war, the Portuguese navigations, the Ottoman succession struggles? These questions are much more difficult to answer for the early sixteenth than for the eighteenth century. Yet their answers have often been predetermined by assumptions about the nature of early modern Muslim states rather than by an analysis of the texts and the actions of those who controlled and engaged in trade. The scope of information available allows speculation on the Ottoman state as an economic actor based on state policy and action, the responses of competing states, the conduct of diplomacy, the rhetoric of legitimation, and the patterns of Levantine commercial behavior. These patterns, reflected in sources on Italian city-state or

Mamluk economic organization and merchant relations, should be employed as suitable options for analyzing Ottoman behavior. Historiographic evaluation of states in Europe has long equated political action with economic motivation; but similar connections generally have not been applied to the Ottoman Empire whose emergence as hegemon in the eastern Mediterranean region coincided temporally with the Italian Renaissance.[32]

In this study, the political and commercial expansion of the Ottoman Empire are inextricably linked. The economies of conquest are not detached from the economies of trade, and the state is granted commercial intentionality as well as a navy to enforce its intentions. A further objective of this work is to present the Ottoman and Safavid states, not as isolated and isolationist blocks cut off from the processes of world trade, but as entities thoroughly incorporated into the Euro-Asian commercial networks that predated the establishment of both these empires.[33] These networks, embodied in the medieval Afro-Eurasian circulation of such commodities as copper and grain, were a powerful force in shaping the foreign policies, diplomatic relations, and expansionist philosophies of the Muslim gunpowder empires of the sixteenth century.

PART I

The Ottomans and Levantine Foreign Policy

The early sixteenth-century Levant was the site for a contest of Muslim arms and of Muslim legitimation which culminated in the Ottoman defeat of its Safavid and Mamluk opponents in Iran, Syria, and Egypt. This dual confrontation mirrored a similar and contemporaneous contest, among Christian monarchs with an eye to expansion, the locus for which was the Italian peninsula. There, the French, Hapsburgs, Spanish, the pope, and city-states like Venice and Milan strove to carve out kingdoms or expand their holdings at the expense of their neighbors. Framing these circumscribed conflicts was the newly emergent contest for world economic hegemony that took as its terrain the sea-lanes of the Atlantic and Indian Oceans. The larger contest for seaborne empire would ultimately determine the course of the more localized conflicts in Italy and in the eastern Mediterranean region. This era of seapower enabled king and sultan alike to cast widely the net aimed at military allies, and to enhance dramatically the scale of sovereign claims made in the conduct of diplomacy. The articulation of those claims, and the reordering of foreign policy and diplomacy in the Levant, which took place as a result of Ottoman and Portuguese expansionist policy, form the subject of the next two chapters. In the course of that reordering, two factors, the rise of a powerful Shi'ite monarch, Shah Ismail, in Iran and the long succession struggle for the Ottoman throne, play prominent roles.

Religious rhetoric provided the terms by which the claims of sixteenth-century monarchs were articulated. The language of submission to divine will was as important to these late medieval monarchs as were the ceremonies of submission which they required from their subordinates. Divine mission was combined with imperial ambition to legitimize the conquests of expansionist powers. The Ottomans used the Mamluks' failure to secure the *hajj* routes and the accusation that they consorted with the "infidel" Ismail as rationales for the seizure of the Mamluk territories. King Emmanuel of Portugal and Christopher Columbus used the redemption of the Holy Land and the gaining of souls respectively as justifications for their voyages of discovery.[1] Shah Ismail utilized the language of jihad to justify his invasions into Ottoman territory while the Ottoman sultan sought a religious decree to sanction the killing of his Safavid foe. Meanwhile European states capitalized upon Shi'ite *vs.* Sunni sectarianism to represent the Safavid and Ottoman monarchs as religious rivals. This language of divine favor notwithstanding, political expediency and commercial imperialism provided the incentives for the military and diplomatic actions which circumscribed the power struggles for the Euro-Asian world.

In 1503, the year in which Portuguese galleys first returned home with a significant cargo of Indian spices, the Ottomans and the Signoria of Venice concluded a peace treaty. It had been exactly half a century since Mehmed II's conquest of Constantinople/Istanbul, a capital worthy of a dynasty with great imperial ambitions. In the intervening years the Ottomans had waged a series of wars against Rhodes, Venice, and the Mamluks which were an expression of those ambitions. Venice, a long time naval power in the Levant, had hoped for control of a port on the Syrian or south Anatolian coast and to that end had attempted a military alliance with Uzun Hasan (1453–1478), the Ak Koyunlu Türkmen ruler in Iran. When Mehmed II defeated Uzun Hasan at the Battle of Başkent in 1473, Venice had been forced to set aside those plans, aiming instead at an alliance which would guarantee its favored position in the port outlets of the overland trade routes from the east.[2] Those outlets were controlled by the Mamluks. The Ottoman-Venetian treaty of 1503 concluded a long period of intermittent warfare over control of naval and trading bases in the eastern Mediterranean.[3] The advantages of this treaty for Venice were the resumption of trading privileges for Venetian merchants in Ottoman territory, and the assurance of some security in the eastern Mediterranean while Venice turned its attention to the internal Italian political situation. The costs were a loss of territory (Modon, Lepanto, Navarino, Durazzo, and Coron) and the payment of an annual indemnity of 10,000 ducats to the Ottomans. Although Venice did not formally acknowledge a vassal relationship with the Ottoman government, the Sublime Porte, the Ottomans viewed this payment as tribute. Venice, among the European states, had provided the bulk of the funding, manpower, and ships for this naval conflict and so bore the brunt of the damage. In 1503, facing the added challenge to its commercial security posed by the Portuguese incursions in the Indian Ocean and the Red Sea, the Signoria required an ally who could safeguard its trade revenues. The Ottoman state would eventually become that ally.

Katib Çelebi, the Ottoman chronicler, found the period of relative stability in Ottoman-Venetian relations which followed this peace treaty somewhat regrettable. He would have preferred to see the Ottoman navy employed in attacking Christian bases rather than in providing security for Mediterranean trade. He wrote that after the Ottoman expedition against Midilli in 1501 the Ottoman fleet was employed only in protecting the Ottoman domains rather than in attacking the infidels, adding:

> When however, the power of the Persian kings in the East began
> to increase, the disturbances of the Rafezis and the retirement of
> Sultan Bayezid Khan, on account of his great age, produced negli-
> gence in the ministers, and tended to injure the prosperity of the
> state; and Sultan Selim, after his accession to the throne, being
> occupied in matters that demanded immediate attention—in pun-
> ishing the Persians, and subjugating the countries of Egypt and
> Syria—the possessions of the infidels thus remained unmolested.[4]

This characterization of the first two decades of the sixteenth century mentions three of the four main factors which influenced the exercise of Levantine diplomacy from 1503–1517. These were: the rise of Ismail Safavi, the development of the Ottoman navy, and the decline of the Mamluk power in Egypt and Syria. The fourth factor was the Portuguese naval expansion and the threat it posed to established trading interests. Of course the chronicler did not tell the whole story. Katib Çelebi was clearly uncomfortable with change, especially the type of change which could adversely affect his own financial position. Nor did the sultan "retire," as Katib Çelebi suggested. Bayezid II (ruled 1481–1512) spent the last years of his reign fighting off the attempts of his sons to occupy the throne before he was prepared to leave it. Ultimately, he was forced to abdicate by Selim I (ruled 1512–1520). Like Katib Çelebi, the Venetians were struck by the new sixteenth century order of things. Accustomed to their long held position of naval supremacy in the eastern Mediterranean, they were now forced to cede that position to the Ottoman Turks. Venetian diplomacy in these early years of the sixteenth century was met with the challenge of redefining commercial and political interests in response to major changes in the political and economic situation in the eastern Mediterranean region.[5] In the course of this redefinition, just who played the part of "infidel" depended on diplomatic necessity.

The contemporaneous attempts to establish Ottoman dominance in the eastern Mediterranean and Portuguese dominance in the Indian Ocean prompted a rearticulation of diplomatic relations. Egypt's commercial survival, like that of Venice, was threatened by the Portuguese. The Mamluks controlled both the inland emporia and the port outlets of the eastern trade: Jidda, Cairo, Alexandria, Aleppo, Damascus, Beirut. They had survived one challenge to their political and commercial hegemony when Sultan Bayezid (son of Mehmed the Conqueror) attacked Syria during the Ottoman-Mamluk wars of 1485–1491.[6] Now the Portuguese threatened to invade the Red Sea and endanger Mecca and Medina. The provision of commercial security for their Levantine trading partners was not the Mamluks' only responsibility. The Mamluk sultan, Qānsūh al-Ghūrī (1501–1516), as nominal overlord in the Muslim world, was obligated to defend Muslim states against attacks by Europeans and to defend the Holy Cities. This duty derived from Mamluk claims to a form of political succession to the caliphs. Challenges to this assumption of political supremacy in the Muslim world were soon to be mounted by the Safavids and Uzbegs as well as by the Ottomans. Though the Mamluk-Ottoman struggle was in a period of stasis at the beginning of the sixteenth century, the Portuguese precipitated a crisis which undermined Mamluk legitimacy and dramatically shifted the balance of power in the eastern Mediterranean in favor of the Ottomans.

Another contender in the eastern Mediterranean, Rhodes, had also actively participated in the Aegean wars against the Ottomans. Unlike Venice and the Mamluk state, however, its economic and diplomatic position was not dependent on the Indian Ocean trade. The Knights of Rhodes, in accordance with their crusading mission, pursued a relatively consistent policy of aggression against both the Mamluks and the Ottomans for over a century. Close links to France and to Genoa as well as commercial competition had also made the Knights intermittently the enemy of Venice. As the sixteenth-century Italian chronicler Guicciardini wrote of Rhodes:

> . . . to the greatest glory of the Order [it] had been, as it were,
> a bulwark of the Christian religion in those seas, although they

were somewhat notorious for the fact that, spending all their days
in piracy against the ships of the infidels, they also at times pil-
laged Christian vessels.[7]

Venice regularly charged Rhodes with failing to distinguish between crusading and piracy, at the expense of Venetian shipping.
Rhodes was also closely associated with Rome, although papal authority at this time was much weakened by challenges from France
and Naples and by the Holy See's efforts to extend its control on
the Italian peninsula. Against the wishes of the pope, who urged
resistance, Rhodes had reluctantly concluded a truce with the Ottomans in 1503, but had not relinquished efforts to mobilize a joint
European fleet to renew the conflict.

While Rhodes, Venice, and the Porte were still engaged in battle at sea in 1501, Ismail Safavi was accumulating political and
military support in western Iran. Hereditary sheikh of the Safavid
order of dervishes and a successful warrior, Ismail quickly moved
to challenge both the Mamluks and the Ottomans for sovereignty
in the Euro-Asian sphere. The speed and scope of his early victories suggested that Ismail might prove a decisive factor in determining the outcome of the power struggle then underway in the
eastern Mediterranean region. Conquering Şirvan and then Tabriz
(in northwestern Iran) in 1500–1501, Ismail became the unknown
quantity in a political realignment which would take place in response to Ottoman and Portuguese expansionism.

The rhythms of sixteenth-century trade were governed by the
attempts of subordinate states to overthrow or circumvent the monopolies of the systems already in place. Ottoman and Portuguese
efforts eventually combined to eliminate the Mamluk middleman
from the east-west trade. In the eastern Mediterranean, the French
sought unsuccessfully to displace Venice as most favored nation in
Ottoman ports. In the Indian Ocean, the Ottomans would seek unsuccessfully to replace the Portuguese as dominant power. Then,
with greater success, the Dutch and English would in turn monopolize the sea trade in the seventeenth century. In the later sixteenth century, the English would seek to bypass Ottoman commercial outlets by negotiating agreements for overland trade with
the Safavids via Muscovy.[8] This commercial outflanking maneuver, however, was unsuccessful. The great triumphs, then, of the
sixteenth-century struggle for control of trade were the establishment of Portuguese hegemony in the Indian Ocean and of Ottoman
hegemony in the Levant. At the turn of the sixteenth century, neither of these triumphs was assured. Hence, a series of alliances

was contemplated and negotiated, their object being to assure the position of each competing state in the new sixteenth-century world order. Often these alliances were temporary and always they were based on material self-interest rather than communal affinities. Such "alliances" would be concluded by the Ottomans and Mamluks against the Portuguese and proposed by Venice and the Safavids against the Ottomans. The first was real and the second only imagined.[9]

Because of its dominant position in the eastern Mediterranean and because of its clearly expansionist policies, the Ottoman Empire became the target of alliances proposed by states on both its eastern and western frontiers. In the end, however, the idea of a grand alliance against the Ottomans was not practicable.[10] It existed more in the imaginations of European writers and statesmen than in the concrete strategies of European policy makers. No concerted attack against the Safavids materialized either, but the Uzbeg-Safavid conflict in eastern Iran enabled the Ottomans to maintain their bilateral Hapsburg and Safavid war fronts for over a century without decisive losses. In the two decades preceding the 1517 conquest of Cairo, the Venetian, Rhodian, Mamluk, and Safavid states held the potential for forming an anti-Ottoman coalition and for maintaining the commercial and political status quo. Yet, diplomatic activity notwithstanding, the pursuit of commercial objectives and the multiple demands on military resources of these states precluded the formalization of any such alliance. On the European side, possible challengers to Ottoman power were preoccupied with the contest for control of the Italian peninsula. The future Pius II's prediction after the fall of Constantinople in 1453 also proved true for the early sixteenth century. He said that Christian Europe was:

> a body without a head, a republic without laws or magistrates . . . every state has a separate prince and every prince has a separate interest. . . . If you lead a small army against the Turks you will easily be overcome; if a large one, it will soon fall into confusion.[11]

CHAPTER 2

The Western Salient:
Venice, Ismail Safavi, and Europe

Modern historiography has been preoccupied with Ottoman firepower as the overwhelming factor in the balance of power in the Mediterranean world in the early sixteenth century, obscuring the importance of the navy in establishing Ottoman supremacy.[1] This preoccupation results from the nature of the sources and from the role played by Ottoman artillery in the battles at Çaldıran, where the Ottomans decisively defeated Shah Ismail in 1514, and Raidaniyah, where they routed the Mamluk army during the conquest of Egypt in 1516.[2] Campaign accounts typically produce histories of conflict. But this conflict-centered vision of history can be balanced to put military engagements in their proper perspective. First, diplomacy can be brought into focus as a means of avoiding wars as well as of ending them. Second, diplomacy and other non-aggressive tactics can be viewed as a means of preserving economic and commercial stability. The image of machismo generated by the campaign accounts can be countered by the evidence of defensive mechanisms, employed by the states of the eastern Mediterranean region: such as diplomatic missions, spies, and noncombat naval strategies. Such mechanisms were utilized by states like Rhodes, whose objective was self-preservation, and by states, like the Ottomans', whose objective was expansion. The conduct of diplomacy in the Levant was altered and its pace quickened by the Portuguese voyages to India, the rise of Ismail Safavi in Iran, and the establishment of Ottoman naval hegemony in the eastern Mediterranean. The simultaneous emergence of these forces in the Euro-Asian sphere suggested the potential for new options in the realms of commerce and politics. It remained to determine which states and which traders would gain and which would lose in the process by which these new options were sorted out.

While the Portuguese were conquering the port towns in the Indian Ocean and brutally making examples of local residents who resisted them, Ismail Safavi was establishing his hegemony in western Persia, disinterring and desecrating the bones of his Ak Koyunlu predecessors.[3] Following his conquest of Tabriz in 1501, Ismail rapidly expanded both his troop strength and the territories under his control. In the ensuing ten year period, he consolidated his power in western Iran, conquered Baghdad and challenged Ottoman and Mamluk sovereignty by invading eastern Anatolia and Syria. As a result, Ottoman and Venetian diplomatic strategy came to depend in part on expectations of Safavid power. For the Ottomans, it was unclear whether Ismail would be a real contender for control of Anatolia or simply a chronic aggravation on their eastern frontiers. One gauge of the Ottoman assessment of that threat is their willingness to commit all their military resources to the anti-Safavid struggle. In fact, they did not do so. A portion of Ottoman military and naval forces was mobilized instead on the Red Sea salient against the Portuguese. Beginning in 1505, the Ottomans sent naval aid to the Mamluks, thus providing some insurance that Bayezid could rely at least on Mamluk neutrality in the event of a major Safavid offensive. It seems unlikely that the Porte would have been willing to provide guns and ammunition to the Mamluks for use in the Red Sea unless it was fairly confident that it could stop any major offensive on the part of the Safavids.

Venetian diplomacy in 1503 was based on expectations that the Mamluk state would provide security for the trade routes bringing goods from the Indian Ocean to the eastern Mediterranean. Events in the following years forced Venice to recast the Ottoman state in the role of provider of security for its eastern commercial interests, despite the potential risks. The growing Ottoman naval power was the weight that shifted the balance in this transformation of Venetian policy. For Venice, it was the Ottoman capabilities for providing naval firepower against the Portuguese that helped legitimize Ottoman claims to the Mamluk territories. For Venetian policy makers, the Ottomans posed, at this juncture, a certain duality. On the one hand, Ottoman military power now represented the promise of security for trade in the eastern Mediterranean and a naval potential sufficient to stop the Portuguese diversion of the eastern trade. On the other hand, it was a constant threat to Venetian possessions in the Aegean. Ismail, as a diplomatic factor, suggested that some balance might be struck in the dilemma of limiting Ottoman power.[4] The dilemma was to find a diplomatic balance that could limit Ottoman power without disabling it. The softening of Ottoman policy toward Venice leading to the peace of 1503 had been mediated by the rise of Ismail and his initial successes. Little was known about the Safavid boy-king, but his successes suggested that he might provide the limiting factor that Venice and other European states were looking for. An elaborate mythology was built-up around the person of Shah Ismail and played a significant role in the development of foreign policy in the eastern Mediterranean region. Various European monarchs initiated correspondence with Ismail. Spies, travelers, and diplomats described the robust young Ismail in glowing terms.

Much of Ismail's support came from the eastern Anatolian frontier areas where allegiance to central governments, either in Tabriz or in Istanbul, was often nominal at best. European observers capitalized on the apparent heterodox religious currents in the frontier area to describe Ismail's followers as an army of sufi devotees, selfless warriors for their faith comparable to the Crusaders. Whereas the motivation of the tribal frontier begs (called "kızılbaş" or "redhead" for their red twelve-peaked headgear representing the twelve Shi'ite imams) could be explained adequately in terms of political interests (maintaining their independence from the Ottomans), instead it was characterized in the European accounts as the flowering of Shi'ite religious fanaticism in opposition to the Sunni Islam of the Ottomans, inspired by the charismatic leadership of Ismail, the deified warrior-sheikh and hereditary claimant to leadership of the Safavi order of dervishes. The elaboration of Ismail's mythology in Europe served the practical purpose of justifying negotiations and possible alliances with a Muslim state. A political alliance with a sufi saint was easier to justify than one with a Muslim king.

Constantino Laschari, a Venetian spy, was one of the first to report to the Venetian Senate on the teenage Ismail and his troops.

> The Sophi |sufi| religion has always fought against the Ottoman royal house because the Ottomans are heretics and usurpers of the territories of many Muslims. Ismail is considered a prophet, rich, just, generous, and divinely inspired. He is much beloved of his sect which is a certain religion—Catholic in their way.[5]

This description, written in 1502, suggested that Ismail was not only powerful but a worthy ally for the Signoria. Laschari predicted that the army the shah was raising would be victorious against the Ottomans. Another flattering portrayal of Ismail was sent to the Venetian Senate in 1507 by Giovanni Morosini, a resident of Damascus. In his attempt to persuade the Signoria to ally with Ismail, Morosini described the shah as valorous, generous, and learned. Adored by his followers, he was called "prophet" and "saint" rather than king or prince. Ismail took counsel with no one, according to Morosini, but had three Armenian priests for advisers. His followers thought of him as "god on earth." Although Morosini admitted that he did not know exactly what Ismail's faith was, he conjectured that it was "more Christian than otherwise."[6]

The political ambitions of the *kızılbaş* and of Ismail himself were translated into religious terms for a European audience. An anonymous Italian merchant wrote in 1508 about Ismail (called the "Great Sophy" or Sufi):

> The Sophy is loved and reverenced as a god especially by his soldiers [the *kızılbaş*] many of whom enter into battle without armor expecting their master Ismail to watch over them in the fight. Others go into battle without armor being willing to die for their monarch crying "Sheikh, Sheikh." The name of God is forgotten throughout Persia and only that of Ismail remembered. Everyone, and particularly his soldiers, considers him immortal.[7]

Ismail was characterized as a benevolent, saintly, Robin Hood-like character, in striking contrast to the familiar image of an aloof and despotic Ottoman sultan. His piety and simplicity inspired rabid devotion and his coming fulfilled prophetic tradition:

> He is adored as a prophet and the rug on which he knelt for Easter was torn to pieces to be used by his followers as Christians use relics. The Turks referred to the Persians as Azamini [*acem*] before the reign of the Sufi, Ismail, but now they call the Persians *kızılbaş*. After Ismail's first victory, the members of his sect flocked to join him because in their books they found it foretold that a prophet of their religion would come and they must support and exalt him.
>
> It is said that Ismail was sent by God to announce that his sect [the Safavi order] was the only true sect whose members would be admitted to paradise and from this it results that the army of Shah Ismail is unpaid just as when we Christians fought the Crusades. They [his army] fight neither for gold nor for the state but for their religion and they believe that if they die they will go straight to paradise and thus they fight most valiantly.[8]

Of course Muslim theology permits no "prophets" after Muhammad, but the messianic representation of Ismail in this account is striking. At a more pragmatic level, also noteworthy is the fact that followers "flocked" to Ismail's standard only "after" his first victory. Victories were necessary to sustain Ismail's charisma as demonstrated by the evaporation of much of his eastern Anatolian support after he was beaten by the Ottomans in 1514. For the time being, however, European accounts of Ismail remained enthusiastic:

> Ismail . . . is known as the Equalizer . . . and the whole of Europe is known here as the people behind the wind. . . . There is no doubt that those who wear the red cap are more like Portuguese than like people from anywhere else.[9]

Several themes are recurrent in these portrayals of Ismail Safavi and his *kızılbaş* supporters. The Ottomans are portrayed as heretics (usurpers of the territories of brother Muslims). Christian Europe justified its attempts at alliance with Ismail by describing the Shi'ites as allied with Christendom by virtue of shared religious opposition to the infidel Sunnis. The *kızılbaş* were warriors for the faith (*gazis*) just like the Crusaders.[10] Their military prowess was the result of religious zeal. They were also willing martyrs for the faith. In the European accounts, Ismail was a saint and a prophet as much as a king. The mystical aspects of heterodox Islam were emphasized, to show an affinity with Christian supernaturalism. The messianic and milennarian content in representations of Ismail was calculated to suggest affinities with contemporary Christian beliefs. The shah became a Christ-like figure: celebrating Easter, distributing his wealth, and inspiring his followers to martyrdom. His dress and the things he touched were "relics." Another point of affinity emphasized in Christian accounts was the devotion of heterodox Shi'ism for Fatima, Muhammad's daughter and the wife of the fourth caliph Ali, comparable to the Christian cult of the Virgin Mary.[11] Ismail was called the "Great Sufi" and his army routinely was referred to simply as "the sufis." This rhetorical transformation, in the European sources, of hardened frontier Türkmen cavalry units into an army of religious fanatics was nothing short of remarkable. Such characterizations lent diplomatic force to the negotiations between the shah and potential Christian allies against the Ottomans. Ismail himself employed the notion of Shi'ite-Christian affinities in his exercise of diplomacy.

Venetian interest in the Safavid shah went beyond myth,

rumor, or speculation. It remained to ascertain the actual nature and extent of Ismail's military potential. Venice made use of extensive merchant and spy networks in an attempt to gain concrete evidence of Ismail's relative power. However great the potential advantages of an alliance, negotiating with the Safavids posed great potential danger to Venice's relations with Cairo and with the Porte. Venice enjoyed favored nation status in its trading relations with the Ottomans and Mamluks and did not wish to jeopardize that position. According to one Venetian compiler, Venice sent envoys to learn:

> many things about Ismail: how he was progressing, the power of his state, and everything about his situation, as it was the custom of Venice diligently to pursue knowledge of the power of other states.[12]

Further, these envoys, well versed in the language and customs of the area, were instructed to engage the friendship of the Safavid ruler without compromising their relations with the sultan in Cairo. Venice was impressed by Ismail's reported military potential but evidently not so much so as to be foolhardy. The mythology of Ismail's prowess and its importance for diplomatic rhetoric could not be confused with relative military capabilities. Neither Venice nor the Mamluks had sufficient confidence in the powers of the "divine" shah to risk jeopardizing their shares in the profits of the oriental trade for the illusory promise of an Ottoman defeat.

The Mamluks, though nominal overlords in the Muslim world were intimidated by Ismail, who threatened their Syrian frontier, as they were by the Ottomans and Portuguese, who threatened their Mediterranean and Red Sea frontiers. This gave Mamluk trading partners, like Venice, increased leverage in negotiations for trading privileges. Ultimately, the Mamluks could not guarantee Venice either commercial or political security in the Levant. Throughout the period under discussion, the primary concern of Venice in its relations with the Mamluks was the preservation of trade revenues from goods arriving overland through Aleppo and, via the Red Sea, through Alexandria. Venetian negotiations focused on obtaining favorable trade conditions in the form of low duties and protection from officials' abuses. In order to protect the trade flow, Venice exerted pressure on the Mamluks to provide both military defense against bedouin raids and naval opposition to the incursions of the Portuguese.[13] Increasingly the Mamluk regime failed to provide this security. Imposts on trade increased in reponse to the demands of the deteriorating military and economic situation in the Mamluk state. Security for the trade routes could not be guaranteed as the regime could not always adequately enforce central governmental controls.[14] Challenges to Mamluk authority took a number of forms, including revolts by the mamluk soldiery (an elite military caste) in Cairo and provincial rebellions in Syria and Arabia.[15] Political instability in Syria was of particular concern to European traders who required access to the Syrian outlets for the Iranian silk trade, the production centers for which were now under Safavid control. Also bedouin raiding on the pilgrimage caravans culminated in the 1505–1506 suspension of the *hajj*, because of disruptions associated with the revolt of the governor of Yanbo in Arabia.[16] This was a grave embarrassment for the Mamluk ruler whose legitimacy in the Muslim world depended upon his ability to protect pilgrims. If he could not protect the *hajj*, neither could he ensure the security of foreign trade.

Breaches of the Venetian-Mamluk commercial treaties occurred in several areas. The most common Mamluk abuses were forced purchases of spices at inflated prices, tariff gouging, and intentional delays of the loading period. The Venetian merchants were periodically subjected to a variety of exactions and affronts to their persons or goods. These included: direct participation of Mamluk officials in the commercial transactions they were expected to supervise; substitution of diluted or poor quality goods and lightweight goods; restriction of trading partners to the sultan's own men; arbitrary refusal to assign goods where credit was owed; arbitrary levying of duties; impounding of merchandise; arrest of merchants; and refusal to loaded ships of licenses to sail. It was such abuses that led the chronicler Ibn Iyās to charge the Mamluk sultan with the ruin of the ports of Alexandria and Damietta in 1502, even before the effects of the Portuguese navigations were felt.[17] Mamluk exactions at the transit exchange points, like Alexandria and Damascus, impeded the flow of goods from India to the Mediterranean just as did the intervention of the Portuguese at the source. This bilateral intervention caused Venice to seek alternatives to its traditional commercial alliances.

The new era of Levantine relations after the signing of the 1503 peace treaty would be an Ottoman era, one in which Ottoman mastery of the trading zones would give the Porte extraordinary leverage in the conduct of diplomacy. It was not merely the extent of Ottoman military dominance which affected this transformation, it was also the willingness which the Ottoman state demonstrated in this period to provide protection for and promote trading ventures. In the context of Ottoman expansion in the Mediterranean and Portuguese expansion in the Indian Ocean, the conduct of Levantine diplomacy can be illustrated by a series of Venetian diplomatic missions between 1504 and 1516. These missions reflect the shift in the balance of commercial power in the Levant to the Ottomans—a shift in diplomacy which reflected the reordering of control of seapower and of trade. The instructions given to Venice's envoy to Cairo in 1504, the year following the approval by the *doge* (elected head of the Venetian republic) of the Ottoman-Venetian treaty, give some indication of Venice's objectives and expectations.[18] The Signoria sent an envoy, Francesco Teldi, posing as a jewel buyer, to Cairo. He was ordered to contact the governor or some other official on his arrival and to obtain a secret audience with the Mamluk sultan. Having once obtained an audience, Teldi was instructed to mention the common trade interests of the Mamluks and Venetians and discuss possible remedies for the damage threatened to their trade because of the Portuguese navigating to India. He was charged with advising the Mamluk sultan that fourteen Portuguese ships had reached Lisbon from India loaded with spices including 5,000 sporta of pepper.[19] Twelve other ships were in transit and sixteen more were being prepared in Portugal to make the voyage to India. Blackmail and bribery of sorts were part of Teldi's diplomatic assignment. He was to warn the sultan that Venetian merchants threatened to go to Portugal to obtain their spices, but that Venice would rather not abandon the traditional routes and arrangements with the Mamluks. The prosperity of the Venetian trade was dependent on established time cycles, trading networks, and the operations of resident agents in the port and transit exchange cities. Financing of these agents' operations and the maintenance of credit were dependent upon a certain degree of continuity in the routes, goods, season, and personnel of commercial transactions, a continuity which the Portuguese navigations threatened to disrupt. The Venetian galley convoy (and its loading period) was called the "*muda*": state-sponsored and defended spice trade convoys, one to Alexandria and one to Beirut, which sailed once, but in the fifteenth century sometimes twice, per year. Teldi promised that the *muda*, stopped during the Aegean war (1499–1503), would again be sent to Beirut and Alexandria that year on condition that the Mamluk sultan blocked the Portuguese navigations and returned the spices to their original routes.

Teldi's message placed responsibility squarely on Qānsūh al-

Ghūrī, the Mamluk sultan, to effect the displacement of the Portuguese from the Indian Ocean. Venice protested its own helplessness saying, "We cannot remedy the navigation because not a single Christian prince will move to make war against the Portuguese." This pleading of the Faith was rhetorical posturing since European history, at the time, clearly shows that shared religious convictions were no impediment to war when opportunity and profit provided the proper incentives. Venice demanded that Qānsūh send envoys to the Muslim kings of Cochin and Cananor and other rulers on the west Indian coast to persuade them not to have dealings with the Portuguese, and to the kings of Calicut and Cambay to encourage them to continue their resistance *against* the Portuguese.[20] The Portuguese had fortified Cochin, a primary pepper shipping port, in 1503. Beyond the coastal areas which could be controlled by means of a seaborne attack, the Portuguese relied on diplomacy and cash to secure their economic interests. Their efforts were opposed by Malik Ayās, the governor of Diu, who had resisted Portuguese threats and bribes. Venice, in short, expected the Mamluks to act militarily and diplomatically to see that Portuguese efforts in the Indian Ocean proved unprofitable. Without Mamluk intervention, Venice feared that the resistance of Calicut and Cambay to the Portuguese might crumble. Conversely Venice hoped that pressure from Qānsūh, as Protector of Mecca and Medina and representative of Muslim sovereignty, might sway the Muslim rulers of Cochin and Cananor from their Portuguese alliances.

Qānsūh did employ extra-diplomatic means in an attempt to meet the Portuguese threat, sending an expedition under Amīr Ḥusain al-Kūrdī to fortify Jidda in 1505. A Mamluk fleet, however, was not launched until 1507. It met with initial success, defeating Almeida, the Portuguese viceroy of India, at Chaul in the Indian Ocean in 1508. The following spring, however, the joint Mamluk and Gujarati fleet was annihilated by the Portuguese fleet at Diu, so the Mamluk expedition had little commercial or military effect.[21] In the Indian Ocean, although shipping in the hands of Muslim traders continued, the hopes of the Venetians that the Mamluk sultan could rally Muslim leaders in India to defeat the Portuguese proved false.[22] Ultimately, although the Portuguese failed to blockade the Red Sea trade, it was only with Ottoman assistance that the Mamluks were able to mobilize a naval force to challenge them.[23] The early years of the sixteenth century were characterized by confusion over just what combination of forces was required to limit the hegemonic ambitions of both the Portuguese and the Ottomans. If Venice could depend neither upon a Christian coalition to deter Ottoman expansion nor a Muslim coalition to deter Portuguese aggression, then some individual power would be required in each case. It soon became apparent that the Safavids would be that power to challenge the Ottomans and the Ottomans would be the power to challenge the Portuguese.

The first major indication of the strength of the Safavid challenge came in 1507 when Ismail mounted against the Zū al-Ḳadr principality an attack which, at a distance, appeared to be a serious political and military threat to the Ottoman eastern frontiers.[24] The Zū al-Ḳadr were a semiautonomous dynasty in southeastern Anatolia which, under the canny leadership of ʿAlā ad-Dawla (d. 1515), contrived to play off the Ottoman and Mamluk sultans, one against the other. The Zū al-Ḳadr principality functioned as a wedge between Ottomans and Mamluks and a stopper against Ottoman expansion into Syria. It was the focus of the Ottoman-Mamluk power struggle for political hegemony in southeastern Anatolia. The importance for Venice of this frontier conflict and its potential escalation lay in the effect it would have on Ottoman-Venetian and Ottoman-Mamluk relations.[25] If Ismail were actually successful in engaging the energy of the Ottomans, it might allow for the reassertion of Venetian colonial activity in the eastern Mediterranean. Giovanni Morosini, a Venetian citizen resident in Damascus, went even further. In a letter to the Venetian Senate describing the battles of Ismail and ʿAlā ad-Dawla he urged the Signoria:

> This is the opportune moment to form an alliance among the Christian princes and Persia to engage in the most holy endeavor to throw the Turk out of Europe.[26]

Not only did Morosini view the Safavids as coconspirators in this sacred mission, he also suggested that Ismail was a supporter of Christianity if not, indeed, a Christian.

If Ismail was defined as an ally and friend of Christianity in an anti-Ottoman strategy, then the Ottomans must necessarily be defined as the enemy. Further, a Safavid attack on the Zū al-Ḳadr, who were nominally subject to the Mamluks, might provoke some form of anti-Safavid joint action on the part of the Ottomans and Mamluks.[27] Ismail thus provided a locus of confusion in the determination of Venetian diplomatic policy.[28] But when Ismail did solicit the aid of Venice in an alliance against the Ottomans, the Signoria was unwilling to compromise the commercial status quo.

In 1508, Ismail launched a successful march on Baghdad, the old Abbasid capital, again prompting speculation in Venice that the Safavid monarch would next direct his victorious armies against the Ottomans. Ensuing events would have far reaching effects on Venice's relations with the Ottoman state and its opponents. The lynchpin of these events was Pietro Zeno, the Venetian consul in Damascus, vantage point for the Venetian Senate's surveillance of Iran.[29] Zeno took his position in Damascus in November of 1508. That same month, he dispatched the customary initial report to the Signoria describing his arrival, presentation of his credentials, the Mamluk officials in Damascus, and current events in the area in which the activities of Ismail figured prominently. After relating the Safavid conquest of Baghdad, Zeno mentioned the many Safavid sympathizers in Syria. This disclosure was echoed short years later by another interested party, the Portuguese civil servant Tomé Pires who noted that there was little recognition of the Mamluk sultan's authority in Syria: ". . . neighboring regions are every day joining the Sheikh Ismail against him."[30]

Safavid military successes, like the defeat of ʿAlā ad-Dawla in 1507, had the potential for consequences ranging far beyond the frontiers of eastern Anatolia; and substantial Safavid support in Syria posed the spectre of revolt against the Mamluk overloads. Such a revolt, coupled with a Safavid campaign, could result in Ismail's controlling a Mediterranean outlet for the Iranian silk trade, the production centers for which were located in Safavid territory. This possibility was of great interest to Venice, a major consumer of Iranian silk. Conversely, the Venetian commodity, which was of most interest to the Safavid shah, was artillery. Ismail followed up his victory at Baghdad with efforts to acquire from Venice the founders and artillery needed to raise an effective challenge to the Ottomans. He sent an embassy to the *doge*, via Zeno in Damascus.[31] It was Zeno's involvement with these Persian envoys which would cause a four-year disruption in Venetian-Mamluk relations and lead to Zeno's eventual incarceration in Cairo.

Ismail's letter to the *doge* commenced with lengthy declarations of friendship and brotherly love. Safavids and Venetians were compelled to fight the Turks "for the love of God." Ismail proposed that they launch a joint attack on the Ottomans. He concluded with a request that was direct and revealing: "send an excellent bombardier, a master craftsman."[32] The Persian messagebearer presented Ismail's demands: that Venice send artillery masters by way of Syria and that the Venetian navy engage the Ottoman sultan, Bayezid, off the coast of Greece while Ismail attacked him in Asia Minor.

Venice responded sympathetically but excused itself, preoccupied as it was with the war against the pope and his allies in the League of Cambrai. This excuse was only the most obvious reason for the Signoria's demurral. Venice was not ready to jeopardize its trade agreements with the Ottomans and Mamluks. Venetian aid to Ismail would be construed as a direct insult to the Ottoman sultan Bayezid, whose forces were arrayed against Ismail in eastern Anatolia. Such an insult could jeopardize the position of the many Venetian merchants trading profitably in Ottoman domains. Nor did Venice wish indirectly to aid the Portuguese by providing artillery to Ismail which might be used in some joint Safavid-Portuguese action against Qānsūh al-Ghūrī. Venice offered Ismail words instead of guns, assuring the envoy of its great friendship for Ismail and animosity against the Turks.[33] The Signoria was indeed militarily and economically debilitated by the struggle against the League of Cambrai.[34] Its promises were guarded: it would cooperate in efforts to stay the land expansion of the Ottomans and the naval expansion of the Portuguese but would prefer that the men, the money, and the supplies came from elsewhere.

In September 1509, the shah's envoys returned through Damascus, having received assurances of friendship but no concrete aid from Venice. Consul Zeno was anxious to speed them on their way, expecting detection by Mamluk spies at any moment. His relief at their departure, however, was short-lived. Zeno's worst fears were realized when Nicolo Soror, a Cypriot, who had accompanied the envoys back to the Safavid court along with some young merchants, was apprehended by the Mamluk governor of Birecik (on the Euphrates river, northeast of Aleppo). On July 16, 1510, Zeno received word from Aleppo of their capture, along with the bad news that the party was carrying incriminating letters from Ismail. The governor of Birecik dispatched the culprits to Aleppo; and the frantic Zeno, sensing a diplomatic disaster, quickly sent word to Venice.[35] Acting on the assumption that information would be tortured out of Soror, Zeno also wrote his hoped for allies in Cairo: the *kadi* (Islamic judge) and the dragoman (interpreter), Ibn Taghribirdī.[36] He protested the innocence of the merchants and of Venice generally, though admitting that Ismail's letters requested aid from Venice against the Ottomans. Soror and one of his attendants, named Zacharia, were sent in chains from Aleppo to Damascus. There Zeno urged them not to implicate the Signoria when they were interrogated in Cairo, but the damage to Venetian-Mamluk relations had already been done. Ismail's letter to Venice not only reiterated the request for an artillery master but also mentioned the exchange of letters and envoys between Venice and the shah.[37]

Although Venice protested to the Mamluk sultan that this Safavid embassy was inconsequential, a request for Venetian artillery aid and military collaboration with Ismail was guaranteed to cause offense in Cairo. Sultan Qānsūh took an extremely dim view of a foreign consul resident in his domains acting as go-between for secret Safavid-Venetian negotiations. Ismail's recent conquest of Baghdad and presence near the Mamluk northern frontiers made Qānsūh fearful that a Safavid invasion was imminent. The official Mamluk position was that the Safavids were heretics. As heretics, military action against them was justified. Later events would demonstrate that a onetime heretic could become a potential ally. Just as the Ottomans used the designation of "heretic" to legitimize their imperial ambitions against the Safavids and later against the Mamluks, so too the Safavids used the designation of "heretic" against the Ottomans to legitimize collaboration with Venice.[38]

One can speculate that Qānsūh was smarting at the failure of Ismail and the *doge* to include him in what appeared to be anti-Ottoman negotiations. It is more likely, though, that Qānsūh suspected that he as well as the Ottomans might be the object of a European-Safavid alliance.[39] He called the Venetian consuls of Alexandria, Damascus, and Tripoli to Cairo and accused them of being traitors who had received messages inviting the Christian princes to attack Egypt by sea while Ismail attacked the Mamluks and the Ottomans by land. The Safavid threat, combined with the Mamluk dependence on the Ottomans for naval aid against the Portuguese, determined that Qānsūh align himself with the Ottomans and against the Safavids, at least for the time being.[40]

An Ottoman ambassador passed through Damascus at about the same time as the Safavid envoy who had cost Zeno so much grief. This envoy was enroute to Mecca with a large quantity of gold for the sacred city. This gift of gold was more than a pious act; it was a declaration of Bayezid's power and claims to sovereignty in the Muslim world. Zeno claimed to have reliable information that this Ottoman ambassador had come to find out about Ismail's conquest of Baghdad and to remonstrate with Qānsūh concerning the Safavid threat. He added that the ambassador brought money for the Mamluk sultan to be used against Ismail. These simultaneous Ottoman and Safavid embassies typify the intricacies of Levantine power relationships at this time. The Ottomans were in a position of relative strength, with both the Mamluk and Venetian states dependent upon them: the Mamluks for naval and military aid and Venice, preoccupied with the League of Cambrai, for peace.[41] Still, they were anxious to avoid conflict on multiple fronts. The quietude of the Ottoman western front was conditioned by the threat of the Safavid attack on their eastern frontier and by the internal tension created by the succession struggle already underway in the Ottoman state.[42]

Regardless of the diplomatic rhetoric of Sunni *vs*. Shiʻi, Ottoman-Mamluk relations in this period cannot be characterized as a friendly union of two Sunni states in the face of the threat from the heretical Shiʻite Safavid state.[43] Rather, the Mamluk state placed itself in dependency status vis-à-vis the Ottoman Empire in response to the imperatives of the Portuguese expansion. This dependency status served only to illustrate Mamluk vulnerability to Ottoman imperial ambitions. The need for ordnance prompted Ismail to apply to Venice just as Qānsūh applied to Bayezid, and with the same rationales: the common foe, the heretic, and self-preservation. Neither the Mamluks nor the Safavids, in fact, had much to offer besides good will in return for the artillery and naval support they wanted. Having already made the Mamluk state dependent on the Ottomans for military aid, Qānsūh had little choice but nominally to support the Ottomans against the Safavids. The Safavids also constituted a direct threat to Mamluk interests in eastern Anatolia, a threat which had already materialized in the form of the attack on the Zū al-Ḳadr principality. Only if the Ottomans and Safavids could neutralize each other in eastern Anatolia was the Mamluk northern frontier safe.

Venice's relations with the Mamluks were further compromised on several fronts shortly after Soror's capture in 1510 when a Rhodian fleet destroyed a Mamluk fleet transporting timber and other naval supplies from Ayas (in the northeastern corner of the Mediterranean).[44] Zeno's correspondence, alternately hopeful that amicable relations would soon be restored then despairing over some new setback, details the deterioration in relations throughout 1510.[45] The Rhodian attack was particularly galling to Venice in view of the fact that the captured fleet was transporting materials for the preparation of a Mamluk armada against the Portuguese, an endeavor the Signoria had been urging on the Mamluk sultan. This insult coupled with the Nicolo Soror incident prompted Qānsūh to order that all "Franks" (Europeans) in his kingdom be detained and their goods impounded. Venetian trade was temporarily halted: ships could not be loaded or unloaded, goods could not be sold, and there was discussion of imprisoning the Venetian merchants and diplomats rather than simply detaining them. The previous century provided precedents for this type of action. In 1464, the Knights of Rhodes had seized Muslim merchants and their goods when a Venetian ship from the Maghreb put into Rhodes because of a storm. The Mamluk sultan, in response, seized all European merchants in Egypt and Syria and had their goods impounded. In 1471, the Venetian consul in Damascus had also been imprisoned and sent to Cairo, again over the question of Venetian relations with Iran.[46] In each case, trade was restricted in retaliation for political indiscretions.

After the impoundment of Venetian goods in 1510, Mamluk customs officials demanded that Venice make good immediately on debts owed and, in general, the temper of hostility towards European merchants prompted official abuses which were detrimental to trade. As negotiations failed, Contarini, the Venetian consul in Alexandria, and Zeno, were called to Cairo and imprisoned, accused of conspiring against the Mamluk state. This episode was one more lesson to Venice in the precarious nature of existence under the Mamluk regime and in the ease with which its investments could be subjected arbitrarily to ruin.

Qānsūh's intelligence operations in Damascus were not as competent as they might have been since the initial passage of the Safavid envoy through Damascus had remained undetected. Once the Venetian maneuvers were discovered, however, Zeno became the scapegoat; blame was directed on an individual rather than on Venetian state policy itself. Both sides wished to avoid a decisive break. Once news of Zeno's negotiations got out, Venice's reaction was not one of support for its representative. To assuage Qānsūh's anger, Zeno was officially blamed for mishandling Venice's interests and souring relations with Cairo. Later, however, after his redemption from prison, Zeno resumed his diplomatic service. Among other posts, he served as envoy to the Ottoman court in 1523.[47] This indicates that official censorship of Zeno was deemed necessary for diplomatic reasons, and either his experience or his family connections insured that his presumed enthusiasm for a Safavid alliance did not ruin his career. In fact, Zeno's correspondence indicates that he proceeded with as much caution as possible and regretted the circumstances which imposed upon him the role of Safavid-Venetian intermediary.

Ultimately Qānsūh's preoccupation with provisions to launch an armada against the Portuguese in the Indian Ocean worked in Venice's favor. In 1509, a preliminary expedition, which Qānsūh had launched against the Portuguese, was destroyed at Diu in the Indian Ocean. By September 1511, because the uncertain diplomatic environment continued adversely to effect trade, the Venetian Senate decided to send an *orator* (special envoy), Domenico Trevisan, to Cairo. With fleets arrayed before the ports of Beirut and Alexandria to remind Qānsūh of Venetian commercial vitality and of the possibilities for large profits, Venice was ready for the reopening of the trade. Trevisan was instructed to settle for good the ill-will from the Zeno affair and to renegotiate a new commercial treaty. He was successful and, in 1512, Mamluk-Venetian relations resumed on a fairly even keel.[48]

Venice's instructions to Trevisan in 1511 provide an interesting contrast to those given its envoy to Egypt in 1504.[49] Trevisan was instructed to conduct his mission with utmost secrecy. It was imperative that he discuss with the Mamluk sultan Venice's desire to eliminate the Portuguese navigations to India, which were damaging to the common interests of the two powers. If the Mamluk sultan asked for artillery masters, ships, oars or such things, Trevisan was to say that Venice would consider it. There was precedent for a Christian power sending arms shipments to Cairo. In 1482–1483, an embassy from the king of Naples arrived in Cairo and attempted to influence the Mamluk sultan in favor of the king's son, then resident at the Mamluk court, as ruler in Cyprus. The king sent a ship loaded with artillery including "a huge cannon," armor, helmets, arquebuses, powder, and balls, much to the sultan's content but much to the stupefaction of the Christian residents of Cairo.[50]

Trevisan made the vacuous claim that the main reason for the formation of the League of Cambrai was the League's members blaming Venice for not joining a Christian alliance against the enemies of Christianity.[51] In effect, Qānsūh should be grateful that Venice had remained an ally, since it had done so only at great cost. Further, Venice suggested that Qānsūh seek aid from the Ottomans. Trevisan was instructed:

> Urge the Mamluk sultan to get from the Turk artillery, lumber, ships and all the things necessary to pursue this effort [against the Portuguese], besides the lumber that they obtain from the gulf of Ayas where it is abundant.

This suggestion that one Muslim power seek the aid of another was not such a reversal of Venetian policy as it might on the surface seem. Rather, the greater threat of the Portuguese outweighed the instinctual Venetian desire to keep powerful competitors at odds with each other.

Venice also anticipated the demands and complaints that the Mamluk sultan was likely to direct at Trevisan. If the question of damages done by the Rhodians was brought up, Trevisan was to explain that Venice did not support piracy and to remind Qānsūh of how Venice had interceded for Arab victims of corsairs. If there were problems with the *muda*, the Venetian state subsidized galley convoys at Alexandria or Beirut, Trevisan was to attempt to resolve any impediments to the loading of goods. He was given full power to negotiate a settlement with the Mamluks, although he had been instructed to consult first with the consuls of Damascus and Alexandria.

This communication demonstrates how Venice's view of negotiations between the main actors in eastern Mediterranean relations had changed. Venice was trying to patch up relations with the Mamluks in the aftermath of consul Zeno's insufficiently discreet negotiations with the Safavid envoy. It was actively pursuing possibilities with the Safavids but was not willing to back such a friendship at the expense of trade agreements with the Mamluks and Ottomans. The Mamluks were not yet willing to support publicly a Venetian-Safavid-Mamluk axis. Meanwhile Rhodian attacks on shipping had further exacerbated the tension between Egypt and Venice.[52] Although the depredations of the Knights on Muslim shipping were nothing new, the attack on the Ayas fleet was a severe blow to Qānsūh's construction efforts on the Suez fleet. It was this blow combined with the secret negotiations between the Safavids and Venice which, added to the Portuguese threat, had so provoked the Mamluk sultan. Qānsūh's condemnation of Venice's negotiations with Ismail had not, however, prevented him from keeping his own diplomatic channels open. A Mamluk envoy was sent to Ismail's camp in the summer of 1510.[53]

The focus of Venetian negotiations with the Mamluks remained the threat of the Portuguese to the commercial revenues of both powers. Since 1504, however, the situation had changed drastically in that Venice now mentioned the Ottoman state as the most likely source of relief. This proposal was an admission that, despite the long-term enmity between the Ottomans and Mamluks, the relative weakness of both Venice and the Mamluks in 1511 justified Venice's proposal of a marriage of necessity. This view signified acceptance that the expansion of the Ottoman sphere of influence was a calculated risk made expedient by the threat of a Portuguese blockade of the Red Sea. What lowered the risk to an acceptable level was the prospect that the Safavids would occupy the Ottomans in eastern Anatolia so that neither Venice nor the Mamluk kingdom would suffer the consequences of the Ottomans becoming too powerful.

At this point, in 1512, Safavid military capabilities were still the subject of speculation on the part of all parties. The Mamluks wished to define Ismail as an anti-Ottoman ally rather than as party to a Safavid-Venetian alliance, which might aim at squeezing the Mamluks out of Syria. Then, too, the possibility of a Safavid-Portuguese coalition could not be ruled out since Ismail had exchanged ambassadors with the Portuguese in India.[54] Thus, Mamluk relations with the Ottomans and Venice were conditioned by Qānsūh's fears that the Safavids and Portuguese might strike an agreement over dividing Syria and Arabia.

The Mamluk sultan's suspicions in this regard were not unwarranted. The Safavids and Portuguese were in direct contention for control of the Persian Gulf, in particular for the right to tax the rich commercial receipts of the island of Hormuz. Ismail was hampered in enforcing both his claims to Hormuz and his aspirations to control the Gulf trade by the lack of a Safavid navy.[55] Despite this regional conflict, however, the broader territorial ambitions of Shah Ismail and of King Emmanuel prompted each to view the other as a potential ally. Both monarchs attempted to keep their options open via diplomatic channels. Duarte Barbosa, the Portuguese civil servant, wrote that Ismail wished to secure the Portuguese admiral, Alfonso d'Albuquerque's, friendship because the shah wished to conquer Mecca.[56] Both the Safavids and the Portuguese coveted Mecca as a sign of their sovereign power and the Red Sea trade as a sign of their commercial wealth. D'Albuquerque, in 1510, proposed to sail into the Red Sea and to burn the Mamluk fleet at Suez so as to prevent the Mamluks from "setting foot in India"; but he was deterred from this endeavor by the deci-

sion to conquer the Indian city of Goa.[57] At Goa he received an
envoy from Ismail who engaged the Portuguese admiral in a verbal
sparring match over the grandeur of their respective masters and
over entitlement to the revenues of Hormuz. The Safavid envoy
was arrogant, suggesting that d'Albuquerque order the minting of
coins in Goa in Ismail's name, an indication of the shah's imperial
aspirations.[58] The admiral refused and instead sent a letter to Ismail along with his own ambassador, Ruy Gomez. The instructions
d'Albuquerque sent with Ruy Gomez are revealing in their elaboration of diplomatic etiquette. The Portuguese envoy was ordered
to elaborate at length on the glory of King Emmanuel's court: its
gold, its richly caparisoned horses and equally richly caparisoned
women, its processions, its nobles, fleets, arms, and even the manner in which the king ate his dinner. D'Albuquerque asked that
Ismail send an envoy to Lisbon, and proposed an alliance which
would be both military and commercial in nature. He proposed to
send Portuguese merchandise into Iran via Hormuz. He further
proposed a joint attack on the Mamluks and Ottomans:

> And if you desire to destroy the Sultan [Qānsūh] by land, you can
> reckon upon great assistance from the Armada of the King my
> Lord by sea, and I believe that with small trouble you must gain
> the lordship of the city of Cairo and all his kingdom and depen-
> dencies, and thus my Lord can give you great help by sea against
> the Turk, and thus his fleets by sea and you with your great
> forces and cavalry by land can combine to inflict troublous inju-
> ries upon them.[59]

D'Albuquerque wished to take the battle to Qānsūh and Bayezid
because he assumed that the Mamluk-Ottoman naval invasion of
India would be renewed. An alliance with Ismail offered Portugal
the land based forces which it could not itself mobilize against the
Mamluk and Ottoman sultans. It offered the shah assistance in
conquering the western end of the Mediterranean-Indian Ocean
trade axis.

    At the same time that the Portuguese were initiating diplo-
matic contacts with the Safavids, in 1510–1511, Venice was trying
simultaneously to smooth over relations with Cairo, explore possibilities with Ismail, and secure aid from the Ottoman sultan,
Bayezid. Venetian diplomacy in Istanbul was directed at securing
aid against the League of Cambrai, ensuring peace to protect Venetian trade through Ottoman territory, and obtaining mercenary
cavalry troops from the Balkans. The aid was not forthcoming but

the Ottoman-Venetian peace was reaffirmed in 1511. It was in part because of this reaffirmation that Venice felt confident in urging Ottoman naval aid on the Mamluks.[60]

When Sultan Selim I came to power in 1512, Antonio Justinian, already in Istanbul, was commissioned by Venice to congratulate the new sultan and to renegotiate the Ottoman-Venetian treaty. It is noteworthy that at this time the Ottoman vezirs demanded and received a clause providing for the provisioning of an Ottoman fleet at the ports of Venetian possessions such as Cyprus. This presaged the provisioning for the Ottoman campaign against Cairo.[61] Previously, during the Ottoman-Mamluk wars of 1485–1491, when the Ottomans had also requested the use of Famagosta on Cyprus to supply their troops from the sea, Venice had refused. The new concessions illustrate the shift in the balance of power since the late fifteenth century. Ottoman naval power, combined with the changing circumstances produced by the Portuguese voyages, left Venice without the power or inclination to resist demands from the Porte that it had rejected with impunity in the preceding century.

The conduct of Venetian diplomacy with the Porte differed substantially from that with Cairo in that, after 1503, relations with the Ottomans were fairly stable. Envoys were sent for two reasons: to reestablish trade agreements and, as was the case in 1509–1511, to request aid.[62] Between Andrea Gritti's 1503 embassy to Istanbul to ratify the peace treaty and Marco Minio's visit to congratulate Süleiman on his accession in 1520, there were only three Venetian special embassies to the Porte. These were Nicolo Justinian in 1512 when the office of *bailo* (resident Venetian ambassador in Istanbul) was left vacant, Antonio Justinian in 1513 to congratulate Selim on his accession, and Alvise Mocenigo and Bartolomeo Contarini (to Egypt first) in 1517 to congratulate Selim on his acquisition of the Mamluk territories and to renegotiate the Ottoman-Venetian treaty.

Within the early sixteenth-century Levant, a certain stability of rule prevailed which promoted the pursuit of commercial interests. A single *doge*, Leonardo Loredano, was installed in Venice for the first two decades of the sixteenth century (1501–1521). Unlike earlier and later periods when a *bailo*'s term might last only two or three years, a single Venetian *bailo*, Leonardo Bembo, was resident ambassador in Istanbul (1513–1519) for most of Selim's reign. Short terms could be the result of sickness, death, removal, or unwillingness of a *bailo* to stay in office.[63] Venice's foreign emissaries often endured lack of funds, abuse by local officials, and disease.[64] Bembo's relatively long term allowed him to establish better contacts at the Porte. It also allowed Venice to enjoy an uninterrupted flow of intelligence from Istanbul. Venetian diplomacy vis-à-vis the Mamluks, however, was prompted by conditions of crisis rather than conditions of stability. Hence special emissaries were sent to Cairo for a set of reasons different from those for which they were sent to Istanbul. The objective of formalizing trade agreements was still the same, but Venetian diplomacy with the Mamluks had other pressing concerns: the Portuguese threat in the Red Sea and the disruptions of the trade caused by Venetian negotiations with Ismail, the attacks of Rhodian corsairs on Mamluk possessions, and the Mamluk failure to provide security and price controls for Venetian trade.

Ottoman stability combined with a narrowing of Venetian political options paved the way to the resolution of these concerns. In the four years, 1513–1517, separating Trevisan's renegotiation of the Mamluk-Venetian commercial treaty and Selim's march on Cairo, two events occurred which accelerated the transformation of Venice's diplomatic policy. These were the decisive Ottoman defeat of the Safavids at Çaldıran in 1514 and the failure of the Mamluk armada to drive the Portuguese from the Indian Ocean.[65] After Sultan Selim's triumphal march into Tabriz, the Safavid capital, in 1514, the battle accounts in the Venetian reports gradually wound down and thereafter dispatches were often filled with "nothing" about the "Great Sophy" other than occasional rumors. Ismail never again led his troops into battle against the Ottomans. The military capabilities of the Safavid army, so long the theme of speculation in the European sources, had been tested and proved lacking. So, too, the Mamluk armada on which such great Venetian expectations for the chastisement of the Portuguese had been riding. The myth of Ismail as the unknown threat had collapsed. Despite a flurry of diplomatic activity and a paper alliance between Qānsūh and Ismail, Venice was now increasingly inclined to recognize the Ottoman Sultan Selim as the last resort for stability and continuity of the trade flow through the Red Sea.[66] An anti-Ottoman axis had failed to materialize. In fact, with the Porte as the only power likely actively to challenge the Portuguese in the Red Sea, for Venice an anti-Ottoman alliance was no longer even desirable. Venice's diplomacy of economic expediency was made easier by the Ottoman appeasement policy in the west which allowed Selim to concentrate on campaigns in the east. Between

1514 and 1516, as conditions in the Mamluk state deteriorated, the continuity of Venetian trade and the safety of Venetian merchants could no longer be guaranteed, at least not by the Mamluks. Venice prepared to negotiate with the Ottomans the trading privileges once dictated by Qānsūh. While Qānsūh mobilized his defenses in expectation of an Ottoman invasion or naval attack on his coasts, Venice prepared to retain its commercial and political privileges under a new hegemony.[67]

By the fall of 1516, the Ottomans had already conquered two of the Mamluk trade depots (Aleppo and Damascus). This conquest gave Venice the advantage in its trade negotiations with the Mamluks. In November 1516, still hedging its bets on the off chance of an Ottoman defeat, Venice sent Tomaso Venier as ambassador to Cairo to attempt to resolve the commercial impasse which had deterred the *muda* for the previous two years.[68] By this time, two years after Ismail's defeat, Venice was bargaining from a more decisive and unambiguous position. The Mamluck sultan demanded 10,000 ducats for the revenue lost from the previous two years' trade. Unruffled, Venier told the sultan that the galleys had been prepared to come every year but that the Signoria did not force its merchants to sail against their will. The merchants claimed that galleys would not be seen at Alexandria as long as the Mamluk sultan continued his price gouging on spice sales. Instead, said Venier, they would go to Beirut since there was news from Damascus that the merchants there were well treated by the Ottomans and the customs dues were low. Venice would deal with the Ottomans if they could not get satisfaction from the Mamluks. Grudgingly Tūmān, the new Mamluk sultan (ruled 1516–1517), confirmed the trade agreements. The transformation of Venetian diplomatic policy was now complete. The naval failures and injurious customs duties of the Mamluks had combined to make the Venetian trade through Egypt less profitable and Venier did not hesitate to throw the Ottoman successes in the face of the desperate Mamluk sultan. Ottoman rule was a viable alternative.[69]

The good treatment accorded the Venetian merchants in the newly won Ottoman cities along with the lure of Ottoman political stability and moderate levies on trade suggested to Venice that Ottoman control of the traditional trade routes from the East might be fiscally advantageous.[70] As for the political and military status quo, the Mamluks did not possess a permanent Mediterranean fleet and hence posed no threat to Venetian possessions or shipping.[71] The Ottomans possessed a large and powerful navy

Plate 3: An indication of Italian-Ottoman cultural exchange. Bellini, Turkish artist. Source: Courtesy of the Isabella Stewart Gardner Museum, Boston, MA.

which had been partially mobilized to support and provision the land campaign against Cairo. Whereas the Mamlucks had shown no inclination or ability to expand their frontiers at Venetian expense, the threat from the Ottoman navy was immediate. Conversely, in the Red Sea this same lack of Mamluk naval power to counter the Portuguese made Ottoman naval interference desirable. Venice was now in the unenviable position of hoping that Ottoman sea power would be selectively applied in the Red Sea against the Portuguese, and withheld in the Mediterranean.

CHAPTER 3

The Eastern Salient:
Ismail Safavi and the Mamluks

Though he failed to meet European expectations, Shah Ismail played a decisive role in the reconstruction of commercial and political relations in the volatile frontier zone linking Antolia, Syria, Iran, and Iraq. There the hegemonic ambitions of the Mamluks, Ottomans, Safavids, and Portuguese intersected. Ismail created a crisis of legitimacy within the Muslim world, taking the battle, through proselytization and arms, into Ottoman territory, and focusing Ottoman attention on the eastern salient. In order to set the conquest of the Mamluk territories in a broader perspective, focusing on the Mediterranean, Red Sea, Indian Ocean axis, which linked Venice to the Ottomans and Mamluks, this study concentrates on sea based foreign relations and trade. An understanding, however, of the historical dynamics of the eastern frontier area, the Zū al-Ḳadr buffer state, and the role of Ismail Safavi in the chronic Ottoman-Mamluk conflict is crucial to any explanation of the change in power relations resulting from the expansion of the Ottoman state.[1] Traditional historiography has focused on the gunpowder successes which enabled the Ottomans to defeat their Safavid and Mamluk foes in the campaigns of 1514–1517. This chapter focuses, instead, on foreign policy as prompting and responding to those campaigns, on the alternatives to military action, and on the processes of negotiation by which Ottoman political and commercial dominance was secured.

By the summer of 1502, there seemed little chance that any state would emerge to challenge the Ottomans. The Porte had demonstrated its naval superiority to all comers in the Aegean wars; the political situation in Europe was chaotic; and odds favored the

Ottomans should a new war break out with the Mamluks. When Ismail appeared on the eastern horizon and the extent and rapidity of his victories became known, the Ottomans' opponents eagerly looked to the Safavid shah as the hoped for "real" threat to Ottoman expansion. But Venetian commercial interests, combined with the Mamluk failure to provide security, resulted instead in a warming of Venetian relations with the Ottoman Porte. This occurred despite the persistent threat to Venetian territories like Cyprus and despite the lure of an alliance with Ismail. Venice was cautious in its approach to Ismail because the promise of a Venetian-Safavid pact was not sufficient to outweigh the benefits of the secure commercial environment which could be provided by Ottoman rule in the eastern Mediterranean. For Rhodes, on the other hand, because of its crusading mission, there was neither this option of rapprochement with the Ottomans nor, after 1503, any concrete promise of an anti-Ottoman Christian alliance. Rhodes actively pursued relations with Ismail. The reason for this is clear. The Safavids diverted Ottoman military attention from Rhodes both by direct pressure at the eastern Anatolian frontiers and by political intrigue to instigate a revolt in Karaman in south Anatolia. The position of the Mamluk state in relation to the Ottomans was similar to that of Rhodes. There existed a traditional enmity between the two Muslim states; and Ottoman political and commercial ambitions, to control the Holy Cities and the revenues of the eastern trade, insured the inevitability of an attack on the Mamluks. Ismail, therefore, offered the Mamluks the same opportunity for relief from Ottoman military pressure that he offered Rhodes.

As early as the end of the reign of Sultan Mehmed II Fatih (the Conqueror), the chronicler Tursun Beg had spoken of an Ottoman plan to conquer Cairo.[2] He reported that in the spring of 1481 the sultan ordered preparations made for a campaign in Anatolia, but no one knew whether it would be against Iran or Arabia. Mehmed II died after crossing the Bosphorus to join the imperial army, so the campaign plans came to nothing. The reign of his son Bayezid, the new sultan, was characterized from the start by ill-feelings between the Ottomans and Mamluks. Tursun relates that ambassadors came from far and wide to congratulate the new Ottoman sultan and all were well-received except the ambassador from Egypt. Bayezid had been angered by the Mamluk sultan's seizure of an Ottoman envoy who was returning from India in company with an Indian ambassador to Fatih Mehmed. When news of Fatih's death reached Arabia, the Mamluk sultan detained these two emissaries and confiscated their goods. This act was considered an insult to Bayezid's sovereignty. Bayezid launched a joint land and sea attack on the Mamluks in 1486.[3] The Ottoman army marched southeast through Anatolia while a fleet armed with artillery sailed to attack the Mamluk coasts. Although this campaign was ultimately driven back, the Ottomans demonstrated their naval power by capturing the fortress of Ayas and pillaging the area nearby. It remained for Bayezid's son, Selim, to reenact this scenario with greater success thirty years later.

When a peace treaty ended the lengthy conflict between Ottomans and Mamluks at the end of the fifteenth century (1485–1491), the Mamluks remained in a position of relative power vis-à-vis the Ottomans. The only decisive defeat the Ottomans had been able to inflict on the Mamluks had been at sea. In southeastern Anatolia and Syria, the Mamluks had maintained their position, a frontier protected by a loose chain of fortresses and buffered by the Zū al-Ḳadr principality centered on Elbistan and Maraṣ. At the beginning of the sixteenth century, however, the balance of power was to shift markedly in Ottoman favor, destroying the relative stasis of a roughly triangular frontier zone between Anatolia, Iran, and Syria-Egypt, centering on the cities of Maraṣ, Diyarbakr, and Aleppo. This zone was crucial for the foreign relations of the Ottomans, Mamluks, and Safavids and, by extension, for the foreign relations of Europe for it served as a focal point in the contention for dominance in the Levant at the beginning of the sixteenth century.

The suspension of open warfare between the Ottomans and Mamluks in 1491 did not signal the end to hostilities between the two states. The first area of contention was the Zū al-Ḳadr principality on the Ottoman-Mamluk frontier. The Zū al-Ḳadrid ruler, ʿAlā ad-Dawla, managed to remain autonomous by playing off the Ottoman and Mamluk sultans one against the other. Bayezid had tried unsuccessfully to depose him during the Ottoman-Mamluk war. A second source of Ottoman-Mamluk hostility was their competition for hegemony on the terrain of Muslim legitimacy. By the turn of the century, the Ottoman sultan was the most powerful ruler in the Middle East, resident in the the capital of the Eastern Roman Empire. But the Mamluk sultan still held the shadow Abbasid caliph and the title "Protector of the Holy Cities," enabling him to assume a form of preeminence over the Ottoman ruler, which was reflected in the honorifics of diplomatic correspondence.[4]

Another source of animosity was Mamluk support for Bayezid's enemies. Cairo had traditionally provided safe haven for contenders for the Ottoman throne including Cem Sultan, who for some years challenged his brother Bayezid's claim to the sultanate.[5] Holding princes hostage was a traditional indication of dominance, useful for the application of political pressure on rival states. Similarly, the harboring of another ruler's dynastic successors was a traditional means of limiting that ruler's power. In the reign of Bayezid, the consolidation of the sultan's power was limited and delayed by the survival of his brother Cem, who was succoured in Karaman and by the Mamluks until his exile to Rhodes and then to Italy.[6] After Cem, a series of Ottoman claimants were also sheltered in the Mamluk and later the Safavid courts.

Cairo was also linked directly to the attempts of Karaman, a principality in southern Anatolia formerly vassal and protege to the Mamluks, to reassert its independence from Ottoman control. For the Mamluks, a revolt in Karaman represented: a means to divert Ottoman attention from the Zū al-Ḳadr area, the existence of a natural ally within the Ottoman state upon which Cairo was dependent for such items as timber, and a means to reassert Mamluk hegemony in the eastern Mediterranean. From 1501 until his death in 1513, a Karamanid pretender, Mustafa, nephew of Kasim Beg, was resident in Safavid and later in Mamluk territory. While he lived, the Ottomans could not rule out the possibility of a revolt. European states, like Venice and Rhodes, conspired with such Karamanid pretenders in order to limit Ottoman expansion. The Karamanid princes would also provide leverage for both Ismail in Iran and Qānsūh in Egypt against the Ottomans.[7]

The rise of Ismail Safavi in Iran provided a new set of alternatives to the states, both European and Asian, contending for hegemony in the eastern Mediterranean. Scholars working on Ottoman-Safavid relations have proposed that Ismail's early successes resulted in an Ottoman-Mamluk rapprochement.[8] Ismail was pursuing an expansionist policy and, at least prior to 1514, Syria, Egypt, and the Hijaz had to be considered Safavid targets just as was Anatolia. This is the reason for the prevalence of the Ottoman-Mamluk rapprochement theory. The rationale for this notion, however, is faulty, because the Safavid threat to the Mamluks was always outweighed by the Ottoman threat, especially after Selim's accession in 1512 to the Ottoman throne. Even the lengthy succession struggle among Bayezid's sons failed to place the Mamluk sultan in the position of aggressor or ascendant power. Hence, the

Mamluk response to Ismail's military and diplomatic initiatives was always moderated by extreme caution and by a strong sense of the Ottoman threat. Ismail, for the Mamluks as for the Venetians and Rhodians, represented a potential for salvation. This salvation was of a very specific kind, freedom from territorial loss to Ottoman conquest. In the Ottoman state itself, Ismail represented an opportunity for Selim to assert his own hegemonic ambitions and claims to his father's throne against those of his brothers. Selim legitimized these claims by saying that his father Bayezid was too weak to meet the Safavid challenge.

In 1502, the nature of the Safavid challenge was only beginning to become apparent. Some of the earliest concrete evidence of Ismail's military capabilities was obtained, as already noted, through the efforts of the Venetian spy Constantine Laschari, a resident of Cyprus.[9] Laschari was sent by the regiment at Cyprus as an agent of the Signoria to contact the Karamanid, Mustafa, in Ismail's camp in Iran. Mustafa had fled to Iran when an attempt to reinstate the Karamanids by installing him as prince and throwing off the Ottoman yoke in 1500–1501 had been put down by the Ottoman army. Mustafa's unsuccessful revolt was contemporaneous with Ismail's successful conquest of Tabriz and with the Ottoman victories over Venice at Modon and Coron in the Aegean. Venice had intelligence of his whereabouts and Laschari was sent specifically to contact him.[10] Laschari left Cyprus with a company of sixty men, masquerading as merchants. Reaching Tarsus on May 18, 1502, he sent a messenger bearing a letter from Venice to Mustafa in Tabriz. When the messenger returned with a reply, Laschari rode to Hisn Keyf, on the Ottoman-Safavid frontier. There he met Mustafa, who had a troop of three hundred cavalry, and they travelled on to Aleppo in Mamluk territory.

Ismail, or his agents, was a party to the Venetian-Karamanid negotiations. Mustafa sought to obtain artillery and galleys from Venice, the same strategy which had been employed by Uzun Hasan, the Ak Koyunlu ruler in the preceding century. Ismail, having seen Venice's letter of support for Mustafa, pledged Safavid support for a march on Karaman to liberate it from the Ottomans.[11] According to Laschari, Mustafa proposed to march first on Amid and then on to Karaman, backed by Ismail whose army was said to number 80,000 cavalry and footsoldiers. Major resistance was not expected. The deposed ruler of Tabriz, Alvand ibn Yusuf Ak Koyunlu, had been unsuccessful in his attempt to secure the support of Qānsūh al-Ghūrī against Ismail. Mustafa estimated that Alvand

and the governor of Amid could not mobilize more than seven or
eight thousand cavalry between them to resist him. The Ottomans,
on the other hand, posed a much more substantial obstacle to Karamanid ambitions.[12]

Bayezid had already mobilized troops that year to send to the
eastern Anatolian frontier in response to Ismail's activity in Erzincan and to the conquest of Tabriz. He had also sent his son Selim
toward the frontier with a force rumored to number 30,000 to
40,000. Ismail had challenged Bayezid verbally and physically by
sending both threatening letters and agents to proselytize in eastern Anatolia. After hearing that two hundred forty Safavid agents
had been sent across the border to mobilize followers for Ismail,
Bayezid ordered his provincial governors to execute Safavid sympathizers.[13] Repressive action against Safavid followers in eastern
Anatolia also prompted Ismail's ambassador at the Ottoman court
to demand the release of *kızılbaş* captives seized and imprisoned by
the Ottomans. Reports from Istanbul and Rhodes also suggest that
a military skirmish took place in the summer of 1502, two to four
days distant from Ankara, between the Ottoman expeditionary
force and some of the Safavid troops. These accounts contradict
each other on who emerged victorious in the combat.[14] Laschari's
report confirmed the existence of extensive support for Ismail in
eastern Anatolia, saying that he encountered numerous Safavid
supporters. At this point, however, Venetian attention was concentrated on the Karamanid prince Mustafa, rather than on Ismail, as
the best bet for resistance against the Ottomans. Not enough was
yet known about Safavid potential. Rumors that Ismail had promised his sister in marriage to Mustafa bolstered Venetian expectations that Mustafa could mobilize considerably more troops than
the three hundred cavalry he already had with him.

Laschari's negotiations with Mustafa indicate that as late as
the summer of 1502 Venice contemplated supporting a revolt in
Karaman. Such a revolt could have affected favorably Venice's negotiations with the Ottomans for an Aegean peace settlement
which was, in fact, concluded later that year. The impetus for Venetian negotiations with Karaman was certainly the news, which
had been circulating in Venice for about a year, of Ismail's early
successes in Şirvan and Tabriz. Laschari's mission confirmed Ismail's support for reestablishing a Karamanid state. Neither was
Venice the only state intrigued with these possibilities. The Grand
Master of Rhodes had responded to similar intelligence by sending
a letter to Mustafa as well. It was probably to this correspondence

that Laschari referred when he said that he feared the Karmanid pretender would be brought to Rhodes. Both Venice and Rhodes viewed Ottoman control in Karaman as sufficiently precarious to warrant intervention. Laschari's report also indicates that the state of Ottoman domestic affairs as well as Safavid offensives made the prospect of Venetian aid to Karaman attractive.

When Karaman had revolted in 1500–1501, Bayezid's son Korkud, had been charged with quelling the rebellion. Venetian intelligence advised that Bayezid had not been pleased with Korkud's performance and, when called to the Porte, Korkud had refused to come for fear of punishment. There were charges that Korkud had, himself, corresponded with Mustafa, inviting him to retake Karaman. This was attributed to Korkud's fears that his own father and brother Ahmed were conspiring to have him put to death. Laschari reported that news of Korkud's disaffection and rebelliousness was common knowledge. He also claimed to have personal knowledge of Korkud from having traded regularly in Karaman before the Ottoman-Venetian war. Laschari suggested to the Venetian Senate that Korkud was willing to negotiate with Venice because he feared that his father and brother ultimately would succeed in disposessing him.[15]

Korkud was the center of rumors about revolt. He was implicated in a conspiracy engineered by the governor of Tripoli in Syria.[16] This Mamluk governor had supposedly offered to supply 30,000 men if the Ottomans would supply 25,000 men to mount an insurrection against Qānsūh al-Ghūrī. This force could then seize Tripoli and pave the way for an Ottoman attack on Cairo. The governor of Tripoli was also on good terms with ʿAlā ad-Dawla, the Zū al-Kadr ruler, who was also nominally a Mamluk vassal. ʿAlā ad-Dawla, maternal grandfather to the Ottoman prince and future sultan Selim, contrived to remain independent until 1515 despite being the focus of the territorial claims of the empires to the north and south. It was an indication of ʿAlā ad-Dawla's autonomy that he was nominally considered a vassal of either the Ottoman or the Mamluk sultan but in practice, though he made demands on both, he served neither. The Zū al-Kadr ruler used to call his supposed sultanic overlords the "goose who laid the golden egg and the goose who laid the silver egg" respectively.[17] The removal of his buffer state was a prerequisite to direct confrontation between the Ottomans and the Mamluks. Rebellion in the northern provinces of the Mamluk state was endemic at this time and the loyalty of the Zū al-Kadr ruler had been extended only reluctantly to either the

Mamluks or the Ottomans. The supposed plan of the governor of Tripoli, and suggestion of Zū al-Ḳadr complicity may, however, have been more a reflection of Venetian aspirations than of political reality in Syria. Venice still coveted a base on the eastern Mediterranean littoral and internal problems or opportunities on the Ottoman eastern frontier were likely to take naval pressure off Venice in the Aegean where the war with the Porte still had not been concluded.

The extent of Korkud's apparent treachery is not known. It is clear, however, that Venice, Rhodes, and the Mamluks all viewed Korkud, if not as an ally, at least as a weak point, politically and militarily, in the Ottoman defenses. For these states, the 1500–1501 Karamanid revolt and the presence of Mustafa in Ismail's camp meant that Ottoman land and naval forces could be turned toward Karaman at any moment. On the Ottoman side, a troop mobilization against Ismail only one year after the Karamanid revolt was clearly a response to the Safavid shah's support for Mustafa as well as to his activities in eastern Anatolia.

Laschari's entire venture sheds light on the situation in this buffer zone between the Ottomans, Mamluks, and Safavids. While Venice was sounding out both Ismail and Mustafa, Ismail sent an ambassador to Sībāy, the governor of Aleppo, with a message of friendship to Qānsūh al-Ghūrī, the Mamluk sultan. The envoy was well received and treated to a military display.[18] As the potential for an Ottoman-Safavid power struggle escalated, Ismail and Bayezid both sent envoys to Cairo in 1502, each attempting to make sure that the Mamluks would not support the other.[19] The Mamluks, for their part, were fearful that Ismail might invade Syria. Until they could ascertain the extent of his power and ambitions they avoided giving assistance to his enemies, and so refused to aid the Ak Koyunlu princes whom Ismail had driven from Tabriz.[20] Meanwhile, the supposed negotiations of the governor of Tripoli and Korkud, combined with the Ottoman military and naval build-up, assured the inquietude of the Ottoman-Mamluk frontier zone.

The relative strength of the Ottoman position is reflected in the language of diplomacy. Bayezid's envoy to Cairo issued a challenge to the Mamluk sultan, which foreshadowed the tone of Ottoman-Mamluk relations in the coming years. This envoy told Qānsūh he had been attacked by bandits at Gazara on his way to Cairo. After a skirmish, the envoy had ordered some of the offending Arab bandits impaled. "This," he informed Qānsūh, "is how my master Bayezid deals with robbers." If Qānsūh could not or would not protect the roadways and caravans against such thieves, the Ottoman envoy sneered, then Bayezid could. Such presumption on the part of a diplomat suggests confidence that Qānsūh would not dare to retaliate. This insult came at a time when Qānsūh's authority was being challenged by his own subordinates. Bayezid's envoy admonished Qānsūh to protect the *hajj* route. He also demanded Cem's daughter, and the Karamanid prince Mustafa in Aleppo, both sheltering in Mamluk territory. Qānsūh supposedly acquiesced to all demands except to the release of the Karamanid, whom he agreed to keep under guard in Damascus.[21] In response to the Ottoman sultan's embassy, Qānsūh sent his own ambassador, Ṭanībāy Khazīnadār, to Istanbul in July of 1503.[22] The content of this ambassador's mission is not known, but Ismail's military potential and his ability to disrupt the Syrian and eastern Anatolian trade were clearly matters of concern to both monarchs.

In 1503, Venice was engaged in its own diplomatic wrangling in Cairo, attempting to shore up strained relations with the Mamluk sultan. The tension was the result of unsuccessful attempts to come to an agreement on customs duties.[23] Benedetto Soranzo, a Venetian envoy, had failed to conclude an agreement; and Qānsūh demanded 80,000 ducats from Venice, threatening to impound all Venetian merchandise and to suspend trade in Syria if this sum were not paid in four months. As a result, Bartolo Contarini, the Venetian consul in Damascus, had written to Cyprus warning that merchants landing in Syrian ports should not disembark from their ships but should attempt to conduct business from shipboard. This was a standard precautionary measure adopted as a result of frequent seizures of merchandise by the Mamluk sultan's agents. This practice allowed the merchants to sail out of port on short notice if threatened rather than unloading all their goods and risking impoundment before they could be sold. Contarini also recommended that the *muda* bound for Alexandria should remain at Candia until an envoy had been sent to Qānsūh to make sure that terms for the trade had been agreed upon. Contarini's precautions were warranted. Three representatives of the Damascene merchant community, who had gone to Cairo that spring to intercede with Qānsūh, had been imprisoned.[24]

Lack of information about Ismail continued to affect the conduct of diplomatic affairs. In 1504, Bayezid sent an ambassador to Ismail, ostensibly to congratulate him on his victories. This was hollow rhetoric indeed since success for the "heretical" leader of the *kızılbaş* was in direct oppostion to Ottoman objectives. The letter, however, was a standard formality, providing an excuse for the Ottoman envoy to spy on conditions in Iran. His formal message was three years late in coming and the object of the mission was doubtless to gather information.[25]

After the initial Ottoman-Safavid skirmishes on the eastern Anatolian frontier and the Safavid defeat of both Alvand and Murad, the Ak Koyunlu princes, in 1502–1503, Ismail's reputation continued to grow. If only the inflated rhetoric of European travelers' accounts were relied upon, Venice and Rhodes should have been expected to conclude alliances with the Persian monarch. In fact, Venice's commercial interests in both the Ottoman and Mamluk states, and the Rhodian failure to secure European backing, mediated against any such alliance. Diplomatically, however, the opponents of Ottoman expansion in the eastern Mediterranean, motivated by opportunism and fear, preserved the potential for an alliance with Ismail right up to the battle of Çaldıran in 1514.

Mamluk concern about Ismail's military potential was particularly acute because of a series of provincial revolts that coincided with Ismail's rise to power. The instability of Mamluk authority in the frontier zones is suggested by the proliferation of charges of insurrection against Qānsūh's underlings in Syria. In autumn 1504, Qānsūh named Ṣudūn ʿAjamī governor of Damascus to replace Qānsūh Burji who had died, and named Khair Beg governor of Aleppo, recalling Sībāy to assume a position at court. Sībāy, however, refused to accept the appointment and would not come to Cairo. This was an act of rebellion against the sultan. In spring 1505, ʿAlā ad-Dawla sent an envoy to the Mamluk sultan, asking clemency for Sībāy and interceding for Dawlat Bāy, the governor of Tripoli, a fellow conspirator.[26] This request implicated ʿAlā ad-Dawla, already suspect for past intervention in Syrian affairs. Such suspicions were warranted. ʿAlā ad-Dawla had given his daughter as wife to Ultībāy, former governor of Tripoli who, along with Sībāy, was accused of plotting to march against Aleppo.[27] The significance of this incident lies in the failure of the Mamluk sultan to compel obedience from his provincial governors and in the assumption, through marriage alliance and promise of arms, by ʿAlā ad-Dawla of a great deal of influence. ʿAlā ad-Dawla constituted a primary bulwark against the Safavids for both the Ottoman and Mamluk states. Hence, there is no incongruity in his acting both as intercessor for Sībāy and as Bayezid's advance force against Ismail in Diyarbakr. Had the Mamluk sultan been secure in his position, Sībāy would have been executed and 'Alā ad-Dawla would not have been granted a concession for supporting the ex-governor of Tripoli's revolt. As it was, Qānsūh was reluctant to send an expeditionary force to the northern frontier. It was to Mamluk advantage to retain the Zū al-Ḳadr buffer zone.[28] This frontier buffer cushioned Syria from the Ottoman-Safavid conflict and allowed the Mamluk sultan to concentrate on the newly emergent Portuguese threat. So, 'Alā ad-Dawla's complicity and Sībāy's insubordination went unpunished. Sībāy was later pardoned and took a position in Cairo. Qānsūh focused his military forces on the Red Sea littoral and adopted a wait and see policy regarding his frontier with the Ottomans and Safavids.

Sībāy, in 1506, was again posted to the provinces, this time to Damascus because the populace had rebelled. Reliable lieutenants in Qānsūh's entourage must have been in short supply indeed since Sībāy's assignment represented posting a governor of highly questionable loyalty to the area of his past offense. The internal political problems of the Mamluk government were such at this time that Qānsūh could ill afford any punitive expeditions against either Ismail or 'Alā ad-Dawla.[29] Mamluk priorities, in fact, were reflected in the summary comment in the chronicler Ibn Iyās' yearbook for 1505–1506. He wrote that affairs with the Ottomans had been calm that year and that grain was abundant. The main problem was the suspension of the *hajj* because of the revolts in Arabia.[30] This suspension of the *hajj* was a realization of the Ottoman envoy's insult, only three years before, that Qānsūh was incapable of securing his own roads. In effect, the failure to protect the *hajj* delegitimated the sovereignty of the Mamluk ruler in the eyes of the Muslim world. The Mamluk sultan's position was so precarious that he could not even protect the pilgrimage much less challenge Ismail. That task was left to the Zū al-Ḳadr ruler.

In the winter of 1504–1505, Bayezid ordered 'Alā ad-Dawla to prepare to march against Ismail in Syria if necessary.[31] The Ottoman sultan's authority was signified by his ability to levy taxes and troops from frontier governors or vassal princes like 'Alā ad-Dawla. That summer Zū al-Ḳadr forces engaged the *kızılbaş* and were defeated.[32] One account ascribes leadership of the Safavid army to Ismail himself and estimates his force numbered 50,000 soldiers. This estimate is certainly exaggerated and, given that the chronicler, Ḥasan Rūmlū, does not even mention the engagement, it is more likely that the Safavids were led by a commander such as Khān Muḥammad Ustājlū, the man named by Ismail as governor of Diyarbakr. The frontier raiding between ʿAlā ad-Dawla and the Kurdish governors subject to the Ottomans against Khān Muḥammad had been escalating since at least 1504.

The events of that summer of 1505 had dramatic effects in the diplomatic sphere.[33] First, there had been a Safavid attack on territory nominally under the Ottoman sultan's rule. Second, Ismail had sent to the Porte an envoy whose insolence almost cost him his life. Stories circulated that the Safavid envoy threw coins minted in Ismail's name at Bayezid's feet. If untrue, these stories still represent the symbolic challenge to the Ottoman sultan's sovereignty. In any case, the envoy's mission served to challenge the Porte and test the willingness and ability of Bayezid to respond. It was rumored that Ismail demanded Trabzon, an ancient kingdom on the Black Sea, now in Ottoman territory.[34] Bayezid responded by preparing for a Safavid attack. Munitions and artillery were transported from the Morea to Anatolia for this purpose.[35]

ʿAlā ad-Dawla also expected a Safavid attack. He sent an envoy in the fall of 1505 to request assistance from Bayezid, whereupon the Ottoman sultan ordered his son, Selim, in Trabzon, to prepare a force to aid the Zū al-Ḳadr monarch against Ismail. Unsatisfied with this precaution, the Zū al-Ḳadrid also applied to Qānsūh for support, sending his own son, in the spring of 1506, to the Mamluk court with an expensive present.[36] The Zū al-Ḳadr ambassadors were graciously received in both capitals. Yet no military aid was forthcoming from the Mamluks and in 1506 at least there was no open combat between Ottoman and Safavid troops. A Safavid army was sent against Sarım Kurd, an Ottoman dependent in eastern Anatolia, but it was routed and its commanders killed.[37] This battle is the only Safavid military action reported for 1506. That year, Bayezid and Ismail again exchanged envoys to test each other's intentions.[38] These missions illustrate the rhetoric, action, and intentions of Ottoman-Safavid diplomacy early in the sixteenth century before either side was certain of the other's capabilities.

On his arrival in Ismail's court the Ottoman ambassador was given the customary presents but then the shah subjected him to ridicule and served him pork to eat. Such mistreatment of ambassadors was common in sixteenth-century diplomacy. Besides the standard travel risks of bandits, illness, and bad weather, envoys often faced murder, mutilation, and various forms of humiliation when they reached their destinations. Far from home, envoys were always in a precarious position and often subjected to whimsical or malicious behavior. The only protection an envoy had, besides the limited avenue of connections at court, was the threat of reprisals. Executing envoys was not undertaken with impunity. Furthermore, a dead envoy could not bring the news of his torment and humiliation back to his master. There was, however, a more compelling reason to avoid consistant abuse of an opponent's envoys. That reason was the very limited sources of intelligence about enemy rulers, their domestic affairs, and the strength of their militaries. Regular ambassadorial missions served to supplement the information gleaned from merchants, travelers, and spies, hence a ruler was well-advised to keep the options of diplomacy open, regardless of intent to negotiate.

Another purpose of such missions, besides intelligence gathering, is demonstrated by the behavior of Ismail's envoy to Istanbul in 1506. This man made use of his visit to contact the representative of another foreign power, Venice, in an attempt to procure artillery. The merchant, Nicolo Justinian, while selling some cloth to the Safavid ambassador, was approached to arrange communication between Ismail and the *doge* so that the shah could obtain Venetian artillery. The conversation, however, was interrupted by the entry of some of the Ottoman sultan's staff. This interruption was probably no accident, for no trust was expended on visiting emissaries. Foreign envoys were carefully watched, their freedom of movement limited, and opportunities for such negotiation were rare. When the Safavid ambassador departed, Bayezid even destroyed the concrete evidence of his presence by collecting all the Safavid money that had been circulated by the members of the envoy's entourage and having it restamped.

The diplomatic maneuvering of 1505–1506 combined with the Ottoman failure to launch a major attack on the Safavids culminated in Ismail's 1507 invasion of eastern Anatolia. This invasion was a watershed event both for Ottoman internal politics and for foreign relations in the eastern Mediterranean. Some sources explain this attack on 'Alā ad-Dawla's territory as prompted by an aborted marriage alliance.[39] These accounts relate that 'Alā ad-Dawla, at Bayezid's behest, attempted to lure Ismail into a trap by promising him his daughter in marriage. The trap supposedly failed and a Safavid party sent to retrieve the promised bride was cut to pieces by 'Alā ad-Dawla's troops. Given the state of Safavid-Zū al-Kadr relations, however, the chronicler Ḥasan Rūmlū's explanation for Ismail's 1507 attack on 'Alā ad-Dawla seems more likely. Rūmlū blamed the attack on the Zū al-Kadr monarch's support for Ismail's rival, the Ak Koyunlu Sultan Murad. Zū al-Ḳadr forces had also been regularly engaged in sorties into Diyarbakr, a territory which Ismail claimed. Another possible reason was Ismail's desire to test Bayezid's response to a direct challenge in anticipation of more extensive attacks. There does not seem to have been any intent on Ismail's part to effect a permanent territorial gain by attempting to hold Maraş. After the attack, he protested to the Ottoman and Mamluk sultans that ʿAlā ad-Dawla alone was the object of his offensive measures, but there is no question that Bayezid and Qānsūh both considered the invasion an act of war.[40] If Ismail intended to test Bayezid, he had not long to wait for the response. But he managed to reach ʿAlā ad-Dawla's territory without engaging in any major battles.

Ismail marched into Ottoman territory in the direction of Kayseri. There he purchased provisions and augmented his army with recruits from the Anatolian populace, then marched on Elbistan. The route taken on the march can be explained on the basis of topographical and military practicality. Ismail avoided the more mountainous terrain of a direct route. His approach from Erzincan allowed him to secure troops and provisions from an area of proven Safavid support rather than attempting to secure food and fodder in Diyarbakr or in hostile Zū al-Ḳadr territory. The route also allowed Ismail to gauge the extent of his proselytising efforts in eastern Anatolia and to impress the Ottomans with a show of force.[41] An initial engagement betwen the Ottomans and Safavids took place prior to Ismail's arrival in Zū al-Ḳadr territory but details are sketchy.[42] The Safavid army strength was estimated at as many as sixty to two hundred thousand men; a more likely estimate, however, is contained in a report that places his cavalry strength at ten thousand men.[43] There is no real disagreement over the outcome of the campaign. Ismail took Maraş and Elbistan and eventually camped at Malatia. ʿAlā ad-Dawla, adopting a hit-and-run form of engaging the numerically superior Safavid force, fled to the mountains east of Maraş.[44]

The Ottoman response to Ismail's invasion was swift. In addition to the forces already mobilized in 1505–1506 under the eastern Anatolian provincial governors, Bayezid sent Yahya Pasha with an army mobilized from the central and western Anatolian *sancak begs* (sub-province governors), including a force of four thousand five hundred *janissaries* (elite Ottoman infantry corps) and three to four hundred pieces of artillery.[45] Also, the troops under the *beglerbeg* (governor general) of Rumelia were transferred

across the Bosphorus to back up Yahya's army. Ismail withdrew
east as the Ottoman army advanced in the fall of 1507. Despite
Ottoman desertions to the Safavids, it seems unlikely that Ismail
was eager to fight this large and well-armed Ottoman force. Neither army was anxious to spend the winter in eastern Anatolia
facing an enemy, harsh climate, and scarcity of provisions. By late
November of 1507, Yahya Pasha had returned to Istanbul, saying
that Ismail had fled, but the conflict between Ottoman and Safavid
subordinates continued on the frontier throughout that winter and
spring.[46]

While still in the area of Elbistan, Ismail had received Amīr
Beg Mūṣilū, former governor of Diyarbakr under the Ak Koyunlu,
who rendered him obeisance. The shah marched east, seizing Harput on the way and executing its governor, Bekar Beg, the son of
ʿAlā ad-Dawla. Crossing the Euphrates, Ismail left a force under
Khān Muḥammad Ustājlū, whom he appointed governor of Diyarbakr, and returned to Khoi with the rest of his army, losing many
men and animals in the snow on the way.[47] Meanwhile, Qaitams
Beg, governor of Amid, refused to submit to Khān Muḥammad.
Forced to winter in the open, the latter's camp was subjected to
raids by the Kurdish begs of Diyarbakr. After pursuing and defeating a sizeable Kurdish force that winter, the Safavid commander
prepared to launch an attack on Amid; and Qaitams Beg sent to
ʿAlā ad-Dawla for assistance. The Zū al-Ḳadr ruler sent a force of
two thousand cavalry under his son Kasim. He was defeated by
Khān Muḥammad who sent his head as a trophy to Ismail. Some
days later Khān Muḥammad took Amid and Qaitams Beg shared
Kasim's fate.[48] Khān Muḥammad continued his battles against the
Kurdish begs in the spring of 1508; and ʿAlā ad-Dawla, grieved
and vengeful, sent two other sons, Blind Shah Ruh and Ahmed, to
attack him. Again the Safavid force was successful and the heads
of Ahmed and Shah Ruh followed that of their brother to Ismail
who was enroute from Khoi to conquer Baghdad.

This series of three defeats decimated the Zū Al-Ḳadr army
and slowed down ʿAlā ad-Dawla's military activities in Diyarbakr.
It is evident, however, that Khān Muḥammad's position was far
from secure. The Kurdish begs continued to resist Safavid rule just
as they were wont to resist any stringent attempts at direct Ottoman rule. Fortresses once taken but not defended by a substantial
force were liable to revolt, and Safavid power was never firmly
established in Diyarbakr.[49] ʿAlā ad-Dawla remained defiant as
well. When Ismail marched on Baghdad in 1508 and took the city,

the deposed Ak Koyunlu prince, Murad, there in exile, fled to Aleppo where he was received by the Mamluk governor, Khair Beg, an ally of ʿAlā ad-Dawla. Then Murad proceeded on to the Zū al-Ḳadr ruler who made him his son-in-law.[50] The chronicler Khvandamīr later mocked Murad's flight, saying he behaved "like a woman," hiding from Ismail.[51] The Mamluk sultan, fearing Ismail's wrath, had refused Murad safe conduct to Cairo, which probably accounts for his taking refuge with ʿAlā ad-Dawla. The Zū al-Ḳadrid, by this action, showed his continued defiance of Ismail and made a statement of his autonomy on both Safavid and Mamluk fronts. Ismail, meanwhile was preoccupied with internal opposition and spent 1508–1509 consolidating his power in Iraq and reasserting it against a revolt in Şirvan.[52]

The events of the summer of 1507 point up the importance of buffer zone politics as an indicator of the policies of the Mamluk, Safavid, and Ottoman states. ʿAlā ad-Dawla, in late summer, sent an envoy to Sībāy, then governor of Damascus, demanding assistance against Ismail. Sībāy owed the Zū al-Ḳadr ruler a favor for interceding on his behalf with Qānsūh in 1505. ʿAlā ad-Dawla also had well-established relations with Ultībāy the former governor of Tripoli, who had been his son-in-law since 1505, and with Khair Beg in Aleppo. Where ʿAlā ad-Dawla utilized his sons on the battle field against the Safavids, he used his daughters in the diplomatic arena to cement local alliances. Khair Beg and ʿAlā ad-Dawla mobilized a force of two thousand cavalry near Aleppo with the intention of engaging Ismail, but this force, ultimately, never encountered the Safavids.[53]

In Cairo, the proximity of Ismail's army caused something of a panic. Qānsūh ordered the Syrian governors to take steps against a Safavid invasion, mobilized an expeditionary force, and authorized payment of campaign bonuses.[54] This planned advance of the Mamluk army was cancelled when an envoy from ʿAlā ad-Dawla arrived in Cairo. Ibn Iyās suggests that Qānsūh refrained from military action because ʿAlā ad-Dawla falsely claimed a victory over the Safavids. More likely, the Mamluk sultan's reluctance to commit an army to battle Ismail was bolstered by the news that the shah had withdrawn across the Euphrates and was thus no longer an immediate threat.[55]

On the Ottoman side, the Safavid humiliation of ʿAlā ad-Dawla and the inadequacy of the Porte's military response provided Prince Selim with material for a critique of the effectiveness of his father Bayezid's reign.[56] As Selim developed a line of political

rhetoric based on the need to meet directly the Safavid threat, Ismail provided him with gross justification for his challenge to
Bayezid. The 1507 Safavid assault on the Zū al-Ķadr was only the
first in a series of direct challenges to the Ottoman sultan.[57] In
1510, Bayezid's authority was further compromised by the Safavid
inspired Shah Kulu revolt in Anatolia and by the diplomatic insult
posed when Ismail sent a battle trophy, the head of the Uzbeg ruler
Shaibānī Khān, to the Porte.[58] Shah Kulu was a kızılbaş sympathizer whose followers thwarted Ottoman attempts to quell their
rebellion in eastern Anatolia for over a year. His revolt symbolized
the widespread rejection of Bayezid's authority by his own subjects
in his own territory.

In terms of foreign relations, a series of Safavid victories beginning with the defeat of ʿAlā ad-Dawla would seem to have provided a likely political context for an anti-Ottoman alliance. Essentially, during Ismail's reign, there were two sets of successful
Safavid campaigns in the western Iranian zone (Georgia to Iraq),
which had a major impact on foreign relations in the eastern Mediterranean region. The first, in 1501–1503, occurred when Venice
and Rhodes were concluding a lengthy war with the Ottoman state
and when intelligence information on Ismail was relatively scarce
in Europe. The second set of military advances occurred in 1507–
1508 by which time considerable effort had been expended in gaining information about Ismail, and the early stages of the Ottoman
succession struggle had weakened Bayezid's authority. Ismail then
pressed his advantage by using his defeat of Shaibānī Khān as justification for claiming the right to rule Mecca and Medina, a title
the Uzbeg khān had also coveted.[59] This challenged the position of
the Mamluk sultan and the ambitions of the Ottoman sultan. Yet
Qānsūh's response was necessarily insignificant and Bayezid failed
to invade Iran to chastise Ismail.

If the years 1507–1512, however, are viewed strategically as a
period of maximum Safavid potential and maximum Ottoman
weakness, the comparison is only relative. Like the Ottomans, the
Mamluks, and Venice, Ismail was engaged on two fronts requiring
substantial overland troop transport. Despite his rhetorical challenges to Bayezid and Qānsūh, at no time after 1507 was Ismail
able to push a military offensive past Diyarbakr in eastern Anatolia.[60] The sluggishness of Ottoman response to the Shah Kulu
rebellion must be attributed, at least partially, to a lack of popular
support and to loyalty problems in the Anatolian military units
rather than to any deficiency in troop strength.[61] This assessment

is supported by the standoff in eastern Anatolia between Ottoman and Safavid forces.[62] The Safavids were not prepared for an actual declaration of war. Ottoman military power and clear naval superiority discouraged an invasion; and Ismail, though bold, was not foolhardy. The 1507 invasion, however, had generated considerable speculation in Europe about Ismail's chances of conquering Anatolia.[63] This speculation was bolstered by the fact that the Ottoman princes, impatient for a chance at sovereign power, were aggressively jockeying for position to end Bayezid's long reign.

The Ottoman succession struggle resulted in political instability which in turn prompted interest in fermenting revolt, particularly in Karaman, on the part of the Mamluks, Safavids, Venetians, and Rhodians. This was less risky than an outright declaration of war against the Ottomans. By 1507, however, both Venice and the Mamluk state were preoccupied with the Portuguese commercial challenge.[64] This threat from outside the Mediterranean made the prospect of interrupting trade within the Mediterranean by antagonizing the Porte even less inviting. Each of these governments had to commit its military and financial resources to threats posed to their territorial integrity. These came, in the case of Venice, from the pope and his allies and, in the Mamluk case, from the revolts of provincial governors and populaces. Rhodes, likewise on the defensive, had insufficient resources to challenge the Porte. In retrospect, Ismail's attack on 'Alā ad-Dawla provided the opportunity for a strategic follow-up by a joint force of Ottoman opponents. In practice, however, Bayezid's enemies did not have the shared interest, information, trust or resources to act in a coordinated fashion. The focus of the Levantine power struggle was already shifting to the Red Sea. As a result, the Safavid momentum gained in 1507–1512 was met with cautious diplomatic maneuvering rather than with vigorous coordinated military effort.

Diplomatic mechanisms remained in effect despite the excitement and military mobilizations resulting from Ismail's attack on 'Alā ad-Dawla. When Ismail invaded Anatolia in 1507, an Ottoman ambassador was present in Cairo and a Mamluk ambassador was in Venice. Ibn Taghribirdī, the Mamluk dragoman, had been sent to Venice to reach a settlement over Venetian trading privileges in the Mamluk territories. Qānsūh was in need of the cash Venetian merchants brought to cover expenses like the bonus payments required by the mamluk troops. Such bonuses were demanded by the officers and often by the troops as well for almost every campaign in those years.[65] Ibn Taghribirdī's sojourn lasted over a year, but a treaty agreement was not formalized by his mission.[66] The Safavid threat operated in Venice's favor by making Qānsūh anxious to consolidate relations with his allies. But this predicament was not sufficient incentive to make him relinquish his demands for the fixed lump sum spice purchases traditionally required of Venice. Nor was it sufficient to interest him in concluding a military alliance with Bayezid at the Mamluk northern frontiers.

The Ottoman ambassador arrived in Cairo in early spring of 1507 and was received cordially by Qānsūh al-Ghūrī. The Safavid threat, presumably, constituted at least part of the rationale for sending this envoy to Cairo.[67] Ottoman diplomacy, however, was geared by broader and more complex motivations than simply stopping the kızılbaş expansion. The subsequent arrival in Cairo of an artillery and material aid shipment from Istanbul in September, following Ismail's attack on ʿAlā ad-Dawla, was not necessarily an indication that this Ottoman ambassador was negotiating an anti-Safavid alliance. Rather, the Ottoman artillery, supplies, copper, and workmen were destined for the Mamluk Suez fleet being prepared for use against the Portuguese. Qānsūh had enemies on both his land and sea confines. He needed to fortify Jidda, with Ottoman aid, and news of Portuguese incursions in the Red Sea had reached Cairo in early spring, just about the time of the Ottoman envoy's arrival. For the time being, Ottoman and Mamluk intentions coincided, neither wished the Safavids or the Portuguese to gain an advantage. For Bayezid, though, the prospect of his Mamluk and Safavid opponents expending their resources and energies against each other was not unappealing. Ottoman aid to Qānsūh, then, was directed primarily at the Portuguese and not at Ismail.[68]

Bayezid could not, after all, be certain that Qānsūh would not negotiate with Ismail. By making the Mamluk sultan dependent upon him for defense against the Portuguese, he helped insure against a Mamluk-Safavid alliance. Spies in Cairo and Istanbul ensured that both sultans were aware of the visits of envoys from Iran. But Ismail could not provide Qānsūh with copper and gun founders. Bayezid could, which is why the famous Ottoman naval captain, Kemal Reis, received such a warm welcome in September 1507 when he arrived in Alexandria with the Ottoman shipment. The Ottoman ambassador who had arrived in the spring was still in Cairo and Qānsūh held a grand reception in honor of the two Ottoman representatives.[69] A similar reception was given for the Safavid ambassador who reached Cairo that December, bearing excuses for Ismail's violation of Mamluk territory during his attack on the Zū al-Ḳadr. The Safavid envoys brought Qānsūh a present worth thirty thousand ducats, and one worth six thousand for the governor of Damascus.

Contarini, the Venetian consul in Damascus, reported that this embassy had a dual mission, to seek aid from Venice and to placate the Mamluk sultan. On their return through Damascus, the Safavid envoys sought an audience with Contarini. He refused to allow a formal visit for fear of angering the Mamluk sultan but arranged to meet them secretly away from his residence. He also refused their request for a Venetian envoy to accompany them back to Iran in the interests of setting up a Safavid diplomatic mission to Venice. Contarini's report suggests that this meeting may well have been the event that set up the Safavid mission to Venice the following year which eventually proved so disastrous for Contarini's successor as consul, Piero Zeno.[70] The caution exercised by Contarini was designed to protect Venetian relations with the Mamluks. Yet the willingness of both the consul and the Damascene governor to meet with Ismail's representatives indicates that Ottoman precautions against a Safavid alliance either with Venice or with the Mamluks were warranted. Ismail was hampered by the lack of resident European ambassadors at his court. Hence, his attempts to sound out Venetian cordiality had to be conducted indirectly.

While the Safavid envoy was in Cairo, he had been treated to a military display in the hippodrome.[71] Qānsūh's display there was a carefully orchestrated event, designed to impress a feared opponent with Mamluk military might.[72] The Ottoman ambassador had already departed but it was common practice to entertain simultaneously envoys of enemy powers. In the practice of diplomacy of the time, embassies were intended as much to gather information as to conclude alliances. Ambassadors presented demands, obtained intelligence on the stability of the administration and troop strength, negotiated commercial arrangements, and participated in ritual gift exchanges which were designed as much to impress and intimidate as to demonstrate good will. These ambassadors became the audience for formal and carefully orchestrated displays of power. Extraordinary measures were taken to frame what they saw and heard. Both Qānsūh and Bayezid kept the Safavid envoys sequestered so that it was difficult for them to engage in court intrigue or to secure intelligence. An ambassador might reside in a city for months with only minimal contact with the court and the sultan. Ambassadors were, after all, messengers in the rhetorical contest for sovereignty and legitimacy within the Muslim world. Thus, every effort was made carefully to craft the images which they bore abroad and carried back home to their own masters.[73]

Ismail's ambassador to Cairo boldly demanded Adana and Tarsus as well as reimbursement for losses to ʿAlā ad-Dawla. These demands, clearly an insult to Mamluk sovereignty, elicited from Qānsūh lavish ceremony and presents but no real concessions. Although the Mamluk ruler may have been somewhat relieved, by the Safavid envoy's protestations of good will, Safavid claims to southeastern Anatolia would require the surrender of Mamluk territory. Both the Mamluk and Ottoman monarchs feared a Safavid conquest of the Zū al-Ḳadr buffer zone. There was another reason for the Safavid mission as well. Ismail intended to attack Baghdad and sent his envoy to Cairo to ensure that he would not face concerted Mamluk and Ottoman retaliation when he did. Qānsūh, however, had been hesitant to advance his army into Syria even when his own territory was threatened. Reluctant to commit the troops and money to his already politically unstable northern frontier, Qānsūh kept his army close to Cairo.

Bayezid was not so reticent. Keeping the Anatolian armies on the alert, he sent a force of up to 35,000 men to the borders of Adana and Tarsus. Perhaps he had direct intelligence of Safavid plans to secure an outlet to the Mediterranean. In any case, such a force could be utilized both to meet a Safavid invasion and to assist in suppressing a revolt in Karaman. The build-up of Ottoman forces at the frontier zone, of course, contributed little to allaying Mamluk suspicions about Bayezid's true objectives.[74]

While this military mobilization was in progress a Safavid envoy arrived at the Ottoman court and remained there from spring until early summer of 1508. The envoy's very presence at the Porte months after the Safavid invasion of eastern Anatolia is witness to the fact that the Safavid and Ottoman sultans were eager to sound out the intentions and potential of their respective adversaries.[75] Bayezid simply could have executed the Safavid envoy, but it was more advantageous to keep the lines of communication open. Bayezid's health was failing and his caution in foreign affairs was dictated by the need to hold off a succession struggle at home. No peace accord was concluded, neither was war declared, so Ottoman-Safavid relations remained at stalemate. But the news of Bayezid's ill health could not but have encouraged Ismail to believe that he could pursue his campaigns in Iraq without fear of Ottoman intervention.

Expectations of Bayezid's imminent death resulted in prema-
ture word of his demise reaching Cairo early in 1509. Qānsūh went
so far as to prepare a memorial service and assigned an envoy to
send to the Porte in May. Soon, much to Qānsūh's chagrin, news
that the sultan was still among the living reached Cairo. The designated envoy, Amīr ʿAlān, journeyed to Istanbul nonetheless in
August 1509 and returned to Cairo in June 1510, rewarded with a
message of good will and a promise of aid from the sultan whose
death he had originally intended to condole.[76] Bayezid had almost
three more years to live, but the extended visit of the Mamluk
envoy represented time devoted to enhancing the Mamluk position
at the Ottoman court in anticipation of the Ottoman sultan's
death. Qānsūh was not the only one deluded by the reports of
Bayezid's demise. In the winter of 1509–1510, it was rumored in
Istanbul that Bayezid was dead. The *janissaries* demanded to see
him, whereupon he appeared on his balcony to reassure them.[77]

The succession of events following on Ismail's 1507 invasion of
Anatolia and Bayezid's illness resulted in the flight of Bayezid's
son, Korkud, to Cairo in 1509. In the event of a sultan's death,
proximity to Istanbul, as well as the support of the army, was a
significant factor in the outcome of Ottoman succession struggles.
Given his father's weakness, Korkud would not willingly have left
Anatolia unless he felt his position there was untenable. Once
abroad, his arrival in the Mamluk domains gave Qānsūh an opportunity to cultivate personally an Ottoman ally.[78] Korkud's visit
lasted over a year, during which time he was royally entertained,
allowed frequent visits to the citadel, and even paid a monthly stipend amounting to two thousand dinars. This latter favor scan-
dalized the chronicler Ibn Iyās, who marvelled at the compliments
paid to Korkud. The Ottoman prince was even permitted to ride a
horse in a court ceremony, a signal honor.[79] Korkud, in his turn
provided some display by sending off one of his officers on the *hajj*
with four thousand dinars to be distributed among the poor of
Mecca. Such largesse could be construed as a symbol of Korkud's
own claims to the Ottoman throne and to patronage of the Holy
Cities.

It is difficult to gauge Qānsūh's intentions regarding the Ottoman prince's claims to the sultanate. Korkud fled because he be-
lieved his life was in danger and his prospects for seizing the
throne, at least immediately, were poor. Qānsūh would not openly
support Korkud's succession bid while awaiting artillery shipments from Bayezid. If Bayezid, however, died while his son was in

Plate 4: Sultan Bayezid II, Lokman, Kiyafet ül-insaniye fi şemail il-osmaniye. Source: British Library, Add 7880, f. 45 recto. Courtesy of the British Library Board.

Cairo, then Korkud would be a Mamluk trump card in negotiations with the new sultan. If Korkud returned to Anatolia and by some chance succeeded his father, then his cordial reception at the Mamluk court would have proved a useful investment.

While Korkud sojourned in Egypt, his brother Selim prepared to mount his first major effort to seize Bayezid's throne.[80] The Ottoman succession struggle coincided with and was in part the cause of three years of provincial unrest in Anatolia. Unrest is reflected in the sources by desertions from the Ottoman army, submission to Ismail of eastern Anatolian governors, and repressive measures taken by Bayezid to punish Safavid supporters. What cannot be measured from the information available is the extent to which rebellion in Anatolia was an indication of support for Safavid ideology or a sign of dissatisfaction with the Ottoman administration.[81] The traditionally independent eastern Anatolian begs resented Ottoman attempts to tighten central government administrative control over taxation and troop deployment.[82] There was, at this time, a general lumping in contemporary narrative sources of all rebellion in Anatolia under the rubric of "*kızılbaş*." This is most apparent in European sources, like the "Diarii" of the Venetian Marino Sanuto, where lack of information characteristically led to an attribution of responsibility for revolt to the "Great Sophy" Ismail, reflecting European hopes for the diminuition of Ottoman power.

The Shah Kulu rebellion against the Ottomans, which occurred in 1510–1511, demands attention for its success and duration if not for its magnitude. Yet, it received only brief mention in Sanuto and less in Ibn Iyās.[83] For Venice, this revolt was an extension of Ismail's anti-Ottoman activities. Shah Kulu, a dervish Safavid sympathizer, who penetrated further into Anatolia than any of Ismail Safavi's own forces and whose defeat required the mobilization of two successive Ottoman armies, did not have a significant or direct impact on foreign affairs. His revolt demonstrated the extent of the turmoil in Ottoman provincial administration and the compromise of authority brought on by Bayezid's age and infirmity. Yet it seems to have remained largely an internal affair. This rebellion and its potential for mobilizing support among the Ottoman populace of Anatolia was cut short by Shah Kulu's death in battle in 1511. Ismail then distanced himself from the movement and its organization when he ordered the execution of some of Shah Kulu's lieutenants for attacking a merchant caravan.[84] In this way, Ismail illustrated the nature of his claims to sovereignty by demonstrating his justice, his protection of commercial interests, and his disavowal of chaotic and undisciplined popular movements.

In a single year, 1510, local chronicles and reports reflect the varied preoccupations in the Mamluk, Venetian, and Safavid states regarding events in Anatolia and Iran. The Persian chronicle of Ḥasan Rūmlū, for example, devotes a great deal of attention to Ismail's defeat of Shaibānī Khān on the Safavid eastern frontiers in 1510, demonstrating the Safavid preoccupation with that monarch's threat to Safavid control in eastern Iran. For Venetian writers, in that same year, the deterioration of Venice's commercial position in Egypt and Syria, brought on by the Mamluk seizure of Ismail's letters to Venice and by the Rhodian attack on the Mamluk fleet at Ayas, was of paramount importance. On the Mamluk side, Qānsūh al-Ghūrī had suffered the loss to Rhodes of his supply fleet following soon after the loss of his Indian Ocean fleet to the Portuguese in 1509. For the Mamluk chronicler, Ibn Iyās, danger lay on all sides, as reflected in that one year alone by the Safavid defeat of the Uzbegs, a Spanish attack on Tunis in North Africa, and the seizure of a Safavid envoy in Syria, who was attempting to mobilize an anti-Mamluk coalition.[85]

Diplomatically, for both Venice and the Mamluks, the important issues were: who was to succeed the Ottoman sultan, and how would that successor alter their positions vis-à-vis the Porte? Ismail had not, in three years, renewed his invasion of Anatolia and the speculation generated in 1507 about a new Safavid offensive had not been answered with any substance.[86] This fact, together with the priorities mentioned above, assured that the response in Venice and Cairo to Ismail's overtures never took any material form. At the end of the year 1510, Yūnus ad-Dawla, Qānsūh's envoy, returned from Istanbul. His five month mission seeking lumber, iron, and ammunition had been very successful. The Mamluk commitment to neutrality in the Ottoman-Safavid conflict was cemented by a huge shipment of arms and material from Istanbul for use on the Mamluk Red Sea frontier against the Portuguese. This Ottoman aid fleet arrived in Alexandria in January of 1511. Bayezid had refused to accept the Mamluk gold in payment for this aid, another factor which insured against Mamluk receptivity to an alliance with the Safavid monarch. Thus, the Ottoman noose tightened around the Mamluk neck.[87]

The years 1510–1512 were characterized by a stalemate of foreign relations in the eastern Mediterranean which, however, was accompanied by an intensification of diplomatic activity as the various states maneuvered for position while the Ottoman wars of succession ran their course. In the fall of 1510, Korkud returned from Egypt, hoping to capitalize on his brother Selim's military challenge to regain the good will of his father, the sultan.[88] The Mamluks, meanwhile, utilizing the Ottoman material aid, prepared another fleet at Suez and remained preoccupied with internal political strife. Venice, with some trepidation, took a hard-line stance against the Mamluks, imposing a moratorium on trade until Qānsūh guaranteed commercial security to Venetian merchants.[89] The Signoria had devoted its attention to defense against the League of Cambrai and then against the emperor, finding it expedient to bypass Ismail's offer of military alliance and to pursue friendly relations with the Porte. For their part, preoccupied with the succession struggle in progress, the Ottomans maintained a policy of cautious truce at their frontiers. In the end, the Anatolian army, which had been mobilized against Ismail, was used to fight the Ottoman dynastic battles.[90] Ismail, though apparently considering a Safavid-Portuguese joint action against the Mamluks, devoted his attention to his eastern borders. He bypassed a second opportunity to invade Anatolia provided by prince Selim's revolt and by the Shah Kulu rebellion.

The embassies of these years suggest that Ismail, Qānsūh, and Bayezid were all eager to avoid any concerted attack by two of their opponents. While one Mamluk ambassador was in Istanbul purchasing arms, Qānsūh sent another, Tīmūr Bāy Hindī, to Ismail in June of 1510.[91] It was only after Tīmūr Bāy departed that the governor of Birecik intercepted Ismail's envoy who was carrying letters to European kings suggesting a joint attack on the Ottomans and Mamluks.[92] This affront, combined with the news of Ismail's victory over the Uzbeg Shaibānī Khān of Transoxania and of the Rhodian attack on the Mamluk fleet at Ayas, could have inclined Qānsūh to attempt a defensive alliance with Bayezid.[93] Circumstances, however, militated against any such alliance. For one thing, Bayezid had assumed a position of superiority by refusing to accept Mamluk money for the military aid which he had supplied. For another, by the time an Ottoman envoy arrived in Cairo in February 1511, the Ottoman succession struggle had escalated to the point that it was no longer clear who was ruling the Ottoman state.[94] Not until after Selim's accession in 1512 were the Mamluks again able to obtain military aid from the Porte for use against the Portuguese. Rather than prompt Qānsūh to ally with the Mamluks' traditional foe, the situation in the Ottoman Empire gave the Mamluk sovereign a temporary reprieve from the threat of an Ottoman attack on his own territory.

The Ottoman state, in 1510–1512, was effectively transformed into a series of armed camps. The Shah Kulu rebellion was not quelled until the summer of 1511. Prince Ahmed was raising an army in Amasia to ensure his own claims to the throne as was his brother Korkud, with limited success, in Manisa.[95] Selim, after an inconclusive battle with Bayezid, withdrew to Caffa to mobilize a larger army; and the refusal of the *janissaries* to accept Bayezid's authority left Istanbul near anarchy from summer 1511 through April 1512.[96] Each contender made efforts to buy the support of the *janissaries*. The situation in the provinces, at this time, puts to the test the strong central government model of the classical Ottoman age, which assumes that the operations of state were dependent upon the consolidation of all authority in the hands of the sultan. The interregnum period, a particularly long one in this case, provides a contrast between the ideal of state embodied in *kanun* (sultanic edict) and the reality of state power in practice. Clearly Bayezid did not control his state at this time, yet it did not succumb, either to provincial revolts or to external invasion.

Failing to secure the throne without the support of the *janissaries*, Prince Ahmed seized Konya. By March of 1512, he had made a last ditch effort to control Anatolia by concluding a marriage alliance with Ismail Safavi, uniting his son with Ismail's daughter.[97] This Safavid support for his primary rival was an important factor in the priority Selim gave to attacking Ismail soon after his accession. The other main factor was the necessity to secure his eastern flank in order to prepare for an invasion of Egypt and Syria.[98]

Venice, the Mamluks, and the Safavids awaited the outcome of the fight for Ottoman sovereignty. The duration of the struggle was disadvantageous to both Venice and the Mamluks. For Venice, the year long instability in Ottoman internal affairs and the chronic insurrection of the *janissaries* compromised the Signoria's commercial position in the Ottoman realm.[99] In February 1512, *janissary* officers had taken advantage of the disintegration of the sovereign's authority in Istanbul to extort money from the Venetian *bailo*. They demanded, and apparently received, twenty-two thousand aspers from the beleaguered Venetian, ostensibly as payment for ships seized by European corsairs. The *bailo*, Foscolo, noted that some of the Ottoman vezirs did not sleep in their own houses at night for fear of their lives. He reflected the sentiments of his government when he said that everyone was waiting to see what would happen next. No Venetian ships were in Istanbul; Venetian commercial shipping into the Bosphorus was effectively suspended until the Ottoman succession was determined one way or the other.

For Qānsūh al-Ghūrī, the battle for the Ottoman throne represented a likely deterioration in his own already fragile position. In Bayezid's last years the Mamluks had benefited from Ottoman material support for use against Portugal and naval support against Rhodes at the same time that the Safavids were engaging Ottoman troops on the eastern frontiers. During the succession battles, material aid was cut off for nearly two years. The Rhodians took advantage of the curtailment of Ottoman naval activity to raid grain shipments in the Aegean and eastern Mediterranean.[100] With the accession of Selim likely, Qānsūh, having supported Korkud, could not be sure what Ottoman-Mamluk relations would be like under the new sultan. The Mamluks, then, feared the possibility of both Ottoman and Safavid invasions. Ismail capitalized on the Ottoman disorders to serve Qānsūh with diplomatic threats and insults.[101] A Safavid envoy came to Cairo in the summer of 1511, mocking Qānsūh with Ismail's successes and suggesting his own master's entitlement to sovereignty over Mecca and Medina.

In June 1512, Tīmūr Bāy Hindī, the Mamluk envoy, returned to Cairo after an almost two-year mission to the Safavid court. He had been abused and humiliated by Ismail and had lost most of his retainers. In this way, Ismail had shown his scorn for Mamluk power. Two days after Tīmūr Bāy's return, an envoy from Ismail arrived in Cairo. He brought Qānsūh rich presents, including two leopards, but his language was coarse and insulting.[102] He claimed Egypt, Syria, and Arabia as Ismail's lawful patrimony as a descendant, so he claimed, of the Prophet. Ismail, like other Muslim lords, before and since, was remiss in adhering to genealogical propriety. The Safavid ambassador's impressive show was countered by a Mamluk military display in the hippodrome. There was, however, little feeling of confidence in the Mamluk court. Ismail's conquest of Iraq and the upheavals in Anatolia had unsettled the whole eastern frontier zone, not to mention Europe. As the traditional enemy of the Porte and as nominal representative of the Commander of the Faithful, Qānsūh could not escape accountability for attempting to meet both the Ottoman and Safavid threats.

The shah was not the only sovereign jockeying for position

during the Ottoman succession wars. ʿAlā ad-Dawla, in March 1512, sent an ambassador to Cairo with magnificent presents. He had continued to engage in periodic skirmishes against the Safavids in Diyarbakr and his embassy to Cairo may well have been aimed at seeking Mamluk backing as a result of Ahmed's alliance with Ismail. If Safavid aid were to ensure Ahmed's success in his bid for the Ottoman sultanate, ʿAlā ad-Dawla's territories could become a Safavid share of the spoils.[103] The Zū al-Ḳadr ambassador was royally received. Again, the importance of the Zū al-Ḳadr principality as a buffer zone was apparent. ʿAlā ad-Dawla's consistency of anti-Safavid policy provided Qānsūh with what little security he had on the northern frontier.[104]

Venice, too, was concerned over both Safavid and Portuguese potential for disrupting the trade through the Red Sea and Syria. The *doge* sent Qānsūh a conciliatory embassy, laden with presents of crystal and cloth, seeking the release of European prisoners and the renewal of trade.[105] A French embassy also arrived in Cairo, seeking to capitalize on the compromised position of Venice in the Mamluk territories in order to enhance France's own commercial position.[106] All this diplomatic activity indicated the extent of the political turmoil generated by the Ottoman-Safavid stalemate and by the Ottoman succession struggle.

This situation changed after the accession of Selim I (ruled 1512–1520). He wasted little time before breaking the stalemate and dispelling the uncertainty. Selim spent the first year of his reign consolidating his power and overcoming his brothers.[107] The struggle was exacerbated by the Safavid shah's attempt to tip the scales against the new Ottoman sultan. Ismail, in addition to supporting Ahmed, had again sent his armies into eastern Anatolia to engage the Ottoman frontier forces.[108] It was in the aftermath of these skirmishes that Selim launched a major invasion of Safavid territory. The Safavid chronicler Ḥasan Rūmlū blamed the foolish behavior of Ismail's lieutenant, Khān Muḥammad Ustājlū, for Selim's attack on Çaldıran in 1514. Khān Muḥammad had sent insults and threats to Selim, suggesting there was some question regarding his masculinity. It is clear, however, that Ismail's invasions of eastern Anatolia and the harboring of Selim's dynastic opponents were reason enough for Ottoman retaliation. Selim could not be viewed as sitting the throne securely until the Safavid challenge was met.

In order to devote his attentions to Anatolia and the eastern frontier, Selim pursued a policy of military neutrality toward the

Mamluks until after the battle of Çaldıran in 1514. The Ottoman envoy, announcing Selim's accession in 1512, brought a message of goodwill to Qānsūh al-Ghūrī. This, in turn, encouraged the Mamluk sultan to reply in kind to the insults which the Safavid monarch had sent to Cairo. Qānsūh sent a hostile reply home with the Safavid envoy, who left Cairo in the summer of 1512.[109] Once this diplomatic question of honor was attended to, Qānsūh immediately turned his attention to practical defensive concerns. He sent one envoy, Ḥamīd Maghrebī to Istanbul to acquire lumber, iron and bronze for the Suez fleet and another, Aq Bāy Tawīl, in 1513, to seek more aid and to gain intelligence about Selim's intentions and plans. Selim cemented the temporary truce with a very generous response, loading the requested materials on a sizeable fleet for the journey to Alexandria. Demonstrating his confidence against both the Safavids and Mamluks, he included cannons of iron and of bronze.[110]

Such displays of friendship notwithstanding, Qānsūh obviously placed no great faith in Selim. In the winter of 1512–1513, he welcomed two Ottoman pretenders to his court, Selim's nephews (sons of his brother Ahmed).[111] These princes proved useless as political leverage, however, since both died the following spring of the plague which was raging in Egypt. The Karamanid pretender, Mustafa ibn Hamza, also resident at the Mamluk court, fell victim to the same epidemic. Even had these claimants survived, in reality the Mamluk sultan was powerless against Selim. Qānsūh devoted his efforts to building the fleet at Suez and to quelling the provincial rebellions that had become endemic in the Mamluk lands.[112] But he lacked even the authority to command obedience from his own troops who refused orders to march to Suez until their demands for bonus pay were met.[113] By the time this expeditionary force finally left for Suez in March 1514, Selim had mobilized his army to invade Iran.[114]

The Ottoman campaign against Ismail, like Ismail's attack on ʿAlā ad-Dawla in 1507, prompted a defensive mobilization of the Mamluk army. This time, however, the army was actually sent out to Aleppo. This reaction gives some indication of the fact that the Mamluks perceived the greatest threat to their territories as coming from the Ottomans rather than the Safavids. There could be little doubt that once an Ottoman army of 40,000 troops was mobilized to march across Anatolia, the strife torn Mamluk kingdom, guardian of the Holy Cities and crossroads of the Asian trade, would be a likely target.

Selim sent envoys to both Mamluk and Safavid courts to declare his intentions.[115] With an air of arrogant confidence, the message of war came to Cairo and Hamadan. At the Mamluk court,
Selim's ambassador announced the plan to attack Ismail and demanded that Qānsūh mobilize his own troops as well. The tone of
the message was that taken with an inferior rather than an equal.
It was at this point that Selim became, rhetorically, master of the
Muslim potentates, and dispensed with the diplomacy of caution.
The natural response of rage, to which his station entitled him,
was one which Qānsūh could not take. Enmeshed in a Mamluk
rebellion over pay for the recent expedition to review the fleet at
Suez, the options available to him were limited, and his response to
Selim's threat was necessarily feeble.[116] A Mamluk force under
Qanī Beg would be sent to Aleppo where it would await the outcome of the combat between the armies of Selim and Ismail. Meanwhile, Qānsūh looked to his own defense. The artillery and defenses of Egypt were assessed and Qānsūh endeavored to stabilize
his northern frontier by proposing a marriage alliance between his
son and the daughter of Sībāy, governor of Damascus.[117] Sībāy's
loyalty was suspect because earlier, as governor of Aleppo, he was
accused of sedition. These suspicions, far from being laid to rest,
were renewed when Sībāy initially refused the marriage alliance,
thus insulting his master. He relented, however, under pressure
and with the added incentive of a 10,000 dinar dowry. This negotiation underscored the weakness of the Mamluk sultan, forced to
bribe his own subordinate into a marriage which, under different
circumstances, would have been considered a mark of favor for the
bride. As a final defensive measure, Qānsūh assigned one of his
lieutenants, Ainālbāy, to accompany the Ottoman ambassador
back to Selim's camp, there to gather information on the course of
the Ottoman-Safavid conflict.

All together, Selim sent three ambassadors to Cairo in 1514 (one
in May, one in July, and one in November). These men articulated
the power and ambitions of their sovereign at the Mamluk court and
gauged the extent of Qānsūh's response to the proximity of an Ottoman army.[118] Despite Selim's aggressive diplomatic style, he wanted
to assure himself that Qānsūh would not launch a military action
against his southern flank while he was engaged on the battle field
with the Safavids. As a result, the Mamluk envoy Ainālbāy was cordially treated at Selim's camp and was given a robe of honor and a
large sum of gold.[119] A year later, after Ismail had been defeated,
Mamluk envoys would not fare so well with the Ottoman sultan.

The tentative and suspicious nature of Qānsūh's response to the Ottoman eastern campaign is evident from both his diplomatic and military behavior. Apprehensive that his own representative would be imprisoned, the Mamluk sultan detained the Ottoman envoy in Cairo until after the return of Ainālbāy. This action was motivated by Qānsūh's wish to await the turn of events before responding to Selim's demands. He also delayed the departure of his army for Aleppo until very late in the campaign season. In fact, the officers did not leave Cairo until August 28, 1514, one day after the battle of Çaldıran.[120] This delay effectively demonstrated that Qānsūh's intentions were not aggressive and that he had no intention either of aiding or of attacking the Ottomans. As news of Selim's victory reached Cairo throughout September, fear mounted that the Ottomans would invade Syria immediately. Accounts of the battle, like those of the Persian chronicler Rūmlū, emphasized Ottoman firepower, saying the Ottoman gunners had "such skill and power in firing their guns that they can hit the indivisible atom a mile away."[121] By the time the formal declaration of victory reached Cairo in November, the grim reality of the force of Ottoman arms was quite clear. Qānsūh sent a message of congratulation but did not celebrate the victory.[122]

Meanwhile, the Mamluk army sent to Aleppo for its defense had run amock, raping and pillaging. Ignoring both the governor and their commanders, the troops' behavior resulted in the flight of many of the citizens of Aleppo. Judging from reports of these depredations reaching Cairo, it is little wonder that the Aleppans welcomed the Ottoman invaders in 1516.[123] The Syrian populace was already disaffected because of the injurious exactions imposed upon it to pay for Qānsūh's infantrymen. Ibn Iyās mentioned an extraordinary tax of twenty dinars per man levied in Nablus, Damascus, and Ghaza. Thus, the population of Syria began to pay dearly for its own "defense" long before Selim's armies actually marched into Syria. Selim spent the winter in Amasia while Qānsūh, expecting an Ottoman naval attack, went to Alexandria to review its fortifications.[124] The Mamluk army, ragged and destitute from famine in Aleppo, straggled slowly back to Cairo throughout the winter and early spring of 1514–1515. The expedition to Aleppo had proved an unmitigated disaster, resulting in further disorganization of the Mamluk army, discrediting the authority of the Mamluk commanders, and causing further disruption and decimation of the population and economy of Syria.[125]

In the aftermath of Çaldıran, Selim's expansionist policy was clear to all his opponents. Italian sources suggest that Ismail orchestrated an anti-Ottoman alliance in the winter of 1514–1515 that included the Safavids, the Mamluks, the Zū al-Ḳadr and the Georgians. The pact supposedly stipulated that none of the participants was to receive envoys from Selim.[126] There is scant evidence of such a treaty but sufficient mention in a variety of sources indicates that some negotiations were going on, prompted by the panic conjured up by Selim's decisive victory at Çaldıran. However, rumors that ʿAlā ad-Dawla was conspiring with Ismail seem unfounded. Such an initiative would have been a complete reversal of Zū al-Ḳadr policy; the rumors may have originated in the Ottoman court in an attempt to legitimize the impending take over of Zū Al-Ḳadr territory.[127] Rumors of an alliance against him appear to have had little effect on Selim. When Ismail sent an envoy to the Ottoman sultan's camp in Amasia, Selim dispensed with diplomatic niceties and had the Safavid messenger detained and beaten.[128]

Ottoman diplomacy toward the Mamluk regime also took on a contemptuous character. While the Ottoman armies mobilized for a new campaign in the late winter of 1515, Selim sent an ambassador to threaten Qānsūh al-Ghūrī. The message was simple and to the point. Selim had decided to aid ʿAlā ad-Dawla's nephew, ʿAlī ibn Shāh Suvār, in seizing the Zū al-Ḳadr territories from his uncle. Selim "invited" Qānsūh to help him assure that this Zū al-Ḳadr pretender would ascend the throne as an Ottoman vassal. This invitation was, in fact, a direct challenge to Qānsūh's sovereignty. Essentially Selim was warning the Mamluks not to interfere in his annexation of the Zū al-Ḳadr principality. Qānsūh was enraged.[129] The following week he received an envoy from ʿAlā ad-Dawla, asking for Mamluk support. Lacking the wherewithal for any concrete assistance, Qānsūh responded by asking Selim not to attack ʿAlā ad-Dawla.[130] Selim replied that he would do as he pleased, for ʿAlā ad-Dawla, Ismail, and Qānsūh were all his enemies. This pronouncement could signify that Selim had intelligence of a proposed alliance among the three, but it needs no explanation other than Selim's confidence in his own military might and in his claims to legitimacy and sovereignty in the Muslim world.[131]

The days of the Zū al-Ḳadr ruler were clearly numbered. Selim was not preoccupied so much with any Mamluk threat as with regrouping his forces after the difficult winter in Amasia. This effort included the replacement of a large number of horses killed at Çaldıran or lost in the winter withdrawal from Tabriz. The sultan also sent to Istanbul for two thousand *janissaries* and ordered that all his *sancak begs* make ready their troops for the campaign.[132] As rumors in Cairo mounted that Selim would attack Egypt, Qānsūh sent an officer named Jānim to Selim's camp to reconnoitre. Intelligence reports also indicated that Selim had launched a fleet the target of which was thought to be Alexandria.[133] The Ottoman fleet never did attack Alexandria. The Mamluks, and the Rhodians, however, once the Ottoman army was mobilized, each took the naval maneuvers as an indication that an attack on their own shores was imminent. Their rationale, generally sound, was that ships were not built and armed unless there was a serious intent to use them. Mamluk spies and envoys had had ample opportunity to survey the extent of the Ottoman fleet in the preceding ten years. Furthermore, the suspicions of the Mamluks were exacerbated by the defection of a Mamluk officer, Qūshqādam, to Selim's camp, where he had a brother and was promptly given a military command. It was feared that Qūshqādam would give Selim detailed information on Mamluk weaknesses and on how best to invade Mamluk territory.[134]

By early summer 1516, Selim defeated ʿAlā ad-Dawla.[135] A number of rationales are advanced in the sources for the Ottoman sultan's attack on ʿAlā ad-Dawla. Ḥasan Rūmlū contends that the Zū al-Kadr ruler had plundered stores accumulated for the Ottoman attack on Ismail Safavi. If in fact Selim had information on a Safavid-Zū al-Kadr conspiracy, then the campaign can be interpreted as a punitive one.[136] If that were the case, however, it would not have been necessary for Selim to justify the invasion by his support for ʿAlī ibn Shāh Suvār.[137] An alternative interpretation is that Selim, having defeated Ismail, no longer required the Zū al-Kadr buffer zone at his southeastern frontier. Because ʿAlā ad-Dawla functioned effectively as an independent prince rather than as a vassal governor, he was now an impediment to the Ottoman expansion. As such, his removal was necessary. If any alliance had been negotiated with Ismail, it was meaningless militarily. ʿAlā ad-Dawla faced Selim's army alone, without benefit of either Safavid or Mamluk aid. Qānsūh al-Ghūrī had done nothing. Although the Venetian consul in Damascus reported that Qānsūh sent an army of 40,000 including 6,000 Mamluks to the frontier, there is no evidence that this army even left Cairo until fall 1515. There was to be no offensive action against the Ottomans. The situation is perhaps best summed up by Justinian, the Venetian *bailo* in Istanbul, who wrote that Selim was openly at war with the Mam-

luks, wishing to destroy ʿAlā ad-Dawla and invade Syria, and that
there was nothing Ismail could do to stop him.[138]

Selim had vindicated Ottoman dynastic honor for the insult
served to his father Bayezid when Ismail sent Shaibānī Khān's
head to the Porte in 1510.[139] Now he sent his own ambassador to
Qānsūh al-Ghūrī with the head of ʿAlā ad-Dawla. The message on
both occasions was the same: "This is what happens to those who
oppose me." With Selim poised to invade, Qānsūh had no choice
but to send an army to Syria. Several factors, however, militated
against a swift response. Order among the mamluk troops was poor
at best, and the recruits were chronically mutinous. The same
month, August 1515, that Selim's envoy arrived, Qānsūh was ready-
ing a force of 6,000 to be sent to Suez, the Portuguese front, thus
limiting military options on the northern frontier.[140] In Syria, the
loyalty of his governors was not assured and Qānsūh was blamed
for failing to send an army to defend against the Ottoman advance
there.[141] Finally, it was unclear whether a force was needed to defend Alexandria against a sea attack. Qānsūh sent only masons to
Alexandria to fortify the sea walls against the Ottoman fleet. He
had no troops to spare.

Nor had he a surfeit of willing diplomats. The lesson of a Safavid envoy who, the previous winter, had been beaten at Selim's
command, was not lost upon the mamluks. When Qānsūh proposed
to send an envoy back to Selim's camp with the Ottoman ambassador, none of his officers would consent to go. Their caution was
warranted. The envoy Jānim, who returned from his intelligence
mission into Anatolia in September 1515, brought disquieting
news. The Ottomans had detained him and only through the intercession of some members of Selim's entourage had he been freed at
all. Further, he confirmed that Selim would invade Syria and reported that an Ottoman fleet of four hundred ships was being prepared to lay siege to Alexandria and Damietta.[142] Another envoy,
sent to Selim's camp by Khair Beg, governor of Aleppo, narrowly
escaped execution at the Ottoman sultan's command.[143] To add insult to injury, Qānsūh also found himself subject to the insults of
Selim's newly installed Zū al-Ḳadrid vassal, ʿAlī ibn Shāh Suvār,
who sent the Mamluk sultan insolent messages from Elbistan.

The Safavids fared no better in diplomatic missions to the Ottoman court. The sultan refused even to give audience to Ismail's
emissary who arrived, in late fall of 1515, at Edirne where Selim
had withdrawn for the winter. When the Safavid demanded, in his
master's name, the return of Kemah fortress and the release of

Persian merchants seized in 1514, Selim replied through his vezirs that instead of releasing the merchants he would take Tabriz as well. Then he had the envoy imprisoned.[144] The Safavid threat thus dismissed, Selim concluded a truce with Hungary to protect his northwestern flank while he launched the campaign against Syria and Egypt.

Qānsūh was left with little in the way of defense besides verbal aggression. When the Ottoman ambassadors, Ruknüddin and Karaca Pasha, arrived at Cairo in the spring of 1516, he castigated them for the conquest of ʿAlā ad-Dawla's territory.[145] Then he sent an envoy to Selim to demand the return of the Zū al-Ḳadr lands, meanwhile offering ʿAlā ad-Dawla's son 30,000 men to help retake his patrimony.[146] This threat, too, was an idle one, since there is no indication that Qānsūh could mobilize such a force to invade El-bistan. Erstwhile Ottoman opponents watched, immobile, to see if the Mamluks could halt the Ottoman advance. But all rumors of alliance notwithstanding, each opponent, Ismail, ʿAlā ad-Dawla, and Qānsūh, in three consecutive years, faced the Ottoman army without benefit of allies.[147]

The states on the Ottoman's eastern frontiers, like those on the western frontiers, failed, then, to achieve any joint military action against the Ottoman expansion. Despite the initial promise of Ismail Safavi as a force to off-set Ottoman power, the Mamluks were prevented from allying with him for tactical, economic, and ideological reasons. The breakdown of authority in the Mamluk army made large-scale military operations difficult and risky, while the preoccupation of the Mamluk sultan with the defense of the Red Sea littoral against the Portuguese siphoned off men and money that could have been used at the Syrian frontier. Ottoman aid for the Mamluk fleet had put Qānsūh in a position of military dependence on the Ottoman sultan. Neither the Safavids nor the Ottomans were viable treaty partners for the Mamluks because both had obvious ambitions to control Mamluk held territory and to claim paramountcy in the Muslim world. On all fronts, the Mamluk state was reduced to a position of self defense, and the state's monetary resources and political legitimacy were not equal to the task. Like Rhodes, the Mamluks could not survive on the glories of an old crusading mythology. They devoted their energies throughout this period to defense at the Ottoman-Safavid frontiers and avoided military offensive outside their own territory until Selim forced it upon them.

As a strategic ally, Ismail could not offer the Mamluks the

incentives: artillery, commercial outlets, troops, and ships that either the Ottomans or possibly Venice could provide. Militarily, he lacked the men and guns to defeat the fully mobilized Ottoman army. Only after Çaldıran, when it was apparent that Selim proposed the elimination of the Mamluk and Zū al-Ḳadr states, did a three-way anti-Ottoman alliance become an alternative. But even then, under crisis conditions, the traditional enmity between Mamluks, Zū al-Ḳadr and Safavids could not be overcome. ʿAlā ad-Dawla had pursued a consistently aggressive policy towards the Safavids and there is no substantial evidence that this policy changed, even in 1515.

CHAPTER 4

Ottoman Naval Development

In the fourteenth century, the illustrious historiographer, Ibn Khaldūn recorded a prediction:

> The inhabitants of the Maghreb have it on the authority of the books of predictions that the Muslims will yet have to make a successful attack against the Christians and conquer the lands of the European Christians beyond the sea. This, it is said, will take place by sea.[1]

This prophesy was realized in the early sixteenth century in the form of the Ottoman navy. Nonetheless, the Ottomans have yet to be granted their place in world history as a seaborne empire. This is nowhere more apparent than in depictions of the reign of Bayezid II (1481–1512). Traditional historiography has characterized the reign of Bayezid as consisting of two halves: before and after the death of his brother Cem.[2] The first half is dominated by Bayezid's struggle to eliminate his brother, the challenger to the throne. Cem, whose unsuccessful bid for the Ottoman sultanate was supported by the Mamluk sultan Qā'it Bāy, died in 1495. Bayezid's reign after Cem's death has been portrayed as a less than illustrious period of quiet consolidation. If, however, the second half of Bayezid's reign is viewed as a period during which a powerful navy was built up, a navy capable of defending and supplying an empire extending far beyond the bounds of Anatolia, then the peaceful characterization of this period becomes somewhat less believable. Bayezid's navy was used to suppress piracy, protect commodities shipping, and intimidate his enemies, present or potential. Ottoman naval supremacy in the eastern Mediterranean

fostered the establishment of cordial Ottoman-Venetian trading relations, permitted the subordination of the Mamluk kingdoms
(through naval and artillery aid) prior to the Ottoman conquest of
Cairo, and allowed for a significant challenge to Portuguese seapower in the Indian Ocean. Seapower was both physical and rhetorical. The threat of the Ottoman navy was used by many states
throughout the Mediterranean to gain diplomatic leverage. Nor
was the Ottoman navy, as traditional historiography would have
it, little more than a group of state subsidized corsairs. Seapower
was a vehicle for developing Ottoman trading interests, securing
the Ottoman coasts, and supporting the transport and provisioning
activities required for Ottoman territorial expansion.

It was at the turn of the sixteenth century that the Ottomans
firmly and decisively set out to use seapower as an avenue to
"world" hegemony. Naval development began in earnest under
Mehmed II.[3] It continued under Bayezid who ordered "ships agile
as sea serpents (*naheng ahang gemiler*)" constructed to fight the
Venetians.[4] The reign of Selim was a period during which the military and naval capabilities built up during Bayezid's reign were
utilized and expanded. The conquest of Cairo provided, in part, the
revenue and the imperial ethos. Anatolia provided the construction
materials and the infantrymen. Upon this foundation Selim was
building a most formidable navy, and planning greater naval conquests at the time of his death. The only obstacle in his path was
the shortage of skilled sailors.[5] These aspirations became operational on a grand scale with an eastward expansion which halted
only at the Indian Ocean in the reign of Selim's son Süleiman.

After the campaign season of 1502, Sultan Bayezid launched
both a major naval reorganization and a broad scale troop mobilization. This troop mobilization in the fall and winter of that year
was a direct result of the military success and diplomatic challenge
of Ismail Safavi in Iran.[6] The naval reorganization was attributed
by Venetian sources to the sultan's wrath over the Venetian victory that year at Santa Maura.[7] The overall victory in the Ottoman-Venetian wars, however, went decisively to the Ottomans
and, by fall of 1502, negotiations were underway for a treaty which
would leave Venice without Modon and Coron and liable for a ten
thousand ducat annual indeminity to the Porte.[8] Hence, the causes
for Bayezid's naval buildup must be sought elsewhere than in mere
vengeance for the defeat at Santa Maura. These causes include the
intentions to expand Ottoman Levantine possessions, to punish

Rhodes for its attacks on Muslim shipping, and to provide naval support for Ottoman campaigns against the Mamluk and Safavid territories. Short years later a fourth cause was added: the provision of direct naval assistance to the Mamluks against the Portuguese in the Red Sea and Indian Ocean.

First, the Ottomans needed a navy revamped to focus outside the Aegean and the Mediterranean. This navy was then directed to purposes of defense and expansion that later proceeded outward in concentric circles; the territorial conquests mirrored the spheres of Ottoman economic interest in the Aegean, Mediterranean, Red Sea, and eventually the Persian Gulf and Indian Ocean. Vigorous shipbuilding activity was underway in the Ottoman arsenals during the wars with Venice from 1499 to 1503. Sadeddin mentions the preparation of a fleet of three hundred ships in the first year of the war.[9] A German knight, Arnold von Harff, claimed, with considerable exaggeration, that he saw that same year eight hundred Turkish war galleys and countless other vessels in the harbor at Istanbul.[10] Bayezid called in the entire Ottoman armada for repairs in the winter of 1500–1501 and ordered the preparation of four hundred ships including two hundred galleys mounted with large cannon, fifty heavy galleys, and four hundred fifty of the smaller galiots and fustas. This work took place at selected sites, with the armada at Midilli alone numbering some one hundred twenty vessels including forty galleys early in 1502. The sultan requisitioned laborers for the fleet, especially carpenters and caulkers, as well as building materials from Chios, a "request" that the Christian administration of the island could not afford to refuse.[11]

This construction cannot be explained only as a requirement of the combat with Venice. By fall of 1502, it was apparent that a peace treaty was in the offing. In the intervening years before the conquest of Cairo in 1517, Venice and the Ottomans were at peace. Their naval relations, though characterized by a healthy distrust, were generally amicable. Yet, just as the peace treaty set aside the threat from the Porte's primary opponent in the Mediterranean, Bayezid began a policy of naval expansion which would ultimately make the Ottomans the dominant naval power in the region. During this same time, the French and Spanish were contenders for naval power in the western Mediterranean, the Portuguese gained control of the Indian Ocean, and the Rhodians remained an insistent, if essentially insignificant, naval threat off the Anatolian coast. Although the Spanish would become a formidable sea power, their success in the western Mediterranean was arguably a function of the direction—east—that the sultan chose for the utilization of his navy.

The Ottoman naval reorganization begun in the fall of 1502 was a three-stage operation. It involved the repair of the fleet, the dismantling of some ships for reconstruction and the building of entirely new ships.[12] Reconstruction efforts were directed at the largest ships which were either taken apart or sold to private entrepreneurs. Materials from the ships, which were taken apart, were used to build heavy and light galleys. These efforts were aimed at producing lighter, more maneuverable ships, which were not only more adaptable to joint naval actions but were also less likely to be captured.

While these efforts were underway Bayezid ordered the mobilization of sixty to seventy thousand men, both oarsmen and sailors. This number is more than even a fleet of three hundred ships could utilize; however, it indicates that the Venetian authors of the reports were impressed with the sultan's levy of seamen. The high number may also be an indication of the divergence between the number of sailors and oarsmen levied and the actual numbers who showed up. In order to finance the naval expansion, Bayezid combined a number of sources of income. He obtained some revenue from the sale of the largest ships. He ordered each of his sons to provide for the construction of six heavy galleys, and a number of his *sancak begs* to finance three light galleys each.[13] In addition, the merchants of Salonica (both Greeks and Turks) were ordered to pay a tithe and to finance mariners.[14]

The fact that only the merchants of Salonica are mentioned as paying the special naval levy does not mean that it was limited to this city alone. There is, however, a certain logic to the idea of levies on the coastal merchants.[15] They were likely to be engaged in commerce supplied by shipping along the Anatolian coast, from the Aegean islands, and across the Mediterranean from Beirut and Alexandria. This shipping was susceptible to corsair raiding especially on the part of the Rhodians. If the naval expansion was aimed, in part, at the protection of Ottoman shipping, then the merchants who profited from it were a likely source of revenue.[16] The bulk of the financing for the fleet, however, came from the imperial treasury supplemented by the special levies such as the oarsman tax (*kürekçi akçesi*).[17]

By the end of the year 1503, the Ottomans had an impressive array of ships at their disposal. In his report to the Venetian Senate, the returning *bailo* of Istanbul, Andrea Gritti, gave a detailed account of the Ottoman fleet and its activities.[18] Gritti counted the Galata fleet as including thirty light galleys, twelve galleys bastarda, two galeazza (unnavigable), and some assorted fustas and gripos. At Gallipoli there were sixty galleys and fustas. Three of these galleys, with thirty, twenty-six, and twenty-two banks of oars respectively, had been constructed by an Italian shipbuilder named Andrea Dere. At Avlonya in the Adriatic the Ottomans had eleven galleys which had been seized during the war and nine fustas (mostly in bad order). At Volissa on the west side of Chios were an additional eight heavy galleys and thirteen light galleys. Gritti's account does not include estimates of naval forces at other Ottoman ports such as Macri and Samsun, but it is clear that Bayezid had a large fleet at his disposal which had not been retired at the end of the war.

The shipbuilder Dere is again mentioned in Leonardo Loredano's report to the Venetian Senate in March 1507. His story illustrates the continuation of shipbuilding activity, gives some insight into the training of the Ottoman sea captains, and emphasizes the competition among states for skilled craftsmen. The sultan's shipwright told Loredano that he had prospered while in the Ottoman service. He indicated, however, that he might consider leaving Istanbul if Venice came up with a sufficiently lucrative offer. This was especially so because Dere's superior, the *kapudan* (captain-general of the Ottoman fleet) Daud Pasha, had died. When Daud was alive, Dere recalled, he would call his shipbuilder to his room and go over navigation charts with him, asking all about the Aegean ports, especially about Zara (a Venetian possession) and its defenses.[19] After hearing this story, Loredano suggested that Venice would be well advised to try to persuade Dere to return to Italy, before the Ottoman navy benefited even further from his knowledge. Good shipwrights were a prized commodity in any case in the Mediterranean, even if they were not possessed of tactical information. In the end, however, Dere, saying that he had served the sultan for many years, seemed content enough to stay where he was.[20]

Lack of a sufficient naval opponent and the expense of keeping large fleets manned insured that much of the Ottoman armada was demobilized at any given time. In the winter, the Ottoman fleet in the Bosphorus, consisting of one hundred twenty or so vessels, was beached and guarded by a large number of sentries. Meanwhile, however, the Ottomans had not ceased to manufacture great numbers of cannon, both iron and bronze, as well as other types of naval munitions. This production was facilitated by a large number of artillery masters at Istanbul working, according to Loredano, continuously. The Porte was able to produce sufficient artillery to arm its own expanding navy and to create a surplus as well. This surplus, in turn, would allow the Ottomans to provide cannon for the Mamluk fleet being prepared at Suez to challenge the Portuguese in the Indian Ocean.

While the bulk of the Ottoman armada remained demobilized in various naval stations, small fleets could be mobilized as needed for the various objectives of the state. Significant among these objectives was the protection of Ottoman commodities shipping through defense of the Anatolian coastal areas. Rumors persisted throughout the Mediterranean after 1503 that the Ottomans intended to launch an armada.[21] But the Ottomans launched no major fleet offensive until 1515. During this time of relative peace, however, fleets of from fifteen to forty vessels were kept regularly cruising in the Aegean. These fleets provided transport, security against corsairs for Ottoman shipping, and general coastal defense. They were also used for commercial purposes and for special diplomatic missions.[22]

Piracy was endemic in sixteenth-century seas, and the newly constructed Ottoman fleet seems to have been used primarily against corsairs. Piratic acts combined with a grain shortage prompted Bayezid in 1504 to send out eight armed galleys and fustas to prevent smuggling and the seizure of grain ships by pirates. These ships were instructed to punish Kara Durmuş, a corsair, who had acquired a small fleet in the course of the Venetian wars and was now operating in the waters near Chios, apparently under the patronage of the *sancak beg* of Manissa, Celal Beg. Kara Durmuş, with a fleet of twenty-two fustas, a brigantine and a galiota, was interfering with Ottoman shipping and raiding the Anatolian coasts. This number of vessels seems large for a single corsair, although most of the ships were the small and maneuverable fustas which could be operated in close to shore.[23] Kara Durmuş may have formed loose and temporary alliances with other small-time corsairs, who united for defensive purposes during some raiding activities while at other times pursuing their interests individually. In 1505, a fleet, numbering fourteen to eighteen ships, under the command of Kemal Reis, a hero of the Ottoman-Venetian wars, was mobilized and charged with the task of pursuing Kara Durmuş and preventing corsairing activities based on Rhodes. This use of Otto-

man vessels in patrolling activity suggests that a uniform definition of "navy" is inadequate to explain the nature of naval action
in the sixteenth century. Visions of large-scale sea battles and of
shipboard Muslim crusaders must give way to a more mundane
version of Levantine sea power.

The Island—Coast Zone and the Nature
of Navies and Corsairs

The term "navy" invokes an image of armed vessels engaging
in battle on the open sea, a seaborne version of an army. In the
eastern Mediterranean, sea warfare was not the primary function
of navies. Rather naval functions were transport, defense of
commerce, support of sieges and land campaigns, and protection
against piracy. Two factors mediated against states maintaining
large navies under sail for continuous periods: technology and
economy.[24] Ships could not remain continuously at sea regardless of
season and weather, in the Red Sea and Indian Ocean even less so
than in the Mediterranean. Storage limitations and crew size determined the number of days a ship could remain at sea without
stopping for provisions of food and water. Warriors transported on
shipboard were bodies that had to be fed and that did not contribute to mobility. The happy medium, of course, was free oarsmen
who might be counted upon to fight should the occasion arise.[25] In
any case, the image of navies as floating armies must be aban-
doned in order to comprehend the development and capabilities of
navies in the period under discussion. The cost of maintaining
ships and crews was much too high for states to support standing
navies of fighting ships.[26]

States adopted varying patterns of naval organization to deal
with their specific limitations of technology and economy. For
Venice, a well-equipped fighting fleet was kept ready in the arsenal for the occasions when mobilization of an armada was necessary; there was bidding for warships and the public debt could be
utilized to pay additional crews.[27] Standard shipping, however, consisted of private ventures or state sponsored galley convoys leased
out to private bidders.[28] The composition and regularity of employment of these convoys was very much dependent upon the prof-
itability of the commerce, as is indicated, for example, by the occasional failure of the Venetian spice convoys to sail to Alexandria in
the years when commercial relations with the Mamluks were
strained.[29]

The Ottomans, because of the ready availability of lumber, shipbuilding materials, and manpower, were able to produce a sizeable armada from scratch in a relatively short period of time.[30] Their chronic problem was staffing the ships with trained seamen.[31] Ships were built in coastal cities near lumber supplies to avoid transportation costs and, in addition, shipbuilding was carried on at the two main Ottoman arsenals of Gallipoli and Galata. Following these centers in importance as naval bases were Midilli, Prevesa, Samsun, and Avlonya. Mariners and navigators were Turks, Greeks, Italians and Dalmatians. The Ottoman navy was commanded by the *kapudan* pasha of Gallipoli to whom the maritime *sancak begs* were responsible for providing both oarsmen and soldiers (timariot cavalry and infantry). As was the case with Venetian commanders who bid for and were elected to their positions, the *kapudan* pasha was not necessarily a naval man by training.[32] This office was an appointed one at the discretion of the sultan.[33]

What was necessary for states like the Ottoman and Venetian was the protection of their commercial and shipping interests, and the ability to provide naval troop transport and artillery support for military campaigns or defense. In times of war, what was possible, and cost effective in terms of fighting ships, was the incorporation of corsair fleets into state naval operations either on a permanent or temporary basis. The distinction between corsairs and navies is problematic but not unresolvable.[34] The problem in part derives from the fact that corsairs figure prominently in accounts of Mediterranean travel whereas official fleets generally receive notice only in times of battle.[35] At the turn of the sixteenth century, only Venice, the Ottoman state, and the Knights of Rhodes possessed regular fleets in the eastern Mediterranean. Despite the prior fame of the Fatimid navy and the vigorous raiding carried on under earlier Mamluk rulers, by 1500 Egypt was no longer a naval power.[36] Mamluk fleets in the Mediterranean were organized only on a temporary basis for special purposes such as embassies and materials transport. Mamluk naval ventures against the Portuguese were carried out only with considerable assistance from the Ottomans and Gujaratis. Other fleets found in the eastern Mediterranean were assembled for corsairing ventures; the three states which possessed navies were forced to engage these corsairs to protect trade. The Ottomans, like the Venetians, were preoccupied with deterring coastal raiding and attacks on state sponsored shipping by these corsairs, particularly those based at Rhodes and along the Anatolian coasts. To defend against such at-

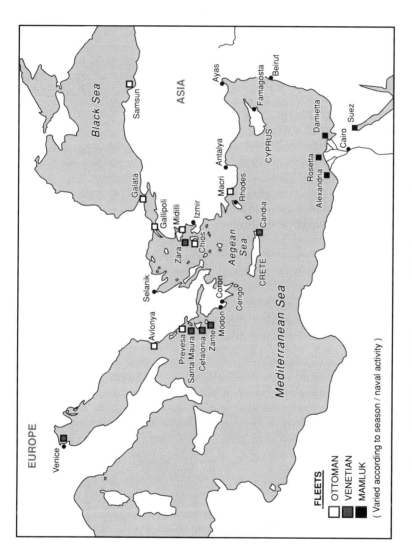

Figure 2. Eastern Mediterranean Ship Concentrations 1503–1516.

tacks small Ottoman fleets cruised almost continuously in the Aegean.[37]

Corsair activity, or raiding, was a means of making naval engagements immediately profitable. Actual fleet battles, such as Lepanto in 1571, were not profitable except in terms of gaining control of territory. Even territorial gains ordinarily required siege operations prosecuted over an extended period of time in the wake of fleet actions which were expensive to both sides in terms of lost ships, ordnance, and especially manpower. In battle, mariners, who had a potential value as slaves if captured, were frequently drowned or perished when ships were set ablaze. Corsair raiding, on the other hand, usually involved less immediate risk. Raids could be directed against coastal settlements or merchant shipping. The latter was the most frequent target in the sixteenth century. In many cases actual battles never took place. Merchant vessels were often ill-armed and when overwhelmed by superior forces simply found it prudent to surrender. Goods and captives were taken for sale or ransom and the ships were burned, disabled, or incorporated into the corsairs' fleets.

Like the term "navy," the term "corsair," along with the image it conjures of independent piracy, needs to be redefined for the eastern Mediterranean.[38] European histories traditionally have made no distinction for Ottoman ships among corsairs, merchant ships, and vessels operating under the authority of the Ottoman navy. As one naval historian notes:

> Early in the sixteenth century, the Turkish rule extended along
> the African shores of the Mediterranean and the maritime power
> of Turkey became very great. It was not on a legitimate commercial basis, however, like that of Genoa and Venice. It was on a
> piratical basis, such as the United States knew in the Barbary
> States in 1789–1815.[39]

Such generalizations fail to reveal the complexities of shipping and naval action which, in fact, existed in the eastern Mediterranean. There were indeed pirates whose sole activities consisted of attacking ships and coastal villages to seize people or property. Individuals were abducted to be sold as slaves, but more often merchandise or livestock was taken.[40] Another important object of corsair activity was the ships themselves.[41] These could be manned to supplement the corsair fleet, or sold. Corsairs operated out of Aegean and Mediterranean ports, the islands, and the North African coast. They were small-time operators, frequently with no more than three or four ships. In peace time especially, they were subject to seizure and execution by the governments in whose ports they took refuge. These punishments illustrate that there was a clear distinction between pirate and naval captain in the minds of Levantine governments. This distinction was based on the targets of the ship captain's activity and on the authority recognized by that captain.[42] Local officials in the coastal towns undoubtedly cooperated, at least by omission, in piratic endeavors since corsairs found ready markets on shore for their booty. But this ready market cannot be construed as indicating either central government policy or a lack of naval vigilance.[43]

The problem of interpretation results from the fact that certain individuals may, at one time in their careers, have served as naval captains (accepting the pay and the authority of the state) and, at other times, as corsairs (entrepreneurs who rejected the authority of the state). Some, who were utilized in the Ottoman navy during the war, were not tolerated in peacetime when their services to the state were no longer required. The use of corsairs in war time may be attributed to the chronic shortage of skilled seafaring men. Kara Durmuş, for example, used the expertise, ships, and recognition he gained in the Ottoman service to launch a postwar career as a corsair. In 1504, he was disarmed and his ships seized. Although he escaped capture, his house was burned by the Ottoman authorities and seventy of his men were executed. This was not only a sign of good will to Venice, upon whose ships this brigand also preyed, but a warning to other corsairs that raids on Ottoman shipping would engender the sultan's wrath.[44]

Because of the small size of corsair operations and lack of land-based military backing, they were liable to reprisals especially while in port. It was expensive and time consuming to man fleets to go searching for corsairs at sea. If they could be cornered while in port, however, they could be captured by a superior naval force operating at the government's behest.[45] For the Ottoman and Venetian states, corsair activity represented disruption of trade and interruption in the provisioning of grain to their capitals. For individual merchants, however, successful corsair operations could prove ruinous. Merchants put pressure on their own governments to resolve the piracy problem, often with little success. The Venetian *bailo* in Istanbul, for instance, devoted much of his peacetime energy to settling claims deriving from seizures of ships, of merchants, and of merchandise.[46]

These complaints, too, provide an avenue for distinguishing

Plate 5: Turkish galleys in a sea battle against Black Sea pirates.
Source: British Library, Sloane 3584, f. 78 recto. Courtesy of the British
Library Board.

the captains from the corsairs. The term "corsair" was used indiscriminately in the sixteenth-century Italian sources. For example, in the multivolume Venetian document compilation of Marino Sanuto, Ottoman commanders are designated two ways, as "*capudan*" or as "*corsaro*." Both were considered the responsibility of the Ottoman government. Against the real corsairs, however, the Ottoman government exacted retribution without waiting for protests on the part of foreign merchants. All of the eastern Levantine states leveled accusations against each other for the raiding activities of corsairs. If the pirates were thought to be based in Ottoman ports, the complaints were directed to Istanbul, demanding that the sultan police his coasts and pay retribution. This was true for the Mamluk, Venetian, and Rhodian rulers as well. Complaints might be lodged by individual merchants or by state envoys and, depending on the status of foreign relations between the two states involved, responses varied. Between Venice and the Ottoman state, in times of peace, the response tended to be a formal statement that the Porte and Signoria did not encourage piracy in their waters and did not condone the activities or corsairs. In effect, the states denied financial responsibility and the burden of defense was placed upon the shipowners either to sail well-armed or to travel in convoy. In times of war, corsairing activities attracted fewer reprisals, but this should be interpreted as resulting from a lack of enforcement manpower as often as not. The argument that states encouraged piratic activity against their competitors in times of war may have some validity but seems questionable in light of the fact that pirates often were indiscriminate with regard to the religion, ethnicity, or port of origin of their targets. A grain ship was a grain ship and hence profitable, whether its owner was Turk or Italian.

Where the distinction between captains and corsairs blurs is in the case of the Knights of Rhodes rather than in the Ottoman case. It was accepted that the Knights, often using a crusading justification for their activities, were in the raiding business. The Knights regularly supported or orchestrated attacks on Muslim (and Christian-owned) shipping. Yet, in certain instances, the Rhodian council specifically prohibited the participation of Knights in such raiding. The council, at specific junctures, when the threat of the Ottoman fleet was greatest, issued instructions that members of the Order were forbidden to arm ships for attacks on Ottoman shipping. In so doing, the council wished to distance the government of Rhodes, however temporarily, from association with the activities of Order members engaged in piratic acts. Targeting non-

Ottoman shipping, however, was still permitted. The implication of such an interdict was that customary practice could be selectively restricted, but, under normal circumstances, the Order permitted and encouraged attacks on Ottoman shipping. Only fear of reprisals prompted the council to deter the entrepreneurial corsairing of the Knights. Both Venice and the Mamluks appealed at different times to the pope to bring pressure to bear on the Knights when their depredations were particularly damaging. This appeal was not without its rationale, although it was prompted by a sense of economic rather than religious affiliation. Since Rhodes received much of its financial backing from mainland Europe the pope was expected to have some authority over the noble Christian families and clerics who provided this funding. The Mamluk sultan, too, as nominal sovereign of the Islamic world, was subject to protests about corsair activities by Muslims in the Mediterranean. Without a navy, however, his leverage was minimal as was the pope's. Venice, because its commercial networks and investments were the most extensive in the eastern Mediterranean, was an easy target for reprisals on the part of Muslim states for the corsairing activities of Christians, whether or not they were Venetians. This was particularly true in the Mamluk territories where Venetian merchants often paid the price of impoundments or seizures in the aftermath of attacks by Rhodians on Muslim shipping.

With the possible exception of Rhodes, then, although the designation corsair was used indiscriminately, there was no question concerning which fleets were part of state naval organizations and which were not. When reparations were sought, it was useful for the plaintiff to attribute responsibility to whatever state controlled the waters where the attack occurred. In times of peace, it was politically expedient for the Ottomans and Venetians alike to punish corsair activities that went unpunished in times of war. The responsiveness of both states to merchants' appeals from 1503 to 1517 is an indication of their desire to preserve amicable relations.[47] This preoccupation with security and redress of injuries was documented in the series of *ahidnames* (treaties) and *fermans* (sultanic edicts) concerning Ottoman-Venetian trading relations. From the Ottoman perspective, both ideological and rhetorical, Venice held a form of vassal status vis-à-vis the Porte. This was by virtue of the unequivocal nature of the commercial treaties and of the position of Venice as tribute-paying state. Venice, of course, rejected this vassaldom verbally, legally, and in principle. In practice, however, there was a type of tacit acceptance on the part of the Signoria in order to protect her merchants and mercantile interests abroad.[48] After the conquest of Cairo, the Ottomans wished to protect the Venetian galley convoys to Egypt and Syria. In turn Venice was expected to protect Ottoman shipping interests while the Ottoman sultans continued their policy of punishing assaults on Venetian shipping. This reciprocity is illustrated by two documents found in the Venetian State Archive, one of which reiterates the Ottoman intent to protect Venetian merchant ships and the other of which demands redress for the attack on an Ottoman sea captain by a Venetian and the payment of an indemnity to the dead man's heirs.[49] Another illustration is the arrival, in November of 1507, of a Turkish galion at Corfu shortly after the Venetian proveditor had executed some Turkish corsairs. The galion captain congratulated the proveditor saying that the sultan would have done the same thing.[50]

These amicable relations are also apparent in the encounters between the Ottoman and Venetian courts in 1507. In January, the *bailo* in Istanbul reported to the *doge* that he had seen the Ottoman captain Kemal Reis, whose ships had sailed "in good company," with the fleet of the Venetian commander in the Aegean. The *bailo* wrote to the *doge* that Sultan Bayezid wanted good relations with Venice and suggested that the Signoria send a special envoy to show honor to the sultan.[51] This desire to promote peaceful relations was not motivated by goodwill alone. In part, it was prompted by the necessity to protect the purchase and exchange of food commodities. Corsair activities had hampered the Venetian navy's ability to procure grain. In May of 1505, the proveditor of the armada, Contarini, obtained grain from "the Turks" at four stera per ducat to make biscuit for the fleet.[52] As this purchase indicates, Ottoman-Venetian relations were based on peaceful coexistence and commercial self-interest. Grain ships were a primary target of corsairs. There is no doubt that the arming of a fleet under Kemal Reis in spring of 1508 was associated with pirates' seizure of sixty grain ships and the ensuing high prices of grain in Istanbul.[53] The degree of cooperation between Venice and the Ottomans at this time was such that the *bailo*, Andrea Foscolo, consented to having Ottoman artillery and munitions shipped to Avlonya on Venetian ships in return for protection against Rhodian corsairs. Although Foscolo was criticized in Venice for transporting Ottoman arms, his decision in this case showed the coincidence of Ottoman and Venetian interests where pirates were concerned. Further indication is given in the treaty arrangements made by

Marco Minio for Venice in 1522. This treaty contained provisions that Venice turn over captured Turkish corsairs to the sultan for punishment. There was also a provision that Venetian vessels must dip their flags to the Ottoman navy, an indication of Venice's subordinate position.[54]

Unlike the pirate captains, Ottoman naval commanders did not function as petty raiders. They acted in the interests of the Ottoman sultan and were an integral part of the state naval apparatus. They were identifiable by their power, the size of their fleets, and, above all, by the nature of their activities. The Ottoman and other Mediterranean states enlisted some corsairs as naval commanders. These drafts had the advantage of providing the state with expert officers and crews ready for action. Venice had an elected *proveditor* general of the armada who sailed with the fleet and exercised overall command (the captain-general was selected only in times of major mobilization).[55] His counterpart, the Ottoman *kapudan*, or admiral, was a pasha who was appointed to the position. He did not necessarily participate in all naval expeditions but some of the *kapudans* were accomplished seamen.[56] The idea that those Ottoman naval commanders who were experienced were little more than pirates with a sultanic *berat* (appointment paper), however, is an illusion. This point is reflected in the memoirs of the *kapudan* Sidi Ali Reis, which describe the practical, educational, and administrative background such a commander was likely to have.[57] Sidi Ali took part in Sultan Süleiman's expedition against Rhodes in 1522 and thereafter in a variety of naval and land campaigns. He wrote that he had seen combat under several senior naval commanders; had cruised the Mediterranean until he knew its evey corner; and had studied the sciences of the sea. His grandfather and father had been Ottoman officials in the Galata arsenal. After long service in the Mediterranean, he was sent in 1553 to command a fleet in the Persian Gulf where, by the mid-sixteenth century, the Ottoman navy had extended the sultan's authority. Although many Ottoman naval captains rose to postitions of prominence through quite conventional channels, as did Sidi Ali, it has been, traditionally, those with a corsairing background who receive the lion's share of attention in European historical accounts.

Corsairing activity, one option in the seafaring career ladder, was institutionalized; it is evident in the careers of the Barbarossa brothers, Oruç and Hayreddin. Bayezid's son, Korkud was Oruç's patron. When Korkud failed to emerge victorious from the succession struggle, which concluded the reign of Sultan Bayezid in 1512, Oruç sailed to North Africa where he was later joined by his brother. Thus, the brothers shifted their base of operations when their link to the Ottoman dynasty put them out of favor, not because of official sanctions resulting from corsairing activity. Once in Tunis, Oruç initiated an agreement with the local ruler whereby the state and the corsair were linked on a percentage basis, for example, port facilities in return for one fifth of the booty.[58] Later the Barbarossas, having pursued their raiding activities off the North African coast with great success, returned voluntarily to Ottoman patronage as naval commanders. This suggests that ultimately the state service was more appealing than the interim career as corsair.

Much less well known in European historiography than the Barbarossas is Kemal Reis, the most prominent Ottoman naval commander in the reign of Bayezid. Kemal Reis was the predominant concern of Venetian naval officers and merchant representatives in the eastern Mediterranean for nearly twenty years. An examination of his career demonstrates how he served the state in war and peace by means of a combination of defense and aggression. Documentation on the early years of his career is sparse, but it is clear that he was in the service of the Ottoman Porte during the early part of Bayezid's reign.[59] In 1495, Kemal returned from the African coast to bolster the Ottoman fleet at Istanbul. There he was assigned three hundred *janissaries* as part of his fighting force.[60] The reputation he gained during the Ottoman-Venetian wars in the Aegean at the turn of the century affected Venetian naval maneuvers until his death. In March of 1501, for example, the mere notice that Kemal had sailed with thirty fustas for the Aegean prompted Venice to dispatch a small ship from Candia to Cyprus to warn the Beirut and Alexandria galley convoys. Later, Kemal was reported to have stormed Zonchio and captured three galleys and a caravelle all in one day. The Venetian captain general at this time had only fourteen galleys, three of which were old and in need of repair, and only two hundred eighty men. His fleet was in poor order, and he felt ill-equipped to deal with Kemal who was perceived as the single most dangerous threat to the Venetian navy.[61]

Kemal's position as an Ottoman naval commander is aptly illustrated by an incident related by the merchant patron of a ship from Chios. The merchant, in Pera in early spring of 1501, encountered Kemal in the harbor. The Ottoman captain's fleet was impressive: eight galiots of twenty to twenty-two banks of oars each, and thirteen fustas with twelve, fifteen, or sixteen banks of oars each.[62] With some trepidation the merchant turned over to Kemal a safe-conduct letter from an official at the Porte. Kemal disdainfully replied that such letters were not for him, but for corsairs (*levends*). The implication of this retort was that an Ottoman naval commander was no threat to merchant shipping. Relieved, the merchant went on his way, concluding his narration with a report that Kemal was received with honor at the Ottoman Porte.[63] Such reports are not the only evidence for the claim that the attribution of "corsair" to captains like Kemal is misplaced and misleading. Not only is it clear that Kemal's primary task after the Ottoman-Venetian war was the suppression of piracy off the Ottoman coasts, but nowhere in the extensive Venetian surveillance reports collected in Sanuto's diaries is there evidence of Kemal's engaging in corsair activities after the Ottoman-Venetian wars.

From the Ottoman-Venetian peace until his death in 1510, Kemal served as a premier Ottoman naval officer. He exercised a considerable degree of independence but acted on orders from the sultan. At sea, a naval commander had discretionary authority much greater than that allowed an army commander because, at least temporarily, there was no higher authority. When he returned to port, however, Kemal, like other Ottoman military personnel was the sultan's servant. On at least one occasion, he was called before Bayezid and suffered his ruler's displeasure for having overstepped his bounds. Despite this strong will and his "scourge of the seas" personna, Kemal's duties consisted primarily in patrolling the Straits and the Aegean for corsairs, protecting merchant shipping, and transporting materials to aid the Mamluks in Alexandria. Although his reputation for naval warfare continued to prompt Venice to keep his movements under surveillance, he made no direct attacks on Venetian shipping after 1502.

Kemal's career, then, illustrates that aggression was not the primary function of Ottoman naval officers. Naval action directed by the Ottoman state and by Venice in the years 1503 to 1517 can be classified as either aggression, defense, or prevention. Aggression, more often than not, was not the primary *modus operandi* of early sixteenth-century navies. In the case of Venice after the peace treaty with the Porte, prevention and defense were the operational modes of the navy. Much energy and planning was devoted to avoiding encounters with hostile ships, providing escorts for merchant shipping, and regulating sailing times to obtain the best possible security. This preoccupation with prevention is demonstrated by the frequency of reconnoitering missions ordered by the proveditor of the armada and his subordinates. Prevention can be considered a formal policy of the Signoria as witnessed by the authority given the governor of Cyprus to withhold license to sail to any vessel if he considered shipping threatened. Only when the depredations of corsairs were frequent, chronic, and costly were punitive expeditions launched. Further, Venice made use of its sophisticated communications network to be advised of the movements of the Ottoman fleets and the activities of the Knights of Rhodes. Such information was crucial for Venice's defensive policy. It was far more likely that Venetian grievances would be negotiated by envoys at the Porte or by merchants in the courts than by naval engagements.

Ottoman naval policy developed in response to one set of priorities in the Mediterranean and another set in the Red Sea and Indian Ocean. In the Mediterranean, Ottoman naval policy was similar to that of Venice. It was primarily defensive and aimed at protecting the trading zones of the Levant. The Ottomans did not require the same extensive type of preventive naval policy as did Venice for several reasons. First, the Ottomans had fewer threatening enemies than Venice, and more ships. Ottoman shipping had little to fear from Venice in peace time. The primary threat came from the Knights of Rhodes and from local, including Turkish, corsairs. Venice, on the other hand, was threatened by the Knights, the Aegean corsairs, assorted Muslim or Christian corsairs who could shelter in Mamluk ports unmolested, and the Ottomans. Although Venetian shipping remained unscathed by the Ottoman navy during this time, the potential threat posed by Turkish corsairs like Kara Durmuş kept the Venetian officers constantly on guard. Venice was so preoccupied wth its own defense and with the provisioning of its remaining bases in the eastern Mediterranean that there remained little money or initiative for other naval efforts, whereas the Ottoman wealth of resources made this a period of naval expansion.

Because of the expansion of the Ottoman navy, the sultan was able to take two forms of offensive action which were not possible for Venice. One was regular punitive expeditions into the Aegean to deal with pirates operating against coastal shipping. The other was periodic cruising by parts of the fleet aimed against Rhodes and Rhodian piracy. Thus, the sultans practiced a type of reactive aggression in the eastern Mediterranean, prompted by assaults on

Ottoman commodities trade or on coastal settlements. The Red Sea and Indian Ocean, however, provided the setting for persistent Ottoman naval aggression. This activity was unrelated to the defense of Ottoman coasts or shipping, but it bore directly on long and short-term Ottoman economic interests. Its motivation was the expansion of Ottoman political and commercial hegemony in the Euro-Asian sphere, the same motivation which characterized the Portuguese in the Indian Ocean.

The Eastern Mediterranean—Indian Ocean Zone

Ottoman provisions for launching a large armada leave little doubt about the naval ambitions of Sultan Selim, who took the Ottoman throne in 1512. Antonio Justinian was drafted as a special envoy by Venice in 1513 to congratulate Selim on his accession and to renew the peace terms. In the course of his negotiations, the Ottoman vezirs wanted to insert two clauses into the articles of treaty. One clause, which sheds light on Selim's long range plans, was a stipulation that, if Selim should launch an armada, Venice would provide it with harbor and provisions in its territories. Three years later this provision would be demanded when Selim launched a fleet to support the land campaign against Syria and Egypt.[64] The second clause was a demand that Venice continue to pay the ten thousand ducat tribute to Selim that had been paid to his father ever since Venice lost the Aegean war. Resorting to diplomatic rhetoric, Justinian said that of course Venice paid tribute to no one but, since this was a "debt," Venice would be content to pay. The vezirs added that Venice must always be the friend of the sultan's friends and the enemy of his enemies, thus attributing client status to Venice. The rhetoric of both sides notwithstanding, Venice was clearly forced into a dependency relationship with the Ottoman state, forced to grant landing facilities as well as tribute. For Ottoman purposes, these concrete gains superceded the rhetorical demands for goodwill. Ottoman insistence on port facilities in Venetian territories, probably Cyprus was intended, indicates that Selim was not completely preoccupied with the Safavid threat in 1513. The year before his decisive defeat of Ismail Safavi at Çaldıran, Selim was making plans for the launching of an armada that could utilize Venetian bases in the eastern Mediterranean. The clear target was the Mamluk territories, key to sovereignty of the Holy Cities and control of the eastern trade. Venice's acquiescence to the sultan's demands indicates its own vulnerability to Ottoman seapower and ultimate inability to resist it. Once Selim was certain of his control over Anatolia, he resumed extensive construction activity in the arsenals. By the second winter of his reign, the Galata and Gallipoli harbors housed two hundred ships and timber was being cut for more. The spring of 1514 saw the arsenal in excellent order and work proceding at a furious pace. Fifty galley hulls had been produced in a single month on the orders of the *kapudan* pasha. Plans were in the works for the construction of one hundred fifty additional galleys; and by that fall, eleven of these were complete as were one hundred and one new hulls.[65] This construction was underway while Selim himself was marching against Ismail in Iran. Troops, money, and provisions were all in demand to supply the army encamped in eastern Anatolia; yet the investment of labor and material in the arsenals denotes that Ottoman hegemonic ambitions already extended beyond the eastern land borders of the sultan's territory. The great expenditure required for such a substantial new fleet was also justified by the need to patrol the south Anatolian coast and to transport troops and provisions in the event of a revolt as well as to launch an attack on the Mamluks.[66]

There was considerable speculation on the possible targets of Selim's naval mobilization. The Italian chronicler, Guicciardini, wrote in the late 1530s that Selim had a burning desire to rule, having often read of the deeds of Alexander and Julius Caesar:

> . . . continually reorganizing his armies and militia, building anew a great number of ships and making new provisions necessary for war, it was feared that he was thinking of attacking, whenever he was ready, either Rhodes, as some thought, bulwark of Christendom in the east, or (as others thought) the kingdom of Hungary.[67]

Ottoman policy was perceived to be expansionist and Venice was not the only state to appreciate the force of Ottoman seapower. In February of 1516, the Mamluk sultan, Qānsūh al-Ghūrī, sent two hundred artillery pieces to Alexandria to defend the coast against an expected Ottoman attack. This was an enormous investment of artillery for a ruler who was threatened on his southeastern frontiers by a Portuguese naval attack and on his northeastern frontiers by a Safavid attack from Iran. The concentration of artillery on the "protected" Mediterranean border indicates that Qānsūh already considered himself to be the object of Selim's naval build-up.[68] The Grand Master of Rhodes, Fabrizio del Caretto (elected 1513), also was fearful that Selim's navy would be directed against his island's shores. This may account for the negotiations between Caretto and Ismail in spring 1515—the Grand Master hoping that an attack on the Ottoman's eastern flank by the Safavids might deter them from naval endeavors in the Mediterranean.[69] An embassy from Rhodes to the pope on March 6, 1516 warned that the Ottomans had prepared an armada "such as no one had ever seen before."

Caretto was rightly apprehensive. Rhodian attacks on Muslim shipping were a constant concern at the Ottoman Porte. Because these attacks had adversely affected Venetian trade as well, the *doge* was unlikely to come to the aid of Rhodes in the event of an Ottoman assault on the island. In effect, no actual aggression on the part of the Ottomans was required in order to keep possible opponents in the Levant off balance. Venice, Rhodes, and the Mamluk state all looked to strengthening their fortifications and consolidating what alliances they had, just in case.[70] Venice, because of its active pursuit of friendly relations with the Ottomans after 1503, was the most secure of these three states.

By 1515, the states of the Levant were terrorized by rumors of the imminent launching of a substantial Ottoman armada. One hundred ships, well armed, were prepared that spring to provision the campaign against 'Alā ad-Dawla and the attack on Syria the following year.[71] This preparation stirred considerable interest in both Cairo and Venice. Apparently, however, the ships were not launched since it is likely that reports from Beirut, Rhodes, or Cyprus of sightings of such a large fleet would appear in the sources. The sultan's plans for the fleet were, nonetheless, soon to be realized. When the Ottoman army marched southeast to claim dominion over Egypt, Syria, and the Holy Cities, the fleet sailed as well, to make sure that the troops were not lacking in food or arms. By early 1517, Cairo was in Ottoman hands.

In the intervening years, between Venice's surrender in the Aegean wars and the conquest of the Mamluk territories, the expanded Ottoman fleet performed the series of mundane tasks which were the antithesis of the chroniclers' preoccupation with naval battles and glorious victories. The routines of chasing pirates and transport, after all, provide scant material for the chronicler's craft. The Porte wished to defend its coasts, expand its commerce, and to provide troop support for its land campaigns. Between 1503 and 1517 there was no Ottoman naval attack on Mamluk or Venetian possessions. There was only one minor engagement, a punitive raid on Rhodes in 1505, which was the direct result of piratic activity.[72] Hence, the myth of Ottoman seapower, which drove the foreign policies of its opponents, was not equivalent to the reality of Ottoman naval action. Also the European fears that the Ottoman fleet would be directed at their shores did not reflect the actual direction of Ottoman hegemonic ambitions in the early years of the sixteenth century. Before the Mamluks were defeated, the Levant experienced a period of quiescence. After their conquest, Selim planned once again to become the aggressor in the Mediterranean. He died before he could launch an assault on Rhodes (accomplished by his son in 1522). This, however, was the sideshow. The real channel of Ottoman aggression proceeded eastward in the direction of Ottoman commercial ambitions. Ottoman offensive action took the route of the Red Sea and Indian Ocean from 1505 on. Initially it took the form of naval aid to the Mamluks against the Portuguese.

Ottoman Naval Aid to the Mamluks

The history of commercial relations along the Indian Ocean/ Red Sea/Mediterranean route is tied to the history of naval alliances. The Mamluk Qalā'ūn (1280–1290) received twenty ships in aid as part of a defensive alliance with the prince of Ceylon. This alliance also guaranteed safe passage for Mamluk merchant ships to the Far East. In the same century the Il-khān Arghūn (ruled 1284–1291), with the aid of Genoese shipwrights, attempted to cut off the Egyptian trade in the Indian Ocean by launching two galleys to blockade Aden.[73] In the fifteenth century, the Ming emperor tried to attain direct control over the Indian Ocean trade by sailing Chinese junks as far as the Red Sea. Meanwhile, the Mamluk sultan, Barsbāy (ruled 1422–1437), in 1425 had taken over the customs of Jidda from the Sharif of Mecca and developed that port to the detriment of Aden. Under Barsbāy, the revenues of Jidda came to 200,000 dinars annually with over one hundred ships anchoring there every year. It was just such revenues which attracted Portuguese efforts to dominate the Indian Ocean, and which prompted local alliances to resist them, as in 1504 when Lopo-Soares was threatened with an Indian-Mamluk naval alliance in response to his pressure against Malabar.[74] In the sixteenth century, the overwhelming naval power of the Portuguese in the struggle for the

Indian Ocean commerce and its rich customs revenues led to an alliance of Qānsūh al-Ghūrī with Gujarati rulers in India.[75] It also prompted the Mamluks to seek aid from their longtime enemies, the Ottomans. The stimulus for this alliance was not only the Portuguese challenge to Qānsūh's political hegemony but also the threat that the customs revenues from the eastern trade and the Mamluk transit monopoly would be lost. For the Ottomans, the stimulus was somewhat different.

The purpose of the Ottoman naval build-up in the reigns of Bayezid and Selim was to actualize Ottoman imperial ambitions in the eastern Mediterranean, and to protect Ottoman shipping. The accrual of naval power combined with the Ottoman richness in building materials and ordnance, however, allowed the Ottomans to increase their influence by means other than direct conquest. With the ultimate objectives of control of the Holy Cities and usurpation of the Mamluks' access to the customs revenues of the eastern trade, the Ottomans sent naval aid in men, guns, and supplies to the Mamluks for use against the Portuguese. This aid symbolized the Ottoman sultans' long-term investment in a struggle for commercial hegemony and for the religious legitimation of sovereignty—a struggle in which the Mamluks and Portuguese shared the same essential objectives.

Mamluk plans for naval operations in the Indian Ocean began in earnest in 1505 when Qānsūh al-Ghūrī prepared a fleet of four galions and four fustas in the Red Sea to be launched against the Portuguese. As overlord of Mecca and Medina, Qānsūh was the Islamic sovereign of record. No sooner had the Portuguese invaded the Indian Ocean than petitioners began to arrive in Cairo to protest their depredations. Envoys from India and Muslim merchants alike applied to Qānsūh for relief from the Portuguese assault on Muslim shipping. The ruler of Calicut attacked Cochin for collaborating with the Portuguese and sent an envoy to Qānsūh demanding assistance against the infidels.[76] Noting both the loss of revenue and the obligation of the Mamluk sovereign to protect fellow Muslims, a merchant complained to Qānsūh that the Portuguese were wreaking havoc with Muslim shipping in the Indian Ocean and seizing all the spices. He alone had lost 30,000 ducats. Another group of merchants were forced to pay a 25,000 ducat ransom to secure their release when the Portuguese seized a Muslim spice ship off India.[77]

Qānsūh promised assistance to these petitioners. Nor were these promises motivated by religious and altruistic sentiments alone. Because the sultan held a state monopoly on the spice trade through the Mamluk territories, each Portuguese seizure of a westbound commercial vessel in the Indian Ocean adversely affected the Mamluk treasury. Initially, Qānsūh took indirect action. Utilizing the Christian presence in the Mamluk territories, he sent some monks of the Church of the Holy Sepulchre to Pope Julius II and to the Catholic kings. If the Portuguese voyages were not stopped, he threatened, he would destroy Christ's tomb and other shrines. The Portuguese argued to the pope that this was an empty threat. They pointed out that Qānsūh made considerable revenue from the pilgrim trade to the Holy Land and that he would not jeopardize this revenue by destroying Christian shrines.

The Portuguese were right. Mamluk options were limited by the nature of their commercial interests and by their position as middlemen in the East-West trade. Muslim and Christian trading interests were interdependent and Qānsūh could not realize his economic objectives by sabotaging commercial operations in his own territory. His options were to fight the Portuguese in the Indian Ocean, to negotiate, to raise customs dues to offset losses from diminished volume in the spice trade, or to find a powerful ally. Because the Portuguese sought not only a monopoly on trade but also the conquest of Mecca, negotiation was out of the question.

Qānsūh increased exactions on European merchants.[78] This adversely affected the trade of Venice as is illustrated by the difficuties suffered by the *muda* of 1504. Cargoes were limited, the spices were not available when the galleys arrived in Alexandria, and the Venetian captains bridled at the increased Mamluk exactions.[79] Although the Beirut *muda* returned to Venice in February of 1505 laden with spices, the *muda* in Alexandria left port under fire from the Mamluks after failing to secure permission to sail. This permission had been contingent on accord between the trading partners over loads and prices. The Mamluks, however, had attempted to squeeze too high an impost from the Venetians. Such struggles show that in the long run an increase in customs was not a productive option for the Mamluk sultan. It damaged his relations with his European customers and posed the threat of a Venetian boycott if the increase in duties and in loading delays offset the potential for profit. Hence, Qānsūh was forced to exercise the military option. Under pressure from the Indian and Venetian merchants alike, and faced with a loss in customs revenues, he began to equip a fleet at Suez. This option, however, was not without its own costs. The Mamluks were no longer a naval power and, in order to pose a real threat to the Portuguese, they were forced to appeal to someone who was. Taking the battle to the Portuguese at sea meant an appeal to Istanbul for aid and a concomitant loss of Mamluk autonomy to the Ottomans.

From the beginning, the challenge to Portuguese hegemony was a coalition effort. The extent of Portuguese seapower was not well known in Cairo, but the rapidity with which Portuguese guns had quelled Muslim resistance in the Indian Ocean made the Mamluks wary. Qānsūh equipped four galions of 500 *botte* each, two barks of 200 *botte*, nine light galleys, three fustas of eighteen banks of oars each and one brigantine.[80] This substantial fleet was staffed with Maghrebis, Turks, and others and was well-armed with artillery.[81] A joint action was planned as early as 1505 with the Mamluk fleet to be supported by the ruler of Calicut, a well-fortified city, which had been armed with cannon through the employment of two Italian artillery masters.[82] There was intense competition for such craftsmen in India; and the shortage of artillery, which afflicted the Mamluks as well, only underscores the importance of the Ottomans, who produced a surplus of cannon, for any endeavor to oust the well-armed Portuguese from the Indian Ocean.

By 1507, there is evidence of Ottoman ships carrying shipbuilding materials to Alexandria with some regularity. The *sancak beg* of Vise and the sultan himself were shipping materials for sale to Alexandria. The *sancak beg*, a boon companion of Bayezid, had three ships of his own engaged in mercantile activity, a heavy galion, a light galion, and a nave. He shipped timber, iron, and wax. Bembo, the Venetian *bailo*, claimed that Bayezid, upon hearing that copper was in demand in Alexandria, sent eight thousand *miera* of Kastamonu mined copper to sell there. Bembo said the sultan had never done such a thing before but that now he "had become a merchant."[83]

There is, however, more to these reports than meets the eye. Bayezid sent his commander Kemal Reis with the fleet that brought the copper to Egypt. Both Kemal and an Ottoman ambassador were received formally by Qānsūh al-Ghūrī in September 1507. Audiences with the Mamluk sultan were not reserved for mere merchants. Kemal brought fifty artillery pieces that Bayezid sent for use against the Portuguese. The cooper was destined for use in more artillery pieces to be cast on site for the fleet at Suez. At the court in Cairo, there was considerable interest in the Ottoman naval commander as well as in the ordnance he brought. Kemal Reis' naval exploits against the Europeans in the Aegean wars were legend and it was hoped that he would join the expedition to India.[84] The Mamluks had need of Ottoman personnel (mariners, craftsmen, and cannon founders) and of Ottoman guns. For their own part, the Ottomans were insuring the security of their southeastern frontiers as well as providing for the expansion of their commercial interests in the Indian Ocean. Ismail Safavi's invasion of eastern Anatolia from Iran that same year provided another incentive for the Ottoman aid. The Ottoman largesse in aid against the Portuguese may be explained in part as an investment to insure that Qānsūh, whose territory was also imperiled by the Safavid threat, would not contemplate an alliance with Ismail.[85] The Safavids posed a land-based obstacle to the eastward expansion of Ottoman hegemony, whereas the Portuguese were a seaborne impediment. Until the Safavid threat was allayed in 1514, support for the Mamluks served Ottoman interests on both the eastern Anatolian and Red Sea salients.

The Mamluk fleet finally sailed from Suez in late summer or early fall of 1507, commanded by Ḥusain al-Kūrdī and an Ottoman naval captain named Selman Reis.[86] Before sailing, Ḥusain al-Kūrdī had been engaged in the task of fortifying Jidda against Portuguese attack.[87] Although initially successful in a battle with the Portuguese off Chaul (near present day Bombay) in January 1508, the combined Mamluk and Gujarati fleets were later destroyed by the Portuguese off Diu, on the northwest coast of India. Ultimately, the effects of this loss were a further consolidation of Portuguese power in India, the subordination of the Mamluk sultan to the Ottomans, and the decision by Bayezid to extend the scope of his military investment in the Indian Ocean.

Even before the news of the disaster at Diu reached Cairo, construction of new ships was underway at Suez. This fleet was to be larger, consisting of thirty light galleys and twenty galions.[88] A captain was appointed with a crew of 1,500 including Turks, Maghrebis, Europeans, black slaves, five hundred gunners, and a captured Italian armorer. Lumber was transported to Suez along with shipwrights and caulkers. Qānsūh armed eleven galions at Damietta for the sole purpose of procuring timber and supplies for the construction of a new fleet, unintentionally frightening both Venice and Rhodes in the process with this unaccustomed Mediterranean naval activity. When reports about Diu did begin to filter in to Cairo, Qānsūh applied to Bayezid for aid to launch the second fleet.[89] Additional pressure was placed on the Mamluk sultan early in 1510 when ambassadors arrived at Cairo from Calicut, Cambay, and Malacca. The failure to defeat the Portuguese had been duly noted in India and these ambassadors came with a threat as well as a petition: if Mamluk assistance was not forthcoming, they would collaborate with the Portuguese.[90] Issuing assurances to the Indian envoys, Qānsūh moved to correct the deficiencies of the last expedition. He also proposed to make an example of the unsuccessful commander Ḥusain al-Kūrdī for his failure. Perhaps in anticipation of such a welcome, Ḥusain collected funds from the ruler and merchants of Gujarat with the stated purpose of returning to Jidda and building a fortress against the Portuguese.[91] The captain had apparently found his experience with Portuguese seapower a sobering one. In any case, hampered by problems of supply, inadequate numbers of mariners, and the revolts and troop insubordination, which were afflicting his state in its final years, Qānsūh was unable to launch the second armada until 1515. This was not due to an insufficiency of Ottoman aid but rather to the difficulties the Mamluk sultan had in governing his own troops and in prompting them to serve on the Suez campaign.[92]

Mamluk naval vulnerability and dependence on the Ottomans is illustrated by the destruction in 1510 of the fleet which Qānsūh had mobilized to procure lumber at Ayas in the northeastern corner of the Mediterranean. This venture operated only with the acquiescence of the Ottoman sultan who could easily have destroyed such a convoy with his own fleet. But the Mamluks were subject to minor naval powers as well as to the dominant one. The Grand Master of Rhodes, utilizing intelligence on Mamluk ship movements, feared that the Ayas fleet represented an Ottoman-Mamluk alliance to attack Rhodes. Seizing the initiative, he sent a fleet of seventeen to eighteen Rhodian ships, which destroyed the Mamluk lumber convoy in the harbor at Ayas. In the course of the battle, the Mamluk commander was killed and those of the crew who could flee and swim escaped to shore leaving their ships to the Rhodians.[93]

Arriving only three months after this humiliation of the Mamluk sultan by Rhodes, the Ottoman aid fleet symbolized the eclipse of Mamluk sovereignty and the ascendance of the Ottomans. The envoy sent by Qānsūh to Istanbul to request this aid brought with him a purse of 40,000 ducats. He arrived at Bayezid's camp in Edirne with sixty mounted attendants, an impressive retinue, to present his request for artillery and lumber for the armada against the Portuguese.[94] The ambassador was rewarded with an Ottoman pledge of lumber, iron, artillery, sails, masts, all sorts of equipment, and a fleet to provide safe-conduct and transport to Alexandria. Bayezid refused payment for the aid. This boon allowed the ambassador to spend the Mamluk money in Istanbul on additional equipment, a great windfall for the market there. This embassy, in effect, was a public statement of Mamluk dependence on the Ottomans. Nominally sovereign of the Islamic world, Qānsūh had become a petitioner and Bayezid the magnanimous benefactor, using his naval power to extend both his influence and his reputation into the Red Sea.

Bayezid, again, sent Kemal Reis to command the fleet escorting the Mamluk envoy back to Alexandria. The sultan ordered all ships, including Venetian ships, bound for Alexandria detained until this escort fleet was ready to depart, thus insuring that the fleet would sail in as great a force as possible.[95] When it did sail, the fleet was comprised of twenty-five to thirty-five ships including eight galleys. Its cargo included iron, wood, oars, arrows, 300 *makahil* (firearms), forty kantars of gunpowder, copper, artillery, and other supplies.[96] Such a large fleet is indicative not only of the substantial nature of Bayezid's military aid but also a precaution against the depredations of corsairs enroute. Shortly after departing Istanbul, the fleet was disbursed in a storm, several ships lost, and the commander Kemal Reis drowned. The rest of the ships regrouped and reached Alexandria, but the loss of Kemal was a severe blow to the sultan's navy. By December 1510, the artillery and lumber from these vessels was on its way to Cairo and thence to Suez.[97] Zeno, the Venetian ambassador in Syria, naively attributed this artillery shipment to Bayezid's wish to repay the great honor paid to his son Korkud at the Mamluk court as well as to his intention to pursue an assault on the Portuguese.[98] Quite the contrary, Bayezid feared his son was trying to secure Mamluk support for an attempt to seize the Ottoman sultanate for himself. As the scions of the Ottoman household were already jockeying for position in the succession struggle, Bayezid had good reason to suspect Korkud's motives for enjoying the hospitality of the Mamluk sultan.[99] The aid shipment, thus, served two purposes: to advance Ottoman interests in the Red Sea and Indian Ocean salient, and to buy insurance against Mamluk collaboration in any attempt to challenge or overthrow Bayezid.

Additional military aid from Istanbul to Cairo continued in the following years, enhancing Ottoman power in Suez and making Ottoman administration of the naval efforts against the Portuguese more direct. While laborers and shipwrights built vessels and manufactured gunpowder at Suez, Qānsūh sent a convoy of ten or eleven ships to Istanbul in 1512 to purchase lumber for the Red Sea fleet.[100] This convoy, which coincided with the accession of Selim as Bayezid's successor, was loaded with 160 sporta of pepper and other spices. It is likely that the spices for lumber exchange was negotiated directly with the Porte making both sultans merchants in pursuit of political objectives.

By this time, the position of the Mamluk sultan was quite desperate. Selim wasted little time after his seizure of power in preparing to settle the Ottoman score with Shah Ismail in Iran. As pressure thus built on Qānsūh's northern frontier, the Portuguese commander Alfonso d'Albuquerque launched an attack on Aden in the spring of 1513. Although their siege against the fortress was unsuccessful, the Portuguese managed to burn a large number of merchant ships in the harbor.[101] This attack intimidated the Mamluks and reaffirmed the immediacy of the Portuguese threat in the Red Sea. Not only was the Suez fleet itself threatened but also Qānsūh's legitimacy as protector of the Holy Cities came into serious question if the infidels could sail at will off the western Arabian coast. Under this duress, he was forced to allow the Ottoman sultan, his major competitor for sovereignty in the Islamic world, to take charge of the armed resistance against the Portuguese.

When, in April 1514, Qānsūh traveled to Suez to review the troops and survey the progress of fleet construction, the admiral who welcomed him was the Ottoman Selman Reis with a force of two thousand Ottoman soldiers. This Ottoman contingent outnumbered the mamluks. The mamluks resisted participating in the Suez expeditions, which involved fighting at sea, fighting on foot, absence for more than one campaign season, and fairly remote chances of a safe return. Further, the concentration of arquebusiers on the Portuguese front and of artillery on the Suez fleet ultimately reduced the Mamluk firepower available to resist Selim's invasion of Syria and Egypt that occured a year after the Suez fleet sailed. Much of the remaining artillery was concentrated on port defense at Jidda and Alexandria.[102] The cost of producing this fleet was staggering in terms of money, as well as in reputation, to the Mamluk sultan. Armed with canon of iron and bronze the twenty or so ships had cost Qānsūh over 400,000 dinars.[103] For the Ottomans, the provision of naval supplies had been a worthwhile investment. When the Suez expedition departed in August of 1515, it was commanded by the Ottoman admiral Selman and signified the arming of Ottoman ambitions to oust the Portuguese from the Indian Ocean.[104] This expedition elucidates both the grand design and the power depth of the Ottomans. Despite the campaigns in eastern Anatolia and Iran, Selim was already making operational the plan to extend his realms and his commercial interests beyond the Safavid lines. Thus, the shipping of artillery and military supplies by the Ottomans to their traditional enemies in Egypt is not as incongruous as it might seem. The shipments served the military and diplomatic objectives of the Porte against the Portuguese and against Ismail Safavi, who was negotiating with the Portuguese.[105] Earlier they helped insure that Qānsūh did not actively support the claims of Korkud against his father Bayezid. Both Selim and Bayezid capitalized on the adverse conditions brought on by the Portuguese navigations. The Portuguese focused Ottoman attention politically and economically on the Red Sea, and Mamluk weakness provided the opportunity for concrete Ottoman gains. After Çaldıran, Selim was able to pursue Ottoman interests aggressively, but the way had been paved by the Ottoman intervention in the Red Sea and Indian Ocean under Bayezid. The presence of Selman Reis and an Ottoman force in the Suez in 1514 and 1515 was a calculated intervention. Selman and his troops were an Ottoman advance force. Selman could serve a diplomatic function with the local monarchs in the Indian Ocean if the fleet succeeded against the Portuguese. Whether the fleet sailed or not, the presence of an Ottoman force on the Red Sea littoral was a symbol of Sultan Selim's military power. An Arabic chronicle called the arrival at Kamran of the fleet under Selman the "beginning of the coming of the Turks to the Yemen."[106] He might well have said, "to India".

Once the Mamluk territories and Cairo had been conquered in 1517, the way was then open for the Ottomans to pursue Indian Ocean hegemony from bases in the Red Sea and later the Persian Gulf. Selman Reis returned from the ill-fated Indian Ocean expedition of 1515 and set about fortifying Jidda where he successfully warded off a Portuguese foray into the Red Sea in 1517.[107] This was a decisive engagement because of the timing, just after the Ottoman conquest when government authority in the onetime Mamluk territories was still contested. The Ottomans had not yet consolidated their power in the Hijaz and the Yemen, so the Portuguese could have followed up a victory at Jidda with an attack on Mecca. Lest there be any doubt about Selman's intentions, a letter he wrote to

Sultan Süleiman some years later reveals that Ottoman military efforts against the Portuguese were inspired by the desire to relieve the Europeans of their lock on Indian Ocean customs revenues.[108] Selman suggested that an Ottoman Hormuz would be a very profitable colony indeed. He did not, however, get to pursue his designs on Hormuz. Instead he was later commissioned to command a fleet supporting the installation of Khair al-Dīn Ḥamza at Zabid for purposes of reasserting Ottoman rule in the Yemen. Despite Selman's apparent disappointment in this regard, the Ottomans did extend the scope of their naval endeavors into the Portuguese sphere. Both the Yemen and the Persian Gulf were used as bases of naval operations from which the Ottomans attempted to challenge Portuguese hegemony in the Indian Ocean.[109] Under Selim's son, Sultan Süleiman the Magnificent, a heavily armed and staffed expedition was launched in 1538–1539 against Diu, a key base for the conquest of India. A Hungarian captive, who participated in this abortive Ottoman sea campaign, wrote that the fleet consisted of fifty warships and four galleys.[110] The size of this formidable force alone suggests the extent of Ottoman ambitions in South Asia. Enroute, the Ottoman commander occupied Aden, hanging its recalcitrant governor on a ship in the harbor before the eyes of the citizens. By 1547, the Ottomans controlled the head of the Persian Gulf, had forty four galleys at Suez and, according to the Portuguese, were sending vessels from Suez to Mocha.[111] Thus, the conquest of the Mamluk kingdoms provided more than title to the Holy Cities and to the wealth of Egypt. Just as the Portuguese feared after their loss at Jidda, the conquest provided the Ottomans with a base for the attempt to extend their rule into the Indian Ocean. Süleiman the Magnificent continued the naval efforts of his father and grandfather, distilling the image of Ottoman grandeur into formidable fleets.[112]

Naval aid to the Mamluks in the early sixteenth century has been used, along with the stepped-up exchange of envoys between the two powers, as evidence that Ottoman-Mamluk relations were friendly during this period.[113] In the broader context of Euro-Asian power relations, however, it is clear that Ottoman naval aid to the Mamluks was a calculated move to expand the Ottoman sphere of influence into the Mamluk territories, thus paving the way for their conquest. Qānsūh's defensive measures indicated that he had little doubt about Selim's actual intentions, but the Ottomans were the only Muslim power to possess the artillery needed to combat the Portuguese, and to preserve some semblance of Mamluk legitimacy. The Ottoman-Mamluk enmity was preserved intact, economic expediency forcing Qānsūh to accept aid in the form of money, manpower, and materials. In effect, this was a form of submission, a humiliation of the Mamluk military status which the Ottoman sultan heightened by insisting that he not be reimbursed for his assistance.[114] The Porte's superiority in artillery and sea power were underscored by the sultan's largesse. The importation of Ottoman personnel and financing was coupled with an increase in Ottoman influence. The next step was to admit that the Ottoman sultan was the logical successor to the role of protector of the Holy Places and defender of the trade routes and the *hajj* against the infidel. As Selman Reis suggested, there was no reason to suppose that the Ottoman navy could not extend the hegemony of the Porte to the Indian Ocean, just as it had to the Red Sea.

PART II

Traders, Trade Goods, and Trade Zones

The economies of trade in the Levant both mirrored and drove the economies of conquest. Military, naval, and diplomatic action were geared to protect the provisioning of cities as much as to acquire control over agricultural lands and the entrepôts of trade. Conquest was a relative term.[1] It could include claims to possession and legal entitlement, physical occupation of space with the seizing of territory and the garrisonning of troops, control of crucial centers and routes, the leverage to collect taxes and levy troops, or merely the wherewithal to scare off opponents. Conquest was not fixed in time and space. It was negotiable, like commerce. The conquered space need not be occupied. This was most visible in the control of the maritime routes of trade. No chain of fortresses could be built at sea to remind travelers and merchants alike of the current claimant. But naval hegemony was established nonetheless. How else could the Portuguese, with a few well-armed ships and periodic disciplinary expeditions, control the Indian Ocean with slips of paper granting the right to sail? How else did the Venetian *luogotenente* forbid ship departures from Famagosta at the mere rumor of an Ottoman fleet sighting? Conquest was fallible. It could be breached as the corsair cannon breached the sides of carracks loaded with grain or spices—and it was. The willingness to challenge the power of the current naval hegemon depended upon calculations of profit and risk, of speed of escape, and possibility of pursuit. States, like the Gujarati kingdom at Diu, undertook these risks, as did individuals. Others, however, calculated the risks and found them too great. Then, diplomatic protocols took the place of attempting to elude competitors with more powerful navies. States, like Venice and the Mamluk state, undertook to negotiate for the protection of their trading ventures rather than to defend them with arms or manage them through stealth. They applied to the power that controlled the seas.

The rulers, however, were not equivalent to the sum total of commercial relations. Trading power was diffuse; it was invested in many centers, "lawful" (by each governing body's own definition) or unlawful: sultans, governors, sea captains, merchants, toll collectors, *kadi* courts, market inspectors, port authorities, corsairs. Hence, commercial relations were entered and exited at many levels besides those of international diplomacy or state law. There was no absolute distinction between state commercial interest and the individual commercial interests of those who were servants of the state.

The nature and extent of state participation in trade also varied by commodity. In the Aegean island-coast zone, radiating both east and west into the Mediterranean, grain was the commodity that launched ships, prompted diplomatic protests, set the outer limits of campaign strategies, and, in general, geared the economies of conquest and of trade. Historical analysis of the Ottoman state and of Euro-Asian empires in general has fixed upon control of agricultural estates as the great motivator for expansion and conquest. Among the European city-states, Venice stood apart in the scholarship: a seafaring nation powered and fed by the wind in the sails of merchant ships. Debate on the sixteenth-century Signoria focuses on when and how Venice turned to mainland agricultural investment as an alternative and replacement to long-distance trade.[2] High grain prices provided the incentive for the Venetian aristocracy's interest in agriculture (with 1589–1598 wheat prices in Venice nearly twice as high as in 1567).[3] Because the demand was also quite high in the earlier years of the century and because Ottoman pashas were, by definition, controllers of large agricultural estates in the form of *timar* grants, the Ottoman state, like Venice, must become the object of scrutiny for patterns of grain speculation.[4] There is no question that Ottoman *askeri* speculated in grain and other commodities. At issue are the mechanisms of this commercial participation and its meaning for determining the nature of the Ottoman economy.[5] As the assessment of documentation on the behavior of Euro-Asian states and elite commercial investors progresses, the simple dichotomy between reactive and aggressive economies must necessarily give way. The Ottoman Empire need not be only an agrarian-military state just as Venice need not be only a commercial-naval state.

In fact, the Ottomans were a dynasty spurred to conquest of markets as well as fiefs, a military bureaucratic class whose investments were distributed outside of *timar* holdings and *evkaf* endowments, and a great (and conscious) naval power that aimed to control and tax trade at its points of initiation, transit, and exchange across broad expanses of sea. That said, another particular of the nature of historical evaluation requires scrutiny. Admitting that the Ottomans were "involved" with trade, how was this involvement manifested? The scholarly focus on luxury trades smacks of indolent and licentious Oriental palace structures whose sole rationale is consumption: rich foods for the sultan, fancy silks for the palace women. The trade in luxury goods was important, not merely because of a fascination with these goods as object, but because luxury goods had a high cash-conversion rate—small space requirements for transport and high and consistent demand. The Ottoman palace, like its successful European counterparts, did indeed consume at a spectacular rate. The Ottoman state, however, like its competitors in the Levant, to the extent that it actively sought control of trade, was motivated by two essential factors: the desire to insure a steady supply of grain and foodstuffs, and the intention to bolster the central treasury by expanding the number and volume of customs posts.

Points of Ottoman behavior, then, which require particular scrutiny are: What indications are there that Ottoman policy was directly concerned with control of commerce? How can Ottoman military and naval action be explained in terms of exerting control over or protecting existing trade? To what extent, at what levels, and with which goods were members of the Ottoman elite classes engaged in commercial activities? The preceding chapters have discussed Levantine diplomacy and Ottoman naval development in terms of Ottoman expansion eastwards. This section will treat distinctive commodities in each of the three spheres of Ottoman conquest and expansion: grain in the island-coast zone, silk in the Anatolia-Syria zone, and copper and spices in the eastern Mediterranean-Indian Ocean zone.

In each case, these trade goods were consistently in demand throughout the period under discussion. Grain of course possessed a demand factor far surpassing that of the other goods. The grain trade prompted the highest incidence of banditry, piracy, and smuggling as well as the most aggressive attempts at state control. Examination of the grain trade opens a small window revealing the involvement of the masses, who are often invisible in other considerations of commerce in the sixteenth century. The documents may speak of the people, "without bread" or "forcing a ship to unload" in port during times of shortage, where otherwise these generally invisible consumers escape remark. To a lesser extent the demand for copper, including bits and pieces of old pots, reveals the lower strata of society who utilized the copper in the form of low denomination coins to purchase their bread or to pay taxes.

More apparent is active intervention on the part of the state in two forms: state attempts to regulate or block the flows of trade, and participation by members of the state military-bureaucratic classes in trading ventures. Competition for shares in the silk, copper, and spice trades existed at both the state and merchant levels, at both ends and at intervals along the trade routes. During this period, Euro-Asian rulers attempted to demonstrate their ability to control trade by periodically implementing stoppages or blockades of the flow of goods. Attempts by the Mamluk and Safavid states to control pepper and silk shipments westward were only relatively successful. Demand for copper in the East was so great that suppliers found they could sell in Egyptian markets as much copper as they could acquire. In the island-coast zone, the Ottoman was the state most consistently assured of adequate grain supplies and surpluses, giving it significant leverage in diplomatic affairs. The Ottoman sultan sometimes suspended grain exports not only in order to insure internal supplies but also to demonstrate in a concrete and potentially devastating fashion his power over life in dependent states. When sultan or shah attempted to apply a tourniquet to one area of Ottoman-Safavid economic life-blood, the silk trade, he found he was cutting his own throat in the process. The Mamluk sultans suffered similar discomfiture when they attempted to block or delay the spice trade through their kingdom in order to put political pressure on their trading partners, especially Venice. Except in the case of Ottoman grain, the export of these commodities was too vital to the economies of their producers or middlemen to allow for lengthy suspensions. In the case of grain, the strength of the Ottoman economy permitted the imposition of stringent regulation on exports but could not prevent the smuggling and speculation which were a reflection of high demand.

Consistent demand prompted the intervention of states and the participation of the *askeri* class in trade. Both were interested in predictable sources of profit—states to create or pad revenue surpluses and *askeri* to find alternative investments and shelters for their own wealth. Members of the military-bureaucratic classes were involved in the disposition of these trade goods, in particular the Mamluk notables in the spice trade and the Ottoman *askeri* in the grain trade. Safavid sources are few for this period and do not reveal the extent of notable involvement in the silk trade.

Consistent demand prompted variability of routes. When political intervention in the form of wars, tax increases, or extortion by officials put pressure on merchants and peddlers, routes were altered. When the vagaries of transport prevented the arrival of buyers at a site in a timely fashion, routes were altered. Silk routes seemed to vary the most in response to the vagaries of war, customs exactions, and merchant competition, although pepper shipments were also rerouted overland through Syria and Anatolia rather than via the Red Sea and Mediterranean. The sea route remained the route of choice for the trade in copper because of its weight and bulk. For grain, the sea route was also the most expeditious, enhancing transport distances, but it carried the potential for entire loads spoiled through exposure to moisture.

No synthetic theoretical framework has been devised for assessing the nature, mechanisms and impact of interregional and international trade in the early Ottoman state.[6] Suraiya Faroqhi addresses the possibilities for such a framework, contrasting the work of Pirenne, Raymond, Lapidus, and Antoine Abdel Nour to assess the relative weight of political conditions, interregional, and international trade in determining the fortunes of sixteenth-century Ottoman cities. She postulates that Ottoman intervention with trade and traders was "more regular, impersonal and bureaucratized" than was the case under Mamluk rule. In this model, the sultan and Ottoman high officials did not normally enter the market as sellers; and market manipulation, as described by Lapidus for Mamluk Syria and Egypt, was rare. Faroqhi suggests that when market manipulation did occur "the Ottoman central administration was quick to point out the pernicious consequences that could be expected to ensue." This of course poses the question of divergence between the rhetoric of the official sources and the actual conduct of trade. Stressing bureaucratic rules and institutionalized checks and balances, Faroqhi concludes that in the Ottoman case there is neither an "all powerful and overwhelming state" nor the "extremely fluid and unorganized state or urban society," which Lapidus describes in Mamluk Syrian cities.[7] In effect, Faroqhi's model suggests that Ottoman notables had less economic power and discretion than was the case with the Mamluk emirs, that the Ottoman state was much more predictable and unified, yet still fairly opaque and impersonal.

Without suggesting that the Ottoman pashas in the early six-

teenth century were a pack of opportunistic rapacious individuals
(as Ibn Iyās describes the Mamluk emirs), there is an alternative
model which gives more leeway to individual endeavor than Faroqhi's model. This model poses a state and pashas that intervene
more consciously and often than Faroqhi suggests. It assumes an
independence and flexibility of trading mechanisms, and of merchants and *askeri*, which are not closely regulated by the state, at
least not in any immediate way. Chaos on the one hand and a pervasive, rule-geared state system are not the only alternatives. Lapidus' model is still important, and applicable to the Ottoman case,
in terms of the significance of overall political security for the
smooth operation of trading mechanisms already in place.[8] Be-
neath this umbrella of security, there exist three levels of activity,
among others, on the basis of which the Ottoman involvement in
trade can be assessed. First is that of state regulation. This varied
for different types of goods, dependent in part upon the distances
those goods traveled, the distance from the administrative center
that transactions took place, and the importance of those goods in
foreign policy considerations. The second level is that of individual
opportunism or endeavor. At this level, the actions of the sultan,
his family, vezirs, pashas, state agents, tax farmers, and merchants can be analyzed individually, by class, or by commodity involved. If the behavior of individuals comes into conflict with the
rhetorical definitions or ideals of class (by class here is meant
groups defined by function, birth, and economic status: dynasty,
askeri, tujjar), then assumptions about characteristic definitions of
groups and group ethos within Ottoman society require alteration.
The third level is that of demand. When demand for a certain good
alters substantially or, conversely, remains consistently high, does
the opportunity for profit prompt individuals to alter their behavior and participate in trade in an uncharacteristic fashion? If not,
are there certain trading mechanisms and networks not corresponding to state boundaries or single state rules (Levantine patterns of trade) in which Ottomans, like their class counterparts in
Egypt, Italy or elsewhere, participate in what can be considered a
characteristic fashion, for example, the investment of notables' surplus revenues in international trade, or the export of controlled
commodities in times of scarcity? State regulation or regulariza-
tion of trade does not in the Ottoman case presuppose lack or prevention of investor initiative. Rather, investor initiative can always be assumed to be at some tension with the interests of the
state, particularly where grain is concerned, but also where engag-

ing in "non-traditional" functions by the *askeri* is presumed ideologically to compromise the interests of the state.

The Ottoman sultan and pashas had the ships, the control of commodities, the surplus capital, and the existing Levantine commercial networks to provide the incentive and opportunity to participate as investors in international trade. The instance of Bayezid II shipping large quantities of copper to Alexandria is only one indicator of the incentive which high demand provided to the Ottoman elite classes. By 1594, the Venetian *bailo*, Matteo Zane, reported that Ottoman elites (pashas, sultans and *"tutte le persone de condizione"*) were engaged in what was considered "honorable" trade—each with several large vessels sailing in his name to Alexandria and other ports. Zane said this trade utilized the sultan's materials to arm and equip the ships and took place with the cooperation of arsenal officials who benefited from it.[9] The sultan himself, according to Zane, condoned this practice and had a score of his own galleons which, when not at war, navigated to Alexandria. These vessels protected the *hajjis* traveling to Mecca from Christian corsairs and returned to Istanbul loaded with provisions like sugar and rice, which supplied the palace and surrounding areas. (This account suggests the varied functions of Ottoman vessels: military, commercial, provisioning, defense, and legitimation. It also suggests that the sultan could combine his duties, of protecting the *hajj* and feeding his people, with trading ventures.)

Breaking down the assessment of Ottoman commercial behavior by individual or class action helps dispell the Frankenstein monster image of the Ottoman state as exceptionally unconscious, or somehow running by itself without benefit of consistent plan or regulation. The Frankenstein image is now more a question of behavior than of looks. Historians no longer represent the bloody and destructive "Terrible Turk" of the late medieval sources. But they continue to produce images of a state whose economic function is rough, reactive, unsophisticated, unconscious, and subordinated overall to the impetus to conquer and control agricultural land. This image is almost an automatic side effect of analyzing economic behavior at the state level in an era when communication was so slow. That is, Ottoman sources, land and tax registers, often suggest the long-term enduring nature of economic activity, rather than the ad hoc, variable nature of economic activity found in sources like commercial letters, bills of exchange, or customs registers. Faced with a changing situation, the response time of the central government in altering commercial law might be slow. But members of the state system, fully integrated into commercial networks, were ready to respond rapidly to ground level changes in commercial situation, such as fluctuations in supply or demand.

State manipulation of trade was both conscious and unconscious. Bruce McGowan, for example, has approached the question of trade from the Balkan end of the empire and from the perspective of world systems theory. He concludes that "the Ottoman role in the emergent world trade system was neither deliberately chosen, nor understood, nor effectively controlled by the Ottoman authorities."[10] How exactly a sixteenth-century state, Asian or European, could deliberately choose its role in a world trade system is a debatable question. Sixteenth-century states inherited their roles in Levantine trading networks to a large extent and the Ottoman state was not an exception in this pattern. Intentionality cannot be presumed to exist in a vacuum outside of the context of trading customs, merchants groups, contract conventions, trading mechanisms, and methods of enforcement. These patterns limited the success of any late medieval state, particularly those states whose borders traversed large expanses of territory, in implementing stringent controls and regulations on trade. Nor could any such state be aware of all of the ramifications of its attempts to control or alter patterns of trade. McGowan has made a case for just such "unconscious" developments in sixteenth-century Europe, where waterside population densities created a hierarchy of land use that pushed crops unable to pay high rents outward and away from the demographic field.[11] The Ottoman Empire then, according to McGowan, contributed to the evolution of land use patterns in Europe, because imports of Ottoman grain permitted alternative use of these lands. The argument that all phases of the development of trade were not conscious or well understood does not, however, militate against the notion that the Ottoman state and its agents consciously attempted to control and manipulate trade.

CHAPTER 5

The Aegean, the Mediterranean, and the Grain Trade

The grain trade in the Mediterranean, like the lumber trade immortalized in Phoenician engravings, long predated the Ottomans. This trade was as profitable as shortages, hoarding, and luck in escaping bandits could make it. Its distance and duration were circumscribed first by weather, transport technology, and preservation methods and second by the dictates of lords and generals attempting to feed their capitals, supply their troops, and get their shares of the sale price. The trade in grain, along with that in other commodities, linked the Ottoman state into Euro-Asian trading systems, stretching from the western Mediterranean to the Indian Ocean. Maurice Aymard has distinguished the Ottoman system as inevitably separate from European world commerce as a result, in part, of the low state regulated grain prices which the sultans attempted to enforce.[1] But Ottoman participation in long established patterns of cereal exchange suggests an integrated rather than a partitioned Mediterranean system. This system, in turn, connects southeastern Europe to the unified world systems posed by Fernand Braudel and K. N. Chaudhuri for Asia.[2]

When, in the fourteenth century, the descendants of Osman were newly establishing their supremacy on Anatolian soil, already there existed a trade network from South Hampton to Alexandria that was plied by Italian ships. The Ottomans inherited their position as trading partners of the Genoese from the Byzantines whose rule they supplanted. Huge sums were invested in the medieval Genoese-Byzantine grain trade as illustrated by petitions for damage compensation made to the emperor Andronicus II.[3] Like his Byzantine predecessor, the Ottoman sultan, and his governors and customs agents were in a position to profit handsomely

131

from Balkan and Anatolian grain surpluses. In the reign of Sultan
Bayezid I (1389–1402), Genoese merchants were buying Anatolian
grain, combining this source of supply with major exports from
Caffa and from Sicily.[4] Genoese convoys of two or three galleys also
carried on a regular trade with Syria, supplying the Italian mainland or, when unlucky, the many pirates attracted by grain profits.[5]
The competition between pirates and merchants, in turn, prompted
the activity of merchant-state navies to protect the government
share in grain trade revenues and to insure the food supply for
their populations. With the merchants and pirates came the ships
of the rulers. At this early date, Gian Giacomo Musso, in his study
of medieval Genoese commerce, describes the Genoese documents,
saying ". . . the most frequent reason for which naval movements
appear in the registers . . . is grain provisioning."[6] The same was
true for naval movements in the sixteenth century, which were
often motivated by provisioning rather than combat objectives.

Levantine states, which controlled grain reserves, enjoyed the
wealth and prosperity that a grain surplus wrought, but all did not
have the military and, more specifically, naval might to maximize
control of these agricultural resources. The ability of state authorities both to control and to protect grain wealth was an important
indicator of that state's ability to maintain its sovereignty and to
expand its commercial ventures. Wealth accrued to Sicily, for example, to the extent that it acted as a grain emporium for the Mediterranean basin. Sicily used its grain resources to finance its
rulers and to draw foreign currency into the realm, just as the
Mamluks used the spice trade.[7] This cereal wealth, however, made
Sicilian shipping a prime target for corsairs and a choice prize in
the European struggle for territory.

Besides feeding the Aegean and Adriatic regions, Sicilian
grain was exported to North Africa, there to be exchanged for
slaves and gold. In the sixteenth century, however, under the
Spanish administration, control of the grain trade produced internal and external strife. Tax free Sicilian wheat provided biscuit for
the Spanish fleet and cut-rate grain as compensation to Venice for
war damage done by the French to Venetian shipping.[8] In 1512,
Moncada, the Spanish Viceroy in Sicily from 1509–1517, placed a
new tax on grain exports, alienating merchants and landowners.
Spanish soldiers returning from North Africa commandeered grain
stores, further exacerbating the tension between locals and the
Spanish administration. The King of Spain's death in 1516 provided the occasion for this widespread discontent to manifest itself,

and Moncada's move to reduce food taxes did not prevent rioting soldiers from sacking his palace and forcing him to flee to Messina.[9] This scenario is reminiscent of the chaos in the Mamluk kingdom at the same time and of the depredations of the Mamluk troops retreating from Aleppo.

The food needs of the army and populace, the opportunity for official profiteering, and the diplomatic leverage attached to grain exporting capabilities created currents of conflict in the Ottoman case as in the Sicilian. This conflict was inextricably linked to the demand generated by states suffering chronic dearth, like Venice—one of the states actively competing for both Sicilian and Ottoman grain stores. The Ottomans had capitalized on grain scarcity in order to advance their expansionist policies even before the conquest of Constantinople. They wrote treaties to institutionalize the nature and limits of competition. In 1419, the Venetian *bailo* in Constantinople and the ambassador of the Ottoman sultan in Edirne negotiated a pact which couched Mehmed I's attempt to consolidate his power in Rumelia in terms of cordial and secure trading relations with Venice. The pact stated that all the merchants of Venice might trade in Ottoman realms "on land or sea without interference" and that Ottoman merchants would enjoy the same privileges in the realms of the Signoria "without injury or impediment—*senza danno et senza impazo*."[10] Neither state, of course, could guarantee such carefree trading. In the case of Venice, access to the grain stores of the Ottoman kingdom (newly restored in Rumelia and Anatolia after Timur's conquest in 1402) and circumventing Genoese predominance in the Byzantine state, were clear priorities in the negotiation of any such treaty.

Tied to the competition for grain stores were the competitions for other types of trade goods and for political position. Early in the fifteenth century, for example, Süleiman, the son of Sultan Bayezid I, attempted to bargain trading privileges in return for Venetian political support. Süleiman sought allies in his bid to succeed his father and Venice sought favorable trade arrangements for horses, lumber, and Ottoman grain.[11] These relations signify that, at this early date, Venice utilized power struggles in Rumelia (and Anatolia) to enhance its trading position and its access to the Ottoman commodities trade. Later, Venice would attempt to negotiate with individual governors in Rumelia to acquire grain, horses, and even cavalry troops.

But access to Ottoman grain stores would not be guaranteed in the centuries that followed. Where grain had provided leverage to enhance Ottoman bargaining power, it would become a commodity to be guarded zealously and withheld from states competing with the Ottomans for hegemony in the Levant. Venice, in later treaties, placed a priority on attempting to secure grain guarantees.[12] But assuring the provisioning of cities, armies, and fleets in the Aegean was a struggle that required constant vigilance. Governments mobilized for this struggle through preemptive treaties, state intervention in the grain trade, export restrictions, import incentives, and even piracy. As Musso has pointed out, it was not easy to distinguish between public and private when it came to so general a need as grain.[13] Where grain was concerned, the Ottoman sultan in the sixteenth century could not distinguish between his obligations to feed his palace, tend to the poor, maintain order, and secure the fair share of the treasury in customs taxes. To insure the foreign reputation of his empire, the sultan had to control piracy, protect merchants, and prevent smuggling. To preserve order, Istanbul had to be provisioned, as did the troops. To insure prosperity and a full treasury the provincial farmers could not be overtaxed by governors or central government agents. Surpluses, however, were generated on a regular basis, allowing Ottoman pashas to exploit both their agricultural lands and Levantine grain shortages to good advantage.

Few scholarly efforts have been made to assess the Ottoman state as conscious participant in the economic organization of the early sixteenth-century Levant.[14] These efforts ordinarily emphasize the state's efforts to prevent grain exports and fail to focus on state and *askeri* participation in grain sales to foreigners. One scholar has aptly characterized the Ottoman state for the eighteenth century, though his words apply equally well for the sixteenth: "The Ottoman government was neither the tyrannical monster depicted by the late 18th century French traveler Baron de Tott nor the disinterested, passive observer of the capital's provisioning portrayed by the modern Turkish scholar Lütfi Güçer."[15] Neither aloof nor monstrous, the Ottoman state of Bayezid II and Selim I can be characterized as a decidedly interested party where the grain trade and other forms of commerce were concerned. This interest is reflected both in state policy and in the actions of individual Ottomans. Ottoman state involvement in the grain trade was both active and reactive, taking legal measures to control, channel, and exploit the grain trade as well as military and naval action to prevent threats to that control: smuggling and piracy.

Ottoman state policy, like that of the Italian city states, came into play most vigorously to guarantee the provisioning of its territories and military. This required not only supervision of agricultural lands and distribution of grain surpluses but also vigilant action against pirates. High demand and chronic shortages made piracy along the Anatolian coasts a profitable business. It was grain transports rather than luxury-goods bearing vessels which attracted the most corsair activity. Shortages in Venetian or Rhodian territories, for example, prompted the exploitation of three diverse options: (a) buying from Ottoman territories, (b) raiding Ottoman grain shipping, or (c) purchasing grain from any available provider, with no questions asked. Venice, for one, continued to count on the option of grain purchases from both Ottoman and Mamluk territories. In 1503, the Venetian *proveditor* of the armada noted that a combination of ship seizures and high prices resulted in a three day period when there was no bread at all in Corfu. He complained that the sultan's ban on grain exports ultimately caused this dearth, suggesting thereby that Corfu had come in the past to rely on Ottoman grain stores. The following year, grain was so scarce on another Venetian possession, Candia, that the populace forced a ship stopped in port to discharge its grain cargo for distribution.[16] Impounding grain from ships in port was common during shortages, although these impoundments were ordinarily accomplished by the military authorities rather than by popular actions. In 1510, Cyprus, ordinarily a grain exporter, had so little food that only imports of grain from Syria and Egypt kept the island alive.[17]

Escalating grain prices only increased the temptation for raiding. Rhodian based pirates preyed on Ottoman and Venetian grain shipping alike.[18] In 1512, the Rhodians captured eighteen Turkish grain transports causing the price of wheat in Istanbul to increase from nine to fourteen aspers a measure.[19] Piratic acts, in turn, brought out squadrons of the Ottoman navy on search and destroy missions. Nor were corsair activities discriminating in terms of religious predilection—Ottoman vessels were the targets for Muslim as well as Christian corsairs and Ottoman naval commanders brought Turkish pirates, like Kara Durmuş, to justice with impunity.[20] Grain was nondenominational and in times of shortage the market did not inquire at whose expense stolen or smuggled grain had been acquired.

Piracy and shortages affected naval policy in a variety of ways, related to the ability of a state to mobilize and pay for ships and sailors. Shortages required not only the acquisition of grain from alternative sources but also the requisitioning of ships for the transport of that grain. Rhodes regularly compromised its very limited naval capacity to send ships to Sicily or the Italian mainland to secure grain. Venice, when faced with famine, needed to convert ships utilized for other types of merchandise into grain transports, thus reducing the yield of customs duties on merchant ships entering the port (the customs tax on imports did not apply to grain). During the 1528 famine, this loss amounted to as much as 12,000 ducats.[21] The Ottoman state, with more vessels at its disposal but, like its competitors, always short of qualified seamen, also made arrangements to insure the availability of ships for grain transport.[22] Military campaigns, which diverted grain surpluses as well as ships (used more for provisioning campaigns than for actual combat), could easily strain the provisioning capabilities of a state, even a large grain producer like the Ottoman state.[23] Grain stores were drawn from areas of eastern Anatolia as well as from Cyprus, Syria, and Egypt to provision the intermittent Ottoman campaigns against the Safavids. One gauge of the degree of subordination of the eastern Anatolian begs to the central government was their willingness to supply provisions on demand for these campaigns. Often the begs refused provisioning orders, protesting that their own stores were low or insufficient to meet the government's demands. The *janissaries* of Istanbul alone during this period consumed in the area of 150,000 stera or 9,300 tons of grain a year.[24] This strain impacted on collateral areas not necessarily involved in the combat but subject to seizure or forced requisitioning of provisions. Such was the case for Cyprus during the 1515–1516 Ottoman campaign to conquer the Mamluk territories.

The effects on shipping in the eastern Mediterranean of the Ottoman mobilization for the Egyptian campaign were already apparent in 1516 in the form of ship seizures for transport and Ottoman interference in the staples trade. In November 1516, the Venetian *luogotenente* in Famagosta blamed the "disturbances in Syria" for Cyprus's failure to send money for the galleys and biscuit for the Venetian armada in Corfu. The biscuit was kept in Famagosta in anticipation of an Ottoman attack. In December 1516, Haidar Mustafa Aga arrived in Nicosia with a letter from Sultan Selim demanding provisions for the Ottoman army. Although Cyprus protested a scarcity of provisions, most of Haidar's demands were met. The Ottomans paid well for the provisions and Haidar Aga was provided with transport on a Venetian ship to Syria.[25] By the following year, the Ottomans had replaced the

Mamluks and, as collectors of the Cyprus tribute, could dictate the terms of its payment.[26] By the last quarter of the sixteenth century, the Ottomans had conquered Cyprus, gaining control of this important naval base, grain, and sugar producing region.

The Ottoman state directed its provisioning control attempts to certain target areas: city markets, ports, customs stations, and coastal waters where smugglers could be more readily intercepted. Legal controls were enforced via governors and *kadis*, for example, the 1548 Damascus law prohibiting sale of grain except at the designated market. There were also physical controls, such as discretionary punishments meted out by naval captains who apprehended smugglers.[27] When distribution problems, shortages, or campaigns required crisis response, the Ottoman state intervened through commandeering grain, releasing legally mandated stores, or forcibly altering normal distribution patterns.[28]

The environment of endemic grain shortage in the early sixteenth century conditioned the naval and diplomatic relations discussed in the first four chapters of this work. Grain trading, shortages, and piracy all prompted the formulation of state policy on the part of Levantine states and also dictated, to a large extent, the movements of state navies. It was not solely at the level of state organization, however, that grain was a prime motivator. The grain trade also drew in powerful members of the state military apparatus acting as individuals, for profit. While it is unproblematic that the aristocratic members of Italian city-states speculated in the Levantine grain trade, the understanding of the "sultan's servants" as mere instruments of the Ottoman ruler's exercise of power has militated against analysis of direct *askeri* participation in commerce. According to the paradigm, based on title and the idealization of group identity, a soldier is not a merchant and a *kul* (or slave) of the sultan does not initiate economic action or decision-making. This understanding requires redrawing in light of the notion that if it acts like a merchant it can be called a merchant. The Ottoman state was not *only* a military/agricultural formation and the Ottoman statesman was not *only* a soldier. Both participated consciously in economic planning, decision making, and events.

It would be surprising to find that powerful members of the military establishment in a state which produced grain surpluses did not involve themselves in the grain trade. The early decades of the sixteenth century can be characterized as years of expanding opportunity for investment, particularly in the eastern trade, for

Ottoman entrepreneurs. The situation is the converse of that faced by the Venetian nobility later in the century. Just when the establishment of Ottoman naval hegemony in the Levant and the Portuguese incursions in the Indian Ocean began to circumscribe commercial opportunities for Venetian nobles, who began to invest in land and food production, these same factors were providing the Ottoman agricultural aristocracy with new options for investing their surpluses of wealth in commerce.[29]

Ira Lapidus has discussed how the ideal of sultanic monopoly was subverted in practice in the fourteenth- and fifteenth-century Mamluk kingdom. Lapidus points out that the fortunes accumulated by Mamluk emirs, and itemized in confiscation records, included "vast stocks of grain." Grain payments made to the mamluks were converted to cash in the urban markets and "emirs and officials thus became the grain dealers par excellence of the medieval Muslim city."[30] Emirs speculated in the grain trade, buying up the payments in kind of lesser officials and participating in interregional grain trading. They exploited the pervasive power of the military to force merchants and subordinates to buy grain at inflated prices, reflecting similar abuse of foreign buyers by the Mamluk state.

The Mamluk case suggests some of the avenues open to Ottoman pashas who accumulated similar personal treasuries and who had access to grain surpluses. For one thing, the Ottoman pashas were also subject to the confiscation of their estates. Thus, the protection of accumulated wealth and the insurance of support for heirs required both a diversification of investments and the sheltering of those investments in the names of various agents.[31] Chronic grain shortages and consistently high demand for exports also provided, as they had for the mamluks, a strong incentive for Ottoman notables to speculate in the grain trade and to enhance this commercial activity with the political leverage and channels of influence associated with their *askeri* status.[32] Finally, central government levies of provisions for military campaigns diminished the grain stores available for disposal by various local authorities and thus was resisted both directly (through insubordination) or indirectly (through smuggling and the illegal sale of grain targeted by the government).

The greatest opportunity existed in Rumelia where grain could be shipped overland as well as by sea to Aegean and Adriatic markets, thus avoiding naval surveillance.[33] Nor can the relatively low Ottoman grain prices, emphasized by Maurice Aymard, be used to

suggest that the whole Ottoman territory comprised a single unified zone for purposes of assessing the grain trade. Low prices do
not characterize the Ottoman state absolutely since prices fluctu-
ated by region, demand, and scarcity and also because attempts to
regulate grain prices were only relatively successful.[34]

How then did Ottoman pashas and agents function as merchants? Although they could not dispose of the land itself, Ottomans who controlled agricultural lands had some discretion in the
disposal of the revenues and goods of those estates. European
states, merchants, and smugglers capitalized upon this fact to deal,
legally or illegally with the estate holders. For example, under Sultan Süleiman, Venetians regularly negotiated for Ottoman grain
with the various Ottoman begs, purchasing grain on credit from
the *hass* (royal domain) estates of Mustafa Pasha, Gözelce Kasim
Pasha and, in 1536, 487,000 akçe worth of grain from Ayas Pasha.[35]
A ferman to the governor of Herzegovina in 1533 ordered that he
assist Venetian merchants in his province in the purchase of grains
and see that no one molested them.[36] This was only one instance of
imperial Ottoman intervention on the part of foreign merchants
seeking grain purchases. In 1551, the grand vezir Rüstem Pasha
sent his own ships with grain to Venice, contracting with the *bailo*
for 200,000 stera of wheat in September and October alone. Venetian raconteurs were impressed with the income at the disposal of
Ottomans like Rüstem Pasha, one envoy noting that the income of
Ottoman pashas, particularly that of the grand vezir, increased
dramatically in times of grain shortage.[37] Interdictions on grain exports between 1560–1590, although making open export more difficult, encouraged creative arrangements between European agents
and Ottoman merchants and begs.[38] Documents from Topkapı Library indicate that in 1552 Balkan *kadis* were charged with the
task of confiscating grain and with attempting to prevent flagrant
abuse of state regulations on grain sales.[39] While this illicit traffic
in grain continued in the Balkans, however, the Porte also authorized the sale of grain from the same area to France. This grain
ultimately ended up in the hands of Venetian merchants.

Besides the disposal of grain surpluses, pashas had the opportunity for indirect control of commerce through such avenues as:
(*a*) sons or agents who engaged directly in trade, (*b*) connections
with foreign merchants and envoys negotiating trade agreements,
and (*c*) complicity in or toleration of piratic activity. Agents of
pashas were trading in Ancona during Selim's reign.[40] Venetian
diplomatic dispatches frequently mention connections with pashas

as significant for the success (or failure) of commercial negotiations or reddress of abuses of merchants.[41] When the goods of foreign merchants were seized and not redeemed, who disposed of them? Such questions require investigation. Ottoman officials had various means of applying leverage to the foreign traders operating in Ottoman territory and this leverage could be translated into commercial privilege. When the Ottomans wished to negotiate with Rhodes, for example, in 1504, for the release of an Ottoman official, the *kapıcı başı* Kemal Beg, they offered Rhodian captives who were in the possession of the *sancak beg* of Manissa. This governor was apparently the patron of a corsair, Kurdoğlu, and profitted from the fruits of his labors in return for the provision of safe harbor.[42] Clearly, grain smuggling also required the cooperation of local begs and customs agents. Rather than dismissing such activity as indicative of the "Oriental" penchant for "corruption," such activities should be viewed as the natural response of grain producing regions to demand from areas of scarcity—the continuation of pre-Ottoman patterns of trade, which were at odds with periodic central government regulation.

Finally, the long association of Venice and the Ottomans in Istanbul, along with the existence of a resident Venetian *bailo* whose task was, in part, to establish close relations with influential pashas, provided members of the Ottoman *askeri* class with access to the networks of Levantine trade long dominated by Venice.[43] The affairs of foreign merchants in Istanbul cannot readily be extracted from the context of diplomatic negotiations, provisioning arrangements, and security and financial concerns. One of the *bailo's* primary tasks, besides negotiating favorable trade agreements and accumulating intelligence information, was to intercede for the Venetian merchant community in the day-to-day conduct of commercial affairs. Such intercession took place via the vezirs, pashas, and the *kapudan* pasha of the navy. The commercial interests of Ottoman officials could intersect or conflict with those of Venetian and other foreign merchants. The *bailo* Zane, for example, complained that the Ottoman *kapudan* pasha, as both a holder of large estates and naval commander, was meddling in Venetian attempts to import Turkish grain in the course of his efforts to impose stringent controls on grain smuggling.[44] He argued that the Ottomans were indebted to Venice for helping protect Turkish grain transports in the Aegean, suggesting that shared interests in suppressing corsairs should facilitate Venetian acquisition of Turkish wheat. Zane was right in suggesting that the interests of Ven-

ice and the Ottoman *askeri* were inextricably linked. As his predecessor, Antonio Erizzo noted in 1557:

> . . . the friendship of Venice is most useful to the sultan, bring-
> ing as it does the Venetian merchants to his territories, whose
> trade brings great benefit, both public and private; first by means
> of the customs taxes that these merchants pay for the goods they
> bring and carry away, and second by means of the earnings that
> his subjects make by means of the sale of their goods to the Vene-
> tians.[45]

The organization of the grain trade at the level of the individual Ottoman merchant remains obscure for the early sixteenth
century. From the European sources, more is known concerning
the affairs of individual pirates than of the affairs of Ottoman merchants, although it is clear that the time is long past to abandon
the refrain that Turks were not particularly interested in engaging
in commerce.[46] The longtime presence of European merchants in
Istanbul required networks of Ottoman trading partners.[47] These
trading partners were not only obscure Muslims and *dhimmis*
(non-Muslim subjects) of the *tujjar* class, but also prominent members of the Ottoman governing class. In this they were not unlike
their aristocratic counterparts in Venice, rulers and men of commercial affairs whose trading interests in Istanbul linked them inextricably to the success of Ottoman expansion.[48]

CHAPTER 6

Trade on the Eastern Salient

> . . . trading in merchandise is so necessary that without it the
> world would not go on. It is this that enobles kingdoms and makes
> their peoples great, that enobles cities, that brings war and peace.
> . . . Pope Paul II was originally a merchant and he was not
> ashamed of the time he spent in trade . . . nowadays it is carried
> on throughout the world, and particularly in these parts it is held
> in such high esteem that the great lords here do not do anything
> else but trade.
>
> Tomé Pires, *Suma Oriental* (1512–1515)

The mystique of capturing the oriental trade permeates the
imperial ambitions of the gunpowder empires in the Age of Discovery: Ottoman, Mughul, Safavid, Portuguese. The rhetoric of dominance claimed the sea lanes of the Indian Ocean and the caravan
routes of Iran as well as the Holy Cities of the prophets. Once the
Portuguese laid claim to all customs ports washed by the eastern
seas from Africa to Southeast Asia, the sovereign states of Asia
seemingly had no choice but to respond. They responded to the Portuguese challenge in proportion to the nature and extent of their
investments and firepower.[1] The clash, of Ottoman and Portuguese
in the Indian Ocean, or of Mamluk and Portuguese in the Red Sea,
was never reducible to the simple Christian *vs.* Muslim dichotomy
so entrenched in the language of traditional historiography.[2] The
audience-driven conventional rhetoric of sacred trusts and crusading missions so endemic in the chronicles and diplomatic dispatches
of this era should not be permitted to obscure what amounted to
the military articulation of commercial acts. Religion was a mo-
bilizer of popular sentiment, a legitimizer of kingly commands, a

customary tool for insulting rivals for political and economic sovereignty. Yet, it was money in the form of trade goods which lured the Portuguese to the Indian Ocean, prompted the Indian rulers to resist them, and, in turn, drew the Ottomans there to challenge them. Of course honor was another motivating force, but honor, like piety, is more difficult to measure than profit, and profit brought honor in terms of the abilities to establish courts, maintain armies, and defeat opponents.

In this context of competition for honor and for profits, the Ottoman expansion early in the sixteen century upset the balance of power in the Levant and required the renegotiation of customary commercial and diplomatic relations. Yet this renegotiation was neither based entirely on adversarial relations nor was its outcome determined strictly by military force. The Ottoman state, Venice, Mamluk Egypt, and Safavid Iran, all were in contention for control of trade at two levels: inter-regional commodities trade and long-distance international luxury trade. The interests of these states, however, coincided in several areas of commercial endeavor. One was the desire to preserve the status quo in those areas of trade where resources were redistributed to the mutual benefit of two or more states. For example, the lumber trade from Anatolia to Egypt was mutually beneficial to both the Ottoman and Mamluk states, despite chronic hostility in their political and military relations. The Mamluks required Ottoman timber for constuction and naval projects which could, in turn, contribute to their own defense. The Ottomans made the lucrative lumber trade a state monopoly and used their forest resources to bargain for imports of spices, a Mamluk state monopoly. In addition to the customs revenues and the benefits of exchanging Anatolian lumber for Egyptian pepper to supply the palace, the Ottomans also profitted from leasing the sultan's ships for the cross-Mediterranean transport of lumber to Alexandria.[3] Another trade good, which represented the shared interests of traditional foes, was the silk trade from Iran. Acting as middlemen for the lucrative trade in this luxury item, both the Ottomans and Venetians gained substantial customs or resale revenue in the exchange.[4] As the Safavid Ismail rose to power, his relations with the Ottomans were also conditioned by the necessity to transport silk to its commercial outlets through both Ottoman and Mamluk territory.

Another shared interest of the eastern Levantine states was the imperative to prevent the rerouting of international trade by an outside power to the detriment of those states which monopolized customs duties on the old routes. The classic case of this shared motive is the threat of the Portuguese navigations to the interests of the Ottomans, Mamluks, and Venice in the Indian Ocean spice trade. Given these common objectives among competitors, the question becomes: Which of the competitors was in a position to resist, control, or alter patterns of trade? The answer clearly is the Ottomans, but the reevaluation of Mediterranean trade, prompted in part by the Annales school, has not yet incorporated the Ottoman state as an economic actor with full participatory rights. Further, the Ottoman naval investment of the Red Sea and Indian Ocean remains cast in terms of a "holy war" to protect the Hijaz. In fact, the Ottoman naval development of the late fifteenth and early sixteenth century, coupled with a conscious economic policy of commercial expansion, placed the Ottoman Empire in a unique position in the Euro-Asian world to determine the outcome of the struggle for control of trade.

The research of Eliyahu Ashtor, Frederic C. Lane, Vittorino Godinho, and Niels Steensgaard has supplanted the traditional scholarship of Wilhelm Heyd, which indicated that the Portuguese navigations cut off the flow of trade from India through the Red Sea to the Mediterranean.[5] Yet their research, by contrasting the fifteenth with the mid to late sixteenth century, does not banish the assumption that the early sixteenth-century eastern Mediterranean was a commercial backwater. In fact, despite the Portuguese incursions in the Indian Ocean, the open conflict between Ottomans and Safavids, and the sultan's preparations to conquer the Mamluk territories, trade remained very active in the eastern Mediterranean region. It is not yet clear to what extent the Euro-Asian trade was in fact displaced toward the oceanic edges in this period. But it is clear that the overland trade north and west from the Persian Gulf and Iran through Anatolia was highly resilient. Ottoman merchants competed with the Venetians and French for spice loads in Alexandria, for the Egyptian copper market, and for the overland trade through Aleppo and Damascus. The conduct of the Venetian *muda* continued with Ottoman tolerance and even cooperation. Indeed, the whole rhythm of Levantine trade came to be predicated on Ottoman policy and on predictions of Ottoman action and intent.

The Eastern Salient: Silk and the Further East

The silk, spice, and copper trades provide illustrations of the inextricable linkages between economies of conquest and economies of trade. As luxury items, spices and silk have garnered the lion's share of attention from past generations of economic historians. Yet the luxury trades were interdependent and interoperational with the commodities trades and, in this discussion of the eastern salient, copper will play the role that grain must play in any discussion of the conduct of Mediterranean trade. Copper draws the examination of oriental trade processes past the Levantine port outlets and Anatolian customs stations to the Indian subcontinent where the demand for copper was as crucial as the control of spice resources for an understanding of the mechanisms of trade. Copper was at once a trade good and a trade currency, shipped to the East to pay for silk and spices alike. Hence, a discussion of copper, as a trade good, which defined policy, will follow the discussion of silk here and lead into a case study of the Venetian *muda* to illustrate the interconnections of Levantine state policy, state navies, and the intersecting zones of commodities and luxury trade.

The silk trade geared the economies of Ottoman exchange between Europe and the Orient in the period predating the conquest (1516–1517) of Egypt and Syria.[6] For silk, the Italian merchants crowded the *hans* (commercial warehouses) of Bursa and fretted over the fifteenth-century conflicts between Ak Koyunlu and Kara Koyunlu dynasts in Iran and between Mamluk and Ottoman along the Syrian littoral. Silk, like pepper, drew the Europeans into Ottoman domains, bringing brocades, woolens, and especially cash into the Ottoman coffers—transaction fees for the right to purchase the raw silk, bags of pepper, and a box or two of rhubarb from the caravans arriving overland from Iran. Silk provides a case study for: the flexibility of routes, the modes of negotiation, the nature of government policy and intervention in trade, the durability of commerce in areas of chronic warfare, and the participation of state agents in the mechanisms of trade.

Shah Ismail's military recruiting and religious proselytizing challenged the sovereignty of the Ottoman sultan by attempting to command the allegiance of the governors and populace of the eastern Anatolian provinces. But Ismail, by gaining control of the centers of Iranian silk production and by threatening the frontier customs collection points, compromised Ottoman economic interests as well. At issue were both the domestic operation and control of silk production and trade, and the authority to dictate the commercial policy of competing states. Thus, the silk trade prompted Ottoman diplomatic intervention at a state to state level, aimed at confirming Ottoman dominance in the pecking order of Muslim sovereigns. It also prompted intervention at a more local level, aimed at protecting the interests of individual merchants and the interests of the central treasury in individual transactions. The nature of Ottoman government intervention in the Iranian silk trade was a function of the scale of profits to be made and of the potential for damage, physical and ideological, to be wrought on the Safavid enemy.

Government controls attempted to regulate the interests of domestic entrepreneurs as well as those of competing states. Points at which Ottoman government interest intersected with the silk industry were guild controls, customs collections, palace purchases, impounding of foreign merchants and merchandise, frontier border controls, and participation by *askeri* or state agents as investors in trade.[7] Government restrictions insured the Ottoman share of customs revenues, allocated the collection of those revenues to selected individuals as favors or for profit, and attempted to implement political policy in the form of restrictions on the flow of trade. To circumvent government restrictions or the extra-legal exactions of greedy customs-station collectors, merchants altered routes, customs stations, or packaging methods. For example, a silk caravan might travel via Van rather than Erzurum to secure a lower customs rate, or simply pay a lump sum to avoid the careful itemization of goods by customs agents.[8]

Of course a sufficient military force allowed one to ignore customs tolls with impunity. Such was the case in the fifteenth century, when the Ak Koyunlu leader Uzun Hasan scorned the efforts of the Ottoman sultan, Mehmed II, to add a customs tax on Iranian silk loads at Tokat to the one already imposed at Bursa. Uzun Hasan sacked Tokat.[9] Most merchants, however, lacked the military wherewithal of dynasts like Uzun Hasan and simply changed routes or paid what was demanded instead. In the sixteenth century, when Shah Ismail, in his turn, challenged the Ottoman sultan's control of the Anatolian customs stations, Ottoman and Venetian merchants scrambled to maintain the commerce through eastern Anatolia or shifted loads down to Aleppo for export by sea.[10] An alternative to changing routes was to maneuver for reductions in the amount or number of customs charges. On the western end of the silk route, in Bursa, Florentine merchants attempted to outbid Venetians for silk loads and negotiated for tax breaks from Bayezid and Selim. The Florentines secured their investment by negotiating a clause in the *ahidname* (treaty or granting of privilege), which released them from paying a second brokerage fee in Istan-

bul once they had paid in Bursa.[11] When negotiation or route
change was not an option, merchants circumvented toll charges by
repackaging goods. In Syria, under the later Ottoman administration, route changes and even boycotts by merchants occurred in
response to increases in customs exactions by officials. It was rou-
tine practice to overload camels and other animals outside the city
of Aleppo (even doubling the load weight) to minimize charges imposed by the load, even though taxing by the load was illegal according to imperial regulations.[12] Nor were the merchants the only
ones to adapt in response to the need to maintain profit levels.
States, too, were competitors and found economic incentives to at-
tract customs revenues. In later centuries, for example, the Ottoman government responded to decreased trade volume by lowering
customs duties at Erzurum on the silk route from Iran.[13]

Control of urban trade entrepôts and centers of production was
an important factor in determining the Ottoman avenues of conquest. Cities had prospered along the traditional trade routes and
these cities provided centers for the administration of commercial
regulation by successive dynasts. Although supply and communication difficulties prevented the Ottoman sultan Selim from retaining control of the Iranian silk centers of production after his march
to Tabriz in 1514, the Syrian commercial centers, like Aleppo and
Damascus, were accessible to troop garrisoning and supply by sea,
allowing the Ottomans, after 1516, to control the outlets for the
Iranian silk trade to the Mediterranean. Aleppo and Bursa were
major entrepôts of the silk trade before and after the Ottomans
added Aleppo to their string of commercial centers reaching eastward toward South Asia.[14] Customs receipts in Bursa on the silk
trade amounted to 40,000 gold ducats in 1487; 33,000 gold ducats
in 1508; and 43,000 in 1512, dropping under Selim's reign.[15] This
drop reflects route alterations rather than solely the success of Selim's measures to thwart the Safavid trade. Aleppo under the late
Mamluk administration provided an alternative to Bursa for European merchants who wished to compete for silk loads nearer the
source of production and to skip the Ottoman middleman. Under
early Ottoman rule Aleppo remained an important silk entrepôt,
although its role diminished in later years.[16] Conquest of a trading
city like Aleppo, allowed the Ottoman state to expand its options
for commercial control and exploitation and to limit the options of
its competitors.

Each competitor, Ottoman, Mamluk, and Safavid, attempted
to capitalize on its location along the silk route. The Ottoman-Safa-

vid battle for control of eastern Anatolia was fought in the markets as well as on the bloody battlefields like Çaldıran. Once he had conquered the Mamluk territories, Selim I utilized economic force in an unsuccessful attempt to subordinate the beaten but unconquered Safavid foe, Shah Ismail. He imprisoned Iranian merchants and boycotted the silk trade, just as the Mamluk sultan in the past had impounded merchants and goods in an attempt to force Venice to come to more reasonable terms of trade. This attempt to halt the silk flow, however, was both economically disadvantageous and frustrating in terms of enforcement. The demand for and impetus of the silk trade were too strong, and the profits too great. Here the economies of conquest had to be subordinated to the economies of trade. While demand was high, the Ottomans found their interests best served by facilitating the silk trade rather than in using it to enforce an economic stranglehold on Iran.[17] Of course the Ottoman conquest of Syria in 1516 cut off the Iranian option of sending silk loads through Aleppo rather than through Anatolia. After the conquest, Iran's only options for circumventing the Ottoman middleman were shipping the silk out from the Persian Gulf or shipping it overland north through Muscovy as proposed unsuccessfully (later in the sixteenth century) by the Englishman Anthony Jenkins. Thus, the Ottoman state remained the primary broker for Iranian silk destined for the ships and markets of Venice, France, and northern Europe. Venice was a survivor in the shift from Mamluk to Ottoman domination of the eastern Mediterranean silk outlets, retaining its position as favored commercial partner until the seventeenth century.[18]

Copper and Spices

While silk brought prosperity to the Venetian merchants plying their trade in the markets of Bursa and Aleppo, it was the spice trade that monopolized cargo space in the holds of Venetian vessels loading at the port outlets of Alexandria and Beirut. The spice ship convoys, second seaborne link in the long trade flow from India to Suez, Suez to Alexandria, Alexandria to Venice and beyond, were organized to capitalize upon the European demand for Asian spices, a demand which was satisfied only through the concomitant eastward flow of some form of cash. In this exchange one of the common forms of payment was copper.

The conduct of the Venetian *muda* illustrates the process of the Ottoman capturing of the eastern trade and the interrelations of the spice, copper, silk, and grain trades. Spices were a key commodity linking the trade of the Anatolia-Syria and the eastern Mediterranean-Indian Ocean zones. The loads of caravans coming west through Anatolia and of ships from Syria usually combined sacks of Indian spices and quantities of Iranian silk. The limitations imposed by transport technology and weather required that the successful merchant attempt both to diversify his investments and to accumulate stores of goods, coordinating purchases with both caravan arrivals and with caravan or ship departures. Cash on hand, official connections, and advance bidding were required to insure a merchant his share of silk and spice loads. Copper was a trade good which could be substituted for money on the western end of the east-west trading axis because of the consistently high demand for copper in Egypt and India. The Venetians and Ottomans alike used copper to pay for the spices of the Indian Ocean traders and their Mamluk kingdom middlemen. The Porte and the Signoria were naval powers and their ships enabled them to provide the flexibility of transport which made trade in copper profitable.

Major sources of copper to supply eastern demands were Spain, Morocco, Germany, and Anatolia.[19] Like the lumber trade, the copper trade to North Africa and India predated the Ottoman Empire. At the beginning of the eleventh century A.D. the Geniza documents show Jewish merchants in Fustat trading in copper imported from Spain and Morocco. The copper was sold in bars, large and small, cast in various shapes, hammered, or in pieces and fragments gathered in bags or bushels.[20] Jewish merchants carried on an active copper trade in Aden and, in the twelfth century, ran a bronze factory in India, which processed copper, tin, and old bronze vessels shipped from the West.[21] A proposal was made to the Venetian Senate in 1377 to ship copper to Alexandria, despite the pope's ban on such exports; and fourteenth-century Italian notarial records show copper transported from Famagosta on Cyprus to Alexandria.[22]

By the time the Ottomans gained control of Anatolia in the fifteenth century, Venetian merchants were regularly exploiting the Oriental demand for copper with high-volume exports east through Alexandria. Venetian merchants based their trade on imports of German copper which were re-exported east to exchange for grain, silk, spices, and other commodities. The Germans often exchanged their copper for silk in Venice and, in the fifteenth cen-

tury, much of this copper was, in turn, channeled through Alexandria.[23] Even as middlemen, the Venetians could count on profit
from copper transactions in Egypt. But along the east-west trading
axis, copper mines were to be found much closer to the Egyptian
markets than Germany.[24] The rich copper mines of Anatolia were a
source for copper supplies which the Venetian merchants could not
have failed to notice.

The chronicler Kritovoulos mentions the Anatolian copper
mines in the time of Sultan Mehmed II, who conquered Constantinople in 1453, describing the Black Sea port of Sinop as follows:

> . . . a coast town, the best and richest of those on the Euxine
> Sea. It ruled over an immense countryside and was already a com-
> mon emporium for the whole region as well as for no small part of
> lower Asia. It gets the use of many products of the seasons from
> land and sea. . . . The greatest of these is copper, which is abun-
> dantly mined here, and is distributed everywhere in Asia and Eu-
> rope, and brings in large incomes in gold and silver for the inhabit-
> ants.[25]

The Genoese were exporting this copper from Sinop as early as the
later part of the fourteenth century.[26] Inebolu was also a point of
departure for copper shipments into the Black Sea.[27] The Conqueror thus inherited not only the mines near the Black Sea coast
but the trading networks which provided options for the profitable
export of copper.

These options for export, along with Ottoman domestic needs,
prompted Mehmed II's successors to implement stringent controls
over the mining and distribution of copper. High demand, however,
as in the case of the grain trade, insured that some Ottoman copper
found its way into external markets and sometimes the sultan
himself was responsible for these exports. Bayezid made use of
these resources to ship copper to Alexandria early in the sixteenth
century, lured, as the Venetian *bailo* commented, by the opportunity to "become a merchant" and secure substantial profits.[28]
"Anatolia has perfect mines of pure copper," Bernardo Navagero,
the Venetian representative at the Porte, noted with unabashed
admiration in 1553, ". . . and it is easily transported out via the
Black Sea."[29] At the end of the sixteenth century, copper continued
to be a major commodity in the Venetian shipload registers, and at
least some of this copper was shipped from Istanbul.[30] For example,
Venetian registers for 1599 include a bark with over 4,000 livres of
copper destined for Fortore; a galion which foundered with 5,923

Plate 6: Two *Kayık* and sailing boats in front of a town. Hafiz, *Divan*, 1538. Source: British Library, Or 13324, f. 144 verso. Courtesy of the British Library Board.

pieces of copper coming from Rhodes and Istanbul; and a nave with 18 sacks of copper captured enroute to Istanbul. *Mühimme* (important affairs) documents, from late in the reign of Süleiman, reveal both Ottoman controls on the mining and distribution of copper and information that copper was shipped overland into Syria. Whether this copper was intended for re-export for the eastern trade or was designed to meet local coinage, vessel, and founding needs is unclear. What is apparent, is that the Ottomans continued to participate in the trade of Anatolian copper established under their predecessors, overland through Anatolia and by water, via the Black and Mediterranean seas. Widespread demand for copper ensured that export remained an option for augmenting the Ottoman treasury and that regulation of the copper supply could inflict hardship. The sultan, for example, attempted to inflict such hardship on the Safavids in the 1560s by preventing strategic goods, among them copper, from reaching Iran.[31]

Copper was a strategic material because it was used for cannon founding.[32] Control of the resources for founding, both founders and copper mines, as demonstrated earlier, was one root cause for the success of Ottoman expansion eastwards. Copper facilitated Mamluk military subordination to the Ottomans; and Venetian access to gun founders and to copper resources was an important rationale for Shah Ismail's attempts to conclude an alliance with Venice. Just how crucial was the demand for copper is illustrated by the resolution of conflicting demands when supplies were limited. If copper were needed for coinage the cauldron makers did without.[33] If copper were needed for guns? In 1463 Venice withdrew copper coinage from circulation for recasting into cannon.[34]

Thus, guns and money helped fuel the demand for copper that was used for cannon founding and coinage as well as for cookware, jewelry, vessels, utensils, and decorative items.[35] Venice produced a variety of coins of silver/copper alloys, and copper coins, as in the Ottoman state, were valued much higher than their weight in metal would suggest.[36] Revenues from the control of copper coinage were already the subject of tax farms in the sixteenth-century Ottoman Empire, and, after the conquest of Syria, the copper coin *mukataa* in Aleppo, like the silk scale *mukataa*, was a sought after tax farm.[37] Yet, even in the Ottoman state, where rich silver and copper mines gave the sultans great power as trading partners, copper specie was periodically in short supply. Shortages, and hence demand for copper coinage traced through the history of the Ottoman Levant all the way to the twentieth century. An imperial ferman to the Bursa *kadi*, for example, mentions shortfalls in the distribution of copper for coins in 1595 and 1598 which in turn created hardship for the populace, dependent upon small coins for bread and other small day-to-day purchases. As late as 1876, when Sultan Abd ül-Hamid called for the withdrawal of copper coinage in common use, towns counterstamped coins to avoid the hardship that taking them out of circulation caused.[38] The proliferation of local copper coinage and the common shortfall of coins in circulation to supply local needs thus links the early modern state in the nineteenth century to that in the sixteenth. Multiple local coinages in India created the same type of demand on the subcontinent as was found in the Levant—alleviated there, however, by imports rather than by distributions from local mines.[39]

Duarte Barbosa, the Portuguese agent and chronicler, noted such imports early in the sixteenth century, discussing the large quantities of copper brought to Chaul in India:

> . . . here they sell a quintal of copper for 20 cruzados and upwards. It is used in the interior and in the kingdom of Gujarat. They coin it into money; and make thereof also cauldrons for boiling rice. The Portuguese bring copper here, as well as much more which comes from Mecca.[40]

Of course the copper was not from Mecca, but rather channeled through the Red Sea via Egypt and points west. Copper coinage came into India from the east as well, smuggled out of China in the thirteenth century, for example, for use in the spice trade.[41] The Indian demand for copper in this period was essentially insatiable, ensuring that copper—as much as Ottoman and Italian merchants could bring—would find a willing market in Alexandria and points east.

The significance of copper in the east-west trade was not lost on observers in the early sixteenth century. Describing Jidda in the reign of Selim I, Barbosa mentioned spices first as the major incoming commodity and copper first among the exports east:

> whither every year ships from India were accustomed to go with spices and drugs and thence went back to Calicut with much copper, quicksilver, verdegris, saffron, rosewater, scarlet cloth, silks, camlets, taffetas and divers other goods which are sent to India, also with much gold and silver.[42]

At Hormuz, Barbosa noted the great quantities of copper arriving on ships from Aden as well as the great quantities of silk arriving for re-export from the lands of Shah Ismail.[43] From Hormuz the copper was shipped on to Cambay and to other Indian ports. Some, however, remained in the Yemen where, as in India, it was used to mint coins.[44] The African coasts, too, participated in the consumption that drew western copper like a magnet through the Red Sea and beyond. When the Portuguese conquered Mombasa, on the East African coast, they found a "great store of copper" among the booty taken there.[45]

The Portuguese were able to seize the Mombasan king's hoard of copper, but they were not able to staunch or capture the flow of copper to Indian shores. Although copper, according to one source, was "worth its weight in gold in India" in 1513 because of the Portuguese blockade on the Red Sea, the following year it was "extremely cheap and plentiful in Diu, many ships having recently arrived from the Red Sea laden with copper."[46] This continuity in copper trade illustrates the limitations of conquest. The establishment of Portuguese dominance in the Indian Ocean was illusory, circumscribed by the number of Portuguese ships and by the number of instances in which Portuguese ships and permits were eluded. Demand for copper, as with that for Iranian silk during the Ottoman-Safavid conflict, ensured that the disruptions of war would be only temporary. Portuguese cannon could not cover all the sea lanes at once, nor all the landing places. So, regulation of the Red Sea to Indian Ocean trade depended upon the timing of enforcement patrols by Portuguese vessels. Even when enforcement of shipping controls was successful, the profits might be lost, as illustrated in 1531 when a captain from Diu, enroute back to India, scuttled his ship, laden with copper and lead, near the Yemeni port of al-Shihr, rather than allow the Portuguese to seize its contents.[47]

Copper provided a currency as common as silver to pay for Venetian or Ottoman pepper purchases in Egypt. Like silk, it provided a link between the Levantine and Indian Ocean zones of the Asian trade: brought to Egypt on the *muda*, shipped overland to Suez, and thence to India. Where the Venetian *muda* has long been associated with the spice trade, it must come to be associated with the copper, silk, and grain trades as well. This association is illustrated by the conduct of the Venetian *muda* in the period during which the Ottoman state extended its control over Egypt, Syria, and the Hijaz.

The *Muda* as Case Study, 1501–1516

The *muda* was a characteristic trading formation of the late medieval Levantine economy: a convoy of state controlled and taxed galleys leased to private individuals or partnerships. It represents the interrelated nature of state and private commercial venture whereby state policy negotiated for the benefit of individual merchants (who in turn constituted the state) and state navies provided security for private commerce in return for a share of the profits. The term *muda* was used for the Venetian state sponsored and regulated galley convoys and for the actual loading periods of these convoys. The primary object of the *muda* was the acquisition of Indian spices (and silk loads) from the Mamluk middlemen for resale across Europe. Considerable scholarship has been devoted to the Mamluk spice trade by historians like Lane, Ashtor, and Godhino.[48] The Ottomans, however, have tended to figure in this paradigm only as the military power which conquered the Mamluk territories just as these territories were losing their position of prominence in the east-west trade. The spice trade was significant historically for its relatively high margin of profit. Even before the Ottomans usurped the Mamluk position as middleman, Ottoman merchants competed for a share in these profits and Ottoman state policy governed the direction the transformation of the Levantine spice trade would take. Conversely, Venetian merchants strove to maintain their position in the face of competition and Venetian diplomacy was geared toward the preservation of its merchant communities and of state profits from the Egyptian and Syrian trade entrepôts, regardless of which Muslim power dominated these outlets. It is within this context of commercial interest that the diplomatic initiatives, presented earlier, evolved.

In the period under study, Venice tended to conduct one *muda* of three galleys in Alexandria and one *muda* of two galleys in Beirut annually, although in the past the *muda* sometimes had been conducted twice a year to those ports.[49] Sailing times varied, as will be discussed below. The preferred loading period, however, was in autumn with ships leaving Venice in August or September. Fleets frequently missed the departure deadlines and were launched in late autumn to load in December or January, or in winter to load in February or March.[50] The terms of the *muda*, or loading period, were agreed upon by the Venetian and Mamluk states. But in practice the details frequently were negotiated by the Venetian galley captains and consuls with the local Mamluk customs officials and city governors of Beirut and Alexandria. Regular trade from Venice to Istanbul was carried on during this period as well but not organized at the same level as were the *mudas*.

Externally, there can be no doubt that the Portuguese attempts to monopolize the Indian Ocean spice trade had an effect on the availability of spices for the *mudas*. Within the eastern Mediterranean, however, commercial policy and the conduct of the trade itself were affected by a number of variables, independent of Portuguese influence. These variables were: the availability of security for the vessels at sea, the availability of security for merchants and their goods in port, weather, plague/sickness, war, banditry, competition, timing, provisioning, and the desire to preserve established trading patterns and modalities. The following is an attempt to present the eastern Mediterranean trade in terms of these variables and in the context of broad scale commercial policy not limited to the spice trade.

In March of 1501, at the height of the Ottoman-Venetian war, the Venetian galleys were at Beirut and Alexandria loading spices. The Alexandria galleys loaded 2,570 colli or loads of spices; and the Beirut galleys 3,200 loads.[51] The captain general of the Venetian armada, overall commander of the fleet, fearful of an Ottoman attack, sent an escort of five to eight light galleys to accompany the Beirut galley convoy to Candia, where it stopped to get bread. Shortly afterward the convoy's captain, Marin da Molin, sailed by Zonchio ignoring the plight of the city, under siege by the Ottoman naval commander, Kemal Reis. For this act, da Molin was later accused of cowardice. But he faced the dilemma posed by the dual nature of Levantine ships as primarily transport and, only secondarily, fighting vessels. By definition, the task of the *muda* was to deliver its merchandise safely to Venice. Da Molin's decision not to risk his sailors and cargo to defend his countrymen against a superior force was perhaps ill-advised. Yet it is a reflection of the strong motivation to preserve commercial activity, regardless of political conflict. This held true for mercantile endeavors in the Ottoman territories as well. For example, while the war in the Aegean raged, European merchants imprisoned in an Ottoman fortress near Istanbul were freed after paying a 10,000 ducat fine. The sultan then issued them a safe-conduct, allowing them to come and go with their merchandise without impediment.[52] This favor served two purposes as far as the Ottoman state was concerned: an infusion for the treasury and the preservation of trading apparati with a view toward the conclusion of hostilities.

The following year, in 1502, as the war activity wound down, the primacy of commercial continuity is illustrated by negotiations over the conduct of the *muda*. The Venetian galleys again required an escort. It was not the Ottoman navy, however, but Mamluk exactions which interfered with the conduct of the trade. The Mamluk sultan, Qānsūh al-Ghūrī, attempted both to delay the loading period and to increase the fixed price per load. The galley captain, Marco Venier, agreed after much negotiation, saying that his overwhelming desire was to avoid disrupting the *muda*. The Mamluk sultan, noted the Venetian vice-consul Venier, was very anxious to obtain Venetian silver. Hence, he could not afford to press his demands in such a fashion as to discourage the *muda* altogether. Nor were these exactions directed exclusively at Venice. Mamluk Muslim subjects were also the target of increased duties on trade. Despite the high prices, Venice, because of its favored status in Alexandria, was given precedence in loading over a French vessel, which was already in port when the Venetians arrived.[53] Like the Venetians, other traders continued to come to Alexandria, and to make a profit. Venier reported that Turkish ships arrived and departed daily, traveling between Alexandria, the Anatolian coast, and Istanbul. Many of these ships were engaged in commodities trading. The luxury trade in spices and other eastern goods, however, attracted Ottoman subject merchants as well as representatives of the Ottoman state.

By early autumn of 1502, reports from Alexandria indicated that an excellent *muda* was in the offing. Alvise Arimondo, the Venetian consul, reported that 3,000 *schibe* of spices had arrived in Tor on the Red Sea, followed by 1,000 *schiboti* and that thirteen ships were at Jidda with more spices.[54] An enormous nave of 3,000 *botte* was in the Red Sea with 7,000 *schibe* more. These loads were expected in Cairo by mid-December or January, with approximately one third of the loads from Tor destined for Damascus. Spices were apparently plentiful. The Ottoman ambassador in Cairo in December 1502 obtained an undisclosed quantity of spices from the Mamluk sultan.[55] This was an instance of two states, each of which had monopolies on certain products deemed essential or desirable by the other, dealing directly rather than operating through middlemen. Because the Ottoman state, at that time, had greater political leverage than did Venice over the Mamluk sovereign, the Ottoman ambassador paid a lower price for his pepper.

Despite the availability of spices and the relatively low open market prices, Venetian interests were again partially frustrated by Qānsūh al-Ghūrī's manipulation of the trade. This took two forms. First, Qānsūh had demanded that Venice send an ambassador who would confirm the trade agreements. Venice had been remiss in expediting the emissary's voyage, and, in March of 1503, he was still at Candia. This delay may have been influenced by Venice's desire to await the settlement of the peace treaty, signed that very month by the *doge*, with the Ottomans before conducting further negotiations with the Mamluks. For the Mamluk sultan, this demand for an ambassador from Venice was a means of asserting his authority and also an opportunity to take advantage of other trade opportunities while keeping the Venetian convoy as a captive buyer. He detained the galleys until the envoy arrived. Then, while negotiations were still in progress, Qānsūh authorized the sale of pepper. Genoese ships, which had been waiting in the harbor for twenty days, took advantage of this authorization, at Venice's expense.[56] Qānsūh, then, forced the captain of the Venetian galleys to purchase 300 sporta of pepper at 105 ducats fixed price each. This was 90 sporta over the annual fixed price load which Venice, in return for its privileged position, was required to purchase from the Mamluk sultan at above market price. By the time the galleys returned to Venice in late summer 1503 with 1,100 loads of spices, the *muda* had suffered losses both in market timing and in exchange value, having paid well over market price for almost one third of its cargo.[57]

    The Beirut galleys had returned considerably earlier, in late spring, with a cargo of 350–400 loads of spices, and 200 loads of silk, as well as quantities of Syrian grain.[58] Although it was impractical to ship grain long distances overland, the silk trade through Syria had options in terms of route. Aleppo and Damascus were transit points at which the silk could be sold to European merchants such as those supplying the Venetian *muda*, or sold to Ottoman merchants, for example, and transported overland through Anatolia. Price, customs, and volume would determine, in part, who won out in this competition at selected entrepôts. The option to choose an alternate trade route and pay the lowest customs and shipping tolls was also a factor in the competition for profits. Until the Ottoman conquest of Syria in 1516, Italian merchants could skip the Ottoman middleman by buying their silk or spice loads in Syria. After the Ottomans gained control of all the Levantine outlets, Venetian customs payments invariably contributed to Ottoman coffers.[59]

    While spices had been plentiful in Alexandria, they had not been so in Beirut, but the Beirut *muda*, at least, had managed to maintain some semblance of a time schedule. Thus, both supply and timing problems exacerbated by local officials in Damascus and by the Mamluk sultan in Alexandria, combined to thwart the potential of the Venetian *muda* in the two years (1502–1503) before the effects of the Portuguese navigations were felt in Cairo. If the advance reports of incoming loads were correct, then Venice accounted for only a fraction of the actual total purchases of spices unloaded at the Red Sea ports. Competition from Ottomans, North Africans, and Genoese provided the Mamluks with alternate customers, while they still maintained their income from the Venetian traders.

Thus, in the case of this particular *muda*, the Venetians were competing with the Ottoman state, with the Genoese and with Tunisian merchants. Competition gave force to the attempts by the Mamluk sultan to alter the existing trade agreements with Venice. The course of this *muda* indicates as well that the political relations of the competing states were inextricably linked to decision-making regarding the manipulation and sale of trade goods. The nature of the evidence, of course, is fragmentary. It suggests, however, the probability that such instances of competition were common rather than exceptional.

After 1503, Portuguese intervention at the source of the spice supply replaced Ottoman intervention in the Mediterranean as a major concern of Venice. Mamluk exactions and European competition, though, remained important factors in the spice trade. Neither the news of the Portuguese voyages to India, nor the Mamluk levies at Alexandria prevented Venice from sending a new *muda* at the end of 1503. In October, the Senate debated whether to hold the Alexandria galleys at Corfu to avoid buying high and selling low, but this measure was not taken.[60] When the galley convoys finally reached Beirut and Alexandria in November, neither had large quantities of spices for the Venetian merchants. The consul in Damascus wrote that the major portion of the spices had been sent overland through Anatolia, rather than to Beirut on the coast. This is an indication that merchants were purchasing spices at Tor and Jidda and shipping them overland to Bursa and Istanbul, for sale to the Porte and to European merchants. This apparent diversion of spices through Ottoman territory may reflect increased corsair activity along the sea routes as well as a lack of confidence in the timely arrival of the *muda*, although part of this spice trade routinely went overland.[61]

The problems encountered by the *muda* at this point seem to have been a question of supply, timing, and Mamluk recalcitrance, rather than of shifting trade patterns. It remains to be documented whether or not the volume of trade routed overland through Anatolia increased markedly during this time or whether routing vacillated from year to year depending on the competition.[62] Venetian merchants, for example, may have been willing to pay above market price, to guarantee loads, and still make a profit. The sellers in Syria, however, could not count upon the arrival of their buyers

because of the fluctuations in the timing of the *muda*. That being
the case, depending on the arrival time and volume of the caravan
trade, local merchants may have opted to ship overland immediately rather than risking an extended delay in hopes of securing
a higher price. The effects of such lack of coincidence were buffered
by the existence of resident agents (representing the interests of
European investors in the Syrian cities), who could compete for the
caravan merchandise as it came in. The competition could be stiff.
As one Venetian merchant in Damascus noted: "We willingly pluck
out both our own eyes in order to pluck out one of the competition's."[63] These agents also still labored under the same difficulties
as did the galleys competing for spice loads in the port of Alexandria. Their transactions, ultimately, were subject to the whims
and abuses of Mamluk officials.

The details of negotiations in Alexandria in the winter of 1503
help pinpoint the logistical problems faced by the Venetian galley
captains. The Mamluk customs officer was absent from the city
when the galleys arrived and the loading had to await his arrival.
Worse still, the Mamluk governor chanced to be ill, and died in the
midst of the negotiations. Then loading had to await the confirmation of his successor.[64] The Venetian vice-consul reported that communication back and forth to Cairo took eight to ten days each
time confirmation of purchase agreements was required. Further,
Qānsūh al-Ghūrī demanded a reckoning of the galleys' cargoes, saying that the Venetian merchandise was insufficient to satisfy two
Muslim merchants, and intimating that the Venetians' trade was not
worth his trouble. The vice-consul responded that the *muda* was dependent upon good treatment, placing the onus on the Mamluk sultan for the conduct and continuity of a profitable exchange.

The sultan's bargaining position was that the existence of alternate buyers allowed him leeway in setting terms. The Venetian
position was that investors in the trade for the sultan's goods had
other options and their continued investment was dependent upon
Mamluk goodwill, guaranteed prices, and freedom from officials'
abuses. Conditions in the Syrian and Egyptian commercial centers
at the end of the Mamluk period demonstrate why one of these
alternative options, for Venetian merchants, was to trade through
Ottoman controlled outlets. Again, the higher price had to be
weighed against the possibilities of long delays, no security, and
unanticipated exactions. In fact, Qānsūh's intervention in the trade
was limited primarily to delaying tactics. He was operating from a
position of military weakness vis-à-vis the Ottomans. Once the
peace treaty between the Venetian *doge* and Bayezid was signed in

1503, the Mamluk sultan found himself unable to take too cavalier a stance with Venice.[65] Mamluk vulnerability to the rapidly expanding Ottoman navy was all too apparent, and the temporary cessation of hostilities on the western front allowed the Ottomans to turn their attention eastwards to the Holy Cities and to the customs depots for the eastern trade.

Qānsūh was caught between diplomatic and economic imperatives. He had to balance cash requirements fed by inflated spice prices, against the possibility of a suspended *muda*. Between 1503 and 1516 the need to preserve commerce on both sides ensured that the *muda* was conducted more often than not. But the dynamics of the Venetian-Mamluk trading relationship gradually changed after 1503, reflecting the ascendant Ottoman position in the eastern Mediterranean. Ottoman military energy was no longer focused in the Aegean. This meant that the Ottoman navy could be directed, with impunity, against Alexandria. For Qānsūh al-Ghūrī, the Ottoman and then the Portuguese naval threats enhanced the value of Venice, a naval power, as an ally. Unlike the relationship between the Ottoman state and Venice, where the Signoria's subordinate position was quite clear after the humiliating treaty of 1503, the relationship between Venice and the Mamluk state was characterized by a more equivalent symbiosis. For the Mamluks, Venice was not only a source of silver but also potentially an alternative source for artillery. The Mamluks were dependent on Ottoman artillery resources, especially Kastamonu copper for founding.[66] Countering the weight of Venetian goodwill and potential aid, was the Mamluk sultan's need to preserve his authority. With intermittent revolts in Syria and Arabia, and chronic sedition among the Cairene mamluks, Qānsūh could not afford to let the Europeans dictate commercial terms. The mechanics of the *muda* negotiations, year by year, were dependent on a certain sense of reciprocity. In 1503, Venice expected its share from the Mamluks in the forms of spices and military action against the Portuguese. As the decade progressed, the security provided for Venetian trade by Bayezid in Istanbul, and by the Ottoman fleet in the Aegean, became a more successful form of reciprocity than that provided by the Mamluk sultan in Cairo and by the Mamluk fleet in the Indian Ocean.[67]

One indication of the the Ottoman-Venetian rapprochement, after the peace treaty was signed, was the loosening of restrictions in Venice on Ottoman merchants. In February 1504, a complaint was brought before the Senate concerning Ottoman subject merchants, Maronites and Jews, who had arrived with the galleys returning from Alexandria. In this case, the plaintiff protested that it was illegal for these merchants to unload their wares, and had been so traditionally. While the Senate debated the matter, the merchandise was sequestered. When a vote was taken, however, the sultan's subjects were granted permission to trade.[68]

While these Ottoman merchants were given freedom to trade, Venetian investors were still awaiting the return of the Beirut *muda* fleet, which had departed Venice in 1503. A combination of adverse conditions limited the success of this venture. Initially the convoy had been delayed in the Adriatic by bad weather. Then it was delayed for a month at Tripoli by adverse weather conditions and by the death of its captain, Piero Nadel. By the time the galleys arrived at Beirut in December, they had missed the scheduled loading period. Because the merchants trading spices in Syrian entrepôts needed some assurance that the Venetian buyers were, in fact, coming, timing was important for the purchase, as for the eventual sale, of the spices. With no assurance of buyers with the requisite goods at Beirut, the spices could be shipped overland from Damascus to Anatolia.[69] At Beirut and Tripoli combined, the Venetian captain found only 120 loads of spices. At Damascus, the Venetian merchants secured hardly any of the 500 loads on the market in late autumn.[70] When the Beirut galleys finally returned, there was plague on board; and over forty crewmen died. The galleys were quarantined for over a month before being allowed to discharge their cargo at Venice.[71] Thus, the venture of the Beirut galleys could be, and was, disrupted at various stages of the voyage. Delays of even a few months could totally alter the year's merchandise and credit cycles.

The disruption in the timing of the *mudas* was such in 1503–1504 that the Venetian Senate took extra precautions to ensure the timely departure of the *muda* the following year. In March 1504, the Senate determined that the Beirut galleys should leave by August 15 in order to conduct the loading for all of October. Despite news from Alexandria that Qānsūh had sold spices to Muslim merchants at high prices, quantities at Alexandria were promising in September. Three Muslim merchants had purchased 36,000 ducats worth of spices in July, but the Venetian *luogotenente* at Cyprus reported that there were still enough spices for four shiploads at Alexandria. Venetian agents had contracted for these spices in exchange for a good quantity of copper.[72] This transaction illustrates the significance of copper as a commodity, beneficial to Ottomans and Venetians alike, in the competition for spice loads in the Mamluk territories. The Ottomans could utilize their own copper resources, shipped from the Black Sea to the Mediterranean.

The Venetians were middlemen, primarily using copper mined in Germany.[73]

Although the amounts and prices of Venetian spice purchases in Alexandria were governed by treaty, the form of payment was not fixed. The standard Venetian-Mamluk agreement for the *muda* stipulated that Venice purchase 210 sporta of pepper at eighty ducats (or more) fixed price, regardless of market price. In the negotiations of Ibn Taghribirdī, the Mamluk ambassador to Venice in 1507, two of the articles demanded by Venice were that the purchase of no more than 210 sporta at eighty ducats be required and that the sultan must accept copper in payment of the Venetian debt on behalf of all creditors, and at higher than market value.[74] This stipulation was partly in response to abuses which characterized the 1504 *muda* during which the Mamluk customs official in charge of loading forced the merchants into an agreement to exchange sixteen kantars of copper for each sporta of pepper. Since the market price of copper was 12 ducats per kantar, the pepper cost the merchants 192 ducats per sporta. Having acceded to this forced exchange, the merchants loaded the pepper.[75] The *muda* was then forced, under the threat of imprisonment of the merchants, to accept an additional 250 sporta at the inflated price. Cargo on the already loaded ships had to be rearranged to accommodate this additional load. The purchase price was not paid in full at the time of loading. Rather the Venetian merchants were indebted to the sultan for the payment of the copper within a fixed period of time. Qānsūh attempted to shorten the repayment period to six months, but through negotiation Venice avoided this demand.[76]

The Mamluk sultan's attempts to raise cash are illustrated not only by these exactions but also by his demand that Venice borrow money from local usurers in order to pay cash rather than taking the pepper on account. The difficulties experienced during this particular *muda* point up certain potential advantages Ottoman merchants in Alexandria had over Venetian merchants in the competition for eastern goods. Demand for Anatolian commodities, like lumber and copper, in Egypt gave Ottoman merchants an alternative to cash exchange; Venice had to import the copper paid for spices and transport it further distances. In addition to the customs advantages Muslim merchants routinely obtained over "franks," spice customers like the Ottoman ambassador could even dispense with the tedious official negotiations required from the Venetian captains in the Egyptian markets.[77] Nor did Qānsūh have the political leverage vis-à-vis the Ottomans to exact inflated prices or inflict unreasonable penalties. The increasing dependence of the Mamluk sovereign on Ottoman naval aid, as the decade progressed, would also shield Ottoman merchants from the effects of Qānsūh's cash flow dilemmas.

Venice's position was not so secure and, ultimately, the struggle over payments for the 1504–1505 Alexandria *muda* culminated in violence. Venice's consul in Alexandria, along with some merchants, was imprisoned and the Venetian galleys were instructed not to leave the harbor without license to sail. Qānsūh ordered that the captain of the *muda* turn over his sails, to insure against his departure. If he refused, the governor of Alexandria was instructed to bombard the Venetian ships with his shore batteries. The captain did indeed refuse to surrender his sails, despite the jeopardy in which this act placed the imprisoned consul and merchants. On March 15, 1505, under fire, he sailed out of the harbor.[78]

This incident resulted in the suspension of the *muda* for one year.[79] Although surpassed in duration by reprisals taken later, after the 1510 Rhodian attack on the Mamluk fleet at Ayas, the Mamluk actions during the 1504–1505 *muda* were unsurpassed in degree of severity. This can be attributed to the shock administered that year to the Mamluk government by the combined effects of the Portuguese navigations and of provincial revolts. Revolts in Arabia were such that the *hajj* had to be suspended in 1505, a severe blow to Qānsūh al-Ghūrī's prestige.[80] The Mamluk failure to protect the pilgrimage routes was emphasized by the Ottomans in order to bolster their own claims to hegemony in the Islamic world. The relative weight of the revolts in determining reprisals taken against Venetian merchants can be gauged by the fact that exactions were greater in 1504–1505 than in 1510–1511. This was despite the fact that the effects of the Portuguese navigations were only beginning to be felt in 1504, whereas they peaked in 1509 with the destruction of the Mamluk fleet and the Portuguese blockade of the Red Sea.[81]

The reputation of the Mamluk state at this time was that of a state militarily incapable of controlling its own subordinates and incapable of rebuffing seaborne aggressors. Mamluk naval impotence compared unfavorably to Ottoman naval vigilance. Once past the customs stations and loading docks, merchants shipping in Ottoman waters were safer than those shipping in Mamluk waters because of Bayezid's active campaign against corsairs. The contrast was not lost on the Venetian captains. For example, the *muda* of 1507 was plagued by the activities of a corsair named Piero Navarro. News of his presence nearby delayed the convoy, enroute to Alexandria in November, at Candia. The Beirut convoy was also forced to fight off an attack by Navarro later that winter.[82] These and similar corsair activities prompted the launching of an Otto- man fleet to combat the pirates even though the season, December, was not ordinarily a launching period.[83] The Alexandria convoy eventually returned with a rich cargo. It had, however, been de- layed at Candia all winter awaiting the outcome of negotiations between the Mamluk sultan and the Alexandrian consul over safe- conduct and trading terms.[84] This scenario illustrated the coinci- dence of Ottoman and Venetian trading interests as contrasted to the difficulties suffered by Venice as a result of the Mamluk inabil- ity to continue to balance cash needs against the desire to main- tain an orderly *muda.*

Between 1505 and 1507, when Venice and the Mamluk state renewed the fragile commercial agreement between them, the Ot- toman sultan had impressed Venice with his efforts to protect mer- chant shipping. Not only had Rhodes been chastised for its support of raiding activities, but Ottoman cruising fleets provided insur- ance against attacks on Venetian as well as Turkish vessels in the Aegean.[85] In a report dated January 18, 1507, Bembo, the Venetian *bailo* in Istanbul, commented upon the good relations desired by the Ottoman sultan and on the friendly behavior accorded the proveditor general of the armada by the Ottoman naval captain Kemal Reis. Venice's preoccupation with corsair activities is in- dicated by the Senate's order, issued in January 1507, to arm thirteen additional galleys in order to increase the fleet cruising strength from seven galleys to twenty.[86] At this time, there were 120 Ottoman galleys and fustas at Gallipoli alone. When compared to Venice's projected fleet strength of twenty galleys for the year, it is evident why the Ottoman navy represented the logical solution to the problem of defense for commercial shipping in the Aegean and eastern Mediterranean. Hence, although Ottoman and Vene- tian merchants might be competing for goods and prices at the cus- toms stations in Alexandria and on the overland routes through Syria, once vessels put to sea Ottoman and Venetian efforts com- bined to insure that the goods reached port. This was particularly important for the continuation of the commodities trade.

In May of 1506, the Venetian Senate voted to send three gal- leys to Beirut. It was noted in the proceedings that the decision was made despite the abuses in Alexandria because there were good quantities of spices in Damascus.[87] The potential profit factor here outweighed the calculated risk of Mamluk government exactions—by now Venice was familiar with both. Thus, spurred by the Venetian consul in Damascus's promise that the galleys would have a cargo of 2,000 colli of spices and 300 colli of silk, the Beirut *muda* sailed in the fall.[88] Risk was calculated not only on the basis of avoiding problems with officials but also on the basis of projected success in bargaining for caravan loads which had not yet arrived. The consul in Damascus noted that Venetian merchants had contracted for one-half of the cargo of a silk caravan from Aleppo and hoped to obtain the other half as well. Resident agents in the major entrepôts cultivated their contacts so that such bargaining could proceed year-round. Even when the *muda* was suspended in 1505, the Venetian merchant community had not remained idle, awaiting the outcome of negotiations. The Mamluk sultan had been unable to enforce his demand in 1505 that the Venetian consul and merchants in Damascus come to Cairo. There the trade for Iranian silk continued with the Venetian merchants competing with merchants who shipped overland to Bursa. Damascus based merchants also traded securely in Iran.[89] Further, individual Venetian merchants continued to trade with Egypt in 1506 even though the Alexandrian *muda* did not resume until 1507.[90]

From the time the Alexandria *muda* sailed in 1507 until 1510, Mamluk-Venetian relations remained on a fairly even keel. Then commercial transactions were again seriously disrupted as a result both of Venice's negotiations with Ismail Safavi in Iran and of the Rhodian attack on the Mamluk fleet loading timber at Ayas. In the intervening years, Venice was engaged in the struggle on the Italian mainland with the League of Cambrai. The Mamluks, like the Ottomans, were preoccupied with Ismail's 1507 invasion of eastern Anatolia, 1508 conquest of Baghdad, and 1510 defeat of Shaibānī Khān.[91] The fiscal demands of military contestation for Venice, and of defense preparations for the Mamluks, helped ensure the relatively tranquil conduct of the *muda* between 1507 and 1510.

Ottoman commercial interests were affected just as were those of Venice by the threat of Ismail rerouting the overland trade. Certainly the military power and political expedients of these two states differed, but the response of the Porte to the Safavids was moderated by concern for the investments of resident Ottoman merchants in the eastern Anatolian trade and by the ambitions of the palace to control the Indian Ocean trade. Venice, meanwhile, hoped to benefit from Ismail's initiatives without sacrificing commercial advantage in Egypt and Syria. Even in the period between 1511 and 1513, when Venetian-Mamluk relations were again disrupted by Venice's negotiations with the Safavids, the *muda* was not again suspended. This belies the supposition that the *mudas* had become unprofitable, because Venetian commerce in the Mamluk territories operated on the basis of both continuity and profit. Differences brought on by external threats like Ismail and by the Mamluk-Venetian struggle to dictate commercial terms were resolved, at least temporarily, in favor of this profit motive.

Despite the military threat generated by Ismail's rise to power, the trade in the Mamluk territories continued as it did on the eastern Ottoman frontiers. Although the Mamluks were aware that Ismail had sent letters to Venice suggesting a joint land and sea attack on Egypt, the Mamluk sultan allowed the Venetian galleys to return to his harbors.[92] In February and March of 1512, the convoys returned to Venice with 1,600 colli of spices and 350 colli of silk from Beirut and 1,044 colli of spices from Alexandria.[93] The implications of this continuation of the *muda* trade for Ottoman expansionist policy are evident. If the Ottomans annexed Egypt and Syria, they gained not only territory and prestige but also control of the customs revenues from the profitable trade through the Red Sea. This middle ground could then be used to extend Ottoman hegemony over the sources of production in the Indian Ocean region.

Two factors contributed to the unwillingness of Qānsūh to prolong the suspension of the Mamluk-Venetian commerce. One was the preoccupation of the sultan with the preparation of the Suez fleet to be used against the Portuguese. The other was the increasingly precarious military and fiscal position of the Mamluks. By the end of 1510, both a Safavid invasion from the northeast and a Portuguese invasion via the Red Sea from the southeast appeared distinctly within the realm of possibility. In sum, Qānsūh needed both friends and funds. Ottoman and Safavid ambassadors arriving in Cairo in 1511 were portents of the impending collapse of Mamluk hegemony. In February of 1511, the Ottoman ambassador arrived formally to announce the coming of an Ottoman aid fleet. Qānsūh had tacitly accepted a type of vassal status to Bayezid. In June, Ismail's ambassador arrived to announce the defeat of his Uzbeg rival, Shaibānī Khān, and to deliver some mocking verses to the Mamluk sultan.[94] Even the Grand Master in tiny Rhodes managed to challenge the Mamluk sutan with impunity. He sent Qānsūh a letter, saying that the Rhodian attack on the Ayas timber fleet was prompted by the threat of a Mamluk-Ottoman alliance. He warned of the possibility of a new crusade, although this threat represented more of rhetoric than of substance.[95] Mamluk sovereignty was thus compromised on all fronts. In view of this and of the humiliating destruction of the Mediterranean and Red Sea fleets, the Mamluks were wise to discourage hostilities with Venice. From Qānsūh's vantage point, it began to appear that the Ottomans would not have to trade for long as foreigners in the Mamluk domains. In fact, he had only to wait for an Ottoman change of venue.

Three events are of particular note in elucidating the conduct of trade and shipping in the final years of Mamluk rule and in illustrating the stages by which the Ottomans replaced the Mamluks as commercial and political lords of the eastern Levant. These events are: (a) the Portuguese conquest of Kamran Island in the Red Sea in 1513; (b) the Ottoman defeat of the Safavids at Çaldıran in 1514; and (c) the Ottoman campaign of 1516–1517 into Syria and Egypt. The effects of these events on shipping and trade policy shed light on the relative weight of different factors in the conduct of Levantine trade. Significant in this terminal period of the Mamluk regime is the extent to which Portuguese or Ottoman military and naval endeavors did not interfere with trade, rather than the extent to which they did.

Events in Cairo in 1513 reflected the intensity of the perceived threat of a Portuguese invasion of the Red Sea. Plague was raging in Cairo and the army was mutinous.[96] Yet a large expedition to Suez was organized to bring cannon to the fleet. Suspecting that the Portuguese might attack Suez, Qānsūh also sent a troop of mamluks to increase the guard at the arsenal there.[97] The Portuguese attack did materialize in the form of an assault on Kamran. This attack, however, did not cut off the spice trade through the Mamluk domains.[98] Quantities of spices were available in Cairo and were "reasonably" priced that summer of 1513. But the galleys had other problems, the last *muda* having been infected with plague, and many resident merchants having succumbed. In Damascus, the merchants had escaped the plague, by and large, and looked to a profitable trade with merchants from Mecca and Cairo.[99]

In Cairo, the news of the taking of Kamran and of an attack on Aden caused an uproar. The sultan prepared an expedition to Suez, which departed in March of 1514.[100] He feared, not only that the Portuguese might attack Suez, or capture Jidda, but also that a successful raid on Jidda might lead to the capture of Mecca itself. Such a defeat would make good the Safavid envoy's taunt in 1511 that Qānsūh was undeserving of the title of Protector of the Holy Cities. Shortly after Qānsūh returned from Suez, he was faced with a series of revolts in Cairo followed by the news that Selim, who had emerged victorious from the Ottoman succession struggle, was now marching to attack Ismail.[101] Soon, the Ottoman armies would defeat the Safavids on the broad, dreary plain of Çaldıran on the eastern Anatolian frontier. Selim's success (attributed to superior artillery) against Ismail, culminating in the sack of the Safavid capital Tabriz, left Qānsūh with an even more powerful enemy threatening to transgress his northern frontier. For the rest of the Mamluk period, Qānsūh's desperate efforts to maintain sufficient authority to defend his north and eastern frontiers prevented him from exercising any vigorous commercial sanctions against Venice and, by 1516, Venice was able to use the Ottoman expansion as leverage in its negotiations with the Mamluks for commercial privileges.[102]

While the Çaldıran expedition caused the Mamluks to fear that an invasion of Syria was imminent, it had little effect on the conduct of the *muda*. In June of 1514, Qānsūh wrote to Venice encouraging the merchants to come and trade under the old capitulatory terms. He promised security and good treatment if the Venetians adhered to the agreements. Qānsūh even threatened his own officials with punishment if the Venetian merchants were not well treated.[103] The Mamluk sultan was no longer in a position to dictate terms. The Beirut *muda* that year returned loaded with 2,010 colli of spices, more than in the previous years.[104] The silk loads from Iran, however, did not come that year because of the war.

Thus, Venice enjoyed a period of relative prosperity in the *muda* trade while the inevitability of the conquest of Cairo became apparent. This prosperity was not coincidental. It was conditioned by various facets of the assertion of Ottoman hegemony in the eastern Levant which either promoted or compromised Venice's competitive capabilities. These were: naval security provided for trade, the security of trade in Ottoman cities, Ottoman military and diplomatic pressure on the Mamluks, Ottoman commercial interests in the overland trade through Syria and in the sources of the trade in the Indian Ocean and, finally, the Ottoman usurpation of the prestige factor in the contest for Islamic world sovereignty. The years 1514–1516 saw a continuation of cordial relations between the Venetians and the Ottomans. Although the provisioning needs of the 1516 campaign against Syria and the long absence of Selim from the capital resulted in some temporary abuses (grain exactions and arbitrary treatment of merchants in Istanbul by Ottoman officials), in general the land campaigns had a marginal effect on the actual conduct of the eastern Mediterranean Venetian sea trade.[105] Venice had witnessed the advantages of Ottoman rule over

a period of years. Now that Ottoman naval development had insured the political and military success of the Ottoman expansion,
cautious foreign policy had insured that Venice remained in a position to benefit. Venetian merchants had still to compete with their
Ottoman counterparts in the ports and in the caravan route entrepôts, but the Ottomans now controlled both ends of the Red Sea-
Aegean axis. The rhythms of trade had not been broken, merely
altered to serve a new master.

After the conquest of Cairo, Sultan Selim pursued his aggressive naval policies, building a new fleet in the Red Sea and preparing for an assault on Rhodes. His death in 1520 left those tasks to
his son Süleiman. By 1525, the Ottoman naval commander, Selman Reis, was urging the sultan to challenge the Portuguese king
for the customs revenues of the Persian Gulf trade. He reported to
the grand vezir Ibrahim Pasha that the financial rewards of an
Ottoman attack on the Portuguese would be substantial: from Hormuz alone the Portuguese garnered 100,000 florins on the 10 percent customs duty for the fifty to sixty ships which stopped there
annually. Selman also had an eye for the customs possibilities of
exports like the red dye produced in the Yemen.[106] Süleiman did
challenge the Portuguese and continued the policy of aggression in
the Indian Ocean, even launching a fleet of fifty-four ships to lay
siege to Diu in 1538.[107] Still, the Ottoman capturing of the Levantine outlets of the eastern trade was never complemented by the
establishment of Ottoman hegemony over the Indian Ocean and
the spice-growing regions. Why the Ottomans did not, in the end,
succeed in dominating the Indian Ocean is a complicated question.[108]

Andrew Hess was the scholar who, in 1970, insisted that the
Ottomans in the early sixteenth century were a seaborne empire
rivaling the Portuguese:

> . . . the naval history of the powerful Ottoman Empire should
> have occupied a major position in the modern interpretations of
> sixteenth-century maritime history. Yet, with few exceptions, the
> histories dealing with the impact of Western naval power on the
> Muslim world contain a limited amount of information on the
> actions of a sixteenth-century state capable of defending itself
> against the West.[109]

Hess argued that Western historiography tended to be one-sided
and to inflate the impact of Western technology in the sixteenth
century. He cast the Ottomans in a dominant role as imperialists
and seafaring successors of the Byzantines. Still, he concluded that
the ambitions of the Ottoman and Portuguese empires were inher-

Plate 7: Sailors in a Storm. Anonymous, Wonders of Art and Nature.
Source: British Library, Harleian 5500, f. 53 recto.
Courtesy of the British Library Board.

ently different and, therefore, Ottoman accomplishments could not be measured using a standard of "Western objectives." The long range naval expansion of the Portuguese was a sign of "deep internal changes in Western society" while the Ottoman expansion "revitalized a traditional orthodox Muslim community through the creation of a seaborne empire that added to the glory of a great Islamic state."[110] For Hess, the clash of the Ottoman and Portuguese empires was a continuation of the old Muslim-Christian conflicts; the Ottoman investment of the Red Sea and Indian Ocean was essentially a defensive response, in the tradition of the *gazis* (warriors for the faith), aimed at protecting the Holy Cities. The difference between the two empires lay in the nature of their objectives. Where the Portuguese intended to monopolize the sea trade and gain naval supremacy on the open sea, the Ottomans sought to conquer territories and tax agricultural lands.[111]

While it is clear that the Ottomans failed in their bid to challenge the Portuguese in the Indian Ocean, the questions of competing seafaring technologies and of Ottoman commercial intent remain at issue. John Guilmartin has argued compellingly that neither ship type nor cannon technology were crucial in the Ottoman-Portuguese contest for naval supremacy in the sixteenth century.[112] While "Portugal and the Ottoman Empire led the world in cannon technology at the beginning of the sixteenth century," numbers and type of cannon, tactics, manpower, the availability of small arms, and the setting of fires were often the factors which determined outcome in sea battles.[113] Ottoman fleets could hold off Portuguese fleets, as is illustrated by the account of Sidi Ali Reis in 1554, and often naval encounters were indecisive.[114] No naval power could *control* the seas, not the Ottomans in the Mediterranean or the Portuguese in the Indian Ocean. If, then, control of the seas was a question of rhetoric rather than of physical presence, the differentiation of the Ottoman and Portuguese empires by economic objective becomes less evident. It is true that the Ottomans did not relinquish their territorial ambitions to pursue an all-out onslaught on the commercial revenues of the Indian Ocean trade. But this does not preclude an interest in commercial endeavor unattached to colonial conquest. The Ottomans, under Selim I, also failed to follow up the conquest of Tabriz in 1514 with a major investment of troops and an attempt to control the silk producing regions of Iran, turning instead to conquest of the Mamluk territories. In each instance, it was not a case of the lure of commercial *vs.* agricultural tax revenues, but a question of relative gain, distance, terrain, and ease of access. Title to the Holy Cities was a clear priority in terms of the legitimation of Ottoman sovereignty. But sovereignty was legitimized by commercial wealth as well as by religious position. At no time in the reigns of Selim or Süleiman did the Portuguese truly endanger Mecca. Had the Portuguese succeeded in taking Jidda in 1517, the Ottomans would have quickly taken it back. Thus, the Ottoman naval operations in the Indian Ocean and Persian Gulf after the conquest of Cairo were neither purely defensive nor purely a manifestation of *gazi* impulses. This is not to discount religion, Islam or Christianity, as a significant cultural force in the articulation of empire. It is rather to say that drawing the historiographic battle lines as religious boundaries obscures commercial and political motivation. While neither the Portuguese or Ottoman empires can be said to have revolutionized naval warfare in the early sixteenth century, both can be said to have been engaged in operating on a global commercial scale.

Under Selim there was every intention of extending Ottoman control over commerce to India; neither Hapsburg military power nor Spanish seapower ultimately prevented Ottoman expansion into the Indian Ocean. Rather, logistical problems of distance and failure to subjugate the Yemen, along with the internal dynamics of Süleiman's court and his focus on the western front, were major factors. Also, the fact that the Portuguese were not really successful in cutting off the trade through Egypt and Syria made a substantial commitment in the Indian Ocean less imperative.[115]

Prior to the reign of Süleiman, however, this outcome was not assured.[116] The Portuguese expected the Ottomans to attack their bases in the Indian Ocean and, once Cairo was in Ottoman hands, they had not long to wait before such an attempt was made. In fact, a letter written by Johan de Chamara from India only six months after the Ottoman capture of Cairo suggested that the only way to contain the Ottomans would be to stop their advance at the Red Sea. Chamara described a proposal by the Portuguese commander to mobilize a large fleet in India, take Jidda, and blockade the Red Sea before the Ottomans could advance their fleet into the Indian Ocean. He pointed out that the Ottomans should not be permitted to gain control of the sizable store of artillery at Jidda and that the need to transport lumber from Anatolia would delay the construction of an Ottoman fleet in the Red Sea. Should the Ottomans be allowed to construct such a fleet they would become more powerful than the Portuguese and supplant them in India. Chamara added that the Ottomans were in regular contact with the governor of Diu who was urging them to oust the Portuguese.[117] Here was an assessment of economic competition on a grand scale. The focus of this competition was control of the customs revenues of the east-west trade and its instrument was seapower. There is no inherent reason to assume that economic motivation was present in the case of one dominant naval power and absent in the case of the other.[118] The Portuguese, whom distance and objective (control of trade) limited to armed collection of duties rather than to absolute territorial conquest, would seem to have viewed the Ottoman state as a competitor in the same vein.

CHAPTER 7

Conclusion: The Ottoman Economic Mind in the Context of World Power

This study challenges the notion that the sixteenth-century Ottoman Empire was merely a reactive economic entity, driven by the impulse to territorial conquest. Instead, matching the zones of Ottoman territorial expansion to zones of commercial interest, this work incorporates the Ottoman state as inheritor of Euro-Asian trading networks and participant in the contest for commercial hegemony in the economic space stretching from Venice to the Indian Ocean. The development of Ottoman seapower was crucial to this endeavor. The navy, in this era, was not a water-borne wing of the military, but an avenue by which the state could engage in long-distance trade, a defensive mechanism for protecting the exchange of commodities, a transport system, and a force for intimidation in the conduct of diplomatic relations. Seapower enabled the Ottoman Empire to subordinate both Venice and the Mamluk kingdom in Syria and Egypt to dependency relationships articulated in the context of the Portuguese threat to the eastern trade. It also provided the Ottoman *askeri*, the military-administrative class, access to avenues of commercial investment and accumulation of wealth.

The early sixteenth century was a crucial period during which the Ottomans extended their control over Egypt, Syria, and the Holy Cities of Mecca and Medina, capturing control of all the Levantine outlets of the eastern trade, and challenging Portuguese dominance in the Indian Ocean. At this time, the establishment of Ottoman hegemony in the Levant was complicated by the rise to power in Iran of the charismatic warrior shaikh, Shah Ismail Safavi, the ruler who reunited Iran under one sovereign and effected its conversion to Sh'ite Islam. In the European sources, Ismail was

175

represented as a messianic figure leading an army of dervish religious fanatics who perceived him as immortal—a savior whose
armies would stay the Ottoman expansion and preserve the territorial integrity of Christendom. In the Ottoman and Mamluk sources,
he was both a "heretic" and a powerful military opponent, challenging their authority in Anatolia and Syria, and laying claim to
the Holy Cities. In both cases, these representations served the
rhetorics of legitimation and functioned to clarify the distinctions
between ally and enemy. Shah Ismail, Ottoman seapower, and the
profits of the eastern trade were the forces which shaped the articulation of Levantine diplomacy and the struggle for primacy within
the Muslim world in the Age of Discovery. Emphasizing these
forces, this study has assessed Ottoman expansion, linking economies of conquest to economies of trade.

   This work proposes a reframing of sixteenth-century history
by which the Ottoman Empire is incorporated more thoroughly
into the contexts of European, Euro-Asian, and world history. The
objectives of this reconceptualization are: to imagine the Ottoman
state as protagonist rather than obstacle; to refocus attention on
frontiers not privileged by the Age of Discovery theme; and to expand the understanding of Euro-Asian relations beyond the boundaries imposed by rhetorics of difference.[1] This reframing could be
extended to the cultural sphere. That is, the Ottomans could be
figured into equations of the construction of culture in the Mediterranean and Euro-Asian spheres rather than represented as detached defenders of "tradition" until they "discovered" Europe in
the nineteenth century. Here, however, the focus is limited to
themes of commerce and politics. By granting economic intentionality to the Ottoman state and to the Ottoman notable class,
this study allows for the inclusion of the Ottoman Empire in the
scholarly discussion and comparative analysis of late medieval and
early modern states, rather than supporting its exclusion as somehow unique, inert, and aloof.[2] The Ottomans were conscious participants in the Levantine trading networks among which their empire emerged. Their state can be compared to European states on
the bases of ambitions, commercial behaviors, and claims to universal sovereignty. The Ottoman state behaved as merchant, for
profit, and to create, enhance, and further its political objectives.
These objectives included the acquisition and exploitation of commercial entrepôts and production sites. The empire, fractionalized
into its component parts and people, was preoccupied with things
commercial. Pashas and vezirs, far from disdaining trade, were at-

tuned to commercial opportunities and to the acquisition and sheltering of wealth to which those opportunities could lead.

Granting economic intentionality and a "consciousness" of trade to the Ottomans does not presuppose the anachronistic application of eighteenth-century paradigms of commercial behavior. It does, however, demand that the principles of analysis applied to economic behavior be equivalent for the Ottoman and European states. If this seems obvious, it need only be pointed out how often Middle Eastern states are identified by the simple religious designator "Islam" in the same breath that European or other states are identified geographically.[3] In the Ottoman case, it is vague generalizations about the nature of Islamic states and romantic notions about the disdain of military classes for commerce which, all too often, underlie the approach to representing economic behavior.

Once the Ottomans are assumed to be conscious and interested, a new set of questions can be examined, such as the connection between merchant activity and the Ottoman "notables." Of course, such a class must be presumed to exist. Issawi, for example, noting that declining "intellectual standards," parochialism, and the fusion of religious and secular authority acted against economic interest in Middle Eastern states wrote: "Islam, like most other non-Western civilizations, never had bodies enjoying power comparable to those of European feudal landlords."[4] The Ottoman *askeri* in the sixteenth century defy this assessment.

If an Ottoman notable class existed and involved itself in trade, how conscious were these men of their role and how do they compare with European counterparts? Ugo Tucci has developed a moderating paradigm for assessing Venetian merchant notable intentionality which works well for the Ottomans and provides a useful alternative for the antiquated "did not know and did not care" model for Ottoman trading policy.[5] Tucci proposes that there were limits to the sixteenth-century economic vision of the Venetian merchant investors:

> . . . few appear to have widened their vision beyond the mechanics of geographical price variation in which a profit would be made in an elementary way, to the pursuit of bold increases of profit or the nourishing of ideals of accumulated wealth over and above what sufficed for a tranquil old age and the conservation of a family's social position.[6]

Surely no more elevated standards need be applied to the Ottomans in order to accept that their behaviors were consciously oriented to commerce. This standard does not contradict the assessment that the sixteenth-century Ottoman Empire was in a protectionist, premercantilist stage as characterized by Inalcık:

> . . . the Ottoman trade policy was that the state had to be concerned above all with the volume of goods in internal markets so that the people and craftsmen in the cities in particular would not suffer a shortage of necessities and raw materials.[7]

It does, however, suggest that protectionist state policy did not deter the notables, including members of the dynasty, from profiting from certain types of export activity or from investing surplus revenues, in cash or in kind, in international trade. Nor does it deny a state policy which envisioned enhancing this participation in trade, particularly via naval development. This enhancement proceeded along the widening circles of the commercial zones detailed earlier. Notable participation involved, or rather necessitated state policy involvement, for the state could not be divorced from the actions and interests of its power brokers. State policy cooperated in, planned, designed conquest along the lines of, and acted against the extension of these commercial interests. It could even ignore these interests, but it could not be detached from them because of the layers of participation by the state's own personnel.

How does one proceed to analyze the sources once one accepts the necessity of a notable commercial intent paradigm? Exploitation of the *mühimme* registers for the later sixteenth century (where they exist) can be used to delineate the microlevel relations of Ottoman economic function—not center-bureau oriented through focusing on law, but relation oriented through focusing on local and individual economic behaviors.[8] It is evident that the interests of Ottoman merchants and notables often intersected with those of European merchants and notables, as illustrated in chapter 5. The disposition of Balkan and Anatolian grain surpluses shows a clear pattern whereby Ottoman provincial governors and pashas can readily be compared to their medieval predecessors and to European notable counterparts.[9] This proposal does not resolve the problem of the dearth of registers for the early sixteenth century. Bits of evidence and narration, in this earlier era, by accretion, suggest that the trading networks and merchant behaviors of the late medieval period did not disappear with the Ottoman conquest, but were continued, even if articulated in a different administrative language, and exploited to establish the bases of Ottoman rule and dominance. The mechanisms of trade, like the mechanisms of

conquest, were flexible, responding to variations in economic practices already in place in the conquered territories. Hence, the networks of trade survived the advent of newly successful armies and
the demise of onetime hegemons.

There is evidence of the direct participation of members of the
Ottoman dynasty and of *askeri* in trade. Particularly striking is
their exploitation of long established grain export mechanisms and
networks. The pashas were not the only servants of the sultan who
stood to benefit from speculation in the grain trades. High demand
prompted non-elites and minor functionaries to participate as well.
Also important were the Ottoman investments in the copper, lumber, silk, and spice trades. It is clear that the Ottomans were attracted by the prospect of capturing the oriental trade, rather than
simply by the possibilities of territorial conquest, and that state
agents urged the sultans to conquest for commercial wealth. Ottoman naval development was directed to the acquisition and protection of that wealth and to the provisioning and support of campaigns which would consolidate Ottoman control over the outlets
and production sites of the oriental trade. The Ottomans used their
navy to dominate the eastern Mediterranean region and to effect,
without direct military engagement, a diplomacy of submission on
the part of competing states like Venice and the Mamluks. The
Portuguese threat in the Red Sea and Indian Ocean enhanced the
position of the Ottomans in the Euro-Asian sphere because they
were the only power with the artillery and naval resources to resist
the Portuguese.

Further, this study illustrates the inadequacy of Christian-
Muslim or Oriental-Occidental polarizations for explaining the
evolution and articulation of political and economic policy among
the contender states in the Levantine world at the turn of the sixteenth century. Alliances were formed across communal lines and
were motivated by attempts to preserve the traditional balances of
power. The profit motive, the competition for commercial hegemony, and sometimes expansionist ambitions prompted states to
alter or accept alterations of those balances. Just such a reconfiguration of alliances took place at the turn of the sixteenth century. Thus, Venice shifted its support from the Mamluk to the Ottoman state as dominant power in the eastern Mediterranean
during the early years of the century. So, too, Shah Ismail provided
the occasion for a new series of interstate negotiations in direct response to the expansionist policies of the Ottoman and Portuguese
seaborne empires. For the Ottoman dynasty, seapower, firepower,

and the command of resources like copper allowed the pursuit of ambitions for world sovereignty at the expense of neighboring states. It was this active seeking of trading profits, world sovereignty, and the legitimation of that sovereignty in the form of control of the Holy Cities that brought them into conflict with states like the Portuguese which also had great imperial ambitions.

The tribal origins, Islamic faith, and slave-state military ethos of the Ottomans did not absolutely determine and restrict their economic consciousness and action, any more than they restricted Ottoman naval development. The Ottoman dynasty and its attendant power-brokers, the *askeri*, however Muslim in faith or "tribal" by heritage, were fully acculturated and participant citizens in the commercial world of the turn of the century Levant. The use of religious rhetoric, as illustrated by the conduct of sixteenth-century diplomacy, was a strategy employed by all the contenders for power in the Euro-Asian sphere. It served to legitimize sovereign claims, rally military and popular support, and disarticulate the competing claims of other states. Why then, has Islam been singled out, and selectively applied to the Ottoman and Safavid states, as an impediment to elite participation in long established commercial behaviors? Islam's recognition of merchant activity, dating to the time of the Prophet, is well known; participation in commerce by governmental officials in medieval Islamic states is recognized as a commonplace. Even in the Mamluk case, the arguments of tribal origin and slave-state military ethos have not prevented the study of the mamluk caste as commercial entrepreneurs. The answer for the exclusion of the Ottomans, then, must lie in the nature of the threat that the Ottomans posed to European sovereignty and in the attempt of European historiography to distinguish itself from the Ottoman "other."[10] Historiography privileges outcomes, and the Ottoman state became the primary threat in the Euro-Asian sphere to European dominance in the early modern era.

The success of the Ottomans in overcoming the military challenges of European states, in uniting the Holy Land to the rich agricultural heartlands of the Eastern Roman Empire, and in gaining effective control over the outlets to the eastern trade focused the attention of Europe in a dramatic fashion just when its internal social unity was being fragmented by the Reformation.[11] At the same time, the Ottomans had developed a navy which threatened European control of the western Mediterranean. These accomplish-

ments reinforced notions of the Ottoman state as a military jug-
gernaut before all else—notions which were articulated in the
European diplomatic correspondence and chronicles for rhetorical
political purposes. These rhetorical images were then incorporated
into European histories of the Ottomans and coupled, in modern
historiography, with the knowledge that the Ottoman state would
come to lose the contest for world hegemony to the voyaging empires of western Europe. But this image of the Ottoman state and
of the Ottoman *askeri* was neither the image shared by the European traders in the Aegean who negotiated grain sales from Ottoman pashas in the Balkans, nor that of the Venetian merchants
who competed with Ottoman traders for the silk and spice loads in
Aleppo and Damascus, nor that of the French and Genoese captains who watched the Ottoman ships unload copper at Alexandria
and sail back to Istanbul with cut-rate pepper.

Whether or not and when the term mercantilism, broadly construed, is used to characterize the Ottoman state, an evaluation of
various forms of Ottoman commercial behavior demonstrates that
Ottoman commercial regulation was not purely protectionist, it
was selectively so. Starting with an anonymous and ubiquitous
state or with state policies driven predominantly by interdenomi-
national or "tribal" animosities does not facilitate this analysis.
The dilemma is resolved instead by observing how the Ottomans
functioned within the macrolevel of the "world" trade system
reaching from the Levant to East Asia and at the microlevels of
large and small merchant activity.[12] The Ottoman economic mind
can be assumed to reflect the Levantine trading patterns employed
by Ottoman predecessors and competitor states who possessed the
wherewithal to manipulate trade. Then specific instances of Ottoman commercial behavior and the actions of individual members of
"the state" can be used to test the assumption that the empire
of Osman did not stand apart and aloof from the trade of the
Oikoumene.

In assessing the Ottoman economic mind then, in the early
sixteenth century, it may be more advantageous to assess options
perceived, ambitions articulated, and actions taken by individual
members of the state rather than to pose the question: Was there
mercantilism? Decisions made by the state and actions taken by
the *askeri* were prompted by a long term plan to conquer customs
outposts and by the short-term lure of hefty profits. The Ottoman
state cannot then be portrayed as purely reactive in its economic

behavior. In a world where Indian merchants came to Bursa to trade and where the Portuguese Ludovico d'Varthema met Chinese merchants selling silk in Bengal, the Ottoman sultan was subject to the same temptation urged on the English king by his agent, Robert Thorne, in 1527: "Come, be a merchant, like the king of Portugal."[13]

Notes

Chapter 1. Introduction.

1. Thomas Goodrich, "Ottoman Americana: The Search for the Sources of the Sixteenth-Century Tarih-i Hind-i garbi," *Bulletin of Research in the Humanities* 85 (Autumn 1982): 269–294 discusses the extent of Ottoman information about the Americas in the sixteenth century and concludes, as had Bernard Lewis in various writings about Arab states, that the Ottomans were little affected by this information and disinterested in cultures assumed to be inferior to their own, pp. 271–273. The question of interest here is, however, relative. Perhaps the question might better be posed as: In which direction did the most profitable interest lie?

2. *The Venture of Islam: Conscience and History in a World Civilization,* v. 2 (Chicago: University of Chicago Press, 1974), pp. 330–362. The inclusive level of analysis posed by Marshall Hodgson remains useful for developing assumptions about the Ottoman role in commerce, as does his geographic designation of the "Afro-Eurasian Oikoumene." Hodgson uses this designation to comprehend a geographic and cultural sphere in which the exchange of goods and the communication of ideas were not analyzed by continental blocks, political entities, or polar divisions of occident and orient. What Hodgson has done in terms of a synthetic model for intellectual history and civilization, K. N. Chaudhuri has attempted to do for trade. *Trade and Civilization in the Indian Ocean: An Economic History from the Rise of Islam to 1750* (Cambridge: Cambridge University Press, 1985), p. 190. Although Chaudhuri's point of departure is South Asia, his work also opens ways to envision the Indian Ocean from the Ottoman side.

3. H. G. Koenigsberger, George L. Mosse and G. Q. Bowler, eds. *Europe in the Sixteenth Century* (London: Longmans, 1989), p. 229. This work attributes universalist claims to three "European" empires: those of

Charles V, the Ottoman, and the Muscovite, an apt characterization but only after the period of the present study.

4. See George Ostrogorsky, *History of the Byzantine State* (New Brunswick, N.J.: Rutgers University Press, 1957) on the scope of the Byzantine Empire.

5. Written by the Venetian ambassador to the *doge*, quoted in Halil Inalcık, "The Turkish Impact on the Development of Modern Turkey," in Kemal Karpat, ed. *The Ottoman State and Its Place in World History* (Leiden: Brill, 1974), p. 52. See also Bernard Cohn, "Representing Authority in Victorian India," in Eric Hobsbawm, ed. *The Invention of Tradition* (Cambridge: Cambridge University Press, 1989), pp. 211–263, discussing the title of Caesar applied to Queen Victoria's claims to India.

6. *Architecture, Ceremonial, and Power: The Topkapı Palace in the Fifteenth and Sixteenth Centuries* (Cambridge: MIT Press, 1991), pp. 12–13. See Gülrü Necipoğlu on the myth of Alexander as incorporated into Ottoman court ceremony and symbol. See also Kenneth M. Setton, *Western Hostility to Islam and Prophecies of Turkish Doom*, Memoires of the American Philosophical Society, v. 201 (Philadelphia: American Philosophical Society, 1992), pp. 30–36, on prophecies of the Ottomans seizing the "Red Apple," symbol of Rome, of Constantinople and, in general, of world dominion; and Lucette Valensi, "The Making of a Political Paradigm: The Ottoman State and Oriental Despotism." In *The Transmission of Culture in Early Modern Europe* (Philadelphia: University of Pennsylvania Press, 1990). Edited by Anthony Grafton and Ann Blair, pp. 180–184, on the Venetian image of the Ottomans as claimants to world empire.

7. On sources for Ottoman information about Ming (1368–1644) China see Ildikó Béller-Hann, "Ottoman Perceptions of China," *Comité International d'Études Pré-Ottomanes et Ottomanes VIth Symposium, Cambridge, 1rst–4th July 1984*, Series Varia Turcica no. 4 (Istanbul and Paris: Isis Press, 1987). On Süleiman's designs on India from the account of a contemporary Hungarian captive named Huszti see Lajos Tardy, *Beyond the Ottoman Empire: 14th–16th Century Hungarian Diplomacy in the East*, trans. János Boris, *Studia Uralo-Altaica* 13 (Szeged: 1978): 152–158.

8. Halil Inalcık, *The Ottoman Empire: The Classical Age* (London: Weidenfeld and Nicholson, 1973), p. 128. In 1528 Egypt and Syria provided one third of the budget income of the entire Ottoman Empire. See also Halil Sahillioğlu, "1524–1525 Osmanlı Bütçesi," in *Ord. Prof. Ömer Lütfi Barkan'a Armağan* (Istanbul: Gür-Ay Matbaası, 1985).

9. See Naim R. Farooqi, "Moguls, Ottomans, and Pilgrims: Protecting the Routes to Mecca in the Sixteenth and Seventeenth Centuries," *The International History Review* 10, no. 2 (May 1988): 198–220, on the rhetoric of *hajj* route protection. The charge that he was incapable of defending

the *hajj* was a mortal blow to the prestige of an Islamic ruler. Of course, such a charge was in practice often motivated by objectives that had little to do with piety and much to do with political ambition.

10. "Eastern Mediterranean region" is a term used in this work to designate the area of the eastern Mediterranean Sea and its surrounding territories (Egypt and the north African coast, Arabia, Syria, Anatolia, the southern Balkan peninsula, Italy, and western Iran) extending beyond the immediate coastal areas. This designation is meant to include the eastern Mediterranean trading networks and their hinterlands. It is distinguished from the Euro-Asian sphere that extends eastward to India and does not include the African coast west of Egypt. Both areas are grounded on the trading routes which traverse them.

11. Throughout this work, by "Syria" will be understood the territory that in a later historical context came to be called "greater Syria," a territory which encompassed the modern states of Syria, Jordan, Lebanon, and Israel/Palestine.

12. For one thing, the Hapsburgs were not a sea power. On Hapsburg ambitions in this area see Lawrence Sondhaus, *The Hapsburg Empire and the Sea: Austrian Naval Policy, 1797–1866* (West Lafayette, Indiana: Purdue University Press, 1989), p. 2. "In decades of warfare against the Turks, the Hapsburgs provided the Christian alliance with its land power and left naval matters to the Venetians."

13. Andrew Hess, *The Forgotten Frontier, A History of the 16th Century Ibero-African Frontier* (Chicago: University of Chicago Press, 1978). Hess' work points up the fact that later outcomes have focused historiographic attention on certain frontiers while neglecting others. Furthermore, the "nation-state" model, based on latter-day Europe, promotes the insistence on viewing late medieval states as blocks of territory rather than as entities flowing into and out of one another. Hess' work subverts this anachronistic paradigm.

14. Goodrich, "Ottoman Americana," p. 270 divides the "politico-military zones" of Ottoman expansion or interest into five in the latter sixteenth century: Muscovy and Poland, the Safavid Empire, the Hapsburg Empire (all based on land expeditions) and the Hapsburg Mediterranean and Portuguese Indian Ocean and Persian Gulf (based on sea expeditions). The utility of such zoning depends upon whether Ottoman objectives are defined primarily in terms of military conquest or in terms of economic interests and trade routes. Notable work on zone definition for trading purposes can be found in Fernand Braudel, *Civilization and Capitalism 15th–18th Century*, trans. by Siân Reynolds, v. 3 (New York: Harper and Row, 1984), pp. 339–344; and K. N. Chaudhuri, *Asia Before Europe: Economy and Civilization of the Indian Ocean from the Rise of Islam to 1750* (Cambridge: Cambridge University Press, 1990), pp. 1–41.

15. Inalcık, *The Ottoman Empire,* pp. 121–139, on the Ottoman routes of trade and their evolution.

16. Chaudhuri, *Trade and Civilisation,* pp. 98–118, 186–191 surveys the Indian Ocean route and its commodities in this study and challenges the notion that the wind system in the Indian Ocean was the sole explanation for the segmentation and zones of the transcontinental trade, p. 103–4. Chaudhuri poses social conventions, local knowledge, quality of political institutions, and the types of merchant communities as alternate factors determining commercial frontiers. Such factors can be analyzed for the Ottoman trade as well, and help explain why trading zones are coincident neither with state borders nor with state policy.

17. Even Andrew Hess, whose pioneering study challenged the traditional historiography on Ottoman seapower, concludes by emphasizing this commerce *vs.* agriculture paradigm as epitomizing the differences between the objectives of the Portuguese and Ottoman seaborne empires. See Andrew Hess, "The Evolution of the Ottoman Seaborne Empire in the Age of the Oceanic Discoveries, 1453–1525," *The American Historical Review* 75, no. 7 (1970): 1916.

18. Cemal Kafadar, "A Death in Venice (1575): Anatolian Muslim Merchants Trading in the Serenissima," *Journal of Turkish Studies* 10 (1986): 191–218 addresses the role of Ottoman traders in Venice and assigns the Ottomans a more conscious role in commercial expansion. Halil Inalcık, "Capital Formation in the Ottoman Empire," *Journal of Economic History* 29 (1969): 109 points out that many of the wealthy deceased in Bursa late in the fifteenth century were *çelebis,* sons of high ranking members of the administration. This, too, suggests that it may have been common policy for some members of the *askeri* class to invest in trading ventures, either directly or through intermediaries.

19. Numerous studies have been made on the investments of the Venetian notables and their diversification in the sixteenth century from commercial transactions to mainland agricultural land, for example the contributions of Nicolai Rubenstein, Ugo Tucci, and Brian Pullan in J. R. Hale, ed. *Renaissance Venice* (Totawa, New Jersey: Rowan and Littlefield, 1973). In the Ottoman case, the focus on the land-based financing of the *askeri* class must be expanded to include commercial activities as has been demonstrated for the eighteenth century by Rifaʿat Abou-El-Haj, *Formation of the Modern Nation State: The Ottoman Empire, Sixteenth to Eighteenth Centuries* (Albany: State University of New York Press, 1991).

20. This image is beginning to change. Recently, Janet Abu-Lughod, *Before European Hegemony: The World System A.D. 1250–1350* (Oxford: Oxford University Press, 1989), pp. 320–347 has devoted an entire chapter to the question of Ming seaborne activity and the Chinese potential for world system hegemony. Abu-Lughod connects the scrapping of the Ming

navy to the economic collapse of China by the mid-fifteenth century and links that, in turn, to the ". . . final fragmentation of the larger circuit of thirteenth-century world trade in which China had played such an important role" (p. 345). On criticism of aspirations to world hegemony and the imperial voyages of the Ming Chinese and the Portuguese see Robert Finlay, "Portuguese and Chinese Maritime Imperialism: Camões's *Lusiads* and Luo Maodeng's *Voyage of the San Bao Eunuch*," *Comparative Studies in Society and History* 34, no. 2 (April 1992): 225–241.

21. For example, see a recent collection of essays, James D. Tracy, ed. *The Rise of Merchant Empires: Long-Distance Trade in the Early Modern World, 1350–1750* (Cambridge: Cambridge University Press, 1990) on merchant empires in the early modern world. This work is inhabited, when they are even mentioned, by "hostile Ottomans." Although the chapter by Habib Irfan discusses some of the analytical problems posed by facile comparisons of Asian and European trade, in other contributions the Ottomans appear in the tired old roles of consumers and disrupters of trade: pp. 30–32, 271, 361. Carla Rahn Phillips even tries to explain why the Ottoman Empire was not included in this volume, citing Wallerstein that the Ottoman Empire was "a separate world system . . . for the whole of the period considered here it remained a separate, autonomous system, linked with Europe by a trade in luxury goods," (p. 34). We are, in effect, forced to choose among several unpalatable alternatives: whether the Ottomans had a "system," whether they only acquired one in the reign of Süleiman I, whether they only copied one from the Europeans, or whether they never thought of one at all. James Tracy's preface claims that the topics addressed by the participants were "truly universal in scope," (vii). But since this is a volume dealing with "the growth and composition of European overseas trade and the participation of indigenous merchant networks in long distance trade" from 1350–1750, the answer to that claim is: "Not universal enough."

22. Many of the challenges concerning this trade posed by the pioneering work of Halil Inalcık remain unanswered. See Halil Inalcık, "Bursa and the Commerce of the Levant," *JESHO* 3, no. 2 (1960): 131–147 and 1969, 97–140. On the role of the *askeri* such an examination has long been suggested. See Inalcık, "Bursa I, XV Asır Sanayı ve Ticaret Tarih Vesikalar," *Belleten* 24, no. 93 (1960): 46–101; and *The Ottoman Empire*, pp. 125–129 on "notables" leading caravans and on ship ownership by pashas; and "Osmanlı Idare, Sosyal ve Ekonomik Tarihiyle Ilgili Belgeler: Bursa Kadi Sicillerinden Seçmeler," *Türk Tarih Kurumu Belgeler* 10 (1980–1981): 1–91.

23. Mehmed Genç, "Ottoman Industry and the Eighteenth Century: General Framework, Characteristics, and Main Trends." Paper presented at the "Manufacturing in the Ottoman Empire" conference, Fernand Braudel Center, State University of New York at Binghamton, November

1990; Daniel Goffman, *Izmir and the Levantine World 1550–1650* (Seattle: University of Washington Press, 1990); Suraiya Faroqhi, "Towns, Agriculture and the State in Sixteenth Century Ottoman Anatolia," *JESHO* 33 (1990): 125–156; Bruce Mc Gowan, *Economic Life in Ottoman Europe: Taxation, Trade and the Struggle for Land, 1600–1800* (Cambridge: Cambridge University Press, 1981).

24. Frank Perlin, "Proto-Industrialization and Pre-Colonial South Asia," *Past and Present* 98 (1983): 30–95. Perlin warns against "arbitrary evolutionist schema" in discussing a theoretical model for assessing production, markets, and the role of the Mughals and Indian merchants in broad commercial networks. Abu-Lughod, *Before European Hegemony*, in her attempt to draw a thirteenth- and fourteenth-century world system, has also challenged notions of the cultural limitations on hegemonic power, seeking explanations of economic causality in their stead.

25. Wilhelm Heyd, *Geschichte des Levantehandels im Mittelalter*, 2 vols (Stuttgart: J. G. Cottascen, 1876); Frederic C. Lane, *Venice, A Maritime Republic* (Baltimore: Johns Hopkins University Press, 1973), and other works; Niels Steensgaard, *The Asian Trade Revolution in the 17th Century* (Chicago: University of Chicago Press, 1973); Vittorino Malaghes Godinho, *Le Économie de l'Empire Portugais au XV'e e XVI'e Siècles* (Paris: S.E.V.P.E.N., 1969); Eliyahu Ashtor, *Levant Trade in the Later Middle Ages* (Princeton: Princeton University Press, 1983).

26. Albert Hourani, *A History of the Arab Peoples* (Cambridge: Harvard University Press, 1991), p. 215, 231–232. This is one of the few general histories that emphasizes Ottoman commercial and naval power. Still, Hourani argues that the Ottoman naval investment in the Red Sea was purely defensive, and that the direction of Spanish attentions to the New World allowed for the balance of Ottoman-Spanish naval power in the Mediterranean.

27. Fernand Braudel in his pioneering work, *The Mediterranean and the Mediterranean World in the Age of Philip II* (New York: Harper and Row, 1972) pp. 666–667; Will Durant, *The Renaissance: A History of Civilization in Italy from 1303–1576 A.D.* (New York: Simon and Schuster, 1953), p. 284 understood better Ottoman-Venetian relations at the turn of the sixteenth century. Venice, Durant wrote, agreed "that trade was more important than Christianity," and so declined to participate in another crusade.

28. For example: Perry Anderson, *Lineages of the Absolutist State* (London: Redwood Burn, Ltd., 1980), pp. 512, 515–516. Anderson emphasizes the use of Greek seamen by the Ottomans, stating that Ottoman seamanship was relatively short-lived and artificial. Anderson does not use Ottoman sources but this same thesis is echoed by Colin Imber, who does: "The Navy of Süleiman the Magnificent," *Archivum Ottomanicum* 6

(1980): 211–282. Such ethnocentric analyses of navies are then used to characterize states and their economic behavior. On the Ottoman state system, Anderson explains that the "Turkification" of the Islamic political order decisively accentuated the military cast of the original Arab system at the expense of its mercantile component.

29. See Palmira Brummett, "Rhodes: the Overrated Adversary," *The Historical Journal* 36, no. 3 (1993): 1–25.

30. Pasha was a designation of military rank applied to high ranking officials, commanders, and governors who, as members of the *askeri* class held military rank although not necessarily consistently serving in a military capacity. Beg (otherwise *bey* or *bek*) is used in this work either as a title (a generic term meaning chief) or to designate provincial governor status.

31. It has been argued that merchants in Italy circumvented tax farmers and state control, for example, by buying tax farms themselves. Amiya Bagchi, *The Political Economy of Underdevelopment* (Cambridge: Cambridge University Press, 1982) has argued that it was large scale traders in India who were investing in industrial entrepreneurship and the same paradigm has been posed for Venice, but in the Ottoman case it has been assumed that state (dynasty and *askeri*) and merchant interests remained carefully distinguished.

32. Connections between the Ottomans and the Reformation are more frequent than those between the Ottomans and the Renaissance. See, for example, Robert Schwoebel, *The Shadow of the Crescent: The Renaissance Image of the Turk (1453–1517)* (Nieuwkoop: B. De Graf, 1967); Peter Burke, *The Italian Renaissance: Culture and Society in Italy* (Princeton: Princeton University Press, 1986) excludes the Ottomans; Daniel J. Boorstin, *The Discoverers* (New York: Vintage Books, 1985), pp. 543–544 mentions them to illustrate the lack of Muslim receptivity to the printing press. The Ottomans, in such scholarship, generally qualify only as representing the antithesis of a mentality inclined toward discovery.

33. Andre Gunder Frank, "A Theoretical Introduction to 5,000 Years of World System Theory," *Review* 13, no. 2 (Spring 1990): 155–250 has reviewed proposals for models of world systems theory in the pre-Ottoman period. He suggests, for example, pp. 229–230, possibilities for analyzing large trading networks in Euro-Asia before 1500. These were the trading networks which the Ottomans inherited and in which they were active participants. Conversely, Bernard Lewis, *The Muslim Discovery of Europe* (New York: W. W. Norton and Co., 1982), p. 300 characterizes the sixteenth-century clash of empires in terms of "jihad" and portrays the peoples of Islam as, "Walled off by the military might of the Ottoman Empire, still a formidable barrier even in its decline."

Part I: The Ottomans and Levantine Foreign Policy

1. Aziz S. Atiya, *The Crusades in the Later Middle Ages* (London: Butler and Tanner Ltd., 1938; New York: Kraus Reprint, 1965), pp. 256–259.

2. See John E. Woods, *The Aqquyunlu: Clan, Confederation, Empire* (Minneapolis and Chicago: Bibliotheca Islamica, 1976), pp. 127–128 on the machinations of Venice with Uzun Hasan; and V. Minorskii, "La Perse au XVe Siècle entre la Turquie et Venise," *Publications de la Société des Études Iraniennes* 7 (1933): 12–13, 15–16.

3. For Venice in the context of European relations and the wars with the Ottomans see Frederic C. Lane, *Venice, A Maritime Republic* (Baltimore: Johns Hopkins University Press, 1973), pp. 241–243. Also Kenneth Setton, *The Papacy and the Levant (1204–1571)*, 4 vols. (Philadelphia: The American Philosophical Society, 1978–1985); Sydney Nettleton Fisher, *The Foreign Relations of Turkey 1481–1512* (Urbana: University of Illinois Press, 1948). This latter study of foreign relations explores the European sources. On the tribute paid by the Venetians in the fifteenth century see Momcilo Spremiç, and Mahmud Şakiroğlu, "XV Yüzyılda Venedik Cumhuriyetini Şarkta Ödediği Haraçlar," *Belleten* 47, no. 185 (1983): 382–390. For Ottoman-Venetian wars and relations see the documents and commentary of S. Tansel, *Sultan II. Bayezit'in.*

4. Katib Çelebi, *History of the Maritime Wars of the Turks*, trans. by James Mitchell (London: Oriental Translation Fund, 1831), pp. 23–24. For a more contemporary account see Sadeddin, *Tac üt-Tevarih*, 2 vols. (Istanbul: Tabhane-yi Amire, 1279/1863–1864); and Selahattin Tansel's treatment of Bayezid's foreign relations in, *Sultan II. Bayezit'in Siyasi Hayatı* (Istanbul: Milli Eğitim Basımevi, 1966).

5. See Andrew C. Hess, "The Ottoman Conquest of Egypt (1517) and the Beginning of the Sixteenth-Century World War," *International Journal of Middle East Studies* 4 (1973): 55–62, for a good analysis of the changing political and economic forces at this time.

6. Bayezid, who ruled from 1481 to 1512, is technically Bayezid II. Bayezid I was defeated and killed by Timur at the beginning of the fifteenth century. Because only Bayezid II is considered in this study, however, he will be referred to simply as Bayezid.

7. Francesco Guicciardini, *The History of Italy*, trans. Sidney Alexander (New York: Macmillan Co., 1969), p. 334. Guicciardini was writing in the mid-sixteenth century.

8. Steensgaard, *The Asian Trade Revolution*, pp. 212–236.

9. There were clear precedents for Muslim-Christian alliances. At-

iya, pp. 249–250, 256–259 points out the correspondence between Timur and Henry III of Castile early in the fifteenth century and between the Mongols and the pope, proposing anti-Mamluk and anti-Ottoman actions in the thirteenth and fifteenth centuries.

10. Using Hungarian diplomatic sources Lajos Tardy, p. 112 has argued that the Hungarian King Matthias had concrete plans for a Central Asian or Mamluk alliance against the Ottomans, which were broken up by his death in 1490. But Tardy admits that by 1503, when Wladislas II signed a truce with the Sublime Porte, Hungary was "a country on the verge of total collapse, torn by internal strife" with no real pretensions for worldwide diplomatic initiatives against the Ottomans.

11. Quoted in Paul Coles, *The Ottoman Impact on Europe* (New York: Harcourt Brace and World, 1968), p. 100.

Chapter 2. The Western Salient.

1. The treatment of the Ottoman navy in Ismail Hakkı Uzunçarşılı, "Bahriyyah," in *Encyclopedia of Islam*, 2d edition, 2: 945–947, "bahriyyah," skips from 1470 to 1538 in its short account of Ottoman naval history. This is not uncommon in secondary sources.

2. Herbert Jansky, "Die Eroberung Syriens durch Sultan Selim I," *Mitteilungen zur Osmanischen Geschichte* II, 4 (1924–1926): 173–241; Adel Alouche, *The Origins and Development of the Ottoman-Safavid Conflict (906–962/1500–1555)*, (Berlin: Klaus Schwartz, 1983); Ghulam Sarwar, *History of Shah Isma'īl Safawī* (Aligargh: by author, 1939); George Stripling, *The Ottoman Turks and the Arabs 1511–1574* (Urbana: University of Illinois Press, 1942); P. M. Holt, *Egypt and the Fertile Crescent 1516–1922, A Political History* (Ithaca: Cornell University Press, 1966); Muhammad Bakhit, *The Ottoman Province of Damascus in the 16th Century* (Beirut: Librairie du Liban, 1982), "Events" section.

3. For Ismail's extension of his power bases in western Persia see Faruk Sümer, *Safevi Devletinin Kuruluşu ve Gelişmesinde Anadolu Türkmenlerinin Rolu* (Ankara: Güven Matbaası, 1976), pp. 15–40.

4. Donado d'Lezze, *Historia Turchesca*, edited by I. Ursi (Bucharest: Academiei Romane, 1910), p. 268. D'Lezze says that nothing of moment occurred between the Ottomans and Venetians in the years after the peace of 1503 because of the threat from the Safavids.

5. Guglielmo Berchet, *La Repubblica di Venezia e la Persia* (Torino: G. B. Toravia, 1865), pp. 23–24.

6. Ibid., pp. 153–157.

7. Anon., "Travels of a Merchant in Persia," in *Travels in Tana and*

Persia, Hakluyt Series 1, no. 49 (London: Hakluyt Society, 1883), p. 206. See Said Amir Arjomand, *The Shadow of God and the Hidden Imam* (Chicago: University of Chicago Press, 1984), pp. 105–110 on the *kızılbaş* allegiance to Ismail. Also, Franz Babinger, "Marino Sanuto's Tagebücher Als Quelle zur Geschichte der Safawijj," in *A Volume of Oriental Studies Presented to Edward G. Browne*, ed. T. W. Arnold and R. A. Nicholson (Cambridge: Cambridge University Press, 1922), pp. 44–47.

8. Theodoro Spandugino, *La Vita di Sach Ismael et Tamas Re di Persia Chiamati Soffi*, in Sansovino, *Historia Universale dell'Origine et Imperio de Turchi* (Venice: 1582), pp. 98–100. Similar accounts of willing martyrs were common in the Western press during the Iran-Iraq war, nearly 500 years after Ismail's time.

9. Tomé Pires, *Suma Oriental*, Hakluyt Series 2, no. 89 (London: Hakluyt Society, 1944), pp. 23, 26–29. This account, by the Portuguese chronicler, was written in 1512–1513.

10. Pal Fodor, "Ahmedī's Dāsitān as a Source of Early Ottoman History," *Acta Orientali Hungaricae* 38 (1984), p. 41–54. Fodor points out (p. 51) the importance of holy war against fellow Muslims in this early fifteenth century work: ". . . the idea of a sacred commitment to the holy war . . . crystallized within the Ottoman dynasty since Murād I during the fights against their coreligionists [rather] than against the Christians, and came to constitute the ideological legitimation of the dynasty's claim to power."

11. The link between Mary and Fatima was carried into modern orientalist scholarship as well. Gibb's obituary on fellow orientalist Massignon says he pursued "themes that in some way linked the spiritual life of Muslims and Catholics and enabled him to find a congenial element in the veneration of Fatima, and consequently a special field of interest in the study of Shi'ite thought in many of its manifestations." See Berchet, *La Repubblica*, p. 265.

12. Girolamo Priuli, "Girolamo Priuli e i Suoi Diarii," ed. by R. Fulin *Archivio Veneto* 22, pt. 1 (1881): 137–248.

13. See Frederic C. Lane, *Venice and History* (Baltimore: Johns Hopkins Press, 1966), pp. 393–394, 403–408 on the costs of protection.

14. Stripling, *The Ottoman Turks*, p. 19; Subhi Y. Labib, *Handelsgeschichte Ägyptens im Spätmittelalter (1171–1517)*, (Wiesbaden: F. Steiner, 1965), pp. 441–480; and for the later fifteenth century see E. Ashtor, *Levant Trade*, pp. 450–479. Note that all citations to the work of Ibn Iyas in this study will give the pagination from the French edition: Ibn Iyās, *Journal d'un Bourgeoisié du Caire*. Trans. by Gaston Wiet, 2 vols. (Paris: Librairie Armand Colin, 1955–1960), 1: 101/4: 104 followed by a slash (/), then the pagination from the (more complete) Arabic edition, Ibn

Iyās, *Bada'i al-Zuhūr fī waqa'ī al-Duhūr*. Edited by Mohamed Mostafa (Cairo: Franz Steiner Verlag, 1960).

15. See Ibn Iyās, 1: 121/4: 122–123, on the mamluk sedition in 1508 on the occasion of a festival. Demonstrations for more money by the troops were endemic.

16. Ibn Iyās, 1:32/4:36, on bedouin raiding earlier, in 1502.

17. Ibn Iyās, 1:41/4:45–46; Marino Sanuto, *I Diarii*, 36 vols. (Venice: Stefani, Berchet, Barozzi, 1880–1887), 4: 260; 5: 827; 6: 205–206.

18. From the Venetian Archives, Consiglio di Dieci Misti. Reg. XXX, fol. 49 as cited in Louis Mas-Latrie, *Traités de paix et de commerce et documents divers concernant les relations des chrétiens avec les Arabes de l'Afrique Septentrionale au Moyen Age*, 2 vols. Reprint (Paris: Imprimerie Impériale, 1866; New York: Burt Franklin, 1964), 2: 259–263. According to Fulin, Teldi never actually went to Cairo and instead Bernardino Giova was sent in his place. Who bore the actual message is irrelevant to the import of Venice's foreign policy as articulated by the Council of Ten. For Fulin's argument see: R. Fulin, "Il Canale di Suez e la Repubblica di Venezia, 1504," *Archivio Veneto* 2 (1871):194–195.

19. This report refers to the news that was reaching Venice throughout the summer of 1504 on the Portuguese spice shipments. See R. Fulin's edition of Girolamo Priuli's Diarii in "Girolamo," pp. 176–181. Spice weights and measures will be discussed in chapter 6. Ashtor, *Levant Trade*, p. 74, gives the equivalent of a sporta in fourteenth-century Alexandria as 225 kg. On cargoes to Portugal in 1505 see Genevieve Bouchon, "Le Premier Voyage de Lopo Soares en India 1504–1505," *Mare Luso Indicum* 3 (1976):66–68. For an account of the Portuguese spice trade organization including the prices in 1506 see the account of Vincenzo Quirini in Eugenio Alberi, *Le Relazioni degli Ambasciatori Veneti al Senato durante il Secolo Decimosesto, Appendice* (Florence: by the author, 1863), pp. 5–19. Quirino also wrote the Signoria from Antwerp on June 21, 1505 to report that three Portuguese ships had arrived carrying 4,000 quintals of pepper and 50–60 quintals of ginger and nutmeg. Pepper at Antwerp cost 20 Flemish gros per pound. In October of the same year, Quirino wrote that pepper was 18 1/2 gros per pound; ginger from Alexandria 24 gros per pound; ginger from Portugal 17 gros per pound (inferior quality). The ducat = 76 gros, and 100 Venetian pounds equalled 60 pounds Antwerp weight: Great Britain, *Calendar of State Papers: Colonial Series, 1513–1616*, Reprint (London: Her Majesty's Stationery Office, 1862; Vaduz: Kraus Reprint, 1964), pp. 301, 307. For Priuli's reports of the same ships see Fulin, "Girolamo," pp. 190–191. On prices see also Godinho, *Le Économie*, p. 828. For later prices and consumption see Steensgaard, *The Asian Trade*, pp. 154–177.

20. The Gujarati sultans ruled from 1391–1583. For relations of the

Portuguese with the kingdoms in India see Ronald Bishop Smith, *The First Age of the Portuguese Embassies, Navigations and Peregrinations to the Ancient Kingdoms of Cambay and Bengal 1500–1521* (Bethesda, Maryland: Decatur Press, Inc., 1969), pp. 8–60; Bouchon, "Le Premier Voyage," pp. 68–84; Heyd, *Geschichte* 2: 494–501; R. B. Sarjeant, *The Portuguese Off the South Arabian Coast* (Oxford: Clarendon Press, 1963), pp. 14–15.

21. This battle was near the end of the fifty-four year reign of Sultan Maḥmūd I of Cambay (ruled 1458–1511) in the northwest Indian kingdom of Gujarat. He was replaced by his son Muẓaffar II in November 1511. See Joao de Barros, *Da Asia*, Reprint (Lisbon: na Regia Officina Typografica, 1777; Lisbon: Libraria Sam Carlos, 1973), 2, pt. 1: 174–206, 282–310 on the battles at Chaul and Diu. Sarjeant, *Portuguese*, pp. 41–42; E. Dennison Ross, "The Portuguese in India and Arabia," *Journal of the Royal Asiatic Society* (1921), pp. 549–550; Ronald Bishop Smith, *Cambay and Bengal*, pp. 16–19. Sanuto, 11: 76. News of the defeat reached Cairo in 1510. See also Yakub Mughul, "Portekizli'lerle Kızıldeniz'de Mucadele ve Hicaz'da Osmanlı Hakimiyetinin Yerleşmesi Hakkında bir Vesika," *Türk Tarih Kurumu Belgeler* 2, no. 3–4 (1965): 37–38 and Duarte Barbosa, *A Description of the Coast of East Africa and the Malabar in the Beginning of the 16th Century*, Hakluyt Series 1, no. 35 (London: Hakluyt Society, 1866), pp. 22–23.

22. See the account of Vincenzo Quirini in Alberi, *Appendice*, pp. 15–18; R. B. Sarjeant, *Portuguese*, pp. 41–44; Ross, "Portuguese in India," pp. 549–550; Abbas Hamdani, "The Ottoman Response to the Discovery of America and the New Route to India," *Journal of the American Oriental Society* 101, pt. 3 (1981): 326.

23. See Halil Inalcık's review of Ayalon's *Gunpowder and Firearms in the Mamluk Kingdom* in *Belleten* 21 (1957): 503–506; Ibn Iyās, 1: 106/4: 109; and further critique in Mughul, "Türk," pp. 37–41; Salıh Özbaran, "Osmanlı Imparatorluğu ve Hindustan Yolu," *Tarih Dergisi* 31 (1977):66–84; Setton, 3: 19–20, 23; Barbosa, *A Description*, p. 22.

24. Berchet, *La Repubblica*, p. 23. For accounts of Ismail's campaign against the Zū al-Ḳadr see Ibn Iyās, *Bada'i*, 1: 114–115/4: 118–119.

25. After Ismail's attack on the Zū al-Ḳadr, the Mamluk sultan, shaken by this flagrant invasion at his own frontiers, was entertaining a Safavid envoy in Cairo. For the envoy's benefit, aimed no doubt at intimidating the Safavids with Mamluk military prowess, Qānsūh staged a military display in the hippodrome: Ibn Iyās, 1: 120/4: 124.

26. Berchet, *La Repubblica*, p. 23. The letter was sent from Damascus on March 5, 1507. See Hess, "Ottoman Conquest," p. 61, on the frontier conflict; Alouche, *The Origins*, pp. 101–102, 109–110. See Setton, *The Papacy*, 2: 509–526 on the end of the fifteenth century.

27. Arifi Beg, "Elbistan ve Maraşda Zu'l-Kadr Oğulları Hukumeti," *Tarih-i Osmani Encümeni Mecmuası* 25–36 (1330–1331): 358–377, 419–431, 509–512, 535–552, 623–629, 692–697, 767–768.

28. For the articulation of Ismail et al. in the diplomatic correspondence, see Celia J. Kerslake, "The Correspondence between Selim I and Kansuh al-Gawri," *Prilozi za Orientalnu Filologiju* 30 (1980): 219–233; Jean Louis Bacqué-Grammont, "Ottomans," pp. 167–174; Berchet, *La Repubblica*, p. 158; Setton, *The Papacy*, 3: 138; M. C. Şehabeddin Tekindağ, "Yeni Kaynak ve Vesikaların Işiği altında Yavuz Sultan Selim'in Iran Seferi," *Tarih Dergisi* 22 (1967): 49–76; Renate Schimkoreit, *Regesten Publizierter Safawidischer Herrscherurkunden* (Berlin: Klaus Schwarz Verlag, 1982), pp. 110–125.

29. Sanuto, *I Diarii*, 8: 12. Zeno reported early in 1509 that Ismail had taken Baghdad and its ruler had fled to Aleppo.

30. Tomé Pires, *Suma Oriental*, pp. 10–11, 26–29. The same reporter also emphasizes Ismail's Christian connections and adds that "Many Moors say he is a Christian."

31. Sanuto, *I Diarii*, 8: 232, 432.

32. Francesco Luchetta, "L'Affare Zen in Levante nel Primo Cinquecento," *Studie Veneziani* 10 (1959): 183–184; Tansel, *Bayezit*, pp. 245–246.

33. Berchet, *La Repubblica*, p. 25; Bacqué-Grammont, "Ottomans," pp. 165–167; Sanuto, *I Diarii*, 9: 166.

34. On the political machinations leading up to the formation of the League of Cambrai see Frederic Lane, *Venice, a Maritime Republic* (Baltimore: Johns Hopkins University Press, 1973), pp. 242–245. In November of 1512, Venice would use the threat of Selim's bellicosity in an attempt to get the English king, Henry VIII, to pressure the emperor Maximilian I to make peace with Venice. Andrea Badoer, the Venetian ambassador in England, suggested that Selim might view the continuing conflict in Europe as evidence that the Christian powers were weak. In 1514, the same ambassador used the same argument to pressure Henry VIII to urge the emperor again to make peace with Venice, adding that Selim was preparing an armada to invade Italy. See: Great Britain, *Calendar of State Papers, Venice* 2: 67–69, 86, 154–155.

35. Luchetta, "L'Affare Zen," pp. 185–191, dispatches IV–XXII. Sanuto, *I Diarii*, 11: 827–830 includes a report from Cairo.

36. Ibn Iyās, *Bada'i*, 1: 199, 203/4: 205, 210. In April 1511, Ibn Taghribirdī was accused of giving information to the Europeans and thrown into prison at the Mamluk sultan's command.

37. Luchetta, "L'Affare Zen," pp. 190–191; Setton, *The Papacy*, 3:

23–26; Heyd, *Geschichte*, 2: 539. Letters to France and to Zeno were also seized along with the letter to the *doge*.

38. R. C. Repp, *The Mufti of Istanbul: A Study in the Development of the Ottoman Learned Hierarchy* (London: Ithaca Press, 1986), pp. 212–214. Repp discusses the *fetvas* issued to legitimize the Ottoman campaign in 1516 against the Mamluks. One basis for its legitimation was that someone who aided a heretic (in this case the Safavid monarch) was himself a heretic. Hence, it was lawful for Selim to attack the Mamluks. Ibn Iyās 2: 58/5: 60–61. When Selim invaded Syria in August 1516, he sent Karaca Pasha and a *kadi* to Qānsūh with *fetvas* authorizing the execution of Ismail.

39. Ibn Iyās, *Badaʿi*, 1: 184, 199/4: 191, 205. Ibn Iyās reported that the prefect of Birecik had apprehended Safavid spies bearing messages to the Christian princes.

40. Ibn Iyās, *Badaʿi*, 1: 120/4: 124. Tansel, *Bayezit*, p. 116, devotes only a couple of pages to Mamluk-Ottoman relations in Bayezid's reign after 1500. He does, however, mention the Mamluk envoy to the Porte in 1510 who requested military aid against the Portuguese.

41. Fisher, *Foreign Relations*, p. 100, speaking of the period around 1506, describes the reason for the amicable settlement of piracy and naval disputes between the Ottomans and Venice on the basis of "the Sofi's rise and the attack on Venice by the European powers." That is, both states were threatened from elsewhere. The only major engagement during the League of Cambrai was the French victory at Agnadello in 1509; and the League effectively collapsed in 1510 when Pope Julius II (1503–1513) backed out and Ferdinand of Spain became neutral: Setton, *The Papacy*, 3: 54–98.

42. Setton, *The Papacy*, 3: 84–85. For the succession struggle see Çagatay Uluçay, "Yavuz Sultan Selim Nasıl Padişah Oldu?," *Tarih Dergisi* 9 (1953): 54–90; 10 (1954): 118–142; 11 (1955): 185–200.

43. Hess, "Ottoman Conquest," p. 67, describes the end of Bayezid's reign as showing a sudden improvement in Ottoman-Mamluk relations because of the Safavid threat and the Ottoman aid to the Mamluks. Setton, *The Papacy*, 3: 25 not only characterized the Ottomans as the Mamluks' friends but also suggested that Venice was inattentive to affairs in Egypt because of Venetian preoccupation with the League of Cambrai.

44. Özbaran, "Hindustan Yolu," pp. 81–84 discusses the flow of military hardware, timber etc. from Anatolia to Egypt in terms of the economic and strategic importance of the area and of trade to the Ottomans. This flow must be seen also in terms of the extension of the Ottoman political and military sphere of influence.

45. Luchetta, "L'Affare Zen," pp. 190–203.

46. Luchetta, "L'Affare Zen," pp. 200–201. The ambassador, Juan Emo, sent to secure the consul's release, was instructed to make suitable excuses should the Mamluk sultan Qā'it Bāy, complain about Venice sending envoys to Uzun Hasan. Ashtor, *Levant Trade*, pp. 452–453 describes the 1464 incident in detail. Fulin, "Girolamo," pp. 184–187 includes Priuli's account of spring 1505 when Qānsūh imprisoned the consul and merchants and impounded their goods in response to a disagreement over the Venetian ships departing from Alexandria.

47. Luchetta, "L'Affare Zen," p. 109.

48. Sanuto, *I Diarii*, 15: 17–20, 193–207, 246–266; Luchetta, "L'Affare Zen," pp. 171–173; Trevisan was to say that the visit of the Safavid envoys to Venice had been only to relate Ismail's successes and bring messages of friendship, and that no bad effect was intended; Hess, "Ottoman Conquest," p. 67.

49. Mas-Latrie, *Traités*, 2: 271–272 (from Consul di Dieci, Misti. v. 34, fol. 121). Instructions to emissary Domenico Trevisan from the Senate, on going to Egypt, dated 30 December 1511. See also Heyd, *Geschichte*, 1: 528–530; Fulin, "Girolamo," pp. 243–246; Setton, *The Papacy*, 3: 27–30.

50. Joos van Ghistele, *Voyage en Egypte de Joos van Ghistele, 1482–1483*, Collection des Voyageurs Occidentaux en Egypte, no. 16 (Cairo: Institut Français d'Archéologie Orientale du Caire, 1972), pp. 40–41.

51. *Calendar of State Papers, Venice*, 2: 384. On May 12, 1517, the Portuguese ambassador, Don Pietro Civrea, complained to Sebastian Justinian, the Venetian envoy in London, that Venice had been hostile and aided the Mamluk sultan ever since Portugal started its India voyages. Justinian protested Venice's friendship for Portugal and denied the charge, saying that Venice was more zealous for the Christian faith than for a few additional profits.

52. John Wansbrough, "A Mamluk Ambassador to Venice in 913/1507," *University of London: Bulletin of the School of Oriental and African Studies* 26 (1963): 511; for the latter negotiations of Rhodes and Egypt see Bacqué-Grammont, "Ottomans," pp. 171–177. See also Heyd, *Geschichte*, 2: 538, 541–545, on Trevisan's mission.

53. See Luchetta, "L'Affare Zen," p. 189.

54. For the Portuguese negotiations with Ismail seen Ronald Bishop Smith, *The First Age of the Portuguese Embassies, Navigations and Peregrinations in Persia (1507–1524)* (Bethesda, Maryland: Decatur Press, 1970), pp. 8–53; Alfonso d'Albuquerque, *The Commentaries of the Great Alfonso D'Albuquerque*, trans. by Walter de Graybirch, Hakluyt Society Series 1, no. 55, pt. 2, Reprint (New York: Hakluyt Society, 1928; New York: Hakluyt Society, 1970), pp. 111–118; Barros, *Da Asia*, 2, pt. 10:

423–428. On the Safavid-Mamluk embassies see Bacqué-Grammont, "Ottomans," pp. 154–163. Bacqué-Grammont suggests that after Çaldıran Ismail was less inclined to Portuguese proposals against the Mamluks because he now had to view the Mamluks as a possible ally against the Ottomans. Ismail later also sent an envoy to the Grand Master of Rhodes proposing an alliance against the Ottomans and asking him to send to Ismail, Murad, son of Cem and, as Bayezid's nephew, a pretender to the throne. The Grand Master did not comply with this request. See Ettore Rossi, "Relazioni tra la Persia e l'Ordine di San Giovani a Rode e a Malta," *Rivista degli Studi Orientali* 13, pt. 1: 353.

55. Ismail had forced the king of Hormuz, Seyf al-Dīn, to pay tribute beginning in 1503, but d'Albuquerque's occupation of the island in 1507–1508 forced the king to pay the Portuguese instead. See: Hans-Joachim Kissling "Sâh Ismâ'îl Ier, La Nouvelle Route des Indes et les Ottomans," *Turcica* 6: 89–102. Kissling makes the argument that Ismail, too, coveted the Indian Ocean trade and that his willingness to cooperate with the Portuguese was a concession made to advance his efforts to control a trade corridor reaching from the eastern Mediterranean to the Persian Gulf.

56. Barbosa, *A Description*, p. 40, written in 1514–1516.

57. D'Albuquerque, *The Commentaries*, 2: 80. D'Albuquerque took over as Portuguese governor of India, from his predecessor Almeida, in November of 1509.

58. The following year Ismail would extract a promise from the Timurid Bābur to have the shah's name read in the *khutba* (Friday prayer service invocation), and coins struck in his name in Samarqand in return for Ismail sending him troops to conquer that city. See R. M. Savory, "The Consolidation of Safawid Power in Persia," *Der Islam* 41 (1965): 80.

59. D'Albuquerque, *The Commentaries* 2: 111–118. D'Albuquerque calls Ismail the "Very great and powerful Lord among the Moors." His titles for Emmanuel are considerably more grandiose.

60. In 1510–1511, Venice sent ambassador Alvise Arimondo to Turkey to seek Ottoman support: Sanuto, *I Diarii*, 10: 198, 343, 704, 801; 11: 683; Setton, *The Papacy*, 3: 71, 75, 78, 88–90. Late in 1509 Venice had asked Bayezid for 8,000–10,000 Bosnian cavalry. Venice continued negotiations with the Porte and with the *sancak begs* (subprovince governors) of the Morea and Bosnia. The Holy Roman Emperor, Maximilian, in 1510, also attempted to solicit support in the form of Bosnian cavalry from Firuz Beg, the Ottoman *sancak beg*. In the end, Venice attempted to negotiate for a Turkish force of 6,000–10,000 to attack Maximilian. This attack, however, never materialized. Fisher, *The Foreign Relations*, p. 102; Setton, *The Papacy*, 2: 499.

61. Alberi, *Le Relazioni*, Series 3, 3: 46–49.

62. On other requests of European powers for Ottoman aid and on the difficulties of Venice with France and Italy see Setton, *The Papacy*, 1: 534–539. Later, under Süleiman, the Ottomans would become an important counterweight in European diplomacy against the expanding power of the Hapsburgs. On the French-Ottoman alliance in Süleiman's reign see Garrett Mattingly, *Renaissance Diplomacy* (Boston: Houghton Miflin, 1955), pp. 176–177.

63. On the rhetorical crafting of the *bailo's* reports, the *relazioni*, as constructing Ottoman sovereignty and reflecting Venetian ideologies of government see Valensi, "The Making of a Political," pp. 173–203.

64. For lists of Venetian *bailos* and envoys, see Alberi, *Appendice*, pp. 419–435. *A Calendar of State Papers, Venice*, 2: 38, for example, illustrates the problems of Venice's ambassador to England in 1510. Debate in the Venetian Senate suggested that the ambassador was not doing Venice any good but the senators were reluctant to recall him for fear of offending England. Instead they debated, amidst hearty laughter, how far to reduce his living allowance.

65. On Çaldıran see Sharaf Khān Bidlīsī, *Cheref-Nameh ou Fastes de la Nation Kourde par Cheref-ou'ddine*, trans. by Francois Bernard Charmoy, 2 vols. (St. Petersburg: Academie Imperiale des Sciences, 1873), 2: 534–535/ Sharafnāmah, ms. Elliot 332, Bodleian Library, Oxford, p. 207b; Ḥasan Rūmlū, *Ahsan u't-Tavārīkh*, trans. C. N. Seddon, Gaekwad's Oriental Series, no. 69 (Baroda: Oriental Institute, 1934), pp. 68–70; Sarjeant, *The Portuguese*, pp. 48–50; Ibn Iyās, *Bada'i*, 1: 422–424, 431–436/4: 236–238, on Selim's victory at Çaldıran and march to Tabriz. The second armada was finally launched only in 1515 and failed to achieve any success against the Portuguese. By the following year, Selim was already marching to conquer the Mamluk territories.

66. Sanuto, *I Diarii*, 24: 172, 176; Rossi, "Relazioni," p. 353. See also Alouche, *The Origins*, pp. 127–130; Barbara von Palombini, *Bündniswerben Abendländischer Mächte um Persien 1453–1600* (Wiesbaden: Franz Steiner Verlag, 1968), p. 54. On Ottoman-Mamluk diplomacy see Selahattin Tansel, *Yavuz Sultan Selim* (Ankara: Milli Eğitim Basımevi, 1969), pp. 108–221, 233–237.

67. On the negotiations of Mocenigo and Contarini after the conquest see Alberi, *Le Relaziori*, Series 3, 3: 54–60.

68. Sanuto, *I Diarii*, 24: 135–137.

69. Inalcık, "Bursa I," p. 59. The customs charge for foreign or "frank" merchants in the late fifteenth century was 4–5 percent.

70. On the Ottoman treatment of the Christian populace after the conquest see the *berat* (grant of privilege document) from Selim to the

Sinai monastery dated while Selim was still in Egypt, in July 1517: Klaus
Schwarz, *Osmanische Sultansurkunden des Sinai-Klosters in Türkischer
Sprache*, Islamkundlische Untersuhungen Series, no. 7 (1970), pp. 25–30.

71. For one version of Mamluk naval policy and lack of a permanent
navy see David Ayalon, "Bahriyyah," *Encyclopedia of Islam*, 2d. ed., 2:
945–947.

Chapter 3. The Eastern Salient.

1. The chronicling of the day-to-day progress of the Ottoman campaigns of 1514 through 1517 has been done by such historians as Fisher,
Labib and Jansky, op. cit.

2. Tursun Beg, *Tarih-i Abu'l Fath / The History of Mehmed the Conqueror*, Halil Inalcık and Rhoads Murphey, eds. (Minneapolis: Bibliotheca
Islamica, 1978), pp. 64, 156b–157a.

3. Lutfi Pasha, *Tarih-i Al-i Osman* (Istanbul: Matbaa-i Amire
1341/1922), pp. 192–195. The naval attack was aimed at the rear of the
Mamluk army but the fleet was dispersed in a storm. ʿAlā ad-Dawla, the
Zū al-Ḳadr ruler, participated on the Ottoman side in this campaign.

4. Ahmed Feridun Beg, *Mecmua-ı Münşeat üs-Selatin*, 2 vols. (Istanbul: n.p., 1858), pp. 347–351, 354–358, 411–413, 419–427 for Ottoman-
Mamluk communications; Muhammad Harb, *Yavuz Sultan Selim'in Sur-
iye ve Mısır Seferi* (Istanbul: Özal Matbaası, 1986), pp. 26–33, in his treatment of Ottoman-Mamluk diplomacy (which utilizes primarily Ottoman
chronicles) also briefly summarizes the earlier diplomatic relations between Bayezid, the Zū al-Ḳadr and the Mamluks. See for the letters of
1515–1516 and on the composite nature of some of the letters in Feridun
Beg: Celia Kerslake, "The Correspondence," pp. 219–233.

5. See Ismail Hikmet Ertaylan, *Sultan Cem* (Istanbul: Milli Eğitim
Basımevi, 1951), pp 108–113, 122. On the harboring of Ottoman princes at
foreign courts see: Ismail Hakkı Uzunçarşılı, "Iran Şahına Iltica Etmiş
Olan Şehzade Bayezid'in Teslimi Için Sultan Süleyman ve Oğlu Selim
Taraflarından Şaha Gönderilen Altınlar ve Keymetli Hediyeler," *Belleten*
24 (1960):104–110 and "Memluk Sultanları Yanına Iltica Etmiş Olan Os-
manlı Hanedanına Mensub Şehzadeler," *Belleten* 17 (1953): 519–535;
Petra Kappert, *Die Osmanischen Prinzen und Ihre Residenze amasya im
15 und 16 Jahrhundert* (Istanbul: Nederlands Historisch—Archaeologisch
Institut te Istanbul, 1976), pp. 131–139.

6. Lutfî, *Tarih-i*, p. 192; Bayezid, "Letter to ʿAlā ad-Dawla" ms. Or
61, British Museum, London. This letter is an announcement of Bayezid's
victory over Cem detailing the struggle and warning ʿAlā ad-Dawla of the

presence of an Ottoman army in Anatolia should he be tempted to insubordination. See also Halil Inalcık, "A Case Study in Renaissance Diplomacy: The Agreement between Innocent VIII and Bāyezīd II on Djem Sultan," *Journal of Turkish Studies* 3 (1979): 209–230.

7. F. Sumer, "Karaman-oghulları," *Encyclopedia of Islam*, 2d. ed., 4:624. Cem went to Cairo in 1481, attending at the court of Sultan Malik al-Ashraf Qā'it Bāy. In spring of 1482, he was in Aleppo. Ertaylan, *Sultan Cem*, pp. 112–123. Kasim Beg conspired with Cem and with the Grand Master in 1481–1482 to launch an attack on Bayezid from Syria, Rhodes, and Karaman.

8. Stripling, *The Ottoman Turks*, p. 39; Jean Louis Bacqué-Grammont, "Ottomans,", p. 215; Kerslake, "The Correspondence," pp. 230–231; W. W. Clifford, "Some Observations on the Course of Mamluk-Safavi Relations (1502/908–1516/922)," unpublished paper, Chicago, 1985, p. 39.

9. Sanuto, *I Diarii*, 4: 281, 351–357.

10. Sadeddin, *Tac üt-Tevarih*, 2:105–107. Sadeddin suggests that Mustafa had taken advantage of the Ottoman preoccupation with the naval battles at Modon and Coron in the Aegean to make his bid for power. When Mesih Pasha returned from the Inebahtı campaign, he was sent with an army from Istanbul against Karaman in April of 1501. Sadeddin says that Mustafa fled to Tarsus and thence to Aleppo where he was imprisoned. See also Sanuto, *I Diarii*, 4: 43, 309. Another spy, named Murad, was sent from Cyprus to gather information on Ismail. He returned in August 1503: Sanuto, *I Diarii* 5: 196–197, 718. On the Karamanids, see also I. Hakkı Uzunçarşılı, *Anadolu Beylikleri ve Akkoyunlu, Karakoyunlu Devletleri* (Ankara: T. T. K. Basımevi, 1984), pp. 34–36.

11. Sanuto, *I Diarii*, 4: 353–355. The marriage of Mustafa to Ismail's sister was also part of the alliance according to one report. It is unclear whether such a marriage was ever concluded.

12. Woods, *The Aqquyunlu*, pp. 175–177 on Alvand.

13. Sanuto, *I Diarii*, 4: 255, 322, 404–406. In spring of 1502 in Istanbul, Ismail was rumored to be commanding a force of 150,000, a gross exaggeration. See Hanna Sohrweide, "Der Sieg der Safaviden in Persien und seine Rückwirkunden," *Der Islam* 41 (1965): 141–142; Babinger, "Marino Sanuto's," p. 42. See Feridun Beg, *Mecmu'a-i*, pp. 345–346 for a "petition" from Ismail to Bayezid urging him not to interfere with religious visits of the sufis into Iran.

14. Sanuto, *I Diarii*, 4: 417, 432; 5: 488. Hasan Rūmlū does not mention a Safavid-Ottoman engagement in this year. He does mention a battle between the Safavid commander Ilyās Beg Ayqūt Ughalī in Azerbaican with Nasır and Mansur Türkmen, saying the latter, who had 4,000 cavalry, lost the engagement.

15. Sanuto, *I Diarii*, 4: 196, 355–356, 481.

16. This may have been Dawlat Bāy, see Ibn Iyās, *Badaʿi*, 1: 31/ 4: 34. Dawlat Bāy was appointed in 1502 so the reference may have been to his predecessor, Ultī Bāy.

17. Sanuto, *I Diarii*, 7: 286, 442, 529.

18. Sanuto, *I Diarii*, 4: 481. Ibn Iyās, *Badaʿi*, 1: 31, 35–6/4: 34, 39 notes only that a Safavid force had been sighted near Syria, and does not mention the Safavid envoy.

19. In summer of 1502, see Ibn Iyās, *Badaʿi*, 1: 42/4: 46; Sanuto, *I Diarii*, 4: 432, 481. Ismail defeated both Murad ibn Yakub and Alvand Ak Koyunlu.

20. Ibn Iyās, *Badaʿi*, 1: 35–36 /4: 39; Sanuto, *I Diarii*, 4: 334, 716; 5: 34–35.

21. Sanuto, *I Diarii*, 4: 705, 716–717, according to a report from Aleppo in November of 1502. The protection of the pilgrimage route was an important factor in the legitimacy of sultanic authority. On the Ottoman assumption of the *hajj* caravan after their conquest of Syria and Egypt see Jacques Jomier, *Le Mahmal et la Caravane Egyptienne des Pelerins de la Mecque (XVIIIe-XXe Siècles)* (Cairo: Institut Français d'Archéologie Orientale, 1953), pp. 16–21, 52–57.

22. Ibn Iyās, *Badaʿi*, 1: 51/4: 55. See also M. Tayyıb Gökbilgin, *XV–XVI Asırlarda Edirne ve Paşa Livası Vakıflar—Mülkler—Mukataalar* (Istanbul: Ülçer Basımevi, 1952), p. 484 for diplomatic exchange with ʿAlā ad-Dawla that same summer.

23. Sanuto, *I Diarii*, 5: 114–115, 197–198. The Mamluk sultan was angry that the Cyprus tribute, finally paid after two year's delay, had been tendered in "poor quality" cloth. This tribute embassy was headed by Soranzo.

24. Sanuto, *I Diarii*, 4: 260. Representatives of the Damascene merchants had gone to Cairo to intercede with the sultan that spring of 1503 over the question of imposts. He imprisoned three men and demanded 40,000 ducats to be paid on the account of Venice.

25. Fisher, *The Foreign Relations*, p. 94. This groundbreaking study of foreign relations explores the European sources. Fisher, however, tends to take embassies at face value saying, in this case, that Bayezid was unwilling to risk offending Ismail.

26. See Feridun Beg, *Mecmuʿa-i*, pp. 354–356 for communication between Bayezid and Qānsūh on Dawlat Bāy.

27. Ibn Iyās, *Badaʿi*, 1: 64, 67, 73–74, 78/4: 67, 70, 77, 81; Sanuto, *I*

Notes 203

Diarii, 6: 221. Note that this is the second time the sources connect ʿAlā ad-Dawla with a revolt in Tripoli. A 1510 reference in Sanuto, *I Diarri*, 11: 57, alludes to the revolt of Dawlat Bāy and Sībāy, saying that one of them defected to the Ottomans for a time but then returned to Mamluk service. A report from the Venetian consul in Damascus in November 1505 states that a Ramadanid prince had also revolted, seizing Adana and Tarsus and that Qānṣūh was mobilizing troops against him: Sanuto, *I Diarii*, 6: 285.

28. Ibn Iyās, *Badaʿi*, 1: 79–81/4: 82, 84. The Mamluk sultan was faced with not only multiple problems but also the Safavid and Ottoman threats. In September 1505, he reviewed the troops that were divided into three expeditionary corps: one to Mecca against the revolt of the governor of Yanbo in Arabia; one to Karak against the brigandage of the bedouins; and one against the Portuguese on the Red Sea littoral. The latter group, composed of mamluks and reserve troops (Maghrebis, black archers, and Türkmen) left for Suez on November 4, 1505 under the command of Husain Mushrīf and Nūr al-Dīn Maṣlatī. Masons and carpenters were also sent to work on the fortifications of Jidda and the surrounding areas. In short, Qānṣūh had not the manpower even for defense, much less for aggressive action in Syria.

29. Refet Yinanç, *Dulkadir Beyliği* (Ankara: T.T.K., 1989), pp. 80–99 details the career of ʿAlā ad-Dawla and his alternating claims to protection from both Mamluk and Ottoman sultans.

30. Ibn Iyās, *Badaʿi*, 1: 85, 89–90, 93, 95. Repp, *The Müfti*, pp. 206–207 on the difficulties facing pilgrims in the years 1501–1504. Repp describes the delays experienced by Ali Cemalı, soon to be Mufti of Istanbul, when he tried to make the *hajj* in 1503–1504.

31. Sanuto, *I Diarii*, 6: 90, 93.

32. Ibid., 6: 221, 240, 277, 279, 285, 410.

33. Ibn Iyās, *Badaʿi*, 1: 89, 92/4: 93, 96; Sanuto, *I Diarii*, 6: 279, 410.

34. Sanuto, *I Diarii*, 6: 221.

35. Ibid., 6: 277.

36. Ibn Iyās, *Badaʿi*, 1: 89, 92 /4: 93, 96.

37. Rūmlū, *Ahsan*, pp. 39–40; Bidlīsī, 2, pt. 2: 517 / Sharafnāmah ms., p. 202b.

38. Sanuto, *I Diarii*, 7: 14–15.

39. Loredano's *relazione* reported this. See also Sanuto, *I Diarii*, 7: 16; Rūmlū, *Ahsan.* p. 41; and Uzunçarşılı, *Anadolu*, p. 197; Saddedin, *Tac*, 2: 130 also mentions the phony marriage proposal. Fisher, *The Foreign Relations*, p. 95, following Sanuto, cites the failure to deliver the promised

bride to Ismail. Rūmlū, *Ahsan*, p. 41 agrees with Ibn Iyās in citing the conspiracy with Sultan Murad in Baghdad.

40. Merchant, "Travels," p. 196; Sadeddin, *Tac*, 2: 130; Giovan Maria Angiolello, "A Short Narrative of the Life and Acts of Uzun Cassano," in *Travels in Tana and Persia II*, Hakluyt Society Series 1, no. 49 (London: Hakluyt Society, 1883), p. 108. These two latter accounts are so similar they seem to have a common source. On the composite nature of Angiolello's account see George B. Parks, *The Content and Sources of Ramusio's Navigationi* (New York: New York Public Library, 1955), pp. 25–26. Ibn Iyās, *Badaʿi*, 1: 119/ 4: 123.

41. Sanuto, *I Diarii*, 7: 267; Rūmlū, *Ahsan*, pp. 41–42; Merchant, p. 196; Angiolello, "Narrative," p. 109; Zeno, *Travels in Tana and Persia II*, pp. 53–54; Bidlīsī, 2, pt. 2: 518–519 / Sharafnāmah ms., p. 203a.

42. Sanuto, *I Diarii*, 7: 170, 179; Merchant, "Travels" p. 196.

43. Zeno, *Travels in Tana*, p. 53; Sanuto, *I Diarii*, 7: 187, 265–267; Merchant, "Travels," p. 196.

44. Ḥasan Rūmlū reported an initial Zū al-Ḳadr victory by ʿAlā ad-Dawla's son Sarı Kaplan over a Safavid force under Lala Beg. Other sources do not mention it. Since the engagement supposedly took place at the Ceyhan River, located west of Maraṣ, on the road from Kayseri, it may have been the first contact between the Safavid and Zū al-Ḳadr forces. Rūmlū, *Ahsan*, p. 41. Sanuto, *I Diarii*, 7: 267–268 gives a report from Cyprus saying the countryside was depopulated because the people had fled at the Safavid army's approach.

45. Sanuto, *I Diarii*, 7: 150–151, 164. A report from Cyprus in winter of 1507–1508 estimated the total forces mobilized against Ismail by Bayezid as numbering over one hundred thousand men, but these were not all at the front: Ibid., 7: 266–267.

46. Ibid., 7: 259, 263–265. On the withdrawal of Yahya's army and claims of desertions to the Safavids see also: Ibid., 7: 187–188, 265–266.

47. Merchant, "Travels," pp. 194–198. Bidlīsī, 2: 518–519/ Sharafnāmah, ms. pp. 202b–203a; Rūmlū, *Ahsan*, pp. 41–42; Ghulam Sarwar, *History of Shah Ismaʿīl Safawī* (Aligargh: by the author, 1939), pp. 52–54.

48. Rūmlū, *Ahsan*, pp. 42–43, 45; Angiolello, *Narrative*, p. 110; Merchant, "Travels" p. 198; Sanuto, *I Diarii*, 7: 528. The Zū al-Ḳadr force was reported to be between two and seven thousand men. Rūmlū wrote that Khān Muhammad's army numbered two thousand but he also claimed that this same army killed seven thousand men from a larger Kurdish force, so his estimates are, at best, suspect. One report in Sanuto indicates that ʿAlā ad-Dawla himself led this army but escaped, and that the battle took place in December or January: Sanuto, *I Diarii*, 7: 528.

49. Rūmlū, *Ahsan*, pp. 47–48.

50. Khvandamīr, *Habīb al-Siyar fī Akhbār Afrād al-Bashar*, edited by Jalāl al-Dīn Huma'i (Tehran: Kitābkhāne-i Khayām, 1333/1954), p. 486. Khvandamīr said that the revolt was the idea of ʿAlā ad-Dawla. Merchant, "Travels," pp. 199–200; Rūmlū, *Ahsan*, pp. 69–71. Murad died in Diyarbakr in 1514. Caterino Zeno, *Travels in Tana and Persia II*, Hakluyt Series I, no. 49 (London: Hakluyt Society, 1883), p. 55, reports that Murad was not welcome in Aleppo, reflecting the fear of Safavid reprisals. See also Sanuto, *I Diarii*, 7: 710–711; Merchant, "Travels," p. 198. Ibn Iyās, *Badaʿi*, 1: 139–140 / 4: 143, 46, wrote that Murad's envoy came to Cairo in January 1509, but Qānsūh refused to aid him.

51. Khvandamīr, *Habīb*, pp. 489–490.

52. Bidlīsī, 2, pt. 2: 519–521/ Sharafnāmah ms., pp. 203b–204a.

53. Sanuto, *I Diarii*, 7: 188, 221, 267, 269, 527. Ahmad ibn ʿAlī Ibn Zunbūl, "Ghazwat al-Sultān Salīm Khān maʾ al-Sultān al-Ghūrī" ms. Landberg 461, Yale University Library, New Haven, Ibn Zunbūl suggests that it was the interference of Khair Beg in the struggle between ʿAlā ad-Dawla and Selim that precipitated Selim's invasion of Syria in 1515. This is an exaggeration but reflects the close ties between the Zū al-Ḳadr ruler and the governor of Aleppo.

54. Ibn Iyās, *Badaʿi*, 1: 114–115/ 4: 118–119. Qānsūh appointed a commander in chief at Cairo. On the fear caused in Egypt and Syria by Ismail's proximity see also: Sanuto, *I Diarii*, 7: 188, 226, 268, 529.

55. Ibn Iyās, *Badaʿi*, 1: 117, 119 /4: 121–123. The Mamluk soldiery were also demanding extra pay. Reports in Sanuto indicate that Mamluk aid was promised to ʿAlā ad-Dawla: Sanuto, *I Diarii*, 7: 527–528. It seems never to have materialized. The claim that the Zū al-Ḳadr were victorious also reached Istanbul in October: Sanuto, *I Diarii*, 7: 231.

56. Uluçay, "Yavuz," pp. 75–77.

57. Yinanç, *Dulkadir*, pp. 92–95.

58. Şükri, Selim name, Reis ül-Kuttap ms. no. 655, pp. 20b, 50, Süleymaniye Kütüphanesi, Istanbul.

59. Rūmlū, *Ahsan*, pp. 49, 51–55.

60. Diyarbakr refers to the province/area rather than to the modern day city of that name (called Amid).

61. There are numerous reports in Sanuto of Ismail's followers in Anatolia. Many are exaggerated or the result of wishful thinking, but obviously support for Ismail in the provinces was a factor with which the Ottomans had to contend. Sanuto, *I Diarii*, 7: 265 specifically mentions

desertions as a problem in the army under Yahya Pasha, who was sent against Ismail in 1507. See Uluçay, "Yavuz," pp. 61–74; Rūmlū, *Ahsan*, p. 55 on the Shah Kulu rebellion. See also, Uluçay, "Yavuz," pp. 75–76, 78–90 on Selim's letters to Bayezid concerning the eastern frontiers.

62. In the same year that Ismail defeated ʿAlā ad-Dawla, his troops further north along the Ottoman-Safavid frontier lost an engagement to Selim's forces. The following year, in summer of 1508, a Safavid envoy to the Porte demanded the return of Safavid artillery lost during the skirmish. This demand not only affirms the Safavid need for artillery but also illustrates the stated Safavid position that the 1507 attack was not specifically directed against the Ottomans. The envoy claimed that Selim's offensive was unwarranted. Sanuto, *I Diarii*, 7: 631; Merchant, "Travels," p. 196.

63. For example, a report, dated August 24, 1507, by a man who had returned from Konya, was relayed to the Signoria by the Rector of Cyprus. It told of Bayezid's troop mobilization to stop Ismail at the frontier. According to the informant, Ismail was fortifying Erzincan and intended to remain in Ottoman territory. All of Karaman, along with the area surrounding Erzincan would rally to his defense. The source of this report, however, was not well informed in that he thought Bayezid was mobilizing troops to send against ʿAlā ad-Dawla. He reflects, however, the prevalent European notions about the extent of support for Ismail in Anatolia; Sanuto, *I Diarii*, 7: 167, 182.

64. Ibn Iyās, *Badaʿi*, 1: 106 /4: 109. It was precisely in that year, 1507, that a Portuguese fleet sailed into the Red Sea to attack Muslim shipping. Mamluk forces were also engaged in the Hijaz after defeating Yahya ibn Sʿab who had revolted.

65. Ibn Iyās, *Badaʿi*, 1: 115, 119, 160 /4: 119, 123, 164. Ibn Taghribirdī also negotiated the release of Maghrebi prisoners, spending fifty thousand dinars to redeem them. The sultan levied an impost on the Maghrebi communities in Cairo and Damascus to recoup this ransom money. The prisoners ransomed may well have been those seized by the Rhodians in 1507 from a large merchant ship trading between Tunis and Alexandria.

66. John Wansbrough, "A Mamluk Ambassador to Venice in 913/ 1507," *University of London, Bulletin of the School of Oriental and African Studies* 26 (1963), pp. 503–530 recounts the details of Ibn Taghribirdī's mission.

67. Ibn Iyās, *Badaʿi*, 1: 104 /4: 107; Sanuto, *I Diarii*, 7: 128, 152, 164.

68. Ibid. 1: 106 /4: 109; Ibid. 7: 226, 234–235. Moresini, in Damascus, reported to Venice that Bayezid sent artillery in response to Qānsūh's request because Bayezid feared the Safavids, and wanted an alliance. Mo-

resini thought that the artillery was destined for use against Ismail but he was mistaken.

69. Ibn Iyās, *Bada'i*, 1: 115 /4: 119.

70. Sanuto, *I Diarii*, 5: 551. Contarini's dispatch was dated March 4, 1508. Zeno took over duties as consul at the end of 1508.

71. Ibn Iyās, *Bada'i*, 1: 119–120/4: 123–124; Sanuto, *I Diarii*, 7: 286, 442, 529, 533–534.

72. An illustration of the use of diplomatic correspondence to obtain information or to secure neutrality is found in Riazul Islam, ed. *The Shāmlū Letters: A New Source of Iranian Diplomatic Correspondence* (Karachi: The Institute of Central and West Asian Studies, 1971). These documents show the elaborate alternate channels utilized in the absence of formal embassies. They also show the change in tone in correspondence as the balance of power shifted in seventeenth-century Mughul-Safavid relations.

73. For a magnificently illustrated example of the manipulation of symbols of Ottoman power in the context of diplomacy see Gülrü Necipoğlu, "Süleyman the Magnificent and the Representation of Power in the Context of Ottoman-Hapsburg-Papal Rivalry," *Art Bulletin* 71 (1989): 401–417. Necipoğlu illustrates Süleiman's manipulation of symbols in diplomacy, parades, and ceremonies, focusing on the creation of a ceremonial crown.

74. Sanuto, *I Diarii*, 7: 529: one account that year estimates Bayezid's income at three million gold ducats a year, the number of *janissaries* at fifteen thousand men and Ismail's army at twenty-five thousand cavalry (sixty thousand including infantry).

75. Sanuto, *I Diarii*, 7: 631, 634, 636–638, 654.

76. Ibn Iyās, *Bada'i*, 1: 148, 153, 156, 178 /4: 152, 156, 159, 184; Sanuto, *I Diarii*, 9: 546–547. Nicolo Justinian reported in January 1510 from Edirne that Amīr 'Alān had already met with Bayezid. He did not know the agenda of the meeting, but reported rumors of an Ottoman-Mamluk league. It is such reports, rather than actual alliances, which provide the substance for the supposition of an Ottoman-Mamluk rapprochement. The same news of Bayezid's ill-health, which had alarmed the Mamluk sultan, was relayed to Venice, via Corfu in June 1509.

77. Sanuto, *I Diarii*, 7: 631, 663; 8: 12. The *bailo*, Andrea Foscolo, in Istanbul, reported in September 1508 that Bayezid was doing poorly. In Cyprus it was predicted that the sultan would not last much longer.

78. Sadeddin, *Tac*, 2: 131–132 connects Korkud's flight to the struggle with his brother Ahmed. Celalzade Mustafa, "Kitab-i Measir-i Selim-

Han" ms. Hazine 1415, Topkapı Müzesi, Istanbul, p. 42a, says only that Korkud was not in his father's favor. Ibn Iyās, *Bada'i*, 1: 148, 150–153, 157 /4: 152–155, 160 relates that Korkud arrived in Cairo on June 8, 1509 and remained through the following year. See also Uluçay, "Yavuz Sultan Selim," pp. 58–60; and Feridun Beg, *Mecmu'a*, pp. 356–358 for Bayezid's and Qānsūh's correspondence concerning Korkud.

79. Ibn Iyās, *Bada'i*, 1: 165, 178, 180 /4: 167, 184, 186–187. Visitors were usually kept on foot on such occasions. Sadeddin, *Tac*, 2: 131, says Korkud's stipend was three thousand florins a month (although it is unlikely that Korkud was actually paid in gold at all given the Mamluk shortage).

80. Uluçay, "Yavuz Sultan Selim," pp. 77–88.

81. The extent of local Anatolian support for Ismail Safavi has been the subject of a great deal of speculation. Michel Mazzaoui, *The Origins of the Safavids: Si'ism, Sūfism, and the Gulāt* (Wiesbaden: F. Steiner, 1972), for example, gives a complex analysis of the political and religious context for the rise of the Safavid sheikhs; Uluçay, "Yavuz," pp. 54–90; Savory, "Consolidation," p. 93; R. Molov, "Contributions à l'Étude du Fond Socio-Historique du Destan "Koroğlu," *Études Balkaniques* 7 (1967): 113–117; H. R. Roemer, "The Safavid Period," in *Cambridge History of Iran*, v. 6, *The Timurid and Safavid Periods*, ed. Peter Jackson and Laurence Lockhart (Cambridge: Cambridge University Press, 1986), pp. 189–350.

82. E. Dennison Ross, "The Early Years of Shah Ismail, Founder of the Safavi Dynasty," *Journal of the Royal Asiatic Society* (1896), pp. 298–307, 332 on Ismail's followers in eastern Anatolia; Jean Louis Bacqué-Grammont, "Un Rapport Inedit sur la Revolte Anatoliene de 1527," *Studia Islamica* 62 (1985): 155–172. Bacqué-Grammont uses Topkapı documents to illustrate discontent in eastern Anatolia and the oppression by officials, which contributed to the Shah Kulu revolt.

83. Rūmlū, *Ahsan*, pp. 57–58, a more detailed account.

84. Rūmlū, *Ahsan*, pp. 57–58. Ismail did not follow up on the rebellion with a military action. His execution of the offending Shah Kulu followers, however, was more likely intended to bolster his reputation for justice than to mollify the Ottoman sultan. See also ms. Reis ül-Kuttap 655, pp. 20b, 50, Süleymaniye Kütüphanesi, Istanbul.

85. Ibn Iyās, *Bada'i*, 1: 176–177, 179, 184–187/4: 182–185, 190–192.

86. Savory, "Consolidation," pp. 87–124. Ismail attempted to orchestrate an anti-Ottoman alliance with both Spain and the emperor but met with no success.

87. Ibn Iyās, *Bada'i*, 1: 190, 195/4: 196, 201.

88. Fisher, *The Foreign Relations*, pp. 105–106.

89. Sanuto, *I Diarii*, 14: 400, for example, outlines how abuses against merchants continued in Damascus in spring 1512.

90. Fisher, *The Foreign Relations*, pp. 105–112. Venier's embassy later attempted to smooth Venetian-Mamluk relations.

91. Ibn Iyās, *Bada'i*, 1: 178–179, 203/4: 184, 209. Another envoy, Bāshir, was sent to solicit the cooperation of the Indian Muslim rulers against the Portuguese. Bāshir, however, appears to have gotten no further than the Yemen as he returned to Cairo the following April.

92. Ibn Iyās, *Bada'i*, 1: 184/4: 191. Word reached Cairo in August 1510. Sanuto, *I Diarii*, 11: 827–830.

93. Ibid., 1: 185–187, 199, 201/4: 191–192, 205, 207, on the news of Shaibānī Khān's defeat and on the reprisals taken for the Ayas attack.

94. Ibn Iyās, *Bada'i*, 1: 196/4: 202.

95. See ms. Reis ül-Kuttap no. 655, pp. 8a, 9b, 53b, 79b on Korkud in Egypt, Ahmed in Amasya, and the struggles of the brothers.

96. Sadeddin, *Tac*, 2: 182–186; Sanuto, *I Diarii*, 14: 50, 162, 216. Sansovino, *Historia Universale dell'Origine e Imperio de Turchi* (Venice: n.p., 1582), p. 53 mentions Korkud's unsuccessful bid to court the favor of the *janissaries*.

97. Celalzade Mustafa, "Kitab-i," p. 44a says Ahmed joined with the *kızılbaş*. Sanuto, *I Diarii*, 14: 37, 50–52, 162. There is some evidence that either Ahmed or one of the Anatolian governors had defeated some Safavid troops at the eastern frontiers in the winter 1511–1512, but now the threat to Ahmed from Selim was most urgent. Ahmed's army was said to number 40,000, Sanuto, *I Diarii*, 14: 291–292. On the marriage see Sanuto, *I Diarii*, 14: 246, 287, 289, 304. Korkud was forced to flee from Ahmed to Istanbul, see Fisher, *The Foreign Relations*, pp. 109–112.

98. Rūmlū, *Ahsan*, pp. 62–63, Ismail also sent forces into eastern Anatolia shortly after Selim was proclaimed sultan. Bayezid abdicated to his son on April 24, 1512, Sanuto, *I Diarii*, 14: 222.

99. Sanuto, *I Diarii*, 14: 52, 292–293.

100. Sanuto, *I Diarii*, 14: 292–293.

101. Ibn Iyās, *Bada'i*, 1: 217/4: 221–228, 230.

102. Sanuto, *I Diarii*, 15: 356–357.

103. Ibn Iyās, *Bada'i*, 1: 234–235, 240–241/4: 252–253, 257. See also Rūmlū, *Ahsan*, p. 68 for brief mention of 'Alā ad-Dawla's activities between 1508–1514.

104. Ms. Reis ül-Kuttap no. 655, p. 8b on *kızılbaş* in Iraq and Azarbaican.

105. Ibn Iyās, *Bada'i*, 1: 242, 251/4: 259, 265; Sanuto, *I Diarii*, 14: 247, 289.

106. Ibn Iyās, *Bada'i*, 1: 251–253/4: 268–269. Sanuto, *I Diarii*, 12: 308–309. A similar French embassy had come in 1511 bearing rich presents. Envoys were also sent to Cairo representing the interests of the following: Georgia, the Ramadanid principality, Yusuf ibn Sufi Halil, a Türkmen prince, Tunis, the Sharif of Mecca, Prince Mahmud, the Türkmen Ibn Turğul, and also the governor of Damascus and the head of the ill-fated expedition to India, Husain al-Kūrdī.

107. Sanuto, *I Diarii*, 15: 392, 512, 547; 16: 193–194. Ismail was aiding both Ahmed and Ahmed's son Murad. Sansovino, *Historia*, pp. 54–57. Sansovino, who was in the Ottoman military at the time, gives an account of Selim's pursuit of Ahmed. Selim's son Süleiman was sent against Ahmed in 1512. In winter 1512–1513, Selim's forces caught and killed Korkud; see Eleazar Birnbaum, "The Ottomans and Chagatay Literature: An Early 16th Century Manuscript of Navā'ī's *Dīvān* in Ottoman Orthography," *Central Asian Journal* 20 (1976): 157–190. That spring, Selim marched from Bursa and defeated Ahmed in Anatolia.

108. Rūmlū, *Ahsan*, pp. 62–63. Ismail sent Nūr 'Alī Khalifa Rūmlū against Malatia in summer 1512. This army took Tokat and Nıkşehr and defeated Sinan Pasha's Ottoman army near Erzincan. Nūr 'Alī was joined for a time by Murad, Ahmed's son, who later took refuge at the Safavid court.

109. Ibn Iyās, *Bada'i*, 1: 253–254/4: 269–270; Sanuto, *I Diarii*, 14: 410–411, 414–415: Selim also sent an envoy to announce his accession to Venice.

110. Ibn Iyās, *Bada'i*, 1: 267, 303–304/4: 285, 324.

111. Sansovino, *Historia*, p. 57 mentions only Alaüddin, the other was named Süleiman. Ibn Iyās, *Bada'i*, 1: 271–272, 283, 286 289/4: 289, 303, 306, 309.

112. Sanuto, *I Diarii*, 15: 355–356. The Portuguese wreaked havoc on Muslim shipping in 1512 and were said, according to reports from Damascus, to be aided by Ismail. Ibn Iyās, *Bada'i*, 1: 335/4: 359, wrote in March of 1514 that hardly a ship had arrived at Jidda for the past few years and, due to European corsair activity, the trade at Alexandria and Damietta had declined severely as well.

113. Ibn Iyās, *Bada'i*, 1: 299, 302–303, 305–306, 309/4: 319–323, 328, 331. The introduction of new copper money, among other problems like the plague, had caused a great deal of hardship among the populace.

114. Khvandamīr, *Habīb*, p. 543, reports that Selim was eager to conquer Azerbaican and sent an envoy to Ismail to declare his intentions. This account is similar to that in the Ross Anonymous, "Tarīkh-i Şāh Ismaʿīl Safevī," ms. Or 3248, British Museum, London, p. 246b; Ibn Iyās, *Badaʿi*, 1: 337, 339/4: 362, 364. Although Ḥasan Rūmlū, *Ahsan*, p. 68, mentions correspondence sent to the Porte by Khān Muḥammad Ustājlū in the years before Çaldıran, there is no mention of Safavid ambassadors to Istanbul between 1512–1514.

115. Rūmlū, *Ahsan*, p. 68, on the envoy sent to Ismail at Hamadan to declare war. Ismail allowed this envoy to return home and sent word to Khān Muḥammad Ustājlū in Diyarbakr to mobilize his troops: Ibn Iyās, *Badaʿi*, 1: 347/4: 372–373.

116. Ibn Iyās, *Badaʿi*, 1: 348–355/4: 372–382.

117. Ibid., 1: 371–372/4: 379, 399–400.

118. Ibn Iyās, *Badaʿi*, 1: 356–357, 365–366, 373–374/4: 392, 402–404. Ibn Iyās also related the arrival of a false envoy, claiming to be from Selim, who was imprisoned and tortured. This man was rumored to be a spy of Hasan, Ahmed's son and Selim's nephew, who was then resident in Ismail's camp.

119. Ibn Iyās, *Badaʿi*, 1: 366–367/4: 395–396.

120. Ibn Iyās, *Badaʿi* 1: 355, 363/4: 383, 391. The force sent to Aleppo consisted of 3,400 men, veterans and recruits.

121. Rūmlū, *Ahsan*, p. 68

122. Ibn Iyās, *Badaʿi*, 1: 369, 373–375/4: 398, 402–404.

123. Ibid., 1: 371, 378/4: 400, 408.

124. Ross Anonymous, "Tarīkh-i," p. 254b, reports Selim retreated to Amasia out of fear. Khvandamīr, *Habīb*, p. 569, says that because Selim was afraid of Ismail and because he could not get past Tabriz he returned to Anatolia. There he received envoys from Khair Beg, the governor of Aleppo, who offered his submission and urged Selim to send the Ottoman armies against Egypt.

125. Rūmlū, *Ahsan*, pp. 69–70, described the aftermath of Çaldıran with Selim marching to Amasia and Ismail returning to Tabriz. Ibn Iyās, *Badaʿi*, 1: 382–384, 390–391, 398, 413/4: 413–414, 432, 447–448; Sanuto, *I Diarii*, 20: 167, contains a report from Alexandria in February saying that the returning Mamluk army had sacked Gazara.

126. Angiolello, "Narrative," p. 123; Sanuto, *I Diarii*, 20: 109; Zeno, *Travels*, p. 64. Ibn Iyās does not mention an envoy to the Mamluk court from Ismail. A report from Alexandria in Sanuto, however, mentions a

league between Qānsūh, ʿAlā ad-Dawla, and Ismail in July 1515; Sanuto, *I Diarii*, 20: 355.

127. In April 1515 in Istanbul, there were reports of this conspiracy, Sanuto, *I Diarii*, 20: 95–96.

128. Ibid., 20: 40.

129. Ibn Iyās, *Badaʿi*, 1: 401–402/4: 435.

130. On this series of events see: Şükri, "Selim name" ms. Hazine 1597–1598, Topkapı Sarayı Müzesi, Istanbul, pp. 152, 157 on Selim's support for Shāh Suvār who had asked his assistance, and on Qānsūh's request that he not do so; Şükri, "Selim name" ms. H.O. 32, p. 36 on Selim's support for Shāh Suvār; Ibn Iyās, *Badaʿi*, 1: 375, 381, 404/4: 404, 411, 438; Sanuto, *I Diarii*, 20: 109; Uruç Beg (Don Juan), *Don Juan of Persia, A Shiʿah Catholic, 1560–1604*, trans. G. Le Strange (London: George Routledge and Sons, 1926), p. 120.

131. Besim Atalay, *Maraş Tarihi ve Coğrafyası* (Istanbul: Matbaa-i Amire, 1330/1920), p. 51, citing Evliya Çelebi, says that Selim wrote to Qānsūh as to a vassal. When Selim wrote that if the Mamluk sultan did not do as he wished he would come and get him, Qānsūh responded, "Come." The same source says that ʿAlā ad-Dawla read the *khutba* in the name of the Mamluk sultan but took sustenance (*nan u niʿmet*) from the Ottomans. Ross Anonymous, "Tarīkh-i," pp. 139b–140a, relates that ʿAlā ad-Dawla dressed up his men as Ottoman or Mamluk envoys to fool the real envoys when they came into thinking that the messengers of their enemies were visiting his court.

132. Sanuto, *I Diarii*, 20: 40, 95–96, 109.

133. Ibid., 20: 355; Ibn Iyās, *Badaʿi*, 1: 411–412, 423–424/4: 445–446, 459.

134. Ibn Iyās, *Badaʿi*, 1: 415/4: 449–450. This officer fled in April 1515.

135. Angiolello, "Narrative," p. 123; Rūmlū, *Ahsan*, p. 73; Sanuto, *I Diarii*, 20: 109, 383, 385, 403, 472, 556–557; Ibn Iyās, *Badaʿi*, 1: 423/4: 458–459. Both Angiolello and Sanuto contain accounts that ʿAlā ad-Dawla sent an envoy to Selim on the march to protest his friendship, but to no avail.

136. Şükri, "Selim name," ms. H.O. 32, p. 35a. ʿAlā ad-Dawla was already in disfavor when Selim went to winter in Amasia, according to Şükri. This lends weight to the argument that Selim wished to punish the Zū al-Kadr ruler for not participating in the campaign of 1514. Rūmlū, *Ahsan*, pp. 74–75; Angiolello, "Narrative," p. 123; Sanuto, *I Diarii*, 20: 95, 109, 355, 557.

137. Rūmlū, *Ahsan*, p. 77; Sanuto, *I Diarii*, 20: 167. ʿAlī later led the Ottoman left wing in the battle of Marj Dabik, outside Cairo, and served as an Ottoman governor.

138. Sanuto, *I Diarii*, 20: 355, 358; 21: 359.

139. Ibn Iyās, *Badaʿi*, 1: 427/4: 462–463.

140. Barbosa, *Book of Duarte Barbosa*, p. 44 mentions the timber and artillery brought to Suez and the "great sums" spent in the attempt to thwart the Portuguese navigations.

141. Ibn Iyās, *Badaʿi*, 1: 428–431, 437–439/4: 464–466, 473, 475.

142. Ibid., 1: 431, 435–436, 446, 448–449/4: 466, 470–471, 482–485. The Mamluk defenses were further compromised by a revolt of the mamluks in the citadel in December 1515.

143. This spy, for that in fact was his mission, was named Qānsūh. He returned to Cairo in December 1515 bringing more dire warnings of Selim's proposed invasion.

144. Sanuto, *I Diarii*, 21: 456. It is noteworthy that, despite news from the *beglerbeg* of Anatolia that Ismail was preparing a new army, the *bailo* Bembo identified Selim's objective as Egypt.

145. See also ms. TKS E/12282: Qānsūh's communication to Selim; Kerslake, "The Correspondence."

146. Sanuto, *I Diarii*, 22: 485, 583–584; 23: 132.

147. Rūmlū, *Ahsan*, pp. 75–76. Selim's presence in Anatolia may have prompted the revolt against Ismail of Ahmed Çelebi and Bığlu Çavuş in Amid in 1516. Ahmed refused to pay the Amid revenues to the Safavids. Sanuto, *I Diarii*, 22: 413, reported that both Selim and Qānsūh sent envoys to Ismail in spring-summer 1516.

Chapter 4. Ottoman Naval Development.

1. Ibn Khaldūn, *The Muqaddimah*, trans. Franz Rosenthal (Princeton: Princeton University Press, 1970), p. 213.

2. Setton, *The Papacy*, 3: 141, for example on Bayezid's "weak rule."

3. Hess, "The Ottoman Conquest," pp. 62–64 lists the sources for Mehmed II's naval expansion after the conquest of Istanbul. This expansion included the levying of sailors, constructing arsenals, and building ships. Kritovoulos, *History of Mehmed the Conqueror*, trans. Charles T. Riggs (Westport, Connecticut: Greenwood Press, 1970, pp. 53–57). Kritovoulos puts at sixty-seven the number of warships Mehmed transported

overland into the Golden Horn to support his attack on Constantinople. This account also details the nature of hand-to-hand combat and boarding techniques when galleys closed in battle (utilizing infantry armed with battle axes and archers in the rigging).

4. Sadeddin, *Tac*, 2: 86.

5. Levying of both sailors and oarsmen for the fleet was a chronic problem. Ms. Kepeci no. 2544, Mevkufat Kalemi, Baş Bakanlık Arşivi, Istanbul contained references to this problem as early as 1499. The register (*defter*) listing oarsmen levies from Satılmış *kaza* (administrative district) for the naval campaign against Venice shows many men listed as either "sick" or "fled." Another *defter* in the same archive refers to the levying of oarsmen for the Mediterranean early in Süleiman's reign in 1527: Ms. Ali Emiri, Süleiman Tasnifi no. 325, Baş Bakanlık Arşivi, Istanbul. On mariners in the fourteenth century fleet of Umur Pasha, see Halil Inalcık, "The Rise of the Turcoman Maritime Principalities in Anatolia, Byzantium, and the Crusades," *Byzantinische Forschungen* 9 (1985): 179–217. Crew shortages were a chronic problem in European navies as well. See Donald Weinstein, *Ambassador from Venice, Pietro Pasqualigo in Lisbon, 1501* (Minneapolis: University of Minnesota Press, 1960), pp. 20–21.

6. Shah Ismail had conquered Tabriz the year before; in summer 1502, he sent an envoy to the Mamluk sultan. Ibn Iyās, *Bada'i*, 1: 35, 42/4: 39, 46, does not mention this envoy. He mentions only that in August 1502 there was a scare in Cairo over reports of Safavid troops near the Syrian frontiers. That winter an Ottoman envoy arrived in Cairo, perhaps to discuss Ismail's successes. The envoy sent by the Grand Master of Rhodes to Korkud, Bayezid's son, in Anatolia, reported that Ismail had sent two hundred forty agents into Anatolia to proselytize. In response, Bayezid ordered that his governors kill the followers of Ismail in Anatolia, and levy one of every five men in the countryside for the army: Sanuto *I Diarii*, 4: 405–406, 481. See also Pál Fodor, "The Way of a Seljuq Institution to Hungary: the Cerehor," *Acta Orientalia Academiae Scientiarum Hungaricae* 38, no. 3 (1984): 386 on corvee levy of one man per ten households in 1566.

7. Sanuto, *I Diarii*, 4: 403, 480. See Alberi, Series 3, v. 3: 10–13 on the question of prisoners from Santa Maura complicating ambassador Gritti's negotiations with the Ottomans. The Ottoman prisoners had been "sold" and could not be used to secure the release of Venetian prisoners.

8. Venice also returned Santa Maura and negotiated repayment of damages suffered there by the Ottomans, see Tansel, *Bayezit*, pp. 223–224. For a report from the captain general of the armada to Venice on the loss of Modon in 1500 and precautions to be taken against the Ottomans, see Sanuto, *I Diarii*, 3: 688–692.

9. Sadeddin, *Tac*, 2: 90. The ships mentioned are: *kuke* (cog), *kalyon*,

kadırga, and *kayık* (assorted small vessels) listed largest first on down. Halil İnalcık, "Gelibolu," in *Encyclopedia of Islam*, 2d. ed., 2, pt. 2: 983–987. See also İsmail Hakkı Uzunçarşılı, *Osmanlı Devletinin Merkez ve Bahriye Teşkilatı* (Ankara: Türk Tarih Kurumu Basımevi, 1984), pp. 455–479, and Svat Soucek, "Certain Types of Ships in Ottoman-Turkish Terminology," *Turcica* 7 (1975): 233–249. Alberto Tenenti, *Cristoforo da Canal, La Marine Venetienne Avant Lepante* (Paris: S.E.V.P.E.N., 1962), pp. 29–60 gives a detailed description of sixteenth-century ship types. Ms. Maliyeden Mudevver Defterleri, v. 1, no. 23051, p. 9, Baş Bakanlık Arşivi, Istanbul, is an early *defter* from 1496 on fleet expenses and repair. İnalcık, "Maritime Principalities," pp. 205, 207 mentions combined fleets under Umur Pasha of over three hundred ships sailing from western Anatolia in the 1330s and 1340s. For Venetian ships and naval operations, see Frederic Lane, "Naval Actions and Fleet Organization, 1499–1502," in Hale, *Renaissance Venice*, pp. 146–167.

10. Robert Schwoebel, *The Shadow of the Crescent: The Renaissance Image of the Turk (1453–1517)* (Niewkoop: B. De Graaf, 1967), p. 194.

11. Sanuto, *I Diarii*, 3: 1525; 4: 22, 38, 242, 261; Sadeddin, *Tac*, 2: 88–89. New galleys were under construction and fifteen to twenty were completed by March 1501. See also Emel Esin, "İkinci Bayezid'in H. 904–906/1498–1500 Yıllarında Adalar Denizi'ne Seferi," *Erdem* 1, no. 3 (1985): 789–799 on ships built for Kemal Reis.

12. On the Ottoman shipyards and arsenal, see Colin Imber, "The Navy of Süleiman the Magnificent," pp. 211–281. This article relies heavily on the *mühimme defterleri* and hence concentrates on the period after Selim's reign, but it includes a section on the history of the arsenal development in the earlier period; Uzunçarşılı, *Osmanlı Devletinin*, pp. 394–437. An early prewar account of some arsenal expenses for Avlonya and Prevesa ships is found in Maliyeden Mudevver Defterleri, v. 1, no. 23051, pg. 9. See also: Murat Çizakça, "Ottomans and the Mediterranean: An Analysis of the Ottoman Shipbuilding Industry as Reflected by the Arsenal Registers of Istanbul 1529–1650," *Le Gente del Mediterraneo* 2 (no date): 773–788.

13. Sanuto, *I Diarii*, 4: 393–394, 404, 641. As for the sons or pashas of the sultan being asked to pay for ships, the cost of six galleys would be prohibitively high for one person; even vezirs who engaged in merchant activities seldom owned more than one or two galleys individually. On this occasion, however, this mode of financing an armada is mentioned several times in Sanuto's sources. Alberi, Series 3, v. 3, pp. 421: in the *relazione* of the Venetian *bailo* Matteo Zane in 1594, there is a mention that the sultan, at the grand vezir Sinan Pasha's behest, imposed ship costs on his officials, making each *sancak beg*, *defterdar*, *beglerbeg*, and pasha responsible for one ship at a cost of "3,000 scudi each."

14. A Rhodian report says the troop mobilization was for one man from every five households and the other four households had to pay his expenses. The *tahrir defter* (land/revenue survey register) for Gallipoli of 1474 sketches the organization of the *kapudan* pasha's troops and oarsmen: Muallim Cevdet ms. 079, Gelibolu Tahrir Defterleri 1474/879, pp. 26–58, Baş Bakanlık Arşivi, Istanbul. On the Gallipoli troop mobilizations see Ömer Lutfi Barkan, *XV ve XVIinci Asırlarda Osmanlı Imparatorluğunda Zirai Ekonominin Hukukı ve Mali Esasları*, Istanbul Üniversitesi Yayınları, Edebiyat Fakültesi Türkiyat Enstitüsü (1943), pp. 241–242. This document from 1518 does not include information on the ships per se.

15. See Goffman, *Izmir*, pp. 26–27, 82–85 for examples on various levies exacted in the Izmir area in the seventeenth century. See also Halil Sahillioğlu, "16 Yüzyıl Sonu Osmanlı Tacirleri—Vergi Adaleti—(Alī'nin Nasihatü's-salatin'inden)," *Toplum ve Bilim*, no. 6–7 (1978): 157–175 on merchants and campaign financing.

16. Imber, "The Navy," pp. 218–222, 239, 266–267 briefly estimates fleet maintenance costs and discusses levies of oarsmen. He says that arsenal expenses were financed by the treasury, local customs and market dues, and other local sources. He also gives a detailed account of troop levies for the fleet under Süleiman. On the costs and sizes of ships in the early sixteenth century, see Luciana Gatti, "Costruzioni navali in Luguria fra XV e XVI secolo," in *Studi di Storia Navale*, Henri Bresc, ed. (n.p.: Giunti, 1975), pp. 25–72. For studies on the Venetian arsenal, see Robert C. Davis, *Shipbuilders of the Venetian Arsenal: Workers and Workplace in the Preindustrial City* (Baltimore: John's Hopkins University Press, 1991) and on details of labor organization, pay, pilfering and rituals; and Alberto Sacerdoti, "Note sulle Galere da Mercato Veneziane nel XV Secolo," *Bolletino dell' Istituto di Storia della Societa e dello Stato Veneziano* 4 (1962), pp. 80–105.

17. Ömer Lutfi Barkan, "Avarız," in *Islam Ansiklopedisi*, 2 (1970): 15–16.

18. Sanuto, *I Diarii*, 5: 465–466. For mention of Gritti in the Ottoman sources see M. Tayyib Gökbilgin, *XV–XVI. Asırlarda Edirne ve Paşa Livası Vakıflar, Mülkler, Mukataalar*, Series Istanbul Üniversitesi Edebiyat Fakültesi Yayınları, no. 508 (Istanbul: Ülçer Basımevi, 1952), p. 485.

19. Goodrich, *The Ottoman Turks and the New World*, p. 11, points out that Ottoman captains, among them the famous Piri Reis, who authored the geographic guide, *Kitab-i Bahriye*, were important disseminators of geographic knowledge. They were also an important voice for exploration and conquest.

20. Sanuto, *I Diarii*, 7: 18–19. Katib Çelebi, *Maritime Wars*, p. 19–

20 mentions a shipbuilder named Iani, in 1498, who was responsible for the two large *kuke* (cogs) built by Bayezid. He said that this man had learned shipbuilding in Venice. Daud Pasha was *kapudan* from 1498–1502 and *vezir* from 1502–1505. See Hedda Reindl, *Mahner um Bayezid: Eine Prosopographische Studie Über die Epoch Sultan Bayezids II, (1481–1512)*, Islamkundlische Untersuhungen Series no. 75 (Berlin: Klaus Schwartz, 1983), pp. 177–189. On master shipbuilders, Gian Francesco Giustiniano in 1534 and Michele Beneto in 1553 in the Ottoman arsenal see Alberi, *Le Relazioni*, Series 3, v. 1, pp. 17, 67. The Venetian envoy Navagero estimated that there were 300 workers in the Istanbul arsenal in 1553 but many more when an actual armada was being prepared.

21. Sanuto, *I Diarii*, 6: 248. Report from Chios to Venice.

22. Ibid. 6: 63–64. Ottoman fleets of eighteen and twenty-seven ships were reported cruising near Corfu in fall 1506. Sanuto, *I Diarii*, 8: 506, Kemal Reis, for example, was reported leaving the straits for Negroponte in June 1509 with forty ships.

23. Alberi, *Le Relazioni*, Series 3, v. 3: 12–13 puts Kara Durmuş' fleet size at twenty-six fustas and a galiota; Sadeddin, *Tac*, 2: 129.

24. The best treatment to date of naval technology is in John Guilmartin, *Gunpowder and Galleys, Changing Technology and Mediterranean Warfare at Sea in the Sixteenth Century* (Cambridge: Cambridge University Press, 1980). For Indian Ocean technology see: K. N. Chaudhuri, *Trade and Civilization*, pp. 121–159. See also Imber, "Süleyman," pp. 223–225, 227. Imber tends to emphasize the Ottoman technical problems, citing Lutfi Pasha, who said in the 1540s that the "infidel" naval management was superior. Imber says that the Ottoman army remained more formidable than the navy. The Venetian accounts tend to contradict this interpretation.

25. Gulimartin, "The Tactics of the Battle of Lepanto Clarified: The Impact of Social, Economic and Political Factors," in *New Aspects of Naval History*, ed. by Craig L. Symonds (Annapolis: Naval Institute Press, 1981), pp. 41–65. This article discusses, among other tactical factors, the differing use of free and slave oarsmen and the availability of seamen in determining naval development. Sanuto, *I Diarii*, 5: 460–464, in the *relazione* of Andrea Gritti to the Venetian Senate in December 1503, mentions that Bayezid is replacing Christian seamen with "*azaps*," Anatolians, for greater security since the Christians will desert to the enemy in a battle. This contradicts Imber's interpretation of Katib Çelebi that it was Turkish seamen who fled the ships under conditions of combat: Imber, "Süleyman," pp. 260–261. Inalcık, "Maritime Principalities," pp. 209–211 discusses the designation "*azeb*," for Muslim irregulars fighting in both the army and the navy. On oarsmen levy difficulties in the mid-sixteenth century see Alberi, *Le Relazioni*, Series 3, v. 1, pp. 67–68.

26. C. H. Imber, "The Costs of Naval Warfare: The Accounts of Hay-reddin Barbarosa's Herceg Novi Campaign in 1539," *Archivum Otto-manicum* 4 (1972): 203–216, for example, (a *defter* of fleet costs); Frederic Lane, "Naval Actions and Fleet Organization, 1499–1502," in J. R. Hale, ed., *Renaissance Venice* (Totawa, New Jersey: Rowman and Littlefield, 1973), pp. 146–173 on Venice's fleet mobilizations and crew costs.

27. Frederic C. Lane, *Venice and History*, pp. 87–98 on the public debt and pp. 143–284; Lane, *Venice, A Maritime Republic*, pp. 118–171, 354–375.

28. Similar arrangements were used by other European states. The Sicilian fleet in the later sixteenth century, for example, numbered from six to twenty-two galleys, some managed by the government and others leased out. In emergencies, seamen were recruited by lot and the fighting element on the ships was provided by regular Spanish soldiers: see Dennis Mack Smith, *Medieval Sicily 800–1713* (New York: The Viking Press, 1968), pp. 142–143. See also William Ledyard Rogers, *Naval Warfare Under Oars, 4th to 16th Centuries: A Study of Strategy, Tactics and Ship Design* (Annapolis: Naval Institute Press, 1967), pp. 114–116.

29. On the organization of Venetian shipping, see Frederic C. Lane, "Rhythm and Rapidity of Turnover in Venetian Trade in the Fifteenth Century," in *Venice and History*, pp. 109–127; and *Venice, a Maritime Republic*, pp. 336–375. On the suspension of the *muda* convoys in certain years when it was thought unsafe or unprofitable to sail, see Sanuto, *I Diarii*, 3: 1198–1199; Fulin, "Girolamo," pp. 191–192. On the reserve ships in the Venetian arsenal, see Tenenti, *Cristoforo da Canal*, pp. 121, 152–154.

30. See for example Alberi, *Le Relazioni*, Series 3, v. 3, p. 221. The *relazione* of Paolo Contarini in 1583 discusses the Ottoman naval reorganization and production, saying that the *kapudan* pasha had 200 galleys (new and refurbished) in order in the space of three months [no doubt an exaggeration but it gets the point across].

31. Guilmartin, *Gunpowder*, pp. 131–133. Crew shortages were endemic in the Mediterranean. The losses in trained seamen suffered by the Spanish fleet in the battle of Jerba in 1560 resulted in Spanish naval difficulties for years afterward.

32. Lane, "Naval Actions," pp. 155–160.

33. Sanuto, *I Diarii*, 5: 465, *relazione* of Gritti, December 1503. Gritti said the *sancak beg* of Gallipoli was always the admiral, "whose men were obedient down to the last slave." He "appointed men with naval experience as sea captains" to serve under him. Sadeddin, *Tac*, 2: 109–110 on the mobilization of timariot cavalry (*sipahis*) for the navy during the Ottoman-Venetian war. Later, the maritime *sancaks* were placed under the command of Hayreddin Barbarosa, the actual captain of the fleet.

34. On this dilemma, see Gian Giacomo Musso, *Navigazione e Commercia Genovese con il Levante nei Documenti dell'Archivio di Stato di Genova Secolo XIV–XV* (Rome: Ministero per i Beni Culturali e Ambientali, Publicazione delgi Archivio di Stato, 1975), p. 108.

35. Paolo Preto's pioneering work, *Venezi e i Turchi* (Firenze: n.p., 1975), for example, discusses Ottoman-Italian relations in terms of the ill-defined term "corsari." Where the distinction between naval captains and corsairs is clear in the case of the Italian vessels, ships of Ottoman origin automatically tend to be designated "corsair." For an alternative, on "official" European piracy in the Persian Gulf in the eighteenth century, see John R. Perry, "Mīr Muhannā and the Dutch: Patterns of Piracy in the Persian Gulf," *Studia Iranica* 2, no. 1 (1973), pp. 79–95.

36. For a discussion of Mamluk naval activity in earlier times see Ibn Khaldūn, *Muqaddimah*, pp. 210–213; Aly Mohamed Fahmy, *Muslim Naval Organisation in the Eastern Mediterranean from the Seventh to the Tenth Century A.D.* (Cairo: National Publication and Printing House, 1966).

37. For example, see Sanuto, *I Diarii*, 7: 266 on the nineteen ships which left Istanbul to cruise for corsairs in December 1507; and Ibid. 5: 465–466 for 1503.

38. See Guilmartin, *Gunpowder*, pp. 20, 23–34. Guilmartin discusses what he calls the "entreprenurial approach to naval warfare" in the sixteenth century, a combination of naval service and private commercial venture. With regard to Ottoman policy, he adheres to the cliche that as a continental power the Ottomans were essentially concerned with land rather than sea expansion. But, in this analysis of seaborne tactical economies, he places the Ottoman corsairs in the same boat as the Venetian.

39. Rogers, *Naval Warfare*, p. 148. See also Paul Coles, *The Ottoman Impact on Europe* (New York: Harcourt, Brace, Inc., 1968), p. 89 who, at least, also sees corsair activity on the European side.

40. Sanuto, *I Diarii*, 6: 502, for example, contains news that Kara Durmuş raided Candia in fall of 1506; he carried off sixty animals and a woman. This man fought against Venice with the Ottoman fleet during the Aegean war and then afterwards became a pirate, raiding the Anatolian coasts, see Sadeddin, *Tac* 2: 128–129; Sanuto, *I Diarii*, 4: 242; 5: 465. Captives were frequently ransomed for cash rather than sold as slaves, see Sanuto, *I Diarii*, 5: 307. For another example of captives taken for profit in the sixteenth century, see Peter F. Sugar, "The Ottoman 'Professional Prisoner' on the Western Borders of the Empire in the Sixteenth Century," *Études Balkaniques* 1 (1971): 82–91.

41. Sanuto, *I Diarii*, 6: 502. Domengo Delfin added two captured corsair ships to the fleet at Corfu in 1506, so the benefit of conquered vessels worked for the navies as well as the corsairs.

42. Sanuto, *I Diarii*, 5: 460, 958, 973–974; 6: 168. Tenenti, *Cristoforo da Canal*, pp. 148–149 makes the distinction between Ottoman naval officers and corsairs, but he says that Muslim corsairs operated on orders from the Porte. Judging from the reprisals taken by the sultan against corsairs after 1503, Tenenti would seem to be in error.

43. A *firman* (sultanic decree) of Sultan Süleiman I dated 1530 and addressed to the *kadi* (judge) of Gallipoli, lists the protections guaranteed to the Venetians in Ottoman domains. Among them are the Ottoman responsibility to free Venetian subjects who have been captured and sold as slaves, freedom from the seizure of goods or mariners from Venetian vessels, and freedom from extra tax exactions or interference from any Ottoman official. See Christiane Villain-Gandossi, "Contribution à l'étude des relations diplomatiques et commerciales entre Venise et la Porte ottomane au XVIe siècle (1)," *Südost-Forschungen* 26 (1967): 32–35.

44. Sanuto, *I Diarii*, 5: 958, 973–974; 6: 198.

45. Ibid. 6: 198, 223, 502.

46. Gökbilgin, "Venedik Devlet Arşivindeki Türkçe Belgeler Kolleksiyonu," *Belgeler*, no. 5–8 (1968–1971), pp. 14, 25, 28–30, 32–34, 37–38.

47. Sanuto, *I Diarii*, 6: 531.

48. On the indemnity payment agreement between Venice and the Porte, reflecting the "command" form of the Ottoman interpretation, see Kemal Paşazade, *Tarih-i Al-i Osman, Defter VII*, Türk Tarih Kurumu Series 1, no. 5 (Ankara: Türk Tarih Kurumu Basımevi, 1954), p. 515. See also Halil Inalcık, "Imtiyazat," in *Encyclopedia of Islam*, 2d. ed., 3: 1179–1189; Irene Melikoff, "Bāyezīd II et Venise: Cinq Lettres Imperiales (Nāme-i Hümāyūn) Provenant de l'Archivio di Stato di Venezia," *Turcica* 1(1969): 123–149; Luigi Bonelli, "Il Trattato Turco-Veneto del 1540," in *Centenario della Nascita di Michele Amari* (Palermo: n.p., 1910), 2: 332–363; Martin Hartmann, "Das Privileg Selims I für die Venezianer von 1517," *Mitteilungen der Vorderasiatischen Gesellschaft: Orientalistische Studien* 22 (1918): 201–222.

49. M. Tayyib Gökbilgin, "Yeni Belgelerin Işığı Altında Kanuni Sultan Süleyman devrinde Osmanlı-Venedik Münasebetleri," in *Kanuni Armağanı*, T. T. K. Yayınlar Series 7, no. 55 (Ankara: T.T.K., 1970), pp. 173–175, 177, 183. Gökbilgin has done the seminal work on Ottoman-Venetian relations in a series of articles on documents in the Venetian archives, particularly on the evolution of the *ahidnames*.

50. Sanuto, *I Diarii*, 7: 81, 231.

51. Sanuto, *I Diarii*, 6: 531; 7: 231.

52. Ibid. 6: 195. Measures changed by volume and weight from place

to place and over time. A lengthy note on measures is contained in chapter 6. For measures such as the stera/staio, see Inalcık "Ottoman Metrology," and Ashtor, "Levantine Weights and Standard Parcels". See also Gök-bilgin, "Türkçe Belgeler," pp. 34, 37–38 on the Ottoman rice and salt pur-chases from Venetian territory in 1561.

53. Sanuto, *I Diarii*, 5: 307; 7: 538, 613. Pirate depredations on the grain trade affected Ottomans and Europeans alike. Ibid., 5: 354; the proveditor of the armada in October 1503 was detaining grain ships at Corfu because of a food shortage. He said he had been unable to obtain grain from the mainland because Bayezid ordered the *sancak begs* and *subaşıs* (sub-province governors and their timariot lieutenants) not to al-low it. This followed on a spate of grain ship seizures by pirates.

54. Alberi, *Le Relazioni*, Series 3, v. 3, p. 86,

55. Lane, "Naval Actions," p. 157.

56. Daud Pasha, also called Küçük Daud, served from 1498–1502 and actively participated in the Ottoman-Venetian wars. Hersek Ahmed Pasha served from 1504 to 1509, Iskender Pasha from 1512 to 1513, and Cafer Pasha from 1513 to 1520, the year of sultan Selim's death. See Im-ber, "Süleyman," pp. 248–257.

57. Sidi Ali Reis, *Mirat ül-Memalik*, ed. Ahmed Cevdet (Istanbul: 1313), p. 14. For a brief biography of Sidi Ali and his various appointments and salaries under Sultan Süleiman, see Çengiz Orhonlu, "Seydi Ali Reis," *Tarih Enstitüsü Dergisi* 1 (Ekim 1970): 39–56.

58. Svat Soucek, "The Rise of the Barbarossas in North Africa," *Ar-chivum Ottomanicum* 3 (1971): 243–247. Tenenti, *Venezia e i Corsari*, p. 43 gives the sailing time from Algiers to Corfu in 1557 as approximately twenty-two days. See also Hess, "The Evolution," pp. 1903–1906.

59. See Ismet Parmaksızoğlu, "Kemāl Re'is," in *Islam Ansiklopedisi* 3 (1970): 566–568. On the activities of Kemal and the Barbarossas in the western Mediterranean, see Andrew Hess, *The Forgotten Frontier*, pp. 60–65.

60. Kemal Paşazade, "Tarih-i Al-i Osman," ms. Turc 1047, p. 114, Bibliothéque Nationale, Paris. Simon Pepper and Nicholas Adams, *Fire-arms and Fortifications* (Chicago: University of Chicago Press, 1986), p. 156 describes the landing of *janissaries* from ships to support an assault on Elba in 1555.

61. Sanuto, *I Diarii*, 4: 22, 43, 47–48, 71. Sadeddin, *Tac*, 2: 104 also gives the size of Kemal's fleet as thirty *kadırga*. It is possible that the famous geographer Piri Reis accompanied his uncle during these combat missions against Venice and on subsequent voyages: Svat Soucek, "A Propos du Livre d'Instructions Nautiques de Piri Reis," *Revue des Études*

Islamiques 39, no. 2 (1971): 246. Escort ships were a necessity, especially before the end of the war. A report from Nicosia in 1500 says it is impossible to go from Cyprus to Syria with only a few escort galleys: Sanuto, *I Diarii*, 3: 680. Lane, "Naval Actions," pp. 148–149 says the total of Venetian war galleys at sea fell from thirty-five in 1495 to thirteen in 1498.

62. The galiots had two oars per bank from the mast to the focone and one oar per bank on the rest of the ship. The fustas has one oar per bank.

63. Sanuto, *I Diarii*, 4: 88. *Levend* in Turkish does not necessarily mean corsair (it can mean low status unskilled temporary mariner levies, or youthful fighters) but that is the sense in this passage.

64. Tansel, *Bayezit*, p. 178 notes that when Bayezid made a similar request to Venice in 1487 for the use of Famagosta, the Venetians were not willing to cooperate. Alberi, *Le Relazioni*, Series 3, v. 3: 47–48 cites the *relazione* of Justinian read in Venice on February 7, 1514. Justinian was in Istanbul on April 25, 1512 when the *janissaries* acclaimed Selim as Padishah and forced Bayezid to abdicate. He was commissioned on May 30, 1513 to congratulate the new sultan. Selim spoke words of friendship to the envoy and said he was happy to confirm the peace terms to be drawn up by the vezirs Hersek Ahmed, Mustafa, and Dukagin Ahmedzade. See Reindl, *Männer*, pp. 129–146, 302–318. Hersek Ahmed was grand vezir; he had served as *kapudan* earlier, in 1487–1489 and 1504–1509. This may account for his attention to naval affairs.

65. Sanuto, *I Diarii*, 17: 539–540; 18: 421; 19: 84.

66. Sanuto, *I Diarii*, 19: 66. A fleet of six galleys and nine fustas had been sent to the coasts of Karaman in 1514 to act against "rebels."

67. Francesco Guicciardini, *The History of Italy,* trans. Sidney Alexander (New York: MacMillan Co., 1969), pp. 40, 300.

68. Ibn Iyās, *Badaʿi*, 2: 12/5: 14. Ibn Iyās said that Qānsūh had information that Selim had equipped more ships which were approaching the shores of Egypt; Sanuto, *I Diarii*, 20: 386. In May 1515, the *bailo* of Istanbul, Justinian, reported to Venice that Selim had readied a fleet of one hundred ships. This was the fleet that later surprised Rhodes by sailing calmly by after the campaign season ended. Qānsūh, too, had intelligence reports of its preparation.

69. The chronicle of Marulli, published in Naples in 1639, describes these negotiations saying that Selim was putting together the largest fleet that had ever exited Istanbul and that its objective was Egypt. Marulli states that Selim was afraid his enemies would ally themselves with Ismail in Iran. See Bacqué-Grammont, "Ottomans," pp. 169–172 using Fabrizio de Caretto's account.

70. Simon Pepper and Nicholas Adams, *Firearms and Fortifications*, p. 29. The threat of the expanded Ottoman armada caused similar precautions to be taken by the Spanish in North Africa and Naples in the mid-sixteenth century. The Spanish viceroy of Naples built three hundred thirteen watchtower forts along the coast between 1538 and 1571.

71. Ibn Iyās, *Badaʿi*, 1: 411, 435, 446 /4: 446, 471, 483 includes reports on this fleet through summer and fall of 1515. The envoy Jānim, returning to Cairo in September of 1515, reported that Selim had a fleet of four hundred ships in preparation to attack Alexandria and Damietta. Sanuto, *I Diarii*, 20: 361. A report from Edirne relates that Selim had ordered the armada to sail for Alexandria.

72. Sanuto, *I Diarii*, 9: 252. There is also an unconfirmed report from Rome, in fall 1509, of an attack by "Turks" on Siragusa, but this was probably corsair activity.

73. S. M. Imamuddin, "Maritime Trade Under the Mamluks of Egypt (644–923/1250–1517)," *Hamdard Islamicus* 3, no. 4 (winter 1980): 69–72. Atiya, *The Crusades*, pp. 249–250, notes that Arghūn communicated with the pope concerning the expedition against the Mamluks. The Il-khānids, descendants of Hülegu Khān ruled in Persia from 1256–1353.

74. Genevieve Bouchon, "Le Premier Voyage de Lopo Soares in Inde 1504–1505," *Mare Luso Indicum* 3 (1976): 66–68.

75. The Portuguese conquests are related in lurid detail using India Office and Portuguese sources by Sir William Wilson Hunter, *A History of British India*, v. 1., *To the Overthrow of the English in the Spice Archipelago* (New York: AMS Press Inc., 1966), pp. 164–232.

76. Bouchon, "Lopo Soares," pp. 72–73, 84.

77. Sanuto, *I Diarii*, 6: 246, 249.

78. Lane, *Venice*, p. 209; Fulin, "Girolamo," pp. 175, 178; Ibn Iyās, *Badaʿi*, 1: 186–187/4: 192–193.

79. Sanuto, *I Diarii*, 5: 825–827.

80. This is according to a report from Egypt to Venice by Alvise Spandugino in March of 1506. Lane, *Venice and History*, pp. 352–358: the *botte* was based on a cargo capacity measured in terms of wine casks. This was a measure of space, or volume, as well as of weight. Lane estimates the Venetian *botte* for the fifteenth century at 640 kg. occupying 900 liters (.9 cubic meters).

81. Fulin, "Girolamo," p. 192; Mas-Latrie, *Traites*, 2: 257; Barbaro, *A Description*, pp. 22–23, writing in 1515–1516, said this Mamluk fleet, defeated by the Portuguese at Diu, was manned by "Moors, Turks and Maghrebis"; Smith, *Cambay and Bengal*, pp. 11–20: De Almeida, the Por-

tuguese viceroy, attempted to force Malik Ayās, the governor of Diu to surrender Turkish survivors of the defeat, but Malik Ayās refused.

82. Alberi, *Appendice*, pp. 8–9.

83. Sanuto, *I Diarii*, 7: 12–13, 128, 152, *Miera* [?] is not the usual term for copper units in the Venetian sources, which usually identify copper by type (pieces, ingots, fragments), by measure such as kantar or quintal or by value (ducat's or dinar's worth). On the copper trade from Europe, see Eliyahu Ashtor, *Les Métaux Précieux et al Balance des payements du Proche-Orient a la Basse Époque*, Series Ecole Pratique des Hautes Études, Monnaie, Prix, Conjoncture, no. 10 (Paris: S.E.V.P.E.N., 1971), pp. 55–64.

84. Ibn Iyās, *Bada'i*, 1: 115 /4: 119; Sanuto, *I Diarii*, 7: 164; Fisher, *The Foreign Relations*, p. 95. When the Ottoman ambassador was told that Egypt had few guns, Bayezid sent Kemal to Alexandria with a great quantity of copper and many skilled workmen to cast pieces of artillery.

85. Sanuto, *I Diarii*, 7: 534–535.

86. For the varying accounts of this voyage see Sarjeant, *The Portuguese*, pp. 41–44; E. Dennison Ross, "The Portuguese in India and Arabia," *Journal of the Royal Asiatic Society* (1921), pp. 547–551; Ibn Iyās, *Bada'i*, 1: 120 /4: 124.

87. Ibn Iyās, *Bada'i*, 1: 106 /4: 109 says that in 1506–1507, a fleet of twenty Portuguese ships entered the Red Sea and attacked Muslim shipping. He continues that this act made turbans and muslins difficult to obtain in Egypt.

88. Sanuto, *I Diarii*, 10: 110–111.

89. Iby Iyās, *Bada'i*, 1: 156, 176–177, 190 /4: 160, 182–185, 196. Qānsūh had already sent an envoy, 'Alān Bāy, to the Porte in fall 1509. He returned to Cairo in August 1510. Yūnus ad-Dawla, the ambassador, was sent to purchase lumber and artillery; he returned to Cairo in November 1510. See also, Fulin, "Girolamo," pp. 184–196.

90. Sanuto, *I Diarii*, 11: 65, 75–76, 105, 479. It was after the envoys from India arrived that Qānsūh dispatched an ambassador to Selim to ask for artillery.

91. Duarte Barbosa, *The Book of Duarte Barbosa*, pp. 44–49.

92. Sanuto, *I Diarii*, 10: 110 on the Suez preparations in 1510; Ibn Iyās, *Bada'i*, 1: 195, 289, 291, 297, 299, 302–303, 309, 331, 337–343, 422–424, 431, 436 / 4: 201, 309–310, 317, 319–323, 331, 355, 362–367, 457–460, 466–467, 471–472, on the preparations of this fleet from 1510 to 1515. In 1513, for example, the mamluks ordered to Suez refused to report for departure, demanding a bonus payment and threatening revolt. See also, David Ayalon, *Gunpowder and Firearms in the Mamluk Kingdom*

(London: Valentine, 1956), pp. 71–82. According to Ayalon, *al-tabaqah al-khāmīsa* (the fifth corps) a special unit of arquebusiers was formed especially for purpsoes of serving in the Red Sea and Indian Ocean in 1510, in part because of the mamluks' reluctance to serve. This unit, under pressure from the mamluks, was formally dissolved in 1514 but in reality it continued to exist as the arquebusier force needed to fight the Portuguese.

93. Sanuto, *I Diarii*, 10: 432, 636, 799; 11: 76, 105, 227–228, 394. The Ayas fleet was assembled from a variety of sources including a Messinan ship of 500 *botte* purchased by Qānsūh, a Genoese galley seized the previous year, and an 800 *botte* galley, which was a gift to the Mamluk sultan from Korkud, the son (then resident in Cairo) of the Ottoman sultan. See also, Fulin, "Girolamo," pp. 213–214; Bosio, *Dell'Istoria*, pp. 493–494 for the Rhodian version. Ibn Iyās, *Bada'i*, 1: 185–187 / 4:191–192 says eighteen Mamluk ships were lost.

94. Sanuto, *I Diarii*, 10: 21–22, 637, 801; 11: 55, 76. Some reports say two envoys were sent and estimates of the purse range from 30,000 to over 50,000 ducats. The Mamluk envoy had an audience with Bayezid on June 29, 1510.

95. Fulin, "Girolamo," p. 218; Sanuto, *I Diarii*, 7: 164, 294, 589, 621, 661, 873. In July of 1510, this armada, which foundered in a storm on the way, still had not sailed. A letter dated October 16, from Istanbul mentions that it had sailed. It must have departed only shortly before that date because reports from Famagosta on October 17 do not include news of the disastrous storm.

96. Ayalon, *Gunpowder and Firearms*, p. 78.

97. Sanuto, *I Diarii*, 11: 826, 829; Ibn Iyās, *Bada'i*, 1: 195 /4: 201. The report from Cairo says that eighteen ships arrived with lumber, iron, and artillery.

98. Luchetta, *"L'Affare Zen,"* pp. 145–146, 206.

99. Sadeddin, *Tac*, 2: 168–171.

100. Sanuto, *I Diarii*, 14: 500. The ships left Alexandria on April 22 and included either eight naves and three galions or six naves and four galleys. Considering the timing, either Qānsūh was confident of Selim's succession and wished to confirm relations quickly, or he expected the mission to be received by Bayezid.

101. Barbosa, *The Book*, 1: 57–58; Sarjeant, *The Portuguese*, p. 47 citing the "Tārikh-i Shanbāl," an Arabic chronicle, says forty ships were burned.

102. Jean Louis Bacqué-Grammont and Anne Kroell, *Mamlouks, Ottomans et Portugais en Mer Rouge: L'Affaire de Djedda in 1517*, Supplé-

226

Notes

ment aux Annales Islamologiques, Cahier no. 12 (Cairo: Institut Français, 1988), pp. 50–51. Johan de Chamara suggested that the Portuguese in 1517, after their failure to take Jidda, launch a major naval expedition to secure India, take Jidda, and build fortresses on the Red Sea littoral in order to contain the Turks before they became a major threat in the Indian Ocean. Chamara also suggested seizing Diu, saying that its governor Malik Ayās was corresponding with the Ottomans at Jidda.

103. Ibn Iyās, *Bada'i*, 1: 339–341 /4: 356–366. Ashtor, *Levant Trade*, pp. 387–388 cites the prices of ships at the beginning of the fifteenth century as ranging from 400 ducats for small vessels to 9,000 ducats for large trading ships. This latter does not include the price of arming or staffing ships. The gold ducat and dinar were roughly equivalent in value: see Boaz Shoshan, "Exchange Rate Policies in Fifteenth-Century Egypt," *Journal of the Social and Economic History of the Orient* 29 (1991): 28–51. Pepper, *Firearms*, p. 30, estimates the costs of building, rigging and arming a galley in the mid-sixteenth century at 6,000 to 7,000 scudi (taking into account a crew of one hundred fifty oarsmen and one hundred fifty soldiers, sailors, and officers). He estimates the costs of salaries and provisions for each such galley at another 6,000 to 7,000 scudi per year. Also, on the costs of Venetian ships and crews at this time, see Frederic C. Lane, "Naval Actions and Fleet Organization, 1499–1502," in J. R. Hale, ed. *Renaissance Venice* (Totawa, New Jersey: Rowman and Littlefield, 1973, pp. 158–163.

104. Ibn Iyās, *Bada'i*, 1: 422–424, 431 /4: 458–459, 465–466. Six hundred or more of the *tabaqah al-khāmīsa* unit were appointed to participate in the joint Mamluk-Ottoman naval expedition. No sooner were mamluks sent from Cairo to staff the Suez fleet than Ibn Iyās recounted the news that Selim's army was marching against Ismail Safavi and the Zū al-Ḳadr. In August 1515, he reported that the governors of Damascus and Aleppo were blaming Qānsūh for not having properly fortified the frontiers against the possibility of an Ottoman attack.

105. For the continuation of Safavid-Portuguese diplomatic relations under Shah Tahmasp, Ismail's successor, see Manuzzio, *Viaggi fatti da Vinetia, alla Tana, in Persia, in India, et in Constantinopoli* (Venice: n.p., 1545), pp. 101–103.

106. Sarjeant, *The Portuguese*, pp. 48–49.

107. Jean Louis Bacqué-Grammont and Anne Kroell, *Mamlouks*, p. 50. The Portuguese Johan de Chamara, writing from India on August 26, 1517 claimed the Ottomans had taken fifty-two pieces of artillery at Aden and that at Jidda there were forty-eight large pieces of artillery and eight hundred hand firearms.

108. Sarjeant, *The Portuguese*, pp. 50–51. A letter preserved in the

Topkapı archives (E. 6455) from Selman Reis to the grand *vezir*, Ibrahim Pasha, dated June 1515 describes the armaments (ships, cannon, etc.) of Jidda and proposes a naval expedition against the Portuguese utilizing the eighteen ships at Jidda (six bastarda, eight *kadırga*, three *kalyata* and one *kayık*). He said that the Portuguese were very vulnerable to attack and argued that the financial rewards would be substantial. Michel Lesure, "Un Document Ottoman de 1525 sur l'Inde Portuguais et les Pays de la Mer Rouge," *Mare Luso-Indicum* 3 (1976): 137–160. Another document dated June of that same year (Topkapı Sarayı Arşivi, E 5894) details the Ottoman *sancak beg's* administration in Jidda.

109. On negotiations with Gujarat and naval maneuvers in the Indian Ocean, see M. Yakub Mughul, "Türk Amirali Emir Mustafa Ibn Behram Bay'in Hindustan Seferi (1531)," *Tarih Enstitüsü Dergisi* 4–5 (Ağustos 1973–1974): 247–262.

110. Tardy, *Beyond Ottoman Empire*, pp. 155–157. Alberi, *Le Relazioni*, Series 3, v. 1, p. 19: Daniello de Ludovisi's report in 1534 mentions five galions cut in the Istanbul arsenal for this expedition.

111. Salıh Özbaran, "The Ottoman Turks and the Portuguese in the Persian Gulf 1534–1581," *Journal of Asian History* 6 (1972): 56, 73–74. This same report states that if the Ottomans wished they could build as many ships as they wanted because they could obtain lumber "from the great forests of Birecik seven days distant, a large town with great traffic from Persia." This statement demonstrates the Portuguese lack of geographic infomation on the sources of Ottoman timber since the lumber actually only came through Birecik, originating at Maraş. Özbaran cites the *mühimme defterleri* on the Ottoman *tershane* at Basra for the source of the lumber. On timber see also Imber, "Süleyman," pp. 220–221, 228–230. For a detailed account of an Ottoman-Portuguese naval engagement during this period, see Sidi Ali Reis, *Mirat ül-Memalik*, pp. 18–22.

112. See Alberi, *Le Relazioni*, Series 3, v. 3, pp. 108–110, 129–130, 150–153, 164–165, 191–193, 220–223, 374–375 for the reports of the Venetian bailos on the Ottoman fleets in 1526, 1557, 1558, 1561, 1583, 1590.

113. Bacqué-Grammont, "Ottomans," p. 215; Clifford, "Some Observations," p. 39.

114. Halil Inalcık's review of David Ayalon, *Gunpowder and Firearms in the Mamluk Kingdom*, in *Belleten* 21 (1957): 503–506.

Part II. Traders, Trade Goods, and Trade Zones.

1. Inalcık, "Ottoman Methods of Conquest," *Studia Islamica* 2 (1954): 104–129 on the flexible nature of Ottoman conquest and incorporation of the conquered territories.

2. For example: Brian Pullan, "The Occupations and Investments of the Venetian Nobility in the Middle and Late Sixteenth Century," in Hale, ed. *Renaissance Venice*.

3. Pullan, "The Occupations," pp. 381, 403. See also Gabriele Lombardini, *Pane e Denaro a Bassano: Prezzi del Grano e Politica dell'Approvigionamento dei Cereali tra il 1501 e el 1799* (Venice: 1963), pp. 58–60.

4. On *timars*, see Douglas Howard, "The Ottoman Timar System and Its Transformation, 1563–1656." Ph.D. diss. Indiana University, 1987; and Halil Inalcık, "Military and Fiscal Transformation in the Ottoman Empire," *Archivum Ottomanicum* 6 (1980): 283–337. Bruno Simon, "Le Blé et les Rapports vénéto-ottomans au XVIe Siècle," in Bacqué-Grammont, ed. *Contributions à l'histoire économique et sociale de l'Empire ottoman*, Collection Turcica III (Louvain: Éditions Peeters, 1983), p. 275, has periodized the sixteenth century, referring to the years to 1548 as ones of relative general abundance of grain. But this does not account for the periodic scarcities, often quite severe, that affected the eastern Levant in the early sixteenth century.

5. The basic work on this subject has been done by Halil Inalcık, "Capital Formation in the Ottoman Empire," *Journal of Economic History* 19 (1969), pp. 97–140.

6. A descriptive rather than analytical attempt is made in Lütfi Güçer, *XVI–XVIII inci Asırlarda Osmanlı Imparatorluğunun Ticaret Politikası*, but in general much of the analysis of Ottoman economic systems is based on longstanding and unscrutinized assumptions.

7. Suraiya Faroqhi, "Towns, Agriculture, and the State in Sixteenth-Century Ottoman Anatolia," *JESHO* (1990), pp. 130–137. Other scholars who address this question for the seventeenth through the nineteenth century are: Masters, *Origins*; Goffman, *Izmir*; and Sarah Shields, "Regional Trade and Nineteenth Century Mosul: "Revising the Role of Europe in the Middle East," *International Journal of Middle East Studies* 23 (1991): 19–37.

8. Ira M. Lapidus, *Muslim Cities in the Later Middle Ages* (Cambridge: Cambridge University Press, 1984).

9. Alberi, *Relazioni*, Series 3, v. 3, pp. 401–402: Zane suggested that this practice had been a problem in recent years, but the early sixteenth-century sources hint that this was a practice of long standing.

10. Bruce McGowan, *Economic Life in Ottoman Europe: Taxation, Trade and the Struggle for Land, 1600–1800* (Cambridge: Cambridge University Press, 1981), pp. 11.

11. McGowan, *Economic Life*, pp. 5–6. Chaudhuri, *Asia Before Europe*, pp. 251–262 has discussed land use patterns and state control in a

comparative framework for India, China, and the Middle East discerning a "common Indo-Islamic pattern." Chaudhuri, however, is unaware of the extent to which *timars*, like the earlier *iqta*, became hereditary in the sixteenth and seventeenth century Ottoman system, which knowledge would alter his interpretation of continuities in Ottoman notable position vis-à-vis the state. On the *timars* see Howard, "The Ottoman Timar System."

Chapter 5. The Aegean, the Mediterranean, and the Grain Trade.

1. Maurice Aymard, *Venise, Raguse, et le Commerce du Blé Pendant la Seconde Moitié du XVIe Siècle* (Paris: S.E.V.P.E.N., 1966), p. 99 contrasts the integrated Italy with the unintegrated Ottoman territories which instead provided the possibilities for grain speculation. Thus, Aymard focuses on price differential as crucial, at once ignoring price differentials in Europe and consistency of supply in the Ottoman state as factors in the Venetian-Ottoman grain negotiations.

2. Fernand Braudel, *Civilization and Capitalism 15th–18th Century*, v. 3, *The Perspective of the World* (New York: Harper and Row, 1979), pp. 21–44, 484–487. Braudel suggests a single world economy "gigantic, fragile and intermittent," dependent on pendulum swings with India roughly at center. Chaudhuri, *Asia Before Europe*, pp. 231–232 discusses cereal culture, mentioning the sophistication of Mughul fiscal practice and linking it to similar Mamluk and Ottoman practices.

3. David Lopez and Irving Raymond, *Medieval Trade in the Mediterranean World* (New York: Columbia University Press, 1968), pp. 306–310. Lopez includes a series of petitions presented by the Genoese ambassador, Nicola Spinola, for damages due to seizures of grain purchased from the emperor: 1,800 gold hyperpers for 2,000 modii of grain; 1,700 hyperpers damages for seizure of 1,300 modii of Thracian grain in 1285; a complaint that customs officials took twenty-five hyperpers for 500 modi of grain.

4. Gian Giacomo Musso, *Navigazioni e Commercio Genovese con il Levante nei Documenti dell'Archivio di Stato di Genova (Sec. XIV–XV)* (Rome: Archivio di Stato, 1975), pp. 152, 161, 164, 260–261 (contract documents on pp. 235–245). Musso, on pp. 188–193, gives a list of merchants and their provenance in the eastern Mediterranean trade of 1402. See also G. I. Bratianu, *Recherches sur le commerce génois dans la Mer Noire au XIIIe siècle* (Paris: P. Geuthner, 1929).

5. Musso, *Navigazioni*, p. 248, letter dated 1394 describing the "many pirates" in the seas around Alexandria.

6. Musso, *Navigazioni*, p. 221.

7. Henri Bresc, ed. *Studi di Storia Navale* (n.p.: Giunti, 1975), pp.

230 *Notes*

12–15. In this article, Henri Bresc traces the Sicilian grain trade in the fourteenth and fifteenth centuries focusing on transport ships, mostly for the local trade, of the marina Siciliana. Bresc estimates the average load of a Sicilian bark at 45 salme in mid-fifteenth century.

8. Smith, *Medieval Sicily*, pp. 103, 133–140.

9. Ibid., pp. 110–111.

10. Pact in Latin and Italian transcription in George Martin Thomas, *Diplomatarium Veneto-Levantinum sive Acta et Diplomata Res Venetas Graecas Atque Levantis (1351–1454)*, 2 vols., 2 (New York: Burt Franklin, 1966): 318–319. See Inalcık, *The Ottoman Empire*, pp. 17–19.

11. M. M. Alexandrescu and Dersca Bulgaru, "Les Relations de Süleyman Çelebi avec Venise (1400–1410)," in *VIII Türk Tarih Kongresi, Ankara 11–15 Ekim 1976, Kongreye Sunuları*, v. 2 (Ankara: T.T.K. Basımevi, 1981): 996–1006.

12. Simon, "Le Blé," p. 271, for example, on the provisions sought by the ambassador Contarini in 1517.

13. Musso, *Navigazioni*, p. 144.

14. Inalcık, "Capital Formation," p. 120, 128–130, 136–137, is a notable exception, discussing the accumulation of wealth among *askeri* from land holdings. But Inalcık concludes that "the only elements in Ottoman society who can properly be called 'capitalistic entrepreneurs' are the merchants and the money changers." Crucial to this definition is the concept of capitalistic entrepreneur—dependent on state protection and state encouragement of accumulation of wealth by these groups (to the exclusion of other groups). Yet, if focus is directed to the motives and activities of *askeri* and to government cooperation in their grain exporting activities, then the lines between the state, its various component groups, and the big merchant class become less clear. Andre Raymond, *Artisans et Commerçants au Caire au XVIIIe Siècle*, 2 vols., 2 (Damascus: Institut Français de Damas, 1974), pp. 399–416 has attmepted to define the merchant classes in Cairo after the Ottoman conquest, linking the commercial and administrative functions of merchants to their accumulation of wealth and to government policies.

15. Rhoads Murphey, "Provisioning Istanbul: The State and Subsistence in the Early Modern Middle East," *Food and Foodways* 2 (1988): 217. Murphey, pp. 217–263, in this interesting and substantial article discusses the state organization in the eighteenth century of price control, storage, processing, distribution, transport, preventing smuggling, and alleviating grain shortages. Murphey has used this assessment to argue (p. 243) that the Ottomans, self-sufficient in most primary resources, "avoided actively encouraging the promotion of export oriented production . . .," and

were "relieved of the necessity to conduct external commercial exchange." This conclusion fails to distinguish between the interests of individual Ottomans and the rather nebulously omnipresent "state" or to account for greed (even at the highest levels of state and dynasty), motivating speculation in export commerce. See also Aymard, *Venise*, pp. 45–53, contrasting the ideal of government regulation to actual practice. Aymard rightly notes ". . . *la pratique se révele plus souple que le prescriptions officielles.*"

16. Sanuto, *I Diarii*, 5: 354, 973.

17. Sanuto, *I Diarii*, 5: 824; 10: 105; 11: 265. The *luogotenente*, Justinian, purchased 12,000 moza of grain from Damietta (100 moza of Cyprus = 38 stera of Venice). Simon, "Le Blé," p. 276 notes that in 1546 Cyprus imported 10,000 stera from Syria. Lane, *Venice and History*, p. 358 estimates the stera of wheat = 132 litre/62.9 kg. Aymard, *Venise*, p. 172 gives the following measures: 1 stera (staia) of Venice = 83.3 litres, 4 stera = 1 moggio [moza]; 1 kilo of Istanbul = 33 litres, 1 mudd = 20 kilos = 660 litres = 5 quintals. Lütfi Güçer, *XVI–XVII Asırlarda Osmanlı Imparatorluğunda Hububat Meselesi ve Hububattan Alınan Vergiler* (Istanbul: Sermet Matbaası, 1964), pp. 80–81, using the *mühimme defterleri*, notes the levying of Cyprus grain for provisioning the Ottoman army in 1579 after the Ottomans had taken Cyprus. On the Egyptian grain supplies, see for example Raymond, *Artisans*, v. 1, pp. 308–311.

18. Sanuto, *I Diarii*, 10: 255, 389: in 1510, the Grand Master sent out ships with orders to intercept Turkish grain ships to alleviate the shortage on Rhodes. In 1515, the Candians complained that they were the target of similar raids, Sanuto, *I Diarii*, 21: 202–203.

19. Setton, *The Papacy*, 3: 122.

20. See chapter 4. Sanuto, *I Diarii*, 5: 307 mentions six Turkish corsair fustas, which sailed from Valona, and attacked Capo Santa Maria in fall 1503, carrying off a grain ship from Taranto as well as sixty people (who would be ransomed or sold as slaves).

21. Brian Pullan, "The Occupations and Investments of the Venetian Nobility in the Middle and Late Sixteenth Century," in Hale, *Renaissance Venice*, p. 393.

22. Unfortunately such documentation is not yet available for the early sixteenth century. Murphey, "Provisioning Istanbul," pp. 226–230, 252–54, provides documentation for the seventeenth and eighteenth centuries on Ottoman ship leasing, storage, and provisioning.

23. The best treatment of this question is in Güçer, *Hububat*, which illustrates the provisioning patterns for feeding Ottoman troops in the field, on campaign or stationed in garrisons at the frontier. See, for example, pp. 33, 38–41, 77–80, 115–121, 124, 127–128 on provisioning prac-

tices, the *kadis'* involvement in administering provisioning orders, war grain stores, and the commandeering of surpluses for the army. These documents date from the second half of the sixteenth century on.

24. Simon, "Le Blé," p. 272; Halil Sahillioğlu, "1524–1525 Osmanlı Bütçesi," in *Ord. Prof. Ömer Lütfi Barkan'a Armağan* (Istanbul: Gür-Ay Matbaası, 1985), pp. 442–443, for example, notes shipping expenses including 192,000 akçe for supply of ships biscuit and 650,000 akçe for ship expenses at Gallipoli.

25. Sanuto, *I Diarii*, 25: 15–16, 59.

26. See Gökbilgin, "Venedik Devlet Arşivindeki Vesikalar Kulliyatında Kanuni Sultan Süleiman Devri Belgeler," *Belgeler* 1, no. 2, vesika 78 (1964): 202, on the payment in 1519.

27. See Mc Gowan, *Economic Life*, pp. 34–36 on the Damascus law and on Ottoman export bans on grain after 1551.

28. Güçer, *Hububat*, pp. 115–121.

29. Pullan, "The Occupations," in Hale's *Renaissance Venice*, pp. 380–387, argues that the end of the sixteenth century is characterized by the withdrawal of the Venetian nobility from commerce, shipping, and banking in large part due to heavy losses through war and Turkish conquests, discouragements to Levant trade, the collapse of stable credit, and incentives to invest in land and food production.

30. Lapidus, *Muslim Cities*, pp. 50–59.

31. *Evkaf* was the standard form of shelter, yet focus on *evkaf* as "correct" investment diverts attention from focus on commercial investment as also standard practice. On *evkaf* for the disposition of dynastic, military/administrative and merchant class wealth, see, for example, Carl F. Petry, *The Civilian Elite of Cairo in the Later Middle Ages*, Princeton: Princeton University Press, 1981), p. 217; Inalcık, "Capital Formation," pp. 132–135; Gökbilgin, *Edirne ve Paşa Livası*, p. 384 (*evkaf* of Bayezid II's daughter), 488; and Ronald C. Jennings, "Pious Foundations in the Society and Economy of Ottoman Trabzon, 1565–1640," *JESHO* 33 (1990): pp. 326–327 on *evkaf* revenues lent for investments in trade.

32. Raymond, *Artisans*, v. 2, pp. 629–633, 650–657 elaborates on the Egyptian grain trade in the seventeenth and eighteenth centuries, discussing participation of the emirs in the exploitation of grain sales, *mukataa* and the farming of revenues, monopolies on commodities and the role of the *janissaries*. With such information available for the period of Mamluk rule and for later centuries, it becomes unreasonable to presume that the Ottomans of the fifteenth and sixteenth centuries stood aloof from commercial investments and exploitations. For monopolies on wood, stone, and metals under the Mamluks, see Lapidus, *Muslim Cities*, pp. 6–68. Si-

mon, "Le Blé," pp. 274–275, 282 suggests that speculation and contraband grain sales were especially attractive to Rumelian authorities, particularly given the encouragement of Venetian buyers.

33. Braudel, *Civilization and Capitalism*, v. 3, p. 256, has noted how in later years the Danziger merchants manipulated Polish magnates by advancing payments for wheat and rye before it was delivered: "In his dealing with the notables, the merchant was able to dictate terms." A similar phenomenon can be posited for Balkan notables under Ottoman rule, lured by the profits from shipping grain westward.

34. Braudel, *Civilization and Capitalism*, v. 3, p. 292–294 has argued against "a priori definitions" of a "national market" in the case of France, pointing out that there were at least three separate zones in the French grain market. Güçer, *Hububat*, on loads and prices, pp. 33, 66.

35. Gökbilgin, "Yeni Belgelerin Işığı Altında Kanuni Sultan Süleyman Devrinde Osmanlı-Venedik Münasebetleri," in *Kanuni Armağanı*, T.T.K. Yayınlar Series 7, no. 55 (Ankara: T.T.K. Basımevi, 1970), pp. 171–186. Gökbilgin discusses the Venetian grain imports from Ottoman lands in the 1530s.

36. Gökbilgin, "Le Relazioni Veneto-Turche nell'Eta di Solimano il Magnifico," *Il Veltro* 23, no. 2–4 (1979), p. 281–282.

37. Alberi, *Relazioni*, Series 3, v. 1, pp. 88, 406, 411. The envoy, Navagero, suggested that grain demand could double the income of the grand vezir and suggested that Rüstem could enforce purchases at prices higher than the norm. In 1573, another envoy, Constantino Garzone, argued that Mustafa Pasha had an income of "*18 milioni d'oro*" from rents, buildings and other property alone, not to mention *timar* revenues and gifts. Necipoğlu, "Süleyman the Magnificent," pp. 405–406, 417–421 has noted the close ties between Süleiman's administrators like Ibrahim Pasha and various Venetian agents. The "conservatism," noted by Necipoğlu, of Ibrahim's grand vezirial successors, however, apparently did not extend to cutting off grain exports to Venice.

38. Simon, "Le Blé," pp. 277–278; Aymard, *Venise*, pp. 50–51, 60, 95–96, 127–130, 138.

39. Gilles Veinstein, "Un Achat Français de Blé dans l'Empire Ottoman au Milieu du XVIe siècle," in Batu and Bacqué-Grammont, eds. *L'Empire Ottoman, la République de Turquie et la France* (Istanbul: Isis, 1986), pp. 22–23, 26–36. Orders were to Eubée, the *kadi* of Eğriboz and others: Keşan, Kavalla, Gümülcine. Veinstein's article includes facsimiles of the documentation on the exchange with France.

40. Kafadar, "A Death in Venice," pp. 193–194, 196, 199, 211. Rüstem Pasha intervened on the part of a Bursa merchant called Aga Beg trading spices in Venice in 1546.

41. See, for example, Henry Simonsfeld, *Der Fondaco dei Tedeschi in Venedig und die Deutsch-Venetianischen Handelsbeazeihungen*, v. 1 (Stuttgart: 1887, reprint, Scientia Verlag Aalen, 1968), p. 343, noting the Council of Ten's mention of the friendly relations of the agent Baptista Serena with the *sancak beg* of Scutari, Ferisbei [*sic.* Firuz], in 1503. Alberi, *Relazioni*, Series 3, v. 3, pp. 87–88: the 1522 negotiations between the Porte and the Signoria included Venetian demands that ships not be stopped for extra levies at Gallipoli, that the *bailo* could not be brought before a *kadi*, and that all Venetian merchants brought before the *kadi* must have access to a dragoman.

42. Sanuto, *I Diarii*, 5: 958.

43. On the relations of Bernardo Navagero, for example, with Rüstem Pasha in the mid-sixteenth century, see Marie-Mathilde Alexandrescu-Dersca-Bulgaru, "Une Relation Vènitienne sur l'Empire Ottoman à l'Époque de Süleyman le Magnifique," Varia Turcica IV, *Comité International d'Études Pré-Ottomanes et Ottomanes VIth Symposium, Cambridge, 1–4 July 1984* (Istanbul: French Institute of Anatolian Studies, 1987), pp. 136–137.

44. Alberi, *Relazioni*, Series 3, v. 3, pp. 429–430, in 1594.

45. Alberi, *Relazioni*, Series 3, v. 3, pp. 141–142. Raymond, *Artisans*, v. 2, pp. 467–469 on Turkish merchants in Cairo in the seventeenth and eighteenth centuries.

46. Lewis, *The Muslim Discovery*, p. 301–302 minimizes the role of Muslim merchants: "Muslim traders in Europe were few and insignificant, and the Muslim merchant class failed to achieve and maintain a bourgeois society, or seriously to challenge the hold of the military, bureaucratic, and religious elites on the state and the schools." He fails to note the points of reference between commerce and the military and bureaucratic elites. See instead Kafadar, "A Death," on latter sixteenth-century Ottoman merchants in Venice. For later periods, information is more readily available, for example, Masters, *The Origins*, pp. 48–49, 142, 166–169 on those involved in Aleppan trade in the seventeenth century. ". . . it appears that almost all Aleppines who had any excess capital were at one time or another engaged directly in trade or in credit relationships involving commerce. This is the pattern presented in the court records, where we find among those engaged in trade Muslim judges, Greek orthodox bishops, members of the Ottoman military bureaucracy, women and bedouin tribesmen."

47. For a discussion of these merchant communities and their organization in Galata see Halil Inalcık, "Ottoman Galata, 1453–1553," in Varia Turcica III, *Première Rencontre Internationale sur l'Empire Ottoman et la Turquie Moderne, Institute National des Langues et Civilisations Ori-*

entales, Maison des Sciences de l'Homme, 18–22 janvier 1985: Recherches sur la ville ottomane: La cas du quartier de Galata (Istanbul: Isis Press, 1991), pp. 17–116.

48. Pullan, "The Occupations," in Hale's *Renaissance Venice*, p. 384. The brothers Angelo di Francesco and Marco Sanuto, for example, were committed to enterprises both in Istanbul and in Cyprus. Angelo's bank in Venice failed in February 1570.

Chapter 6. Trade on the Eastern Salient.

1. M. N. Pearson, *Merchants and Rulers in Gujarat: The Response to the Portuguese in the Sixteenth Century* (Berkeley: University of California Press, 1976), pp. 83–91 has argued that indigenous cooperation and lack of a concerted resistance allowed the Portuguese to maintain their position in India. This argument incorporates the notion of cost-effectiveness in the debate determining whether or not the Portuguese should be resisted. Part of Pearson's rationale for this evaluation, however, is the assumption that the Indian coastal states (because they were Muslim) were essentially interested only in control of the land. (Malik Ayās here stands as an exception.) This is the same argument that has been applied to the Ottomans to argue against their willingness to invest substantial resources in trade and in its defense.

2. Braudel calls the European merchants and merchants from the Middle East "necessary adversaries," hedging his bets, but the same can be said of the Venetians and Genoese. Braudel, *Civilization and Capitalism*, v. 2, p. 163.

3. See Halil Inalcık, *The Ottoman Empire*, p. 128 and "Bursa and the Commerce of the Levant, pp. 145–148 on the Ottoman lumber trade. Lumber and pitch exported from Antalya in 1477 amounted to 150,000 akçe or about 3,000 gold ducats in customs revenues.

4. Inalcık, "Bursa and the Commerce of the Levant," p. 131–147 on the silk trade.

5. Ashtor, *Levant Trade*; Lane, *Venice and History*, pp. 3–34; Godinho, *Le Économie*; Steensgaard, *The Asian Trade*. See also K. N. Chaudhuri, *Trade and Civilization*.

6. The best treatments of the Ottomans' silk trade are in Halil Inalcık, "Harir," v. 3, *Encyclopedia of Islam*, 2d. edition, pp. 211–218; Inalcık, "Bursa I: XV. Asır Sanayı ve Ticaret Tarihine Dair Vesikalar," *Belleten* 24 (1960): pp. 45–102; Fahri Dalsar, *Türk Sanayı ve Ticaret Tarihinde Bursa'da Ipekçilik* (Istanbul: Iktisat Fakültesi, Istanbul University, 1960).

7. On the profits see, for example, Inalcık, *Bursa I*, pp. 57–61, 84–86, 91–93. These documents indicate the silk customs (*gümrük*) revenues, the sums invested in the Bursa silk trade and the diversification of goods and investments of the Ottoman merchants trading between Anatolia, Iran, and the Mamluk territories in the fifteenth century. See also Lajos Fekete, *Die Siyaqat Schrift in der Türkischen Finanzverwaltung* (Budapest: Akademiai Kiado, 1955), pp. 84–94, 128–137 on the *gümrük* revenues of Istanbul and Galata and other tax farms (*mukataa*) including the tax farms, given for three year periods, under Bayezid II. These documents illustrate the potential for trading revenues accruing to the state in the early sixteenth century.

8. Steensgaard, *The Asian Trade*, pp. 66–67, using Tavernier, shows how merchants shifted routes, i.e. via Van rather than Erzurum, to get lower customs duties, or paid lump sums to avoid being searched by customs agents. Documents from Süleiman's time reflect steps taken to prevent interference with the caravan trade. For example Ms. E 5221/1 Topkapı Sarayı Arşivi, Istanbul, firman to the Birecik *kadi* and *sancak beg*, ordering them to prevent obstruction of the trade from Diyarbakr and interference with the eastern merchants.

9. Inalcık, "Harir," pp. 212–213, 217.

10. We do not have statistics for volume transported by sea *vs.* volume transported by land for this period.

11. Inalcık, "Ottoman Galata," pp. 63–65.

12. Bruce Masters, *The Origins of Western Economic Dominance in the Middle East: Mercantilism and the Islamic Economy in Aleppo, 1600–1750* (New York: New York University Press, 1988), pp. 138–140.

13. Masters, *The Origins*, p. 195.

14. Inalcık, "Bursa Kadi Sicillerinden Seçmeler," *Belgeler* 10, no. 14 (1980–1981), pp. 67, 69, 74, 79–80, 82–83, 86–89 has documented a series of transactions in the Bursa silk trade from the *kadi* records of the late fifteenth century. On pepper transactions in the same records, including the affairs of some Aleppo merchants in Bursa, see pp. 65–67, 71–72, 77, 83, 85–86.

15. Inalcık, *Ottoman Empire*, pp. 123–124. On Aleppo, Bursa, and the silk trade see Faroqhi, "Town, Agriculture and State," pp. 130–133. Without resolving whether international trade was the *crucial* factor in either city's success, as discussed in Faroqhi's article, it can be clearly demonstrated that substantial and regularly arriving silk caravans were very profitable for the state treasury and for the individuals who collected customs and re-exported the silk.

16. Masters, *The Origins*, pp. 61–63: ". . . amounts in deals involv-

ing Iran often dwarfed those expended in other areas of trade." Aleppo natives actively engaged in the silk trade with Iran as capital investors and occasionally as agents. See also Steensgaard, *The Asian Trade*, pp. 43–45 on silk prices in Aleppo in the 1630s; and Domenico Sella, *Commerci e Industrie a Venezia nel Secolo XVII* (Rome: Istituto per la Collaborazione Culturale, n.d.), pp. 27, 49–50 on Aleppo and the decline of Venice's fortunes in the silk trade.

17. Inalcık, "Harir," p. 213 points out the regression in the silk trade during Selim's reign. The boycott, however, suffered the same difficulties the Portuguese suffered in trying to blockade the copper trade through the Red Sea to India. Such blockades were very difficult to enforce in the face of high potential profits.

18. Most of the work on this period in Levantine trade has focused on the spice and silk trades. The type of detailed analysis applied by Inalcık to the Ottoman silk trade and by Ashtor to the spice trade needs to be duplicated for all the commodities of Ottoman international trade. Probably the most profitable sources for this type of endeavor (before the second half of the sixteenth century) are the provincial court records, although these are often not available, and the financial registers of European states like Venice, interpreted to include the Ottomans as a focus of analysis.

19. Lopez and Raymond, *Medieval Trade*, pp. 74–75 note that there were twelve copper foundries in Fez at the turn of the thirteenth century.

20. D. S. Goitein, *Letters of Medieval Jewish Traders* (Princeton: Princeton University Press, 1973), pp. 17–18, 25–26, 86, 103.

21. Ibid. pp. 175, 179–181, 192–195.

22. Ashtor, "Observations on Venetian Trade in the Levant in the XIVth Century," *Journal of the Social and Economic History of the Orient* 5 (1976): 575–577. The proposal to the Senate was rejected but the pope's ban did not remain in effect for long. The provenance of the copper shipped from Cyprus was not given.

23. Lane, *Venice, A Maritime Republic*, pp. 61–64, 142–143, 287, 299. Improvements in technology along with constant demand facilitated stepped up production in German silver and copper mines at the turn of the sixteenth century. According to Ashtor, *Levant Trade*, p. 160, 393, 441: freight charges, according to tariff registers, were five ducats for 470 kg. of copper on the Venetian Alexandria galley convoy in the second half of the fourteenth century. This volume indicates the extent of the copper trade to Alexandria in this earlier era. See also Ashtor, "Observations," p. 537, 575 on copper shipments via Famagosta to Alexandria. One enterprising merchant from Brescia named Bontempelli became quite prosperous in Venice, counting among his ventures a copper mine lease: see Ugo Tucci, "The

Psychology of the Venetian Merchant in the Sixteenth Century," in Hale, *Renaissance Venice*, p. 364. Bontempelli was investing during the late sixteenth century.

24. On *gümrük* applying to ships of Venetians and other *kafirs* (non-Muslims) at Sinop and Samsun in 1481 see Gökbilgin, *XV–XVI. Asırlarda Edirne ve Paşa Livası Vakıflar—Mülkler—Mukataalar*, p. 107, the toll was 4 percent.

25. Kritovoulos, *History of Mehmed the Conqueror*, trans. Charles T. Riggs (Westport, CT: Greenwood Press, 1954), p. 166.

26. Musso, *Navigazioni*, pp. 249–250. A Genoese document mentions the export of ten kantars (*cantara*) of copper "*rame in platinis boni* . . ." in 1395.

27. Documents published by Neşet Çağatay, "Osmanlı Imparatorluğunda Maden Hukuk ve Iktisadiyatı Hakkında Vesikalar," *Tarih Vesikaları* 2, no. 10 (1942), pp. 279–283; and Yaman, "Küre Bakır Madenine Dair Vesikalar," *Tarih Vesikaları* 1, no. 4 (1941), pp. 266–282 for the late seventeenth through the mid-nineteenth centuries, reveal much about mine administration (which must be "*zabt u rabt*," absolutely in order), personnel/labor, revenue, mint and tax arrangements, and appointments but do not address the ultimate disposition of all the copper or reveal information about foreign export. See also Faroqhi, *Towns and Townsmen*, pp. 171–188. Faroqhi estimates the output of the Küre mines in northern Anatolia in 1582 at 302,147 kg. (pp. 179–180). Leasing arrangements with private mine operators could have provided an avenue for marketing of Ottoman copper on the international market because, at least in latter years, these operators were sometimes paid their share in copper.

28. Sanuto, *I Diarii*, 7: 12–13, 128, 152.

29. Alberi, *Relazioni*, Series 3, v.1, pp. 66. See also: Halil Sahillioğlu, "1524–1525 Osmanlı Bütçesi," p. 425. Entries in this budget include 592,095 akçe for "*Küre madeni hasıl*" and (separate item) 36,781 akçe income "*hazinece* [hazinede?] *bakır satışından.*"

30. See Alberto Tenenti, *Naufrages, Corsairs et Assurances maritimes à Venise 1592–1609* (Paris: S.E.V.P.E.N., 1959), pp. 13–14, 147–249, 261–262. Alberi, *Relazioni*, Series 3, v. 3, p. 57: Contarini mentions four Turkish merchant vessels traveling between Alexandria and Istanbul in 1519, but does not discuss the cargo.

31. Suraiya Faroqhi, *Towns and Townsmen*, pp. 54, 108–109, 188. Horses, iron, and silver were other items that the Ottomans wished to keep out of Safavid hands.

32. Cannon founding for the Ottomans has been discussed. On the use of imported copper for cannon founding in India proper see Godinho, *Le Économie*, p. 408.

33. Such hardship could be internal or external. For example, in times of shortage of copper for currency, the cauldron makers might find their supply limited. This happened both in Anatolia and in Egypt. See A. Afetinan, *Aperçu General sur l'Histoire Economique de l'Empire Turc-Ottoman* (Ankara: T.T.K., 1976), pp. 89–90, 93. Cauldron makers of Sivas, Tokat, and Amasia could not get the copper they needed from Kastamonu mines unless they had the proper documents authorizing the purchase. Afetinan mentions annual caravans from Tokat bringing copper to Aleppo, but his treatment is hampered by his failure to cite the specific *mühimme* documents for his examples. Raymond, *Artisans*, pp. 335–337, 358–360 discusses the organization and regulation of the coppersmiths in Ottoman Egypt, pointing out that precautions for minting supplies affected the coppersmiths as they did the goldsmiths. Also on the Ottoman silver and copper mines (of Rumelia) in the late fifteenth century and later see Beldiceanu, *Actes*, v. 2, pp. 81, 161–171, 200, 205, 214, 230.

34. Frederic Lane and Reinhold Mueller, *Money and Banking in Medieval and Renaissance Venice* (Baltimore: Johns Hopkins University Press, 1985), p. 560.

35. Eliyahu Ashtor, *Les Métaux Précieux et la Balance des Payements du Proche-Orient à la Basse Époque* (Paris: S.E.V.P.E.N., 1971), pp. 113–115 notes some uses of copper goods from a Geniza document dated to the Fatimid period. This study, along with the work of Godinho and Frederic Lane, provides the most comprehensive treatment of money and precious metals in this era.

36. Lane and Mueller, *Money and Banking*, pp. 558–562. Coins like the *piccoli* and *torneselli* were largely copper. Lane estimates copper prices in Venice in 1519 at 44 ducats per *migliaio grosso* (477 kg.) or 9.2 gold ducats per 100 kg. Sella, *Commerci*, p. 12 notes that profit for Venetian copper sales in Egypt was 25 percent in the 1390s, with copper in tablets selling in Venice for 82–85 ducats per *migliaio grosso* and in Alexandria for 16–20 dinars per kantar (90 kg.) Ashtor, *Métaux*, notes the value of dinars, gold to silver ratios, and French and Venetian imports into Egypt and Syria in the early sixteenth century (pp. 48–49), prices in Venice (pp. 116–118), and in Egypt and Syria, 9–16 ducats per kantar between 1506 and 1510 (pp. 61–64, 83).

37. In 1520 the *bakır para mukataa* (copper money tax farm) in Aleppo was worth 30,000 akçe. See Inalcık, *Bursa I*, pp. 57 (Bursa), 60 (Aleppo).

38. Ölçer Cüneyt, *Nakışlı Osmanlı Mangırları* (Istanbul: Yenilik Basımevi, 1975), p. 11. The 1604 firman noted that 150,000 akçe worth of copper had been mined, refined, and the ingots registered and marked with the seals of the mint chief and *defterdar* to be sent to the provinces to alleviate the shortage. Cüneyt notes that copper was not acceptable for the

payment of taxes; the coin value of copper coins was more than the actual metal value, and that Edirne, Bursa, Tire, Konya, Mardin, and Amid were common mints for copper coins. See also, Inalcık, "Kadi Sicillerinden," pp. 64, 68–69 on copper for coinage in the late fifteenth century Bursa *kadi* records; and, on mines, Beldiceanu, *Actes*, v. 1, p. 78 on the minting of copper coins in Rumelia. With a new minting, the old coins would be demonetized and sold to the *pul sarrafları* (money changers) at the metal price of copper.

39. Multiple local copper coins was also the norm in Iran where, in the seventeenth century, for example, governors minted the copper coins in their own names and the coins decreased in value when a new governor was appointed: see John Foran, "The Long Fall of the Safavid Dynasty: Moving Beyond the Standard Views," *International Journal of Middle East Studies* 24 (1992), p. 284.

40. Barbosa, *A Description*, pp. 159–60, 191, 194.

41. K. N. Chaudhuri, *Trade and Civilization*, pp. 90, 109, 190–192, 216–217. According to Chaudhuri, copper was the only official coinage in China where gold and silver were used in bullion form.

42. Barbosa, *A Description*, pp. 46–47, 55, 93, 164 written in 1516. See also d'Varthema, p. 90 on quantities of copper at Java.

43. Barbosa, *A Description*, p. 93; Tomé Pires, *Suma Oriental*, p. 12–13, 43–44.

44. Sarjeant, *The Portuguese*, pp. 141, 143, 148, 151 using Arab sources for roughly the same time period as Barbosa.

45. Barbosa, *A Description*, p. 21. Copper was mined in the African interior as well, but the difficulties of transport to the coasts for African copper and the ease and proximity of supply via the Red Sea to Indian Ocean copper trade made European or Anatolian copper a good alternative source of supply for kingdoms like Mombasa.

46. Pearson, *Gujarat*, pp. 51–52. On the prices, demand, and copper use in India from the Portuguese sources see Godinho, *Le Économie*, pp. 371–383, 404–405, 698. The Portuguese continued the trade in copper from Iberia to India via the Cape route.

47. Sarjeant, *The Portuguese*, pp. 63–64.

48. Godinho, *Le Économie*, pp. 702–703, 716–721 on spice quantities in Alexandria and Beirut in the fifteenth and sixteenth centuries. Ashtor, *Levant Trade*, pp. 389–399, 463, 510–512 charts the pepper prices in Alexandria in the fifteenth century and discusses the details of small investors, ship loads and sizes, and trade volumes. Ashtor notes (p. 511) a French account, which estimates that the customs offices in Alexandria were

Notes 241

leased for 250,000 *ashrafis* a year, and that total imports and exports must have amounted to 1.4–1.5 million ducats, including trade with the Maghreb and Turkey. See also Raymond, *Artisans* v. 1, pp. 330–333 on the seventeenth- and eighteenth-century spice merchants in Cairo.

49. Regular fleets also traded to Tunis. Lane, *Venice and History*, pp. 25–34, 128–141; Ashtor, *Levant Trade*, pp. 464–512; Steensgaard, *The Asian Trade*, pp. 53–56; Godinho, *Le Économie*, pp. 713–731.

50. Pullan, "The Occupations," in Hale, *Renaissance Venice*, p. 393. For example, in 1528 several Venetian nobles took shares in the *dazio* (tax on merchandise arriving in Venice by sea) and suffered grave losses in part from the delay of the Beirut and Alexandria galleys which returned after the term of their investment had concluded.

51. Sanuto, *I Diarii*, 4: 38, 47–48. In Sanuto, the term "collo" is used when referring to shipments and the term "sporta" when giving prices. Weights and measures varied from place to place and over time. Godinho, *Le Économie*, p. 717 gives the equivalent of 1 collo as 10 kantar (*cantara*), with 1 kantar approximately equal to 1 quintal. Lane, *Venice and History*, pp. 13–14, estimated that the weight of the collo at Alexandria was 1,120 pounds and that the collo of Beirut was considered equal to 290 pounds but sometimes more. This is a considerable variation, perhaps a function of the bales being broken up for overland travel before reaching Beirut. Lane wrote that the *cantara* at Alexandria used for pepper sales (*cantara forfori*) equalled 94 pounds. This difference would have to be tested against price variations. Halil Inalcık, "Introduction to Ottoman Metrology," *Turcica* 15 (1983): 320, 329 gives the Ottoman kantar (56.443 kg. with variant weight for Bursa) as used in archival sources for the fifteenth and sixteenth century. Load terminology does not necessarily designate a specific weight, and one cannot assume standardized bales, although packing methods at the source could guarantee some uniformity in various types of loads. Commonly used terms for spice measures: cantara, collo, sporta, and quintal are defined by Florence Edler, *Glossary of Medieval Terms of Business: Italian Series 1200–1600* (Cambridge: The Mediaeval Academy of America, 1934), pp. 59, 77, 233, 277, as follows: cantara = weight unit, usually 100 ruotoli, but varying from 100 to 750 pounds; collo = bale or package; quintal = hundredweight; sporta = measure weighing approximately 600 to 700 pounds. Francesco Balducci Pegolotti, *La Practica della Mercatura*, in Giovanni Francesco Pagnini del Ventura, ed. *Della Decima e della Altre Gravezze*, v. 3 (Bologna: Forni Editore, 1967): 56–61, 77, 145, a fourteenth-century source, tends to list trade goods by how they are sold, such as by the hundredweight, by the pound, and so on. In Pegolotti, a cantara of Tripoli = 175 Venetian light pounds (*libbre sottil*); a cantara of Beirut = a cantara of Famagosta, but the Damascene cantara, used for spices, was 80 ruotoli. Pegolotti wrote that the weights of Alexandria, Cairo, Damascus, and Damietta were uniform. Also for weights see Ashtor, "Levantine

Weights and Standard Parcels: A Contribution to the Metrology of the Later Middle Ages," *BSOAS* 45 (1982), pp. 471–488.

52. Sanuto, *I Diarii*, 4: 243.

53. Sanuto, *I Diarii*, 4: 240–241. Ibn Iyās, *Bada'i*, 1: 41/4: 45 wrote that in 1502 the sultan's exactions on merchants were ruining the port trade. The reports in Sanuto show this to be an exaggeration.

54. Ibid., 4: 282, 299, 462. In this case, the *schibe* are distinct from the *schiboti*, which are presumably larger bales, not necessarily weight specific. Edler, *Glossary of Medieval Terms*, p. 262 gives *schibetto* as a term for a bundle, especially a bundle of silk. So this term can denote a variety of sizes depending on the ending applied to the word. Ashtor, *Levant Trade*, p. 397–398, has noted that, at the end of the fourteenth century, caravans coming from the Hijaz to Alexandria brought much larger quantities of spices than those going from the Hijaz to Syria, but that quantities available in Syria were supplemented by the overland caravan trade from the Persian Gulf.

55. Sanuto, *I Diarii*, 4: 705; 5: 34, 59. Unfortunately, the report does not indicate the exact payment made by the ambassador. A Muslim vessel, presumably from Tunis, bought an additional 150 colli. Prices were reasonable: pepper, 72 ducats; ginger, 67 ducats; cloves, 50 ducats; mace, 35 ducats; nutmeg, 25 ducats; cinnamon, 28 ducats (prices given per sporta). In the summer of 1503, pepper at Venice was worth 85 ducats. See Inalcık, "Bursa and the Commerce," p. 138 on pepper prices in the Ottoman Empire; and Steensgaard, *The Asian Trade*, pp. 54–55 on pepper prices in the 1580s. A sporta, according to Setton, *The Papacy*, 3: 19 is approximately 550 lbs., and according to Ashtor, *Levant Trade*, approximately 225 kg. or 495 lbs.

56. Sanuto, *I Diarii*, 5: 197–198.

57. Ibid., 4: 701; 5, 34, 59–60. Qānsūh may have been retaliating for what he called the "poor-quality cloth" used to pay the overdue Cyprus tribute that year. Sanuto, *I Diarii*, 5: 114–115. Lane, *Venice and History*, pp. 109–113 describes how the timing of the galley voyages optimally was set to coincide with the arrival of the shipments from India in the fall and with reinvestment of the profits for new trade goods, such as those from the Flanders and London galleys. When timing was good, investors could turn over their profits twice a year.

58. Competition for grain supplies was a standard in the eastern Mediterranean where grain shortages were endemic. Cyprus, Anatolia, and Sicily were areas of frequent recourse for Venice although these areas, too, suffered from periodic crop failures or shortages. For the grain trade in the latter sixteenth century, Aymard, *Venise*, pp. 93–101, 123–140 mentions the participation by some pashas in the grain trade. See also

Lütfi Güçer, *Hububat*; Rhoads Murphey, "Provisioning Istanbul," pp. 217–263. On the silk trade, see Dalsar, *Türk Sanayı*, pp. 128–129, 135–137, 264–266; Inalcık, "Capital Formation," p. 111.

59. Gökbilgin, *Venedik Devlet*, p. 184. By the time of Süleiman I, Ottoman agents were engaged in the same type of abuses practiced by Mamluk agents in the period under discussion. An Ottoman tax farmer named Ibrahim, for example, attempted to gouge more than the 5 percent customs tolls from Venetian merchants at the Trablus docks. Unlike the Mamluk sultan's participation in such exactions, however, the Ottoman sultan responded vigorously to halt such abuses, responding to a complaint of the *bailo* with an imperial *hükm* (decree) to the *kadis* of Beirut, Trablus Şam and Şam to prohibit such practices.

60. Sanuto, *I Diarii*, 5: 135, 144, 148, 197–198. This was despite the Damascus consul's warning in August not to send the galleys.

61. Ibid., 5: 364, 431. Inacik, "Bursa," pp. 132–136, 142, shows the spice trade conducted in Bursa by the Aleppan and Damascene merchants for the late fifteenth century. It was cheaper, in the Damascene market, for the seller to sell to Muslim rather than "frank" merchants as the duties for both parties were then lower. See Sahillioğlu, "16 Yüzyil Tacirleri," pp. 162–168, 170–174 on Ottoman merchants participating in the Syrian and Indian trade and amassing large fortunes in the latter sixteenth century.

62. For the next century, for example, Steensgaard, *The Asian Trade*, pp. 66–67, has discussed merchants as "customers" of customs agents in eastern Anatolia, suggesting that they shifted routes to secure lower customs rates. In effect, this type of arrangement suggests ad-lib decision-making on the part of the buyers, sellers, and government agents in response to market conditions.

63. Sanuto, *I Diarii*, 19: 304–305, 449, in October 1514.

64. Ibid., 5: 820, 824–826.

65. Ibid., 5: 887–890. Qānsūh's letter to Venice, dated summer of 1503, protested his willingness to abide by the conditions of the trade agreements. He assured the merchants' security, but complained that he was not properly advised of the time of their arrival.

66. Ibid., 7: 12–13, 128, 152.

67. Ibid., 5: 941. Security in Mamluk coastal waters was also poor, as indicated by a report from Damascus that many ships had been lost to Muslim corsairs in the seas near Beirut in autumn 1503.

68. Ibid., 5: 878, 890–891. Pegolotti, *La Pratica*, pp. 137–141 divides the duties for goods purchased in Venice according to whether the merchants were citizens or foreigners (*forestiere*). Rates for foreigners were

approximately double, for example, for spices sold by the hundredweight, a citizen paid twenty-three *denarii picioli* per each light thousandweight (*migliaio sottilo*) and a foreigner paid fifty. If the goods were going to be loaded on shipboard, where additional freight charges were due, the duty (*dazio*) was reduced to twenty *denarii* for foreigners and eighteen for citizens. Pegolotti does not distinguish between Muslim, Jewish, and Christian merchants. No duty was charged for unloading grain in the city. Also in the lists of tolls for goods unloaded in port, Pegolotti does not distinguish between tolls for citizens and foreigners, but between tolls for goods coming in on Venetian armed galleys (no toll) and those for goods coming in on unarmed (merchant) vessels (5 per 100). Thus, there would be a twofold advantage to Ottoman merchants traveling on the *muda*.

69. Ashtor, *Levant Trade*, pp. 165–172. According to Ashtor, ginger was preferentially shipped overland to Damascus in the fourteenth century. Venetians, at that time, alloted 65–80 percent of their investment in spices in Egypt to pepper, and 10–15 percent to ginger.

70. Sanuto, *I Diarii*, 5: 938, 941, 943.

71. Ibid., 5: 1013.

72. Ibid., 6: 43, 64, 93. Prices of spices at Alexandria in July were: pepper, 140 ducats; cloves, 50; mace, 50; nutmeg, 40. Copper was in demand in Egypt, both for consumption there and for export. On the copper trade see also: Sanuto, *I Diarii*, 11: 265; Pegolotti, *La Practica*, pp. 129–130, 135, 138; Giacomo Badoer, *Il Libro dei Conti di Giacomo Badoer, Constantinopoli 1436–1440*, v. 3, in *Il Nuovo Ramusio* (Rome: Libreria dello Stato, 1956), p. 286, which includes fifteenth-century documents on the copper trade with Venice.

73. Perhaps the Venetians also bought Ottoman copper and resold it in Egypt.

74. Wansbrough, "A Mamluk Letter," pp. 200–213.

75. Godinho, *Le Économie*, p. 725, cites the price of pepper in Cairo in 1505 as 192 ducats, apparently using this report from Sanuto. The price, however, reflects an exaction at an inflated price, which the merchants accepted under duress, rather than the market price as implied in Godinho's chart. Ottoman pepper purchases, particularly given the military aid they were supplying to the Mamluks, would have been at a lower rate. For copper prices in the late fourteenth century see Ashtor, *Levant Trade*, p. 160.

76. Sanuto, *I Diarii*, 6: 200–201. It would have been impossible to meet this schedule of payment as the merchants were dependent upon an annual turnover arrangement, the proceeds of one *muda* assuring the payment of the previous year's debt.

77. On market organization and routes, and local profits and consumption see Nelly Hanna, *An Urban History of Bulaq in the Mamluk and Ottoman Periods*, Supplement aux Annles Islamologiques, Cahier 3 (Cairo: Institut Français): 7–32.

78. Sanuto, *I Diarii*, 6: 202–204. No mention of this incident is made in Ibn Iyās, *Badaʿi*.

79. The Beirut galleys sailed again in 1506, bringing home 2,000 colli of spices. Sanuto, *I Diarii*, 6: 487, 519, 522.

80. Ibn Iyās, *Badaʿi*, 1: 89/ 4: 93. For the later period, see Farooqi, "Moguls," pp. 198–220.

81. Sanuto, *I Diarii*, 6: 192 on the Portuguese ships returning to Lisbon in spring 1505 with large quantities of pepper. Barbosa, *A Description*, pp. 21, 219, writing in 1514–1516 mentioned that some of the pepper of Sumatra made its way to Mecca despite Portuguese efforts to stop it. Ibn Iyās, *Badaʿi*, 4: 109 on the Portuguese blockade attempt in 1506–1507 and 156, 182–183 on the defeat at Diu. Godinho, *Le Économie*, pp. 701–703 gives partial figures on Portuguese spice loads for 1513–1519, and estimates as high as 30,000–40,000 quintals for 1506.

82. Sanuto, *I Diarii*, 7: 237–239. Earlier Navarro had seized two Venetian, and one other, caravelles loaded with grain.

83. Sanuto, *I Diarii*, 7: 26, 538. Another fleet under Kemal Reis was sent against grain pirates who had seized sixty ships.

84. Ibid., 7: 551, 589, 682. The Senate, in October 1508, again debated whether to send the *muda* the following year: Ibid., 7: 655. The convoy was ordered by the Senate to proceed from Candia to Alexandria in April 1508 after receiving a safe-conduct from Qānsūh confirming the treaty: Ibid., 7: 596–597.

85. Ibid., 6: 531, 554.

86. Ibid., 6: 520, 529. On the formal recognition of these good relations and on provisions for encounters of ships at sea in the 1513 treaty affirmation see Gökbilgin, "Le Relazioni Veneto-Turche," p. 278. Another possible reason for the cordiality of Ottoman-Venetian relations was the rebuff of an Ottoman ambassador by Naples, the king refusing Ottoman peace overtures in January of 1507. Challenges to the Ottoman navy were more likely to come from Spain or France at this time; and Venetian neutrality, in the event of a clash, could prove useful.

87. Ibid., 6: 339–340.

88. Ibid., 6: 487, 516, 519, 522. Letter of August 1506: the returns from this *muda*, which arrived in Venice in January 1507, were apparently good, although prices had been high in Damascus.

89. Ibid., 6: 207, 220–221, 245–246, 248. Jean Louis Bacqué-Grammont, "Études Turco-Safavides, I Notes sur le Blocus du Commerce Iranien par Selim Ier," *Turcica* 6 (1975): 70–78 on Selim's attempt, only partially successful, to block the silk trade from Iran. The volume of silk trade overland through Anatolia, in the preceding century, (including that of merchants from the Mamluk territories) is treated in Halil Inalcık, "Bursa I," pp. 44–101; Dalsar, *Türk Sanayı*, pp. 267–289.

90. There was, however, competition from the Portuguese, even in the Mediterranean. One report claimed that three Portuguese barks landed at Corfu late in 1506, selling spices and capitalizing on the discomfiture of Venice. Sanuto, *I Diarii*, 6: 502.

91. Ibid., 7: 226. Qānsūh wished to respond to Ismail's advances by rerouting all the spices, which ordinarily went through Damascus, through Cairo.

92. Ibn Iyās, *Bada'i*, 1: 184–185/ 4: 190–191. Sanuto, *I Diarii*, 12: 380–381, 503; 13: 343, 346, 355–356.

93. Sanuto, *I Diarii*, 13: 451, 475; 14: 20, 25–26.

94. Ibn Iyās, *Bada'i*, 1: 195–196, 217, 249/ 4: 201–202, 230, 265–266. The following year, a Safavid envoy to Cairo also brought an insulting message.

95. Sanuto, *I Diarii*, 12: 307–310.

96. Ibn Iyās, *Bada'i*, 1: 283, 289, 291, 297, 299/ 4: 303, 309–310.

97. Ibid., 1: 309/ 4: 331.

98. Sanuto, *I Diarii*, 16: 154–156. The consul in Damascus noted that apparently three ships had reached Jidda with spices, getting past the Portuguese in late summer. Ibid., 17: 156. Barros, *Da Asia*, v. 2, pt. 8: 278–285, on the conquest of Kamran, notes that d'Albuquerque, while there, took the time to gather information on "Prester John" the mythical king of Ethiopia.

99. Sanuto, *I Diarii*, 16: 436, 649. New loads of spices did not arrive that summer in Cairo after the Portuguese invasion of the Red Sea. But, except for cloves and cinnamon, quantities of spices were still available for purchase. Pepper prices in Cairo increased from 120 ducats to 150 at the news of the attack. Prices in Alexandria held steady. Ibid., 17: 155.

100. Ibn Iyās, *Bada'i*, 1: 335, 337, 339–42/ 4: 359, 362, 364–368.

101. Ibid., 1: 342–44, 347/ 4: 368–370, 373. Tomé Pires, *Suma Oriental*, pp. 10–11, a Portuguese civil servant, wrote that at this time the Mamluk sultan had little authority in Syria and that, ". . . neighboring regions are every day joining the Sheikh Ismail against him." The Por-

tuguese were well aware of the Mamluks' internal as well as external weakness.

102. Sanuto, *I Diarii*, 24: 135–137.

103. Ibid., 19: 41–45, according to a report from the Venetian consul in Alexandria, who said this threat was the result of a letter to the Mamluk court from Venice. The consul added that such threats were all for nought unless the governor of the city and the official who supervised the cargo loading (here called *khwaja*) were replaced.

104. Ibid., 19: 304–305, 449. According to a report from Cyprus, the Venetian merchants in Damascus, Tripoli, and Beirut had sold all their goods. This report moderates another one from Damascus, in October 1514, which claimed that quantities of spices were good, but that squabbling among the European merchants was spoiling the trade.

105. Ibid., 25: 15–16, 59.

106. See Michel Lesure, "Un Document Ottoman de 1525 sur l'Inde Portugais et les Pays de la Mer Rouge," *Mare Luso Indicum* 3 (1976): 137–160. This interest of the Ottoman captains and sultan in world empire was symbolized by the map of the New World of Piri Reis presented to Selim in 1517. See Hess, "The Evolution," p. 1911–1912.

107. Tardy, *Beyond the Ottoman Empire*, p. 157.

108. Ultimately the Dutch and British succeeded where the Ottomans had not in capturing the "magnificent possibilities" of eastern commerce, which the English traveler Fitch described to the English public in 1591 after a long tour of India. See Sir William Wilson, *A History of British India*, v. 1 (New York: AMS Press, 1966), p 220–232. Wilson attributes the period of Portuguese sway to its ships. Using a late Lisbon manuscript, Wilson (p. 164–165) notes no fewer than 806 ships were employed in the India trade from 1497–1612, of which 425 returned, 285 remained in Asia, and 96 were lost. This is difficult to document but estimates of ship losses ordinarily run much higher.

109. Hess, "The Evolution," p. 1893–95. Hess argued that the histories of Western commercial activity in the Near East ". . . all have to do with only one side of a multi-cultured contact."

110. Hess, "The Evolution," p. 1919.

111. Hess, "The Evolution," pp. 1914–1917.

112. Hess pointed out in 1970 that the Portuguese did not have a major technological advantage but this notion is still a standard of literature on the Euro-Asian sphere. For example, Bernard Lewis, *The Muslim Discovery of Europe* (New York: W. W. Norton and Co., 1982), p. 39: ". . . the west European empires, with ships built to withstand the Atlantic

gales, had an advantage in navigational skills and naval armament which no Asian country could match."

113. Guilmartin, *Gunpowder and Galleys*, pp. 36–41, 253–273. Guilmartin focuses on the costs of good cannon and cannon balls, ballistics, the lack of change in cannon style, the ability to mass produce, and the availability of skilled manpower in his analyses. He argues that the ideas of the "ship killing gun" and of controlling the seas in the sixteenth century are simply false. The "galley system" did not begin to become obsolete until the seventeenth century. If there were any advantage to be had at the turn of the sixteenth century, Guilmartin suggests (p. 256) that it was held by the Ottomans in siege artillery and by the Spanish, and perhaps the Portuguese, in the use of small arms.

114. Sidi Ali Reis, *The Travels and Adventures*, p. 5–15.

115. For a lengthy description of the Red Sea trade in the seventeenth and eighteenth century: navigation, routes, shipping, prices see Andre Raymond, *Artisans et Commerçants au Caire*, v. 1, pp. 108–125.

116. The Ottomans were well aware of the commercial benefits of the Indian Ocean and Persian Gulf trade and did not abandon efforts to capitalize on these benefits until the 1530s. See the exchange of Godinho and Inalcık in Hans-Georg Beck ed. *Venezia: Centro di Mediazione tra Oriente e Occidente (Secoli XV–XVI) Aspetti e Problemi*, v 1 (Firenze: Leo S. Olschki, 1977): 91–95.

117. Jean Louis Bacqué-Grammont and Anne Kroell, *Mamlouks, Ottomans et Portugais en Mer Rouge: L'Affaire de Djedda en 1517*, Supplément aux Annales Islamologiques, Cahier no. 12 (Cairo: 1988), pp. 50–51.

118. The scholar whose work most clearly emphasizes this conscious motivation for the Ottomans is Salih Özbaran. See, for example, "Hindustan Yolu," p. 82–89 on the economic advantages of the Ottoman conquest and control of the Indian trade routes. Özbaran deals here primarily with the Ottoman interest in the Indian Ocean routes in the 1530s and 1540s, treating the Ottomans as economic and not just political actors.

Chapter 7. Conclusion.

1. Necipoğlu, "Süleyman the Magnificent," p. 424, has contrasted the period from the 1450s to the 1530s to the period thereafter in which the awareness of fixed geographical boundaries heightened the accentuation of "otherness." She employs concrete symbols of sovereignty and artistic production-consumption as measures rather than vague generalizations about religion and culture. Still, even after the mid-1530s the Ottoman physical and cultural boundaries may have been more permeable than her conclusions suggest.

2. This interpretation is reflected throughout in Lewis, *The Muslim Discovery*; also Goodrich, *The Ottoman Turks and the New World*, pp. 6–9 emphasizes the "complacency and insularity" of the Ottomans and notes that New World "colonies drained a good deal of Habsburg energy out of the Mediterranean, which enabled the easier expansion of Ottoman influence." Goodrich concludes, in part because of lack of evidence, that: "The Ottomans acquired the firm conviction that they had nothing of lasting importance to learn from the *kafirs* (infidels) and *putperests* (idol worshippers), who inhabited the non-Islamic world."

3. In Lewis, *The Muslim Discovery*, pp. 34, and 302 for example. Lewis conceptualizes the sixteenth-century world in terms of holy war and uses religion to divide the Islamic world from the rest of the globe. "The contrast has sometimes been drawn between the very different responses of the Islamic world and of Japan to the challenge of the West. . . . Muslim perceptions of Europe were influenced, indeed dominated, by an element which had little or no effect upon the Japanese, namely, religion. Like the rest of the world, Europe was perceived by Muslims first and foremost in religious terms, i.e., not as Western or European or white but as Christian—and in the Middle East, unlike the Far East, Christianity was familiar and discounted." Lewis' work is widely distributed. But we can no longer credit the grouping of highly differentiated political, cultural, and economic units solely under the rubric "Islamic world" for purposes of characterizing or analyzing economic behavior or mentality.

4. Charles Issawi, "The Decline of Middle Eastern Trade, 1100–1850," in D. S. Richards, ed. *Islam and the Trade of Asia* (Oxford: Bruno Cassirer and the U. of Pennsylvania Press, 1970), p. 252–253.

5. The old "super-unconscious" characterization is embodied in Lybyer's notion of the Ottoman conquests: A. H. Lybyer, "The Ottoman Turks and the Routes of Oriental Trade," *The English Historical Review* 30 (1915), p. 588. "They were not active agents in deliberately obstructing the routes. They did not by their notorious indifference and conservativism greatly, if at all on the whole, increase difficulties of the oriental traffic. Nor did they make the discovery of new routes imperative." Although Lybyer's basic conclusions have been drastically revised over the years, their underlying assumptions remain very much intact in new historiography. Goodrich, *The Ottoman Turks and the New World*, pp. 15–16 notes that the sixteenth-century "Ottoman intelligensia does not seem to have been receptive to information from outside the Dar ul-Islam or from outside the Empire itself." Such characterizations are simply not borne out when one considers the active commercial and cultural exchange in which the *askeri* took part even before the sixteenth century.

6. Ugo Tucci, "The Psychology of the Venetian Merchant," pp. 356–357.

7. Inalcık, "The Turkish Impact on the Development of Modern Europe," pp. 54–55.

8. This would explain how the "layers of privilege" in the *askeri* class affected economic action as illustrated by Rif'at Abou-El-Haj, *The 1703 Rebellion and the Structure of Ottoman Politics* (Istanbul: Nederlands Historisch-Archaeologisch Institut te Istanbul, 1984), pp. 10–13, showing, for example, how the confiscation principle was ignored and circumvented, along with endowing of *evkaf*, in order to ensure the continuity of household fortunes.

9. The comparison could proceed along the lines (although not necessarily with the same schematic) suggested by Masters in his study of economic organization in seventeenth- and eighteenth-century Aleppo. Masters looks for shared economic interest and emphasizes client relationships rather than assuming a rigid and closed hierarchical organization of the Syrian urban commercial space.

10. It is true that a language barrier—the limited number of scholars utilizing Ottoman sources and the limited Ottoman sources for the early sixteenth century—has contributed to this problem. But the language barrier cannot account for a drawing of the Ottomans that precludes the notion of *askeri* commercial action. After all, the notable classes in the Arab provinces, where Ottoman became the administrative language and where officials and official documents were gradually Ottomanized after the conquest, have been analyzed as commercial entities. It is the central Ottoman administration which, above all, has been subjected to the exclusion principle.

11. By "unity" I do not mean to propose that Europe constituted a unified cultural or social whole in the sixteenth century. The Reformation, however, altered and restricted the rhetorics of religious unity that could be employed in the languages of diplomacy and legitimation, internally and externally.

12. The large and small merchant question, for example, has been developed for India by Irfan Habib, "Merchant Communities in Precolonial India," in Tracy, ed. *The Rise of Merchant Empires*, pp. 372–399. This article raises a dialogue on theory with the work of Chaudhuri and Steensgaard.

13. On the Indian merchants in late fifteenth century Bursa see Inalcık, "Bursa I," p. 47. Thorne addressed his work to Henry VIII's ambassador at the court of Charles V, suggesting a northwestern route to outflank the Portuguese claims to India: Wilson, *British India*, p. 196; d'Varthema, *Itinerary*, p. 79.

GLOSSARY

ahidname: Treaty or pact whereby the Ottoman sultan granted trading privileges in his domain to merchants of foreign states in return for financial considerations and good behavior. In the early sixteenth century, such an agreement could be revoked by the sultan at his discretion; it had to be renegotiated with each new sultan

askeri: The Ottoman military-administrative class whose members monopolized both the wealth and the political power in the Ottoman state in conjunction with the Ottoman dynasty or family of Osman.

bailo: Venetian civil servant elected to act as resident ambassador in Istanbul. The bailo's term, originally fixed, in practice sometimes lasted until he died, was recalled, or succeeded in obtaining a transfer.

bark: Term for a class of large sailing ships with rounded hulls. Also used for carracks modified with a narrower stern.

bastarda: Hybrid oared vessel combining elements of the galley with various combinations of sails and decks.

beglerbeg: Literally "lord of lords" or commander of commanders. Beg was used to designate provincial governors and military commanders in the Ottoman state.

carrack: Large ship with rounded hull used as a long-distance merchantman, usually for bulk goods. It was equipped with 2–3 masts bearing a combination of square and lateen (triangular) sails.

cog: General term for a class of rounded hulled, high-decked sailing ships, used primarily for transport and commerce. Cogs had a stern rudder, single mast, and square sail.*

fusta: Light, speedy, low draft, oared vessel with one or two oars per bench, frequently used for coastal shipping or raiding.

galleon: Sailing ship with a longer, lower, narrower hull than the round ships, barks or cogs—thus, closer to the hull design of the oared galley.

galiot: General term for a light galley, an oared vessel used primarily for commerce.

galley: General term for a class of oared vessel with an elongated hull, varying in size, ordinarily having 2–3 banks of oars (25–30 benches per side). Galleys were also equipped with sails and were used both for commerce and for combat.

gripo: Small, lateen-rigged sailing ship, which could also be maneuvered by oars.

janissary: Member of the Ottoman elite infantry corps. The janissaries were equipped with firearms and recruited through special levies from the non-Muslim Ottoman population.

kadırga: General term for a galley, usually armed and equipped with 25–26 oar benches.

kayık: General term for a small boat, skiff, with sail or oars.

kızılbaş: Red head. A term used to characterize the followers, particularly the tribal cavalry warriors, of the Safavid shah. They were so called because of the distinctive red twelve-peaked headgear they adopted symbolizing their devotion to the twelve Sh'ite Imams.

luogotenente: Venetian civil servant charged with administering an office, city or territory (i.e. the luogotenente of Famagosta). This officer was elected and, although possessing certain discretionary powers, was subject to the orders of the Venetian Senate.

mamluk: A member of the elite military caste under the Mamluk administration in Egypt, Syria, and Arabia. These soldiers

* In practice the terms cog, bark, and galleon were often used interchangeably.

were organized into military households under their commanders, or amirs. The Mamluk sultan was chosen from among these military commanders. Mamluk (slave) suggests the slave origins of this caste.

maona: General term for a large or heavy galley that was often armed.

muda: The Venetian state-subsidized galley convoys, which traveled annually or twice annually to Alexandria, Beirut, and Tunis. Also used to designate the loading period for these convoys.

mukataa: Ottoman tax farm. The right to collect public revenues, such as land or customs taxes, for a fixed term in return for an advance payment to the government.

nave: General term for round-hulled sailing ships, often applied to large merchant ships.

orator: Elected Venetian civil servant sent to perform a diplomatic mission abroad. An orator was assigned for a specific short-term mission rather than for a resident ambassadorship as was the *bailo*.

palandaria: Lateen-rigged merchant vessel. This sailing ship was often used as a transport for provisions.

pasha: Title designating high Ottoman military rank.

procurator: Elected Venetian official charged with provisioning tasks for a certain area or group such as the army or fleet. The title, actually *procuratore*, was modified by a term indicating the realm of governance such as procurator general of the fleet.

proveditor: Purveyor or superintendent. A Venetian official charged with overseeing a specific branch of government such as the fleet, the salt-works, or customs. The title, actually *provveditore*, was modified by a term indicating the specific task.

sancak beg: An Ottoman sub-provincial governor who administered a district called "a sancak."

timar: An Ottoman military land grant from which the appointee was entitled to collect certain revenues in return for military service.

vezir: Top Ottoman administrative official, appointed by the sultan. The Grand Vezir was the sultan's major administrative advisor and often the commander of military campaigns in the sultan's absence. He was followed in importance by vezirs of lesser rank.

BIBLIOGRAPHY

Manuscript Sources

Ahmad ibn ʿAlī ibn Zunbūl. "Ghazwat al-Ṣultan Salīm Khān maʿ al-Ṣultān al-Ghūrī" Ms. Landberg 461. Yale University Library, New Haven.

Ali Emiri. Ms. 325. Süleiman Tasnifi. Baş Bakanlık Arşivi, Istanbul.

Bayezid II. "Letter to ʿAlā al-Dawla" Ms. Or 61. British Museum, London.

Bidlīsī, Hakim al-Dīn Idrīs. "Hasht Bihisht" Ms. Or 7646. British Museum, London.

Bidlīsī, Sharaf Khān. "Sharafnāmah" Ms. Elliot 332. Bodleian Library, Oxford.

Celalzade Mustafa. "Kitab-i Meʿasir-i Selim Khan" Ms. Hazine 1415. Topkapı Sarayı Kütüphanesi, Istanbul.

Kemal Paşazade. "Tarih-i Al-i Osman" Ms. Turc 1047. Bibliothéque Nationale, Paris.

———. "Tarih-i Al-i Osman" Ms. Revan 1278. Topkapı Sarayı Kütüphanesi, Istanbul.

Kepeci Ms. 2544, Mevkufat Kalemi. Baş Bakanlık Arşivi, Istanbul.

Keşfi, Mehmed Çelebi. "Selim name" Ms. Esad Efendi 2147. Süleimaniye Kütüphanesi, Istanbul.

Maliyeden Mudevver Defterleri, v. 1, no. 23051, p. 9. Baş Bakanlık Arşivi, Istanbul.

Muallim Cevdet Ms. 079, Gelibolu Tahrir Defter 879/1474. Baş Bakanlık Arşivi, Istanbul.

255

Qānsūh al-Ghūrī to Selim I. Ms. TKS E/11282. Topkapı Sarayı Arşivi, Istanbul.

Reis ül-Kuttap Ms. 655. Süleimaniye Kütüphanesi, Istanbul.

Ross Anonymous. "Tarīkh-i Şāh Isma'īl Safevī" Ms. Or 3248. British Museum, London.

Şükri. "Selim name" Ms. H.O. 32. Österreichisches Nationalbibliothek, Vienna.

Şükri. "Selim name" Ms. Hazine 1597–1598. Topkapı Sarayı Kütüphanesi, Istanbul.

Yusuf Ağa. "Kitāb-i Feth-i Sultān Selim Khān" Ms. H.O. 33. Österreichisches Nationalbibliothek, Vienna.

Primary Sources, Printed and Lithograph

Abu Bakr Tihrāni. *Kitāb-i Diyār Bakrīye: Ak-Koyunlu Tarihi.* Edited by Necati Lugal and Faruk Sümer. Türk Tarih Kurumu Yayınları Series 3, no. 7a. Ankara: Türk Tarih Kurumu, 1964.

Alberi, Eugenio. *Le Relazioni degli Ambasciatori Veneti al Senato Durante il Secolo Decimosesto.* Florence: by author, 1863.

Angiolello, Giovan Maria. "A Short Narrative of the Life and Acts of Uzun Cassano." In *Travels in Tana and Persia II.* Hakluyt Series 1, no. 49. London: Hakluyt Society, 1883.

Anonymous Merchant. "Travels of a Merchant in Persia." In *Travels in Tana and Persia II.* Hakluyt Series 1, no. 49. London: Hakluyt Society, 1883.

Badoer, Giacomo. *Il Libro dei Conti di Giacomo Badoer, Costantinopoli 1436–1440.* Vol. 3 in *Il Nuovo Ramusio.* Rome: Libreria dello Stato, 1956.

Barbarigo, Andrea. *Andrea Barbarigo, Merchant of Venice, 1418–1449.* Edited by Frederic C. Lane. New York: Octagon Books, 1967.

Barbosa, Duarte. *The Book of Duarte Barbosa.* Translated by Mansel Longworth Dames. Hakluyt Series 2, no. 44. London: Hakluyt Society, 1918.

———. *A Description of the Coast of East Africa and the Malabar in the Beginning of the Sixteenth Century.* Hakluyt Series 1, no. 35. London: Hakluyt Society, 1866.

Barkan, Ömer Lutfi. *XV ve XVIinci Asırlarda Osmanlı Imparatorluğunda Zirai Ekonominin Hukuk ve Mali Esasları.* Istanbul Üniversitesi,

Edebiyat Fakültesi Türkiyat Enstitüsü Series. Istanbul: Bürhaneddin Matbaası, 1943.

Barros, Joao de. *Da Asia.* Lisbon: Livraria Sam Carlos, 1973.

Berengo, Andrea. *Lettres d'un Marchand Venitien, Andrea Berengo 1553–1556.* Edited by Ugo Tucci. Paris: S.E.V.P.E.N., 1957.

Bosio, Iacomo. *Dell' Istoria della Sacra Religione et Illustrissima Militia de San Giovanni Gierosolimitano.* Rome: Stamperia Apostolica Vaticana, 1594.

Çagatay, Neşet. "Osmanlı Imparatorluğunda Maden Hukuk ve Iktisadiyatı Hakkında Vesikalar." *Tarih Vesikaları* 2, no. 10 (1942): 279–283.

d'Albuquerque, Alfonso. *The Commentaries of the Great Alfonso D'Albuquerque.* Translated by Walter de Graybirch. Hakluyt Series 1, no. 55. London: Hakluyt Society, 1928 reprint, New York: Hakluyt Society, 1970.

Dalsar, Fahri. *Türk Sanayı ve Ticaret Tarihinde Bursa'da Ipekçilik.* Istanbul Üniversitesi, Iktisat Fakültesi Series, no. 116. Istanbul: Istanbul Üniversitesi, 1960.

d'Lezze, Donado. *Historia Turchesca.* Edited by I. Ursi. Bucharest: Academiei Romane, 1910.

Fabri, Felix. *Vovage en Egypte de Felix Fabri, 1483.* Translated by R. P. Jacques Masson. Collection des Voyageurs Occidentaux en Egypte, no. 14, pt. 2. Cairo: Institut Français d'Archéologie Orientale du Caire, 1975.

Fekete, Lajos. *Die Siyaqat Schrift in der Türkischen Finanzverwaltung.* Budapest: Akadémiai Kiadó, 1955.

———. *Einführung in die Persische Paläographie.* Budapest: Akadémiai Kiadó, 1977.

Feridun Beg, Ahmed. *Mecmu'a-i Munşe'at üs-Selatin,* 2 vols. Istanbul: no publisher, 1858.

Firdevsi-i Rūmī. *Kutb-Name.* Edited by Ibrahim Olgun and Ismet Parmaksızoğlu. Türk Tarih Kurumu Yayınları Series 13, no. 5. Ankara: Türk Tarih Kurumu Basımevi, 1980.

Ghistele, Joos van. *Voyage en Egypte de Joos van Ghistele.* Collection des Voyageurs Occidentaux en Egypte, v. 16. Cairo: Institut Français d'Archéologie Orientale du Caire, 1970.

Goitein, D. S. *Letters of Medieval Jewish Traders.* Princeton: Princeton University Press, 1973.

Gökbilgin, M. Tayyip. "Venedik Devlet Arşivindeki Türkçe Belgeler Kolleksiyonu," *Belgeler*, no. 5–8 (1968–1971).

———. "Venedik Devlet Arşivindeki Vesikalar Kulliyatında Kanuni Sultan Süleiman Devri Belgeler." *Belgeler* 1, no. 2 (1964): 119–220.

———. *XV–XVI Asırlarda Edirne ve Paşa Livası Vakıflar—Mülkler—Mukataalar*. Istanbul: Ülçer Basımevi, 1952.

Great Britain. *Calendar of State Papers: Colonial Series, 1513–1616*. London: Her Majesty's Stationery Office, 1862 reprint, Vaduz: Kraus Reprint, 1964.

———. *Calendar of State Papers and Manuscripts Relating to English Affairs Existing in the Archives and Collections of Venice, 1509–1519*. London: Her Majesty's Stationery Office, 1864.

Guicciardini, Francesco. *The History of Italy*. Translated by Sidney Alexander. New York: Macmillan, 1969.

Ibn Iyās. *Badaʻi al-Zuhūr fī waqaʻī al-Duhūr*. Edited by Mohamed Mostafa. Cairo: Franz Steiner Verlag, 1960.

———. *Badaʻi al-Zuhūr fī waqaʻī al-Duhūr*. 2 vols. Translated by Gaston Wiet. *Journal d'un Bourgeoisié du Caire*. Paris: Librairie Armond Colin, 1955–1960.

Ibn Khaldūn. *The Muqaddimah*. Translated by Franz Rosenthal. Princeton: Princeton University Press, 1970.

Ibn Ṭūlūn, Shams al-Dīn Muḥammad ibn ʻAlī. *Mufākahat al-Khillān fī hawadith al-Zamān*. Edited by Muḥammad Muṣṭafa. Cairo: Wizarat al-Thaqāfah wa-al-Irshād, 1962.

———. *Les Gouverneurs de Damas sous les Mamlouks et les Premiers Ottomans, 658–1156/1260–1744*. Translated by Henri Laoust. Damascus: Institut Français de Damas, 1952.

Inalcık, Halil and Robert Anhegger, eds. *Kanunname-i Sultani ber Mücebi ʻÖrf-i ʻOsmanı, II Mehmed ve II Bayezid Devirlerine Ait Yasakname ve Kanunnameler*. Türk Tarih Kurumu Yayınları Series 11, no. 5. Ankara: Türk Tarih Kurumu Basımevi, 1956.

Inalcık, Halil. "Bursa I, XV Asır Sanayı ve Ticaret Tarihi Vesikalar." *Belleten* 24, no. 93 (1960): 46–101.

———. "A Case Study in Renaissance Diplomacy: The Agreement Between Innocent VIII and Bayezid II on Djem Sultan." *Journal of Turkish Studies* 3 (1979): 209–230.

———. *Gazavât-i Sultân Murad b. Mehemmed Hân: Isladı ve Varna Savaşları (1443–1444) Üzerinde Anonim Gazavâtnâme*. Türk Tarih

Kurumu Yayınları Series 18, no. 1. Ankara: Türk Tarih Kurumu Basımevi, 1978.

———. "Osmanlı Idare, Sosyal ve Ekonomik Tarihiyle Ilgili Belgeler: Bursa Kadi Sicillerinden Seçmeler." *Türk Tarih Kurumu Belgeler* 10 (1980–1981): 1–91.

Islam, Riazul, ed., *The Shamlū Letters: A New Source of Iranian Diplomatic Correspondence.* Karachi: The Institute of Central and West Asian Studies, 1971.

Katib Çelebi. *Tuhfet ül-Kibar fi Esfar ül-Bihar.* Istanbul: Muteferrika, 1141/1728–1729.

———. *History of the Maritime Wars of the Türks.* Translated by James Mitchell. London: Oriental Translation Fund, 1831.

Kemal Paşazade. *Tarih-i Al-i Osman, Defter VII.* Türk Tarih Kurumu Yayınları Series 1, no. 5. Ankara: Türk Tarih Kurumu Basımevi, 1954.

Khvandamīr. *Habīb al-Siyar fī Akhbār Afrād al-Bashar.* 2 vols. Edited by Jalal al-Dīn Huma'i. Tehran: Kitābkhāne-i Khayām, 1333/1954.

Kritovoulos. *History of Mehmed the Conqueror* Translated by Charles Riggs. Westport, Connecticut: Greenwood Press, 1970.

Lefort, Jacques. *Documents Grecs dans les Archives de Topkapı Sarayı.* Ankara: Türk Tarih Kurumu Basımevi, 1981.

Lesure, Michel. "Un Document Ottoman de 1525 sur l'Inde Portugais et les Pays de la Mer Rouge." *Mare Luso Indicum* 3 (1976): 137–160.

Levend, Agah Sīrrī. *Gazavāt-Nameler ve Mihaloğlu 'Alī Bey'in Gazavāt-Nāmesi.* Ankara: Türk Tarih Kurumu Basımevi, 1956.

Lewis, Bernard. "A Jewish Source on Damascus Just after the Ottoman Conquest." University of London, *Bulletin of the School of Oriental and African Studies* 10 (1940): 180–184.

Lopez, Robert S. and Irving W. Raymond. *Medieval Trade in the Mediterranean World.* New York: Columbia University Press, 1968.

Lutfi Paşa. *Tarih-i Al-i Osman.* Istanbul: Matbaa-i Amire, 1341/1922.

Luchetta, Francesca. "L'Affare Zen in Levante nel Primo Cinquecento." *Studie Veneziani* 10 (1959): 109–209.

Mas-Latrie, Louis. *Histoire de l'Ile de Chypre sous le Règne des Princes de la Maison de Lusignan.* Paris: Imprimerie Impériale, 1855.

———. *Traités de Paix et de commerce et documents divers concernant les relations des chrétiens avec les Arabes de l'Afrique Septentrionale au*

Moyen Age. 2 vols. Paris: Imprimerie Impériale, 1866; reprint, New York: Burt Franklin, 1964.

Melikoff, Irene. "Bayezid II et Venise: Cinq Lettres Impériales (Nāme-i Hümayūn) Provenant de l'Archivio di Stato di Venezia." *Turcica* 1 (1969): 123–149.

Mughul, Yakub. "Portekizli'lerle Kızıldenizde Mucadele ve Hicaz'da Osmanlı Hakimiyetinin Yerleşmesi Hakkında bir Vesika." *Türk Tarih Kurumu Belgeler* 2, no. 3–4 (1965): 37–48.

Musso, Gian Giacomo. *Navigazioni e Commercia Genovese con il Levante nei Documenti dell'Archivio di Stato di Genova Secolo XIV–XV.* Rome: Ministero per i Beni Culturali e Ambientali, Publicazione degli Archivio de Stato, 1975.

Pegolotti, Francesco Balducci. *La Pratica della Mercatura.* Vol. 3 in *Della Decima e della Altre Gravezze.* Bologna: Forni Editore, 1967.

Pires, Tomé. *Suma Oriental.* Hakluyt Series 2, no. 89. London: Hakluyt Society, 1944.

Piri Reis. *Kitab-i Bahriye.* Türk Tarih Kurumu Yayınları Series 1, no. 2. Istanbul: Devlet Basımevi, 1935.

Priuli, Girolamo. "Girolamo Priuli e i Suoi Diarii." Edited by R. Fulin. *Archivio Veneto* 22, pt. 1 (1881): 137–248.

Richards, Gertrude, ed. *Florentine Merchants in the Age of the Medicis.* Cambridge: Harvard University Press, 1932.

Rūmlū, Ḥasan. *Ahsan al-Tavārīkh.* Edited and translated by C. N. Seddon. Gaekwads Oriental Series, vol. 57 and 69. Baroda: Oriental Institute, 1934.

Sadeddin. *Tac üt-Tevarih,* 2 vols. Istanbul: Tabhane-yi Amire, 1279/1863.

Sahillioğlu, Halil. "1524–1525 Osmanlı Bütçesi." In *Ord. Prof. Ömer Lutfi Barkan'a Armağan.* Istanbul: Gür-Ay Matbaası, 1985.

Sansovino. *Historia Universale dell'Origine e Imperio de Turchi.* Venice: n.p., 1582.

Sanuto, Marino. *I Diarii.* 36 vols. Venice: Fulin, Stefani, Berchet, and Barozzi, 1880–1887.

Schwarz, Klaus. *Osmanische Sultansurkunden des Sinai-Klosters in Türkischer Sprache.* Islamkundliche Untersuhungen Series, no. 7. Berlin: Klaus Schwarz, 1970.

Sidi Ali Reis. *Mirat ül-Memalik.* Istanbul: Ikdam Matbaası, 1313/1895.

Smith, Ronald Bishop. *The First Age of the Portuguese Embassies, Naviga tions, and Peregrinations in Persia (1507–1524)*. Bethesda, Maryland: Decatur Press, 1970.

———. *The First Age of the Portuguese Embassies, Navigations, and Peregrinations to the Ancient Kingdoms of Cambay and Bengal (1500–1521)*. Bethesda, Maryland: Decatur Press, 1969.

———. *The First Age of the Portuguese Embassies, Navigations and Peregrinations to the Kingdoms and Islands of Southeast Asia (1509–1521)*. Bethesda, Maryland: Decatur Press, 1968.

Spandugino, Theodoro. "La Vita di Sach Ismael et Tamas Re di Persia Chiamati Soffi." In Sansovino. *Historia Universale dell'Origine e Imperio de Turchi*. Venice: no publisher, 1582.

Tardy, Lajos. *Beyond the Ottoman Empire: 14th–16th Century Hungarian Diplomacy in the East*. Translated by János Boris. *Studia Uralo-Altaica* v.13, Szeged: 1978.

Thomas, George Martin. *Diplomatarium Veneto-Levantinum sive Acta et Diplomatat Res Venetas Graecas Atque Lentis (1351–1454)*. 2 vols. New York: Burt Franklin, 1966.

Tursun Bey. *Tarih-i Abu'l-Fath/The History of Mehmed the Conqueror*. Edited by Halil Inalcık and Rhoads Murphey. Minneapolis and Chicago: Bibliotheca Islamica, 1978.

Ugur, Ahmet. *The Reign of Sultan Selīm I in the Light of the Selīm-Nāme Literature*. Islamkundlische Untersuhungen Series, no. 109. Berlin: Klaus Schwarz, 1985.

'Urūc Beg (Don Juan). *Don Juan of Persia, A Shiʿah Catholic*. Translated by Guy Le Strange. London: George Routledge and Sons, Ltd., 1926.

Yaman. "Küre Bakır Madenine Dair Vesikalar," *Tarih Vesikaları* 1, no. 4 (1941): 266–282.

Zeno, Caterino. *Travels in Tana and Persia II*. Hakluyt Series 1, no. 49. London: Hakluyt Society, 1883.

Secondary Sources:

Abou El-Haj, Rifaʿat. *Formation of the Modern State: The Ottoman Empire, Sixteenth to Eighteenth Centuries*. Albany: State University of New York Press, 1991.

———. *The 1703 Rebellion and the Structure of Ottoman Politics*. Istanbul: Nederlands Historisch-Archaeologisch Institut te Istanbul, 1984.

Abu-Lughod, Janet. *Before European Hegemony: The World System*. A.D. *1250–1350*. Oxford: Oxford University Press, 1989.

Afetinan, A. *Aperçu Général sur l'Histoire Économique de l'Empire Turc-Ottoman.* Ankara: Türk Tarih Kurumu Basımevi, 1976.

Alexandrescu-Dersca-Bulgaru, Marie-Mathilde. "Les Relations de Süleyman Çelebi avec Venise (1400–1410)." In *VIII Türk Tarih Kongresi, Ankara 11–15 Ekim 1976, Kongreye Sunuları,* vol. 2, pp. 997–1006. Ankara: Türk Tarih Kurumu Basımevi, 1981.

―――. "Une Relation Vènetienne sur l'Empire Ottoman à l'Époque de Süleyman le Magnifique." In *Comité International d'Études Pré-ottomanes et ottomanes VIth Symposium, Cambridge, 1–4 July, 1984,* pp. 136–137. Series Varia Turcica IV. Istanbul: French Institute of Anatolian Studies, 1987.

Alouche, Adel. *The Origins and Development of the Ottoman-Safavid Conflict (906–962/1500–1550.* Islamkundlische Untersuhungen Series, no. 91. Berlin: Klaus Schwarz, 1983.

Anderson, Perry. *Lineages of the Absolutist State.* London: Redwood Burn Ltd., 1980.

Anderson, R. C. *Naval Wars in the Levant, 1559–1853.* Liverpool: Liverpool University Press, 1952.

Arifi Beg, "Elbistan ve Maraşda Zu'l-Kadr Oğuları Hukumeti." *Tarih-i Osmanı Encümeni Mecmuası* 25–36 (1330–1331/1912–1913): 358–377, 419–431, 509–512, 535–552, 623–629, 692–697, 767–768.

Arjomand, Said Amir. *The Shadow of God and the Hidden Imam.* Chicago: University of Chicago Press, 1984.

Ashtor, Eliyahu. *Les Métaux Précieux et la Balance des payements du Proche-Orient à la Basse Époque.* Series Ecole Pratique des hautes Études, Monnaie, Prix, Conjoncture, no. 10. Paris: S.E.V.P.E.N., 1971.

―――. *Levant Trade in the Later Middle Ages.* Princeton: Princeton University Press, 1983.

―――. "Levantine Weights and Standard Parcels: A Contribution to the Metrology of the Later Middle Ages." *Bulletin of the School of Oriental and African Studies* 45 (1982): 471–488.

―――. "Observations on Venetian Trade in the Levant in the XIVth Century." *Journal of European Economic History* 5 (1976): 537–575.

Atalay, Besim. *Maraş Tarihi ve Coğrafyası.* Istanbul: Matbaa-i Amire, 1339/1920.

Atan, Turhan. *Türk Gümrük Tarihi,* v. 1 *Başlangıçtan Osmanlı Devletine Kadar.* Ankara: Türk Tarih Kurumu, 1990.

Atiya, Aziz S. *The Crusades in the Later Middle Ages.* London: Butler and Tanner Ltd. 1938. Reprint. New York: Kraus Reprint, 1965.

Aubin, Jean. "Lettres de Cojeatar à Alfonso de Albuquerque." *Mare Luso Indicum* 2 (1972): 189–199.

———. "Revenues du Royaume d'Ormuz et Dépenses du Roi en 1515." *Mare Luso Indicum* 2 (1972): 233–237.

———. "Le Royaume d'Ormuz au Début du XVIe Siècle." *Mare Luso Indicum* 2 (1972): 77–179.

Ayalon, David. *Gunpowder and Firearms in the Mamluk Kingdom*. London: Valentine, Mitchell, 1956.

———. Review of *Gunpowder and Firearms in the Mamluk Kingdom*, by Halil Inalcik, *Belleten* 21 (1957): 503–506.

Aymard, Maurice. *Venise, Raguse et le Commerce du Blé Pendant la Seconde Moitie du XVIe Siècle*. Paris: S.E.V.P.E.N., 1966.

Babinger, Franz. "Marino Sanuto's Tagebücher als Quellen zur Geschichte der Safawijja." In *A Volume of Oriental Studies Presented to Edward G. Browne*. Edited by T. W. Arnold and R. A. Nicholson, pp. 28–50. Cambridge: Cambridge University Press, 1922.

Bacqué-Grammont, Jean Louis and Anne Kroell. *Mamlouks, Ottomans et Portugais en Mer Rouge: L'Affaire de Djedda in 1517*. Supplément aux Annales Islamologiques, Cahier no. 12. Cairo: Insitut Français, 1988.

Bacqué-Grammont, Jean Louis. "Études Turco-Safavides I, Notes Sur le Blocus du Commerce Iranien par Selim I." *Turcica* 6 (1975): 68–88.

———. "Ottomans et Safavides au Temps de Şah Ismaʿīl." Doctoral thesis, Université de Paris I, 1980.

———. "Soutien Logistique et Présence Navale Ottomane en Mediterranée." *Revue Orientale du Monde Mediterannée* 39 (1985): 7–34.

Bagchi, Amiya. *The Political Economy of Underdevelopment*. Cambridge: Cambridge University Press, 1982.

Bakhit, Muhammad. *The Ottoman Province of Damascus in the 16th Century*. Beirut: Libraire du Liban, 1982.

Barkan, Ömer Lutfi. "Avarız." In *Islam Ansıklopedisi*, 2 (1970): 15–16.

Béller-Hann, Ildikó. "Ottoman Perceptions of China." *Comité International d'Études Pré-ottomanes et ottomanes VIth Symposium Cambridge, 1rst–4th July 1984*. Series Varia Turcica, IV. Istanbul and Paris: Isis Press, 1987.

Berchet, Guglielmo. *La Repubblica de Venezia e La Persia*. Torino: G. B. Toravia, 1865.

Birnbaum, Eleazer. "The Ottomans and Chagatay Literature: An Early

16th Century Manuscript of Nava'i's Divan in Ottoman Orthography." *Central Asiatic Journal* 20 (1976): 159–190.

Bonelli, Luigi. "Il Trattato Turco-Veneto del 1540." In *Centenario della Nascita di Michele Amari*, 2: 332–363. Palermo: no publisher, 1910.

Boorstin, Daniel J. *The Discoverers*. New York: Vintage Books, 1985.

Bouchon, Genvieve. "Le Premier Voyage de Lopo Soares en Indie 1504–1505." *Mare Luso Indicum* 3 (1976): 57–84.

Boxer, C. R. *The Portuguese Seaborne Empire 1415–1825*. New York: Alfred A. Knopf, 1969.

Braudel, Fernand. *Civilization and Capitalism 15th–18th Century*, v. 3. Translated by Siân Reynolds. New York: Harper and Row, 1984.

———. *The Mediterranean and the Mediterranean World in the Age of Phillip II*. New York: Harper and Row, 1972.

Bresc, Henri. "La Sicile et la Mere; Marins, Navires, et Routes Maritimes." In *Navigation et Gens de Mer en Mediterranée de la Pre-Histoire a nos Jours*, pp. 59–67. Paris: Editions du Centre National de la Recherche Scientifique, 1980.

Brummett, Palmira. "Rhodes: the Overrated Adversary." *The Historical Journal* 36 (1993): 1–25.

Burke, Peter. *The Italian Renaissance: Culture and Society in Italy*. Princeton: Princeton University Press, 1986.

Chaudhuri, K. N. *Asia Before Europe: Economy and Civilization of the Indian Ocean from the Rise of Islam to 1750*. Cambridge: Cambridge University Press, 1990.

———. *Trade and Civilization in the Indian Ocean*. Cambridge: Cambridge University Press, 1985.

Cipolla, Carlo, *Guns, Sails, and Empires: Technological Innovation and the Early Phases of European Expansion*. New York: Pantheon, 1965.

Çizakça, Murat. "Ottomans and the Mediterranean: An Analysis of the Ottoman Shipbuilding Industry as Reflected by the Arsenal Registers of Istanbul, 1529–1650." *La Gente del Mediterraneo* 2 (no date): 773–788.

Clifford, W. W. "Some Observations on the Course of Mamluk-Safavi Relations (1502/908–1516/922)," unpublished paper.

Cohen, Amnon, and Bernard Lewis. *Population and Revenue in the Towns of Palestine in the Sixteenth Century*. Princeton: Princeton University Press, 1978.

Cohn, Bernard. "Representing Authority in Victorian India." In *The Invention of Tradition*. Edited by Eric Hobsbawm, pp. 211–263. Cambridge: Cambridge University Press, 1989.

Coles, Paul. *The Ottoman Impact on Europe*. New York: Harcourt, Brace and World, 1968.

Cüneyt, Ölçer. *Nakışlı Osmanlı Mangırları*. Istanbul: Yenilik Basımevi, 1975.

Davis, Robert C. *Shipbuilders of the Venetian Arsenal: Workers and Workplace in the Preindustrial City*. Baltimore: Johns Hopkins University Press, 1991.

Durant, Will. *The Renaissance: A History of Civilization in Italy from 1303–1576 A.D.* New York: Simon and Schuster, 1953.

Edler, Florence. *Glossary of Medieval Terms of Business: Italian Series 1200–1600*. Cambridge: The Mediaeval Academy of America, 1934.

Ertaylan, Ismail Hikmet. *Sultan Cem*. Istanbul: Milli Eğitim Basımevi, 1951.

Esin, Emel. "Ikinci Bayezid'in H. 904–906/1498–1500 Yıllarında Adalar Denizi'ne Seferi." *Erdem* 1, no. 3 (1985): 789–799.

Fahmy, Aly Mohamed. *Muslim Naval Organization in the Eastern Mediterranean from the Seventh to the Tenth Century A.D.* Cairo: National Publication and Printing House, 1966.

Farooqi, Naim R. "Moguls, Ottomans and Pilgrims, Protecting the Routes to Mecca in the Sixteenth and Seventeenth Centuries." *The International History Review* 10, no. 2 (May 1988): 198–220.

Faroqhi, Suraiya. "Towns, Agriculture and the State in Sixteenth Century Ottoman Anatolia." *Journal of the Economic and Social History of the Orient*, 33 (1990): 125–156.

Fisher, Sydney Nettleton. *The Foreign Relations of Turkey 1481–1512*. Urbana: University of Illinois Press, 1948.

Fodor, Pal. "Ahmedī's Dāsitān as a Source of Early Ottoman History." *Acta Orientali Hungaricae* 38 (1984): 41–54.

Fulin, R. "Il Canale di Suez al la Repubblica di Venezia, 1504." *Archivio Veneto* 2 (1871): 175–199.

Gatti, Luciana, "Costruzioni Navali in Liguria fra XV e XVI Secolo." In *Studi di Storia Navale*. Edited by Henri Bresc, pp. 25–72. N.P.: Giunti, 1975.

Gaudefroy-Demombynes. *La Syrie a l'Époque des Mamelouks d'Apres les Auteures Arabes*. Paris: Librairie Orientaliste Paul Geuthner, 1923.

266   *Bibliography*

Genç, Mehmed. "Ottoman Industry and the Eighteenth Century: General Framework, Characteristics, and Main Trends." Paper presented at the "Manufacturing in the Ottoman Empire Conference," Fernand Braudel Center, State University of New York at Binghamton, November 1990.

Godinho, Vittorino Malaghes. *Le Économie de l'Empire Portugais au XVe e XVIe Siècles.* Paris: S.E.V.P.E.N., 1969.

Goffman, Daniel. *Izmir and the Levantine World 1550–1650.* Seattle: University of Washington Press, 1990.

Gökbilgin, M. Tayyip. "Le Relazioni Veneto-Turche nell'Eta di Solimano il Magnifico." *Il Veltro* 23, no. 2–4 (1979): 277–290.

———. "Yeni Belgelerin Işığı Altında Kanuni Sultan Süleyman Devrinde Osmanlı-Venedik Münasebetleri." In *Kanuni Armağanı*, pp. 171–186. Türk Tarih Kurumu Yayınları Series 7, no. 55. Ankara: Türk Tarih Kurumu Basımevi, 1970.

Goodrich, Thomas. "Ottoman Americana: The Search for the Sources of the Sixteenth Century Tarih-i Hind-i garbi. *Bulletin of Research in the Humanities* 85 (Autumn 1982): 269–294.

———. *The Ottoman Turks and the New World.* Wiesbaden: Harrassowitz, 1990.

Güçer, Lütfi. "Le Commerce Intérieur des Céréales dans L'Empire Ottoman Pendant la Second Moitié du XVIeme Siècle." *Istanbul Üniversitesi Iktisat Fakültesi Mecmuası* 7 (1949/1950): 163–188.

———. *XVI–XVIIIinci Asırlarda Osmanlı Imparatorluğunun Hububat Meselesi ve Hububattan Alınan Vergiler.* Istanbul: Sermet Matbaası, 1964.

———. *XVI–XVIIIinci Asırlarda Osmanlı Imparatorluğunun Ticaret Politikası.* Istanbul Üniversitesi, Iktisat Fakültesi, n.d.

Guilmartin, John. *Gunpowder and Galleys, Changing Technology and Mediterranean Warfare at Sea in the 16th Century.* Cambridge: Cambridge University Press, 1980.

———. "The Tactics of the Battle of Lepanto Clarified: The Impact of Social, Economic and Political Factors." In *New Aspects of Naval History.* Edited by Craig L. Symonds, pp. 41–65. Annapolis: Naval Institute Press, 1981.

Hale, J. R., ed. *Renaissance Venice.* Totawa, New Jersey: Rowman and Littlefield, 1973.

Hamdani, Abbas. "The Ottoman Response to the Discovery of America and the New Route to India." *Journal of the American Oriental Society* 101, pt. 3 (1981): 323–330.

Hanna, Nelly. *An Urban History of Bulaq in the Mamluk and Ottoman Periods.* Supplement aux Annales Islamologiques, Cahier 3. Cairo: Institut Français.

Harb, Muhammad. *Yavuz Sultan Selim'in Süriye ve Misr Seferi.* Istanbul: Özal Matbaası, 1986.

Hartmann, Martin. "Das Privileg Selims I für die Venezianer von 1517." *Mitteilungen der Vorderasiatischen Gesellschaft: Orientalistische Studien* 22 (1918): 201–222.

Hess, Andrew. "The Evolution of the Ottoman Seaborne Empire in the Age of Oceanic Discoveries, 1453–1525." *American Historical Review* 75, no. 7 (December 1970): 1892–1919.

―――. *The Forgotten Frontier, A History of the 16th Century Ibero-African Frontier.* Chicago: University of Chicago Press, 1978.

―――. "The Ottoman Conquest of Egypt (1517) and the Beginning of the 16th Century World War." *International Journal of Middle East Studies* 4 (1973): 55–76.

―――. "Piri Reis and the Ottoman Response to the Voyages of Discovery." *Terra Incognita* 6 (1974): 19–37.

Heyd, Wilhelm. *Geschichte des Levantehandels im Mittelalter.* 2 vols. Stuttgart: J. G. Cottaschen, 1876.

Hodgson, Marshall. *The Venture of Islam: Conscience and History in a World Civilization.* Vol. 2. Chicago: University of Chicago Press, 1974.

Holt, P. M. *Egypt and the Fertile Crescent 1516–1922, A Political History.* Ithaca: Cornell University Press, 1942.

Howard, Douglas. "The Ottoman Timar System and Its Transformation, 1563–1656." Ph.D. diss., Indiana University, 1987.

Hunter, Sir William Wilson. *A History of British India.* Vol. 1, *To the Overthrow of the English in the Spice Achipelago.* New York: AMS Press Inc., 1966.

Imamuddin, S. M. "Maritime Trade Under the Mamluks of Egypt (644–923/1250–1517)." *Hamdard Islamicus* 3, no. 4 (Winter 1980): 67–72.

Imber, Colin H. "The Costs of Naval Warfare: The Accounts of Hayreddin Barbarosa's Herceg Novi Campaign in 1539." *Archivum Ottomanicum* 4 (1972): 203–216.

―――. "The Navy of Süleiman the Magnificent." *Archivum Ottomanicum* 6 (1980): 211–282.

Inalcık, Halil. "Bursa and the Commerce of the Levant." *Journal of the Economic and Social History of the Orient* 3, pt. 2 (1960): 131–147.

———. "Capital Formation in the Ottoman Empire." *Journal of Economic History* 29 (1969): 97–140.

———. "Gelibolu." In *Encyclopedia of Islam*, 2d ed., 2, pt. 2: 983–987.

———. "Harir." In *Encyclopedia of Islam*, 2d. ed., 3: 211–218.

———. "Imtiyazat." In *Encyclopedia of Islam*, 2d. ed., 3: 1179–1189.

———. "Introduction to Ottoman Metrology." *Turcica* 15 (1983): 311–348.

———. *The Ottoman Empire: The Classical Age*. London: Weidenfeld and Nicholson, 1973.

———. "Ottoman Galata, 1453–1553." In *Première Rencontre Internationale sur l'Empire Ottoman et la Turquie Moderne, Institut National des Langues et Civilisations Orientales, Maison des Sciences de l'Homme, 18–22 janvier 1985: Recherches sur la ville ottomane: La cas du quartier de Galata*, pp. 17–116. Series Varia Turcica III. Istanbul: Isis Press, 1991.

———. "Ottoman Methods of Conquest." *Studia Islamica* 2 (1954): 104–129.

———. "Military and Fiscal Transformation in the Ottoman Empire." *Archivum Ottomanicum* 6 (1980): 283–337.

———. "The Rise of the Turcoman Maritime Principalities in Anatolia, Byzantium and the Crusades." *Byzantinische Forschungen* 9 (1985): 179–217.

———. "The Socio-Political Effects of the Diffusion of Fire-Arms in the Middle East." In *War, Technology, and Society in the Middle East*. Edited by V. J. Parry and S. M. Yapp, pp. 347–410. London: Oxford University Press, 1975.

———. "The Turkish Impact on the Development of Modern Turkey." In *The Ottoman State and Its Place in World History*. Edited by Kemal Karpat. Leiden: E. J. Brill, 1974.

Issawi, Charles. "The Decline of Middle Eastern Trade, 1100–1850." In *Islam and the Trade of Asia*. Edited by D. S. Richards, pp. 245–266. Oxford: Bruno Cassirer and the University of Pennsylvania Press, 1970.

Jal, Auguste. *Archéologie Navale*. 2 vols. Paris: Libraire de la Societé de Géographie, 1840.

Jansky, Herbert. "Die Eroberung Syriens durch Sultan Selim I." *Mitteilungen zur Osmanischen Geschichte II*, 4 (1924–1926): 173–241.

Jennings, Ronald C. "Pious Foundations in the Society and Economy of Ottoman Trabzon, 1565–1640." *Journal of the Economic and Social History of the Orient* 33 (1990): 273–328.

Jomier, Jacques. *Le Mahmal et la Caravane Égyptienne des Pèlerins de la Mecque (XIIIe–XXe Siècles)*. Cairo: Institut Français d'Archéologie Orientale, 1953.

Kafadar, Cemal. "A Death in Venice (1575): Anatolian Muslim Merchants Trading in the Serenissima." *Journal of Turkish Studies* 10 (1986): 191–218.

Kappert, Petra. *Die Osmanischen Prinzen und Ihre Residenz Amasya im 15 und 16 Jahrhundert*. Istanbul: Nederlands Historisch-Archeologisch Instituut te Istanbul, Uitgaven, 1976.

Kerslake, Celia J. "The Correspondence Between Selim I and Kansuh al-Gawri." *Prilozi za Orientalnu Filologiju* 30 (1980): 219–233.

Kissling, Hans Joachim. "Şah Ismaʿīl Ier, La Nouvelle Route des Indes et les Ottomans." *Turcica* 6 (1975): 89–102.

Koenigsberger, H. G., George L. Mosse and G. Q. Bowler, eds. *Europe in the Sixteenth Century*. London: Longmans, 1989.

Kütükoğlu, Bekir. "Les Relations entre l'Empire Ottoman et l'Iran dans la Seconde Moitié du XVI Siècle." *Turcica* 6 (1975): 128–145.

Labib, Subhi Y. *Handelsgeschichte Ägyptens im Spätmittelalter (1171–1517)*. Wiesbaden: F. Steiner, 1965.

Lane, Frederic C., and Reinhold C. Mueller. *Money and Banking in Medieval and Renaissance Venice*. Vol. 1, *Coins and Moneys of Account*. Baltimore: Johns Hopkins University Press, 1985.

———. *Venetian Ships and Shipbuilders of the Renaissance*. Baltimore: Johns Hopkins University Press, 1934.

———. *Venice, A Maritime Republic*. Baltimore: Johns Hopkins University Press, 1973.

———. *Venice and History*. Baltimore: Johns Hopkins University Press, 1966.

Lapidus, Ira M. *Muslim Cities in the Later Middle Ages*. Cambridge: Cambridge University Press, 1984.

Lewis, Bernard. *The Muslim Discovery of Europe*. New York: W. W. Norton and Co., 1982.

Lombardini, Gabriele. *Pane e Denaro a Bassano: Prezzi del Grano e Politica dell'Approvigionamento dei Cereali tra il 1501 e el 1799*. Venice: n.p., 1963.

Luttrell, A. T. "Venice and the Knights Hospitallers of Rhodes in the 14th Century." *Papers of the British School at Rome* 26 (1958): 196–210.

Lybyer, A. H. "The Ottoman Turks and the Routes of Oriental Trade." *The English Historical Review* 30 (1915): 577–588.

Masters, Bruce. *The Origins of Western Economic Dominance in the Middle East: Mercantilism and the Islamic Economy in Aleppo, 1600–1750.* New York: New York University Press, 1988.

Mattingly, Garrett. *Renaissance Diplomacy.* Boston: Houghton Miflin, 1955.

Mazzaoui, Michel. *The Origins of the Safawids: Sïism, Sufism and the Gulāt.* Wiesbaden: F. Steiner, 1972.

McGowan, Bruce. *Economic Life in Ottoman Europe: Taxation, Trade and the Struggle for Land, 1600–1800.* Cambridge: Cambridge University Press, 1981.

Minorskii, Vladimir. "Mongol Place Names in Mukri Kurdistan." *Bulletin of the School of Oriental and African Studies* 19, pt. 1 (1957): 58–81.

———. "La Perse au XVe siècle entre la Turquie et Venise." *Publications de la Société des Études Iraniennes* 7 (1933): 1–23.

———. "The Poetry of Shāh Ismāʿīl I." *Bulletin of the School of Oriental and African Studies* 10 (1940–1942): 1006a–1053a.

Miroğlu, Ismet. *Kemah Sancağı ve Erzincan Kazası (1520–1566).* Ankara: Türk Tarih Kurumu Basımevi, 1990.

Molov, R. "Contributions à l'Étude du Fond Socio-Historique du Destan "Köroğlu." *Études Balkaniques* 7 (1967): 107–128.

Mughul, Yakub. "Türk Amirali Emir Mustafa Ibn Behram Bay'in Hindistan Seferi (1531)." *Tarih Enstitüsü Dergisi* 4–5 (Ağustos 1973–1974): 247–262.

Murphey, Rhoads. "Provisioning Istanbul: The State and Subsistence in the Early Modern Middle East." *Foods and Foodways* 2 (1988): 217–263.

Necipoğlu, Gülrü. "Süleyman the Magnificent and the Representation of Power in the Context of Ottoman-Hapsburg-Papal Rivalry." *Art Bulletin* (1989), pp. 401–427.

Orhonlu, Çengiz. "Hint Kaptanlığı ve Piri Reis." *Belleten* 34, no. 134 (1970): 235–254.

———. "Seydi ʿAlī Reʾīs." *Tarih Enstitüsü Dergisi* 1 (1970): 39–56.

Ostrogorsky, George. *History of the Byzantine State.* New Brunswick, N.J.: Rutgers University Press.

Özbaran, Salih. "Osmanlı Imperatorluğun ve Hindustan Yolu." *Tarih Dergisi* 31 (1977): 65–146.

———. "The Ottoman Turks and the Portuguese in the Persian Gulf 1534–1581." *Journal of Asian History* 6 (1972): 56–74.

Palombini, Barbara von. *Bündniswerben Abendländischer Mächte um Persien 1453–1600.* Wiesbaden: Franz Steiner, 1968.

Parks, George B. *The Contents and Sources of Ramusio's Navigationi.* New York: New York Public Library, 1955.

Parmaksızoğlu, Ismit. "Kemāl Re'is." In *Islam Ansıklopedisi* 3 (1970): 566–568.

Pearson, M. N. *Merchants and Rulers in Gujarat: The Response to the Portuguese in the Sixteenth Century.* Berkeley: University of California Press, 1976.

Pepper, Simon, and Nicholas Adams. *Firearms and Fortifications.* Chicago: University of Chicago Press, 1986.

Perlin, Frank. "Proto-Industrialization and Pre-Colonial South Asia." *Past and Present* 98 (1983): 30–95.

Perry, John R. "Mīr Muhannā and the Dutch: Patterns of Piracy in the Persian Gulf." *Studia Iranica* 2, no. 1 (1973): 79–95.

Petry, Carl F. *The Civilian Elite of Cairo in the Later Middle Ages.* Princeton: Princeton University Press, 1981.

Pieri, Piero. *Il Rinasciamento e la Crisi Militare Italiana.* Torino: Giulio Einaudi, 1970.

Preto, Paolo. *Venezia e i Turchi.* Firenze: n.p., 1975.

Ramazani, Rouollah K. *The Foreign Policy of Iran, A Developing Nation in World Affairs, 1500–1941.* Charlottesville: University Press of Virginia, 1966.

Raymond, Andre. *Artisans et Commerçants au Caire au XVIIIe Siècle.* 2 vols. Damscus: Institut Français de Damas, 1974.

Reindl, Hedda. *Männer um Bayezid: Eine Prosopographische Studie Über die Epoche Sultan Bayezids II. (1481–1512).* Islamkundlische Untersuhungen Series, no. 75. Berlin: Klaus Schwarz, 1983.

Repp, R. C. *The Müfti of Istanbul: A Study in the Development of the Ottoman Learned Hierarchy.* London: Ithaca Press, 1986.

Roemer, H. R. "The Safawid Period." In *The Cambridge History of Iran.* Vol. 6. *The Timurid and Safavid Periods.* Edited by Peter Jackson and Lawrence Lockhart, pp. 189–350. Cambridge: Cambridge University Press, 1986.

Rogers, William Ledyard. *Naval Warfare Under Oars, 4th to 16th Centuries: A Study of Strategy, Tactics and Ship Design.* Annapolis: Naval Institute Press, 1967.

Ross, E. Dennison. "The Portuguese in India and Arabia." *Journal of the Royal Asiatic Society* (1921), pp. 545–562.

Rossi, Ettore. "Relazioni tra la Persia e l'Ordine di San Giovani a Rodi e a Malta." *Rivista degli Studi Orientali* 13, pt. 1 (1931/1932): 351–360.

Sacerdoti, Alberto. "Note sulle Galere da Mercato Veneziane nel XV Secolo." *Bolletino dell' Istituto de Storia della Societa dello Stato Veneziano* 4 (1962): 80–105.

Sahillioğlu, Halil. "16 Yüzyıl Sonu Osmanlı Tacirleri—Vergi Adleti—(Ali'nin Nasihatü's-salatin'inden)." *Toplum ve Bilim,* no. 6–7 (1978): 157–175.

Sarjeant, R. B. *The Portuguese Off the South Arabian Coast.* Oxford: Clarendon Press, 1963.

Sarwar, Ghulam. *History of Shah Isma'īl Safawī.* Aligargh. By the author, 1939.

Sauvaget, Jean. "Noms et Surnoms de Mamelouks." *Journal Asiatique* 238 (1950): 31–58.

Savory, Roger M. "The Consolidation of Safavid Power in Persia." *Der Islam* 41 (1965): 87–124.

———. *Iran Under the Safavids.* Cambridge: Cambridge University Press, 1980.

Schimkoreit, Renate. *Registen Publizierter Safawidischer Herrscherurkunden.* Berlin: Klaus Schwarz, 1982.

Schwoebel, Robert. *The Shadow of the Crescent: The Renaissance Image of the Turk (1453–1517).* Nieuwkoop: B. De Graf, 1967.

Sella, Domenico. *Commerci e Industrie a Venezia nel Secolo XVII.* Rome: Istituto per la Collaborazione Culturale, n.d.

Setton, Kenneth M. *The Papacy and the Levant (1204–1571).* 4 vols. Philadelphia: American Philosophical Society, 1978–1985.

Shields, Sarah, "Regional Trade and Nineteenth Century Mosul: Revising the Role of Europe in the Middle East," *International Journal of Middle East Studies* 23 (1991): 19–37.

Simon, Bruno. "Le Blé et les Rapports vénéto-ottomans au XVIe Siècle." In *Contributions à l'histoire économique et sociale de l'Empire ottoman.* Edited by Jean Louis Bacqué-Grammont. Series Collection Turcica III. Louvain: Éditions Peeters, 1983.

Simonsfeld, Henry. *Der Fondaco dei Tedeschi in Venedig und die Deutsch-Venetianischen Handelsbeazeihungen.* Vol. 1. Stuttgart: 1887; Reprint Scientia Verlag Aalen, 1968.

Smith, Dennis Mack. *Medieval Sicily 800–1713.* New York: The Viking Press, 1968.

Sohrweide, Hanna. "Der Seig der Ṣafaviden in Persien and seine Rückwirkungen." *Der Islam* 41 (1965): 101–196.

Sondhaus, Lawrence. *The Hapsburg Empire and the Sea: Austrian Naval Policy, 1797–1866.* West Lafayette, Indiana: Purdue University Press, 1989.

Soucek, Svat. "Certain Types of Ships in Ottoman-Turkish Terminology." *Turcica* 7 (1975): 233–249.

———. "A Propos du Livre d'Instructions Nautiques de Pīrī Re'īs." *Revue des Études Islamiques* 41 (1973): 241–255.

———. "The Rise of the Barbarossas in North Africa." *Archivum Ottomanicum* 3 (1971): 240–251.

Spremic, Momcilo, and Mahmud Şakıroğlu. "XV Yüzyılda Venedik Cumhuriyetini Şarkta Odediği Harclar." *Belleten* 47, no. 185 (1983): 382–396.

Steensgaard, Niels. *The Asian Trade Revolution in the 17th Century.* Chicago: University of Chicago Press, 1973.

Strippling, George. *The Ottoman Turks and the Arabs 1511–1574.* Urbana: University of Illinois Press, 1942.

Sugar, Peter F. "The Ottoman 'Professional Prisoner' on the Western Borders of the Empire in the Sixteenth and Seventeenth Centuries." *Études Balkaniques* 1 (1971): 82–91.

Sümer, Faruk. "Karaman-oghulları." In *Encyclopedia of Islam,* 2d ed., 4 (1960): 624.

———. *Safevi Devletinin Kuruluşu ve Gelişmesinde Anadolu Türklerinin Rolu.* Ankara: Güven Matbaası, 1976.

Tansel, Selahattin. *Sultan II Bayezit'in Siyasi Hayatı.* Istanbul: Milli Eğitim Basımevi, 1966.

———. *Yavuz Sultan Selim.* Ankara: Milli Eğitim Basımevi, 1969.

Tekindağ, Şehabeddin. "Selim-Nameler." *Tarih Enstitüsü Dergisi* 1 (October 1970): 197–230.

———. "Yeni Kaynak ve Vesikaların Işiği Altında Yavuz Sultan Selim'in Iran Seferi." *Tarih Dergisi* 22 (1967): 49–76.

Tenenti, Alberto. *Cristoforo da Canal, La Marine Venetienne Avant Lepante.* Paris: S.E.V.P.E.N., 1962.

———. *Naufrages, Corsairs et Assurances maritimes à Venise 1592–1609.* Paris: S.E.V.P.E.N., 1959.

———. *Venezia e i Corsari 1580–1615.* Bari: Editori Laterza, 1961.

Tracy, James D., ed. *The Rise of Merchant Empires: Long-Distance Trade in the Early Modern World, 1350–1750.* Cambridge: Cambridge University Press, 1990.

Uluçay, Çagatay. "Yavuz Sultan Selim, Nasıl Padişah Oldu?" *Tarih Dergisi* 9 (1953): 54–90; 10 (1954): 118–142; 11 (1955): 185–200.

Uzunçarşılı, I. H. *Anadolu Beylikleri ve Akkoyunlu, Karakoyunlu Devletleri.* Ankara: Türk Tarih Kurumu Basımevi, 1984.

———. "Bahriyyah." In *Encyclopedia of Islam,* 2d ed., 2 (1960): 945–949.

———. "Iran Şahına Iltıca Etmiş Olan Şehzade Bayezid'in Teslimi Için Sultan Süleyman ve Oğlu Selim Taraflarından Şaha Gönderilen Altınlar ve Kıymetli Hediyeler." *Belleten* 24 (1960): 104–134.

———. "Memluk Sultanları Yanına Iltıca Etmiş Olan Osmanlı Hanedanına Mensub Şehzadeler." *Belleten* 17 (1953): 519–535.

———. *Osmanlı Devletinin Merkez ve Bahriye Teşkilatı.* Ankara: Türk Tarih Kurumu Basımevi, 1984.

Ünal, Mehmet Ali. *XVI Yüzyılda Harput Sancağı (1518–1566).* Ankara: Türk Tarih Kurumu Basımevi, 1989.

Valensi, Lucette. "The Making of a Political Paradigm: The Ottoman State and Oriental Despotism." In *The Transmission of Culture in Early Modern Europe.* Edited by Anthony Grafton and Ann Blair, pp. 173–203. Philadelphia: University of Pennsylvania Press, 1990.

Veinstein, Gilles. "Un Achat Français de Blé dans l'Empire Ottoman au Milieu de XVIe siècle." In *L'Empire Ottoman, la République de Turquie et la France.* Edited by Batu and Bacqué-Grammont, pp. 22–36. Istanbul: Isis Press, 1986.

Wansbrough, John. "A Mamluk Ambassador to Venice in 913/1507." *Bulletin of the School of Oriental and African Studies* 26 (1963): 503–530.

———. "A Mamluk Letter of 872/1473." *Bulletin of the School of Oriental and African Studies* 24 (1961): 200–213.

Weinstein, Donald. *Ambassador from Venice, Pietro Pasqualigo in Lisbon, 1501.* Minneapolis: University of Minnesota Press, 1960.

Woods, John E. *The Aqquyunlu: Clan, Confederation, Empire.* Minneapolis and Chicago: Bibliotheca Islamica, 1976.

Yavuz, Hulusi. *Kabe ve Haremeyn İçin Yemen'de Osmanlı Hakimiyeti (1517–1571).* Istanbul: Serbest Matbaası, 1984.

Yinanç, Refet. *Dulkadir Beyliği.* Ankara: Türk Tarih Kurumu Basımevi, 1989.

Index